Muzzled

From T-Ball to Terrorism—
True Stories That Should Be Fiction

MICHAEL SMERCONISH

Published by
THOMAS NELSON
Since 1798

www.thomasnelson.com

Published in Nashville, Tennessee, by Thomas Nelson, Inc.

Thomas Nelson, Inc., books may be purchased in bulk for educational, business, fundraising, or sales promotional use. For information, please e-mail SpecialMarkets@ThomasNelson.com.

ISBN 1-59555-050-X (hardcover)
ISBN 10: 1-59555-112-3 (tradepaper)
ISBN 13: 978-1-59555-112-2 (tradepaper)

Printed in the United States of America

07 08 09 10 11 RRD 7 6 5 4 3 2 1

For Lavinia, Caitlin, Michael Jr., Wilson, and Lucky

Contents

Introduction   vii

  1. Photo Finish   1

  2. The Payback   10

  3. Sorry We Got It Correct   28

  4. Dressing for Political Correctness   35

  5. Oh, Yes, It's Ladies' Night   41

  6. It's All about Me   45

  7. God Bless Patrick Cubbage   49

  8. Political Correctness in Full Bloom   56

  9. Seeing Purple   60

10. Trophy Mania   67

11. Getting Maid on Campus   73

12. Naked Tigers   77

13. A Behemoth of an Incident   81

14. Cops and Dancers   93

15. There She Isn't   105

16. Will the Real Rob Morris Please Rise   113

17. It's All about the Wampum   125

18. Intelligently Designing a Curriculum   136

19. I Wish I Were Joking   146

CONTENTS

20. Stamps of Disapproval 157

21. Can't We All Just Get Along? 163

22. Up in Smoke 171

23. Mumidiots 182

24. The Parade at PC and Main Streets 194

25. *24* and There's So Much More 200

26. The T-Word, Shhhh! 206

27. Still Flying Blind 217

28. Is That All There Is? 234

Epilogue: A Letter to My Son 246

Acknowledgments 250

About the Author 257

Notes 259

Index 285

Introduction

MUZZLED.

In a word, it's what we've become. Words and actions in this country have become MUZZLED by those among us in favor of political correctness who would sacrifice the rugged individualism that has been the hallmark of our nation. It's a trend that has been building for a while but is now totally out of control. In the past, this sanitization of that which we say and do would have been debate worthy, but in truth only a minor irritant to our quality of life. In the post-9/11 world, however, domestic political correctness is a cancer that has metastasized into the war on terror where it threatens our very survival.

A bit dramatic, you think? Well, let me explain.

First of all, I get paid to talk. And to write. (*Relax.* This does not mean that you're in store for the usual transcript of some radio or newspaper diatribe masked as a book.) I'm solely responsible for the content of 17.5 hours of morning-drive radio programming every week and a weekly newspaper column for a big city daily of about 650 words. The hardest thing for me is deciding what to say, not actually saying it. To make that determination, I monitor the news 24/7 and start with a 3:00 AM wake-up, so that by the time I go on the air at 5:30, my heavy lifting is done.

I am not complaining. I am a news junkie to begin with. Give me a free afternoon in the sun and my first choice of reading materials is a stack of newspapers. For me, the glitzy on-line versions are a weak substitute. I like perusing the day's news the old-fashioned way, where your fingers get darkened from rubbed off ink, and that is usually what I am doing in my studio at 4:00 AM each weekday. I survive on a steady diet of local and national dailies, and a host of cable television news shows, on most of which I have myself appeared to offer opinions.

Much of what I discuss comes from front-page news. I present a viewpoint and welcome calls. The calls are only superficially screened; I don't weed out those who are disagreeable. As a matter of fact, we usually institute an affirmative action program for those and move them to the front of the line. I don't run a "hatri-olic" (my word, and I am waiting for a mention in *Webster's*) program. I'm not bombastic. I don't hang up on telephone callers except in the most rare of circum-stances. And while my politics tend to be right of center, I'm drinking no one's Kool-Aid and have a handful of views that would be considered liberal. I find this approach—for me at least—is best suited to drawing out competing views from callers on the news of the day, which is what I think makes for good talk radio.

Beyond the headlines and interaction, often the best issue-oriented material comes from my listeners and from my own daily living. Via my Web site at www.mastalk.com, my listeners and readers keep me supplied with information about things going on in their neighborhoods, workplaces, and living rooms. And, as a guy who is married, raising four children, and paying bills, I watch, lis-ten, and try to learn what is making people tick.

There it is. That is my "intelligence" system. It is the way I try to stay pre-pared to discuss everything from the war in Iraq to who's winning *American Idol.* And there is another benefit to the way in which I am plugged in: it enables me to see emerging trends in people's thoughts and actions. My big-picture view of America serves as the basis for my thinking that what began as a change to our lifestyle has now grown into something that jeopardizes our national security. Items that, analyzed on their own, might be just an interesting curiosity but, taken as a whole, paint an alarming picture of who we are and what we are becoming.

So what do I see that alarms me?

There can be no debate as to whether we're MUZZLED here at home when: a Wall Street wunderkind gets fired from his multimillion-dollar job solely because he superimposed his own photograph onto the body of a fully clothed woman's picture in a company circular; a public relations executive working for a leg-endary NFL franchise gets the axe because the thought police can't handle the direct manner in which he tries to combat bad behavior on the part of players in a video he produces; a major American newspaper feels obliged to apologize for having published mug shots of men wanted for murder because they printed no photos of white guys, even though no white guys were then wanted for murder in that city; an advertising salesman is awarded $600,000 after filing a lawsuit based solely on his boss' having given him a copy of the all-time best-selling busi-ness book called (*New) Dress for Success* which he found objectionable; the com-plaint of a single bar patron, who objects to women paying less than he does for drinks, can put an end to the tradition of "Ladies Night" at a local bar, and then across a state; an elementary student is told to read to the class from his favorite book, so long as it isn't the Bible; an honor guardsman at one of the nation's largest military cemeteries is told not to say "God Bless the United States" when presenting Old Glory to the kin of grieving relatives; red ink is shunned in favor of the color purple lest a student's psyche be subject to the double indiscretion of receiving a poor grade and seeing it in an alarming shade; there is serious debate as to whether little leaguers should get trophies just for showing up; a couple of Ivy League entrepreneurs are told that their plan for a room-cleaning business is fine, so long as its name doesn't incorporate the sexist word "maid"; another Ivy Leaguer is almost run off campus because he has the temerity to call a couple of rabble rousing students interrupting his studying "water buffalo"; the Miss America Pageant would rather sink than admit it is really a beauty contest; one of the nation's largest lenders is held hostage for the actions of somebody who once had something to do with a predecessor of the bank—two hundred years ago; and the anti-smoking furor has reached a point where there is legislation pending that could ban smoking in your own car, and even though lung cancer kills more people than breast, prostate, and colorectal cancer, it receives nowhere near the research funding of the others.

These—and many others I am about to expose—are all stories that are true but should be fiction. And while I have endeavored to carefully research the public accounts of each episode, this is no book report. I've spoken to the people involved in these controversies to make sure that I can tell it like it is. By the way, my "sources" are not only random Americans you've probably never heard of yet found themselves in the PC crosshairs but also some folks whose names will ring a bell—like Donald Rumsfeld, Jackie Mason, and Mad Money Man Jim Cramer. (What a carpool that would make.)

At any other time in our history, this would be a collection of enraging, enthralling, and entertaining tales. But now they are also more. While the restraint of words and actions of which I speak has been growing like a snowball for all of my adult life, it has now turned into a matter of survival.

Every slight.

Every insult.

Every look askance.

Today they're all grounds for the proverbial federal case. People are actually on the lookout for indiscretions that in the past would have been addressed with a hand gesture but are now grounds for government action and litigation. But it's worse than that. The MUZZLED, victim-filled society we have created has now invaded and impeded the war on terror.

Do you want to know why four years after 9/11 we still don't look for terrorists at airports and borders by keeping in mind what all the other terrorists have looked like? Isn't it curious that in certain quarters there is more interest in and attention paid to the half-dozen knuckleheads responsible for some truly minor indiscretions at Abu Ghraib than the good work of the 140,000 other honorable service men and women? Have you wondered why there is more attention paid to whether we played Christina Aguilera music too loud for detainee No. 063 at Guantanamo Bay than the fact that this same guy would have been hijacker No. 20 on 9/11 had he gotten past custom's officials when he tried to get into the Orlando International Airport a month before 9/11? It's because we are no longer a country that respects our differences, even when those differences come with rough edges that offend. Instead, we have become a country of kvetchers and apologists, even while at war.

The same thinking that says kids on losing T-ball teams should also get a trophy, or that an "F" grade should be delivered in purple, not red, or that even short people can be cops, or that there is something wrong with calling Miss America a beauty pageant is what puts interrogators in handcuffs at Guantanamo or precludes our looking for terrorists at airports who—look like terrorists! We're literally scared to death to offend.

Perhaps the most egregious recent example of what I am talking about occurred in the immediate aftermath of Hurricane Katrina. A group of Portland, Oregon, firefighters volunteered to help at a time when tens of thousands of people were still stranded in flooded homes in New Orleans and its environs as well as throughout the other storm ravaged states. Before heading into the field, the Federal Emergency Management Agency (FEMA) first gave them training as temporary federal employees. What did that training include? Would you believe: diversity training! Victims were dying in the Gulf States and our government was making sure individuals who had already proven their decency by their willingness to leave their own families and travel across the country to pitch in and assist the rescue efforts were stuck in a hotel room in a sexual harassment class.[1]

If you want to talk real harassment, keep reading. You'll encounter example after blood-boiling example of average Americans who have been bound and gagged by the PC police in every area of life—everything from T-ball to terrorism. I wish it were made up, but sadly it's all too true.

WARNING! If you're standing in a bookstore, sipping a latte, and giving this a quick thumbing before you pull the trigger, let me make your decision easy: this book is *not* for the easily offended. If you are one of them, you are the problem. Keep moving. Find the guy in the Birkenstocks and have him direct you to the stack marked "fiction."

1

Photo Finish

I seem to be on everyone's e-mail list.[1] No matter how hard I try to keep my own e-mail address obscure, I get a boatload of messages every day, not only from people I know, but also from total strangers. I'm not talking about those who communicate via my Web site (www.mastalk.com), which I set up to give my radio listeners and *Daily News* readers an avenue to reach me. I mean that I receive e-mail via an address which I attempt to keep secret. I'll bet it's happened to you, too.

Inevitably, people whom you *want* to have your e-mail address see something interesting they wish to circulate to a number of their friends or business associates. So they send it to you as one of a handful of individuals on their receipt list, and all of a sudden, individuals who are not connected, except by virtue of having one friend or acquaintance in common, see one another's e-mail address. It's the Internet version of the sixth degree of separation, except cyberspace puts us all at one degree of separation.

One positive thing about having my e-mail address exposed: it increases the joke flow. Take any serious news event or matter of less importance but still of public concern: the space shuttle, OJ, Clinton/Lewinsky, any presidential race, or Michael Jackson. Within minutes of serious reportage of such a happening, I receive someone's comedic interpretation of the item. (Thankfully, 9/11 was an exception.)

I've noticed, more often than not, when I scroll to the bottom of the e-mail message following the cyber trail to where it originated, I can decipher an e-mail address with some financial institution connection. It could be an investment-banking house or a stock brokerage. Try it. Next time something comes around, see if you can't do likewise.

Forget the Borscht Belt. Wall Street must be the funniest place on earth. My Internet experience tells me that the most rapidly crafted and most creative jokes seem to flow from that vicinity. I'm not saying the best jokes are written there. But those who work in the financial sector seem to get them first. And they share. I think I can further explain the phenomena.

Information is the lifeblood of Wall Street. Everything they do there is based on having good knowledge. The home to Masters of the Universe has a disproportionate share of Type-A personalities whose livelihood is dependent upon their staying a few steps ahead on matters of financial concern. Those market-related matters are tied to current events. So the movers and shakers on Wall Street make it their business to know what's going on all over the world, and that is why they have such keen insight and the best first impressions into world events.

The high-pressure environment in which they work is also an atmosphere that spawns some levity to prime the intellectual pump. (There've been a few recent incidents that have gotten out of control and portrayed a pinstriped frat house.) You put it all together and you have bright guys, in the loop, sharing a few laughs as they go about their work. I think it's a good thing.

But now I'm worried that this, like many other institutions of American life dealt with in these pages, is imperiled. And my cause for alarm is the case of Andrew Susser and Joel Krasner.

I've never met Andrew Susser, and the only picture I have seen of him is the one that got him fired. More about that in a moment. But from what I have read about him and gleaned from some who are close to him, this guy sounds like a real-life Sherman McCoy. The book version, not the way Tom Hanks played the Tom Wolfe-created visage of Wall Street.

Consider his bio. Susser graduated from prestigious Vassar College in 1986 with a BA in Economics. Maybe an indication of his independent thinking and willingness to challenge conventional norms was in evidence when he co-founded and was editor of the *Vassar Spectator*, an "alternative" campus newspaper.

After graduating from Vassar, Andrew Susser left Poughkeepsie and headed for Wall Street where he spent two years as a market analyst and institutional trading liaison at Merrill Lynch. After that, it was on to Philadelphia where he studied at the University of Pennsylvania. He was awarded two degrees: an MBA from Wharton and a JD from (my alma mater) Penn Law School. After Penn, he had a brief stint at the law firm of Shearman & Sterling, concentrating in the areas of corporate finance and mergers and acquisitions.

But Susser quickly grew tired of putting other people's deals together and decided to get in on the action himself. He landed at Moody's Investors Service where he cut his teeth in the Gaming and Theater sectors as a senior analyst. Andrew Susser then spent two years as a fixed-income Gaming and Lodging analyst at Salomon Brothers and finally landed at Banc of America Securities, LLC, an investment banking unit of Charlotte-based Bank of America Corp. which "delivers capital raising, financial advisory and risk management solutions, bulge-bracket trading and global distribution services, and objective research on global markets and growth sectors to corporations, institutional investors, financial institutions and government entities."[2]

It was here that Susser thrived.

After just five and a half years at Banc of America Securities, Susser was the managing director and head of high-yield bond research, as well as the high-yield analyst for the Gaming, Lodging, and Leisure sectors. From 1999 to 2004, he was a member of the Institutional Investor Fixed Income Analyst All-Star Team, and from 2002 through 2004, he was the No. 1 ranked analyst in the Gaming and Lodging sectors.

During his career, he has been the lead research analyst on many high-yield financings, including those for MGM Mirage, Mandalay Resort Group, Caesar's Entertainment, Station Casinos, Boyd Gaming, Mohegan Tribal Gaming Authority, Aztar Corporation, Stater Bros. Supermarkets, Speedway Motorsports, Vail Resorts, Gaylord Entertainment, and Host Marriott.[3]

By 2004, the not-yet-forty-year-old Susser was enjoying phenomenal success—the kind of achievement that was noted by his peers and the media. Susser had become the sort of guy to whom financial writers at outlets such as *Bloomberg News*, the *New York Daily News*, or even the *Philadelphia Inquirer* might turn to for analysis of the Gaming and Lodging industry.

So far, so good. New York boy done well. Young family. Big income. Recognition by his peers. Unfortunately, it all came temporarily crashing down for Susser at the start of 2005 when he was suddenly fired from his job and forced to forego his reported $4.4 million position.[4]

Andrew Susser was fired because he distributed a report entitled "Checking In" to clients in his area of expertise which featured a cover photograph of a man carrying a woman in high heels across a hotel room threshold. Susser's face had been superimposed over the face of the woman, so it appeared he was the female being carried into the hotel room. That's it. She is clothed. There is absolutely no nudity. And not a word of profanity. The bottom of her skirt is covering her knees. And that is all that is seen in the photograph. Take a look at the picture. (It's at the beginning of this chapter.) Tell me, what is so offensive?

The report was initially distributed in December of 2004 to the immediate high-yield community where it garnered a grand total of *zero* complaints about the cover photo. As a matter of fact, the report was out for a few weeks before there was any reaction. The general consensus among recipients was as Susser intended—it was compellingly funny![5] The report was then distributed to Banc of America Securities' clients around the United States and, thereafter, alas, some unknown person—perhaps not even an intended recipient—raised a beef and touched off a politically correct chain reaction.[6]

When the execs at Banc of America Securities caught wind of the research report, they promptly forced Susser and Joel Krasner, the head of fixed-income research publishing, to "check out." Krasner, who had been hired less than a year before, in March of 2004, was dumfounded. "I had been hired in the Fixed-Income Research Publishing Department to put in place policies and procedures for compliance for research coming into that area. These changes were already made in the equity area, so now it was time for fixed-income research to become more compliant. For ten months, I created manuals, policies, and worked closely with the legal and compliance departments. It was quite a productive ten months," Krasner later told me.[7]

Krasner is a well-known and respected securities analyst with three decades under his belt on Wall Street. His record was clean, his professional credentials intact. Before joining Banc of America, he'd worked in a similar supervisor-analyst capacity for Deutsche Bank. Earlier in his career, he'd spent twenty-five years working, like Susser, as a securities analyst at such Wall Street bastions as Dean Witter and Lehman Brothers.

Krasner has a master's degree in finance and investments, is a Chartered Financial Analyst, has authored books and articles on finance and investments, taught college economics and finance courses, and has instructed CFA candidates at a professorial level. Suddenly, none of that mattered.

Krasner and others have pieced together for me the events that gave rise to his firing and that of Andrew Susser. Krasner said David Goldman then ran the Banc of America Fixed-Income Research Department. Within that department, Goldman managed fixed-income securities analysts (like Susser). Goldman also oversaw Krasner in his role as the person responsible for fixed-income research publishing.

So, when Susser would put together a report, it was then sent to Krasner's department where editors would edit the text, desktop publishers would arrange text and graphics and add a cover, and, finally, supervisory analysts (like Krasner) would be charged with the responsibility to read and make certain it was compliant. So how did this cover get on Susser's report?

In December, Susser's report came into Krasner's department. An editor and a supervisory analyst read it. Because the report dealt with the hospitality industry, the cover that was generated featured a man carrying a woman over the threshold of a hotel room.[8]

Soon thereafter, the publishing department at Banc of America held a holiday party, where the cover photo underwent a slight modification. "At the party there was a conversation about some of the substantive issues in the report. In the midst of that discussion, somebody superimposed [Susser's] face over the woman's face, and everybody chuckled. It was no big deal. That was the total extent of it."[9] Not giving the matter much thought, Susser consented for the new cover to be used.

Initially, the report was met with silence at Banc of America. Then, there was a bit of a buzz when word began to circulate about the infamous cover. The buzz was created by laughter. The consensus, according to those with whom I have spoken, was that the individuals who saw the report with Susser on the cover got a kick out of his face on the woman's clothed body. It was different, and it was head-turning, which was the intended effect.

This, however, did not sit well somewhere up the food chain at Banc of America nor, apparently, with David Goldman, the head of fixed-income research. As one coworker told me, Goldman established a mantra that he was going "to do what was necessary to save his own job." Well, he did. He wanted to show his supervisors that he had it under control, so he fired Susser and Krasner.[10]

Missing was any mention of any complaint by any client.

"Nobody ever complained to me," said Krasner. Krasner himself *never* knew the mocked cover had been used until a few weeks after its publication.

The decision was final. Stunned, the two asked independently if they had broken any regulations. No, was the answer. Nor had they traded on inside information. There was no question about the misuse of client resources. In other words, there was not a whiff of financial impropriety to what they had done, and neither man had any hint of scandal in his work-related past. Nevertheless, each man turned in his Blackberry and laptop, and headed home.[11]

To be certain, they were not offered the opportunity to resign. They were fired. Andrew Susser, a thirty-nine-year-old wunderkind of Wall Street, responsible for significant revenues to his firm, was fired from Banc of America Securities where the powers-that-be were hell-bent on maintaining some killjoy image in the name of political correctness. Ditto for the older, equally respected Joel Krasner.

"Andrew Susser is no longer employed by the company," was all Banc of America Securities spokesman Jeff Hershberger would say at the time, declining to comment on the reasons.[12]

Now that you've heard the story, you are no doubt wondering which feminist group organized, marched, and boycotted Banc of America Securities. What trans-gender association took out an ad in the *Village Voice* to express utter umbrage with Susser dressed like a woman? What, exactly, was the hook that Jesse Jackson used to get himself into the controversy? Surprisingly, none of the above.

Someone close to the controversy told me that there was not a hint of objection from any of Susser's clients outside the firm, nor from anyone on the inside of Banc of America Securities. The worst transgression here was that neither man was given even a small hint of his impending termination.[13]

Industry sources say Susser's bosses should not have been surprised. Susser was known as a young man willing to think and act outside the box. That was what made him successful. His reports were eagerly awaited on Wall Street because of his excellent analytic ability and presentation. "His irreverent sense of humor was always welcome," Barbara Cappaert, Gaming and Lodging analyst at research firm KDP Investment Advisors, reportedly said. "He's a great analyst and I really looked forward to his report every month."[14] (Read that again. Her name is Barbara. She has the right attitude.)

In the politically correct New Millennium, Susser, a man whose research reports "were known for their comic covers," found himself fired.[15] *Bloomberg* reported that clients of the securities firm were similarly shocked. "It's a big loss," *Bloomberg* reporter Tom Parker, high-yield portfolio manager for Barclays Global Investors, said. "He's definitely one of the top Gaming analysts."[16]

There is some good news. This is a story with a happy ending. The hysteria exhibited by Banc of America Securities was not shared on Wall Street where people in the know were startled by Susser and Krasner's termination. Typical were the published comments of Frank Barkocy, director of research at Keefe Managers, who the *New York Daily News* reported as saying, "We're getting all too sensitive in this day and age. People take umbrage at the damnedest things."[17] Or Tim Chriskey, the chief investment officer at Solaris Asset Management, who spoke in support of Susser when he said, "I can't believe he would have meant anything malicious. He was trying to be cute and create some attention. Unfortunately, he created so much attention, it got him fired."[18] Then there was Michael Holland, the founder of Holland & Co., who said, "There had to be something more to this story than simply one choice that was not acceptable to the bank's management. It'd be unfortunate if Wall Street has completely lost its sense of humor."[19]

Marjorie Kelly, editor of *Business Ethics* magazine, sees an emerging trend on Wall Street toward zero tolerance: "There is a new kind of Puritanism which has replaced an era of arrogance and ignorance, an attitude that boys will be boys."[20] Ira Lee Sorkin, a senior white-collar crime lawyer at Carter Ledyard & Milburn in Manhattan, summed up the situation as follows: "We are in a regulatory frenzy. Corporations are acting out of fear, and they don't want to take a chance that employees did something wrong under their watch, so they are basically cleaning house. Someone has to say, 'Enough!'"[21]

As for Susser, he landed on his feet in very short order at a Wall Street investment management firm in New York called GoldenTree Asset Management, LP. GoldenTree has grown quickly since its founding five years ago and already has assets under its management topping $6.5 billion.

When GoldenTree formally announced its "acquisition" of Susser, the firm founder, president, and chief investment officer, Steven A. Tannanbaum, said: "I have worked very close with Andrew over the years, and many of my colleagues have gotten to know him very well both personally and professionally. We are confident he will make a high level impact at our firm as we look for opportunities in this ever more dynamic market."

Better still, GoldenTree Chairman and co-founder Leon Wagner made it clear to the *Wall Street Journal* how the new employer regarded the old employer's decision with his word choice: "The people who worked closely with [Andrew] and for Andrew gave him the highest accolades. What happened was just crazy, and we are more than happy to have him.[22] Unlike the sell-side, our analysts don't have to write reports, funny covers or not. It's liberating to talented people."[23]

The highly decorated businessman is now a portfolio manager covering areas very familiar to him—Gaming and Lodging, Consumer Products, and Supermarkets.[24] Susser has joined three other financial analysts at GoldenTree that have been ranked by *Institutional Investor*. Susser himself, in a public statement when hired, said only, "I could not be happier about joining the GoldenTree team. It is a firm with a great reputation throughout the industry and its success is based on financial analysis of the highest order."[25]

Things were different for Krasner, however, because, unlike Susser, he was not a revenue generator. It took him several months to find suitable employment; he's presently happily employed with RBC Capital Markets in a similar capacity to his role at Banc of America. Along the way he had to overcome the mind-set of some who thought that they would be fired if they hired him.

"Wall Street has become so full of regulation, it is often difficult to operate and get things done efficiently," Krasner now says.

I sought out the resident guru of Wall Street, Jim Cramer—as in TheStreet.com host of *Mad Money* and author of *Confessions of a Street Addict* and *Real Money*—as a sanity check on the Susser/Krasner situation. As I hoped (and expected), this former editor-in-chief of the *Harvard Crimson*, who excels because of both his academic and street smarts, didn't mince any words:

> The scourge of political correctness has hit Wall Street with a vengeance. We've always been a bastion of meritocracy, whoever did the best for their clients and made them the most money then got paid the most money, whoever did the worst got canned. But when Andy Susser, one of the best in the biz, got canned for a hilarious bit of farce, superimposing his head on a woman's body to have a little fun in high-yield research—believe me, it could use it—I knew things had gotten out of control. Can you imagine what would have happened to him if he had made a joke about Muslim terror? He'd be banned for life![26]

I tell this story first because it is incredible, and I don't see the Susser/Krasner situation as some aberrant instance of overreactive behavior. The Susser/Krasner pseudo scandal, SusKrasgate if you will, is becoming the norm. And it alarms me. What happened to Andrew Susser and Joel Krasner is similar to many issues that will be addressed in the forthcoming chapters.

Their story represents society's emerging trigger finger on a cocked and loaded gun, anxious to be fired in the name of sexism, racism, classism, and any other kind of "ism," real or imagined.

This mind-set enabled an African American advertising salesman to be awarded $600,000 after his boss, in an effort to get his workforce to pay attention to their appearance, distributed a business bestseller called *Dress for Success*, which the salesman found to be discriminatory because the book offered gender- and ethnic-specific suggestions. It can be found in the thought process of those school teachers who have sworn off red ink in favor of writing their comments in purple, lest the red ink further alarm pupils who will no doubt be stressed to receive a failing grade and, therefore, don't need the added pain of seeing it in red. It's the fear of religion evident when a national guardsman was fired from New Jersey's largest military cemetery because of his practice of presenting American flags at gravesides while also saying, "God bless you, and God bless the United States." It's what drives Harvard to tell two undergraduates that their room-cleaning entrepreneurial venture could not be called DorMaid because the use of *maid* is sexist. It's why, in New Jersey, the time-honored tradition of bars' having "Ladies Night" is now under attack. I even see it in the mindset that all kids deserve trophies for showing up regardless of whether they succeed after arrival.

We've become afraid of our own shadows, of offending somebody, anybody, even if there is no offense worthy of being offensive! We are overly worried about somebody thinking we're homophobic if we are against same-sex marriage, or racist if we don't embrace affirmative action or reparations.

America, of all places, is in the midst of ingraining a fear of expression, and it exists in the heart of one of America's greatest institutions: Wall Street. Worse, the concern over offending is not just the stuff of schoolyards, corporate sensitivity videos, or ethnic jokes no longer told. No, the real worry here—as will be discussed—is that it has spilled into the war on terror where it compromises our ability to look for terrorists who just "might" look like terrorists.

That is the significance of Andrew Susser and Joel Krasner.

Just one more thing. The name of Susser's successor at Banc of America Securities sums it all up. To replace Andrew Susser—guess who they hired? Larry Bland.[27]

I couldn't make this stuff up.

2

The Payback

Kirk Reynolds didn't want the members of the San Francisco 49ers to join the long and growing list of professional athletes behaving badly. Lord knows there have been plenty of examples of men whose antics off the field have put them in a difficult position. My most recent favorite? The guy who got caught with a Whizzinator. What's a Whizzinator, you ask? (To which I should respond, are you sure you want to know?)

Well, as trumpeted by its Web site, it is: "Undetectable! Foolproof! Reusable!" And what, exactly, does it do? According to Whizzinator.com:

> The Whizzinator is an easy to conceal, easy to use urinating device with a very realistic prosthetic penis. It has been extensively tested and proven to work under real-life conditions!
>
> The Whizzinator is designed to be comfortably worn as an undergarment for extended periods of time!
>
> Used with our organic heat pads, it is guaranteed to maintain body temperature for Eight Hours! And our quality production and materials assures you that the Whizzinator will let it flow, again and again, anytime, anywhere you need it![1]

Get the picture? (Do you want to get the picture?) *Ugh.*

Imagine the surprise of airport security when they stopped Minnesota Vikings' running back Onterrio Smith. When a Transportation Safety Administration officer searched his gear, out, er, flopped his Whizzinator! That is, along with six or seven vials of . . . dried urine.[2] C'mon. You have to laugh at that. Especially when considering that Smith claimed that he was only delivering the Whizzinator to his cousin. By the way, the NFL didn't go for the "cousin made me do it" routine, and given that it was Smith's third strike, he was suspended for the 2005 season.[3]

Then there was baseball's sausage "beat down" involving the Pittsburgh Pirates' first baseman, Randall Simon.

Wait a minute. Did I leave out the NBA? Okay, how about that brawl with fans in the midst of the 2004-05 season in a game between the Pacers and Pistons?

Now let me get back to Kirk Reynolds.

First of all, his team, the San Francisco 49ers, has had some issues of its own, and no doubt a combination of these and other teams' troubles were what caused Reynolds to be proactive. Some would say, too proactive. In 2002, running back Garrison Hearst apologized after initially responding to the "coming out" of former defensive lineman Esera Tualo by telling the *Fresno Bee*: "Aww, hell no! I don't want any faggots on my team. I know this might not be what people want to hear, but that's a punk. I don't want any faggots in this locker room."[4,5]

Then came TO and his Sharpie. Tame by Whizzinator standards, but worthy of mention, nonetheless. Recall that, back in 2003, when Terrell Owens was still with the 49ers, he scored a game-winning touchdown in a key division game against the Seahawks and proceeded to pull a marker from his sock and sign the football for his financial planner who was seated in the stands.[6]

A year later, TO was back in the headlines after subjecting himself to a *Playboy Magazine* "20 Questions" feature in which he questioned the sexual orientation of former 49ers quarterback Jeff Garcia. In the September 2004 issue, TO said of Garcia: "Like my boy tells me: If it looks like a rat and smells like a rat, by golly, it is a rat." And while we're on TO, let's not forget he next caused a stir in the Philadelphia Eagles' locker room when he filmed a segment with Nicolette Sheridan of *Desperate Housewives* fame, which featured her dropping her towel and jumping in his arms. The intro to Monday Night Football was widely debated because it was shown at the outset of the broadcast when young kids were watching. As if that weren't enough, after joining the Philadelphia Eagles and helping them make it to the Super Bowl, TO was dumped by the Birds in his second season. Why? TO wanted to renegotiate a newly minted contract after his first season, saying that he had outperformed his previous deal. When the Eagles balked, he became *difficult*. He arrived at training camp wearing combat fatigues and refused to speak to players and coaches. It only went downhill from there. Finally, he was suspended after telling ESPN that the Eagles "lack[ed] . . . class" for not publicly recognizing his 100th career touchdown catch. In that same interview, TO dissed teammate Donovan McNabb, saying that Green Bay's

Brett Favre would make a better quarterback for the Eagles. After a locker-room fight with former defensive end Hugh Douglas, the team's "ambassador," head-coach Andy Reid finally had enough of TO. Impact player? You betcha.

My point is simply that you cannot evaluate Reynolds's conduct in a vacuum. You have to consider it as a response to men behaving badly. The very men he was seeking to reach. Now let's take a breath and see if we can cut this guy some slack.

Reynolds, responsible for the public relations video created by the 49ers that caused the team to become a PC spectacle, is now the "ex" PR director for the team. Reynolds's intention was to prepare the football players for life in the public eye.

I think of it as the NFL version of those corny sensitivity training videos we've all had to watch in the workplace. (My personal favorite? The vignette in the Infinity Radio video I've had to endure where a guy spills his drink on the front of a woman's blouse at the Christmas Par—er, I mean *Holiday* Party—and then is surprised by her reaction when he tries to wipe it off with his hand.) Only in Reynolds's case, he was determined to make one that held its audience's attention. How did he seek to do that? By using humor. He then learned the hard way that locker room humor doesn't focus when viewed through PC lenses in, of all towns, San Francisco.

The video Reynolds crafted was originally shown to the players during their 2004 summer training camp in Santa Clara, California. The NFL distributes booklets and a video on dealing with the media and community relations that are supposed to be shown to players. Reynolds supplemented the NFL message by addressing the team in person, and then decided to augment that presentation with a video "because of his fear of speaking to groups."[7] (He exhibited no such fear in the video.)

For ten months after the screening at summer camp, there was no word about the video. That is, until a copy was sent anonymously to the *San Francisco Chronicle* and, at the same time, to San Francisco Mayor Gavin Newsom.

There was some intrigue and finger-pointing surrounding the way it came to light. Then 49ers General Manager Terry Donahue had shown a thirty-second snippet of the video to the team owner, John York, just one day before Donahue was fired. Speculation was that Donahue's reason for showing it to York was to undermine Reynolds who, Donahue believed, was fanning the flames not only for his dismissal, but also for that of head coach Dennis Erickson.

Donahue later denied he was the source of the tape. "I didn't make the f**king tape, I didn't release the f**king tape," Donahue told the *Chronicle*. "I'm getting painted with a brush I've never been painted with before, and it's very upsetting."[8] (Interesting to note that five months passed from the time York saw the video until it came to light and the team took action against Reynolds.)

So let's go to the tape. The fifteen-minute video featured Reynolds impersonating Mayor Gavin Newsom in eight of the most un-PC vignettes to come out of San Francisco since Karl Malden patrolled the streets with Michael Douglas. The production values are straight out of *Wayne's World*. But you have to admire the effort.

The stage is set in the very first scene with a close-up of a picture in the *San Francisco Chronicle* which features the face of Kirk Reynolds superimposed on the body of Mayor Newsom (with his hottie then-wife, Kimberly Guilfoyle Newsom). In this scene, "Mayor" Reynolds simply sets up the premise for the training video, telling the players that since they often talk about what they would do if they were NFL commissioner for a day, he now wants to show them his interpretation of a day in his life as mayor: "So follow me, let's go through this great city of San Francisco, and I'll show you what it's like to be the mayor of this great city of San Francisco."

We'll call the first scene Chinatown. "Mayor" Reynolds is outside of a Chinese restaurant called "Joe's" and explains that his office reads everything printed about the team. He requests that the players tell him of any information that ends up in print about them that is incorrect. So far, so good. Good message for the team. But then, an Asian man (played by former 49ers trainer George Chung) ambles by, and Reynolds does a little role-playing by asking him to interpret a sports page written in an Asian language. When Chung begins to speak, it's with a heavy, overdone accent. ("Joe Montana once signed my balls.") Chung deciphers the sports headlines from the mock Asian newspaper: "Tim Latte [a mispronounced reference to Rattay, a Niners quarterback]. He feel good now. He feeling good. No plactice with the team, so most of the time he play with himself."[10] Mayor Reynolds then surmises that would explain his "sore forearm."

The video continues to play on the Asian accent: "[The 49ers] are American and [they] support President Bush and his erection [election]."[11] Reynolds questions Chung on his use of the word "erection," to which Chung replies in a manner oblivious to Reynolds's inside joke: "Yes erection. If you like Bush, then you like erection."[12]

Then Reynolds asks Chung for his character's name. "My name is Suck. Suck. My brother is Suck Young, I am Suck Pung. Everybody in my family Suck."[13] Finally, we get back to the serious message. Reynolds tells the players, "We read everything. If you see anything factually inaccurate, let us know."

I'll bet it played to raves in the locker room—its intended theatre. Unfortunately, you can imagine how it played in the politically correct streets of San Francisco. The point here, at least to me, is that San Franciscans were never the intended audience. And to evaluate the training video through any eyes except the intended audience seems a bit unfair to Reynolds.

It's all about context. Jackie Mason's comedy would sound awfully different if evaluated in a newscast instead of on Broadway. Chris Rock can drop the n-word on HBO, but I sure can't. And while an Italian may get away with a "Dago" joke, that's not fair game for the rest of us. Same thing here. Or, as 49ers safety Tony Parrish put it, "Is the video insensitive? Yes. But . . . it's the same type of satire that has [comedian] Dave Chappelle as the No. 1 show."[14]

More laughs and trouble came in scene three, which delved into the geographically appropriate arena of same-sex marriage. Here we find Mayor Reynolds presiding over the union of two scantily clad women in the Mitchell Brothers Theater on O'Farrell Street in San Francisco. "Now the courts have said we can't do this. Like my predecessor, we make our own rules here in San Francisco. Do you two love each other? Do you intend to love and cherish each other for the rest of your lives? Then show me."[15] The two women proceed to make out with each other and remove their clothes. The film gets blurry.

What was the point? Reynolds sought to explain that the football players should embrace all different types of lifestyles. And he says so: "As you guys learned in diversity training, people have diverse lifestyles. You may have a family worker or coworker with a different lifestyle. Embrace diversity!"

The critics' beef? They said that the overt pornographic features of this scene made light of the "legitimate" institution of gay marriage. I don't know about that, but I bet the scene kept the football players' attention while getting Reynolds' point across. And frankly, nobody got hurt.

The rest of the tape is more of the same, which won't stop me from giving you the blow-by-blow. In scene four, Reynolds walks by a beggar, played by line-backer Julian Peterson, who holds a sign that reads "Will Tackle for Cash."[16] Reynolds tells Peterson to "get a job"[17] and then continues on his way to SBC Park. (The only thing surprising here is that no homeless group of which I am aware complained about the scene.) When Reynolds arrives at SBC Park, he talks about media relations, stressing the importance of beat reporters: "You gotta take care of your locals . . . national stuff will come after that. And we will handle your schedule."

At the end of the scene, Reynolds throws a pitch to the catcher. The catcher then approaches Reynolds and thanks him for his loose policy on "hookers and booze."[18] Kinda dopey. But again, Reynolds is making a point, set in a climate of levity to hold the attention of a rough-and-tumble crowd.

Same thing with scene five which takes place in the Santa Clara Jail. Reynolds explains how the football players should "lean on"[19] the 49ers organization in the event they are arrested for anything. At the end of the scene, linebacker Jeff Ulbrich is shoved into a cell by two uniformed guards. Ulbrich professes his innocence in the fictional scenario by asking, "You got the wrong guy. What did I do?" Reynolds replies in a playful tone, "I'll tell you what NOT to do—drop the soap."[20] Predictable for sure, and, to the extent it is offensive, I ask, to whom? Prisoners? Who cares?

In scene six, Reynolds explains the importance of "keeping one's composure in front of the media." The hilarity of the scene comes when Reynolds does the exact opposite in a mock interview with KPIX-TV. A woman drives by and yells out, "You suck!" A guy drives up and gives him the finger. And then he almost gets into a fight with yet another heckler. His advice to the players? "Keep your composure."

During scene seven, Reynolds explains players must take care in all that they say and do. He's seated in the booth of what appears to be an expensive restaurant. "You gotta eat someplace . . . you need to be responsible for your actions and mindful of your teammates. The National Football League is the most highly visible sport on the planet. Everything you do and say is covered by the media so be careful of what you say and do. If you do something controversial or say something controversial, it will have an impact on this team and your teammates will have to answer questions about it. Remember TO?" When Reynolds is then presented with his dinner bill, he expresses surprise at the cost and says, "This one's on the taxpayers." No biggie.

The final scene got most of the attention. That's probably because of the nudity. Reynolds is taking a shower and is kicked out by a topless blonde. While wrapping a towel around his waist, he reminds the players that some reporters are female. "This brings up an important point. There are women in the locker room." He then tells the players that they should determine when they will be available for interviews.

And finally, after stepping into a women's locker room, Reynolds gives a review lesson: (1) don't get into a "pissing match" with media; (2) if you find yourself in a crisis, we are here to help you; (3) take care of your local media; (4) keep your composure; (5) "diversity is what makes this country great"; (6) "be responsible for your actions." He again references TO, before stating, "What you do and say reflects not only on you, but on the San Francisco 49ers." His seventh point was that they should remember there are women in the locker room and to be professional. The only trouble with the summation is that Reynolds was standing next to three naked women when he delivered it, one of whom then says, "Mayor, let's talk about your happy ending."[21] Ari Gold group hug. Fade to black.

Of course, when it aired on TV and via computer in San Fran, everyone played their expected role, which is to say they expressed shock and horror at Reynolds's conduct. Too bad. I wish someone involved would have stood their ground and simply said RELAX.

The newspapers, the mayor (that is, the real mayor), the team, and its owners made it abundantly clear that they were mortified and offended by Reynolds's training video. The *San Francisco Chronicle* thought he was a bad reflection on the front office and thought others should suffer as well: "Reynolds's crass humor and lesson in diversity insensitivity were inexcusable. But the blame should not fall on his shoulders alone. . . . In the spirit of team sports, the front-office 'team' should bear the brunt of the responsibility. It seems the organization needs both diversity and leadership training."[22]

Gavin Newsom is arguably the most politically correct mayor in the nation. It was he, remember, who initiated same-sex marriage soon after coming into office despite court edicts to the contrary. He wasn't happy he had lent his office to the making of the frat flick. When he finally saw it, he said that the tape wronged the Asian and gay communities. "It wasn't right to do it to the Asian community, particularly the Chinese community. It was wrong to do it to the gay and lesbian community. It was wrong to exploit women as they were exploited in this video."[23] Newson continued, saying, "The video is reprehensible."[24]

Aide Peter Ragone commented: "We didn't know about the content of the video and, if we did, it would have never happened. We find the content outrageous and reprehensible. But that doesn't change the very strong working relationship we have with the 49ers. This is an isolated incident. The 49ers are noted throughout the league for their understanding of diversity and tolerance."[25] Ragone went on to say, "In the future, the mayor's staff will insist on knowing the content of an entire video when it grants requests for filming inside City Hall."[26]

Pressure from these interests caused owner John York to buckle and issue a number of apologies and an official statement professing his contrition. York called the Reynolds's video offensive, inexcusable, and "absolutely contradictory to the ideals and values of the San Francisco 49ers."[27] York's official statement: "The San Francisco 49ers apologize for the inappropriate and tasteless video produced as a part of a player training program this past season. Ostensibly, the video was created to raise player awareness about how to deal with the media and to demonstrate by example how poor conduct can unintentionally make news. Unfortunately, this video is an example in itself."[28] Basically, anyone within shouting distance of the entire episode couldn't stop apologizing.

Did I mention the gay groups? They were upset, too, even though Reynolds harped on the central messages these groups always try to convey: respect, diversity, and alternative lifestyles. It's interesting that Reynolds still garnered support from homosexuals who knew him personally.

Lindsy McLean, an openly homosexual member of the 49er community and former trainer for the football team, said: "Kirk Reynolds is one of the most decent, non-homophobic people I have ever met in the world." McLean went on to say that Reynolds always "treated me with dignity and respect."[29] It seems that McLean was able to demonstrate some refreshing common sense by understanding the locker room content of the training video. When McLean came out in 2003, Reynolds helped him with the large amount of publicity that came with his declaration. I guess the positive things Reynolds has done for the gay community can never outweigh an arguably un-PC video in the eyes of these overzealous PC groups.

In an effort to redeem the 49ers organization in the eyes of the Asian-American community, John York has made several trips to the heart of Chinatown. He attended a packed meeting at the Chinese American Citizens Alliance Hall, in which he apologized on behalf of the 49ers organization: "The 49ers want to apologize directly to you for this very offensive, tasteless, and stupid training video. We are here to listen to you and incorporate your ideas to make sure this never happens again."[30]

For the Chinese-American community, an apology wasn't enough. Rev. Norman Wong of the Presbyterian Church in Chinatown said, "[The 49ers] get an A-plus for confession but the second step is harder: repentance."[31] Asian-American leaders have requested that the football players "spend more time in the community. They want scholarships and internships for their children. They want jobs and contracts for minority businesses."[32] Because the city has decided to build a new football stadium, Doug Chan of the Chinese American Voter Education Committee urged York to give a percentage of jobs and contracts to Chinese Americans and minority-owned businesses whenever the new stadium is built. Chan stated, "Let's start fulfilling promises."[33]

Is this lunacy or what? A guy makes a video with some off-color humor in an effort to hold the attention span of locker room inhabitants and the Chinese community thinks it deserves reparations?

Reynolds wasn't helped by the fact that, in the midst of the controversy, the presence of a more PG-13 predecessor put out by Reynolds in 2003 came to light. It did sport an unknown 49ers staffer burying his face in the bosom of a lap dancer. In the same scene, Reynolds can be seen with a "protuberance" in his pants.[34] But this video did not contain the overt nudity and racial jokes of its successor (although, according to Reynolds, the 2003 video prompted some players to ask for a sequel with "the money shots").[35]

Speaking of the players, most important, in my view, was the reaction of that intended audience. And guess what? They thought it was all a giant overreaction.

Take linebacker Julian Peterson, who was featured in the short fifteen-minute film: "It wasn't meant to harm anybody or be any kind of negative message at all. It was supposed to be an inhouse thing. I know Kirk personally. I know he has not addressed anybody with racial slurs. I'm just so upset this got out of proportion like this."[36] Or cornerback Mike Rumph: "I thought it was one of the funniest things I ever saw. The locker room is like a fraternity. The outside world can't really judge that."[37] Then there was center Jeremy Newberry: "I think they're losing one of the best people in the building. So far, the way he's been depicted in the media . . . is so far from who he is, it's ridiculous."[38]

For his part, Reynolds didn't say much, but was remorseful, articulated all the right things, but still got the boot. He apologized profusely in an interview with the Associated Press, stating: "I'm more sorry than anybody. My intention was to deliver a message important to our team. Certainly the execution and my decision-making were way out of line. I deeply regret it."[39] Reynolds also said that he never meant the video for public consumption. "Did I push too far? I did, but the ideas of the tape are appropriate for the locker room—though some of the subjects were inappropriate for the values of this organization, and mine, frankly."[40]

And just like that, he was gone from the organization for which he worked for eight years, during which time he had established an impeccable reputation. Now that the dust has settled, how does Reynolds look back on the entire incident? Kirk Reynolds recently spoke to me in a forthright manner. He was understandably bewildered and disappointed by the buzz-saw of political correctness that he'd encountered, particularly given an element of the story that has never been publicly revealed: the videotape that caused his firing was not the second one he made, as widely reported. It was the fourth!

Reynolds shared with me how and why he made the first:

I have always been nervous talking to the guys, I get scared in public speaking, so I decided to play off it. I remember that when Steve Mariucci was head coach, he asked me on the first day of rookie camp if I wanted to talk to the guys. And I couldn't do it. I said something like "the next time you hear from me, make sure I have something to drink." So later I decided to play off of that. I did a tape of me drinking, and it worked. Instead of stuttering and stammering, I was able to get my points across. I told a few jokes and guzzled a beer. The guys loved it. A video guy recorded the guys watching the tape and caught their reaction. I was pacing around a bit, rocking back and forth, still nervous. I remember that one of the linemen, Dave Fiore, said, "It looks like you're humping the podium," but guess what, they watched it.

The next two years, I did tapes that made fun of me. They were "day in the life" videos of me as the PR director. In them, I golf, I swim in a Speedo, I eat donuts, and I basically do nothing in about seven different scenes. But I make my points. And they watched. One reason is that each video has had inside team jokes, stuff only the guys would get. And that, too, makes them pay attention, but it would be hard for an outsider to know what is going on.

By the fourth year, I wanted to keep it more current. So year four, it was me as the mayor. In our team yearbook, we always ask the guys stuff like what would you do as commissioner or president, so this time

I thought I would do me as the mayor, tied to the great city of San Francisco.

I wanted to know from Kirk Reynolds why the fourth video got him fired if the first three were kept under the radar screen? He confirmed what many had suspected:

> It was a political issue. It was the general manager of the team blaming the PR guy for getting him fired and knowing there was a racy tape out there that could be used as a weapon to discredit him to save his job. That's even though the GM knew about the making of the video, and knew what was in it even if he didn't necessarily watch it. His roommate was in it and so, too, was his workout partner, but when he sought to discredit a guy who he mistakenly thought was trying to get him fired, he came up with tape, used it like a weapon of some sort.

Despite the controversy that surrounded it, Reynolds told me, the video achieved its purpose:

> The players overwhelmingly thought it was funny and, more importantly, it kept their attention. I knew that after the first two tapes that I made. I knew I was onto something. And I put real value in connecting. If I had just stood up and talked about the importance of the locals, they would have tuned out in fifteen seconds. They would have been sleeping or talking. So this was valuable. Too many mistakes get made if the guys don't listen. If you can connect with even ten of them, you have done service. And I found a way to connect.

After the controversy broke, Reynolds told me about an encounter between Andrew Lawrence from *Sports Illustrated* and safety Tony Parish. Lawrence questioned Parish about the videotape and what he remembered. He recalled several of Reynolds' points from the video, and when prompted slightly, was able to recall them all. As Reynolds told me,

> That was my goal. To get them to remember the points I was making. We had something successful there. And in the role of mayor for a day, I could hammer home those points. I wanted them to be receptive to

things like gay rights. The video itself was a sort of noise to hold their attention while I could stress stuff like that.

If I were to say, "embrace diversity," they won't pay attention. But if I do it using two hot girls, they will pay attention. The most important thing to me was always the message. Those who watched it later lost sight that it was doing the team a service.

In the four years of Reynolds's tapes, no player ever complained about the content.

I had a disclaimer in the beginning. I guess the fact that I had to throw out a disclaimer saying, "I hope no one is offended," you could say, well, I should have known something.

But I was thinking of the religious players, and the nudity, not the Chinese character. After we played it, I actually stuck around afterwards and waited for the more religious guys for their reaction, and none complained, never once said they were bothered.

That Chinese restaurant scene was probably the most controversial of all. And Reynolds told me that this was one of those instances where no one on the outside of the team could properly evaluate what was shown on screen:

You have to understand that the George Chung who is in the scene is a character. And he was always playing a character around the team. He was the team martial arts guy, the one who worked GM Donahue out. He was around the team constantly, but I don't think anyone knew the real George Chung because he was such a character. Well, the day of that scene, just myself and the camera guy went to film it. We went to three different businesses and asked about ten people to read a line on camera. But they all said no. The message we wanted to convey was that we in the PR Department read everything in the press, even the Chinese newspapers. So if something is in print about you, come talk to us because we will already know about it. That's why we wanted a Chinese person to read a line from a newspaper, playing on the fact that the team had been the focus of lots of bad, off-season predictions.

Well, George Chung offered to help us find a person and restaurant to get the scene done. But he didn't get it done. So he said he would do

MUZZLED

it. That's how we shot it in Santa Clara with him and he ad-libbed. The team knew him as a character and everyone had seen him. It didn't strike me as offensive because of who he was. Ironically, the most offensive parts were of a guy making fun of himself. People said, "They have this Chinese guy with buck teeth." Well, those were his teeth! The minute he walked on screen, everyone laughed because they knew him, the only prop he had were his glasses. The last thing we were trying to do was offend anyone. George was being the George we all saw every day and that is why we had it in there. Again, there were so many inside team jokes that no one outside would get it.

Like the scene of Julian Peterson with the cup. Some said that was making light of the homeless because he played one. But Julian had just turned down a long-term contract and a $15.5 million signing bonus and was in a hold out. The team totally connected to that. It had nothing to do with black homelessness. The money was the joke of his sign saying, "Will tackle for cash."

There is one more element to Reynolds's story typical of the PC movement that is muzzling America. It didn't become a story until somebody feigning outrage claimed it was a story. In this case, according to Reynolds, the beat writers knew of the videotape and its contents before it mushroomed into controversy. One local TV guy even saw it before the team viewing. His reaction? He thought it was funny, of course. Nobody saw a story in it. It only became a story when someone used it for a payback. That is the bottom line.

Reynolds told me, "The hardest part was to read or know that people were out there, painting a picture of me as a bigot or racist, and not know who I am. That's the reason the players were okay with me, they know who I am."[41]

And exactly who is he? A (now) forty-year-old guy who's been married to the same woman for sixteen years and who quickly progressed through the managerial ranks of professional football. A guy raised by a progressive college professor father to be open-minded and not the least bit political, despite a political science undergraduate degree from the University of California at Santa Barbara. And a man who now has grown accustomed to phone calls from friends and former colleagues who are anxious to tell him that they know he got screwed but are unable to help him.

Reynolds enjoyed a great reputation among those who covered the NFL. Ray

Didinger covered pro football for twenty-seven years at the *Philadelphia Bulletin* and *Daily News*. He told me: "Kirk Reynolds understood the job of the working reporters, and he did his best to help you. If you wanted time with a player on the 49ers, Kirk made it happen. It is a hard job, being the PR director of an NFL team because you are caught in the middle, between the press and the ball club. The reporters want coaches and players made available, and often the coaches and players don't want to be available. It is up to the PR director to create an environment in which both sides can do their jobs. Kirk did that, through good seasons and bad."[42]

Didinger also shared with me a telling story about Reynolds' character. While Reynolds was the PR chief for the 49ers, a student athlete in the Philadelphia area badly injured his neck in similar fashion to the way it had happened to one of the 49ers. The boy's coach told Didinger that the boy was down-in-the-dumps about his recovery. Didinger placed a call to Kirk Reynolds. That afternoon, Reynolds had the 49ers player on the phone to the Philadelphia teen to lift his spirits.

Dr. Z, writing his "Inside the NFL" column for *Sports Illustrated*, made a similar point: "In a business in which most club PR guys are merely trying to hold a job rather than do one, Reynolds stood out for his honesty and forthrightness, his willingness to take on any challenge. He's dedicated and hard-working, a pleasure to deal with . . . make that past tense, *was* dedicated, because the yahoos got him, the rabble rousers, the people who are the life of the necktie party."[43]

Jeremy Newberry was right—what happened to Kirk Reynolds was ridiculous. There's a time and a place for everything. Isn't that what our mothers taught us? You wouldn't use the same language in the locker room that you use in church, and that's okay. It's not a double standard, it's just plain standard.

When you consider the audience, an all-male NFL team, and you consider the source, PR guy Reynolds trying to get his point across in a way that guys will remember, you come up with a video that serves its purpose, that wasn't meant for public viewing, that was over the top but not painful. So lighten up, Frances! There are bigger problems in sports and San Francisco than a hokey training video. If Kirk Reynolds needs a job, I'd like to be hiring!

Maybe it's just something about video tapes and San Francisco, but not long after the video scandal rocked San Francisco's football squad, another video scandal shamed the city's police department. In December 2005, news leaked regarding a video made by some of the officers in the San Francisco Police Department. You'd have thought from the media coverage that the police video was a secret meeting of SFPD officers in white robes burning a cross, not a home-made tape meant for showing at a holiday party.

"This is a dark day—an extremely dark day—in the history of the San Francisco Police Department for me as a chief to have to stand here and share with you such egregious, shameful and despicable acts by members of the San Francisco Police Department," said Chief Heather Fong at City Hall press conference on the day the video was brought to the attention of city officials.[44]

The mayor—good, old Gavin Newsom—and the police chief described the situation "as videos that mock minorities and treat women as sex objects."[45]

City officials felt the video successfully fulfilled the triple threat of discrimination by describing the video as "racist, sexist, and homophobic."[46] In the words of the *New York Times*, "The videos include scenes of uniformed and plainclothes officers mocking the homeless, women, Asians, African Americans and gay men." An editorial in the *San Francisco Examiner*, written before all of the details of the video were made public, slammed the officers and stated that the officers "should ask themselves whether they would want the tape . . . discovered by their boss."[47]

What the editorial board of the *Examiner* did not know at the time was that showing the video to their boss was the whole point. The twenty-eight-minute video was "created for . . . the Bayview Station's Christmas party."[48]

So what is racist about the video? One portion of the DVD shows an African American officer with a dog collar around his neck, in a cage, eating out of a bowl of dog food and, according to one source, was "the image of greatest concern to authorities."[49] Left underreported, of course, was that the dog image is a known joke among the officers and was not meant to portray African Americans as inferior. The officer in the DVD "earned the nickname 'Dog' after he complained that he was being treated like one by a station sergeant" after being summoned into a superior's office.[50] The officer had been teased about his nickname for weeks and prior to when the video was taken "a lieutenant at the station opened a can of dog food for the officer as a joke."[51]

If turning the parody of an individual officer's nickname into an overall degradation of African Americans seems a stretch, the claim that the video mocked Asian Americans as bad drivers is a total leap of faith. The video shows an Asian American bicycle officer having trouble riding his department-issued bike and depicts the officer about to crash into the captain's car.[52] City officials were "concerned the skit could be interpreted as a takeoff on the stereotype of Asians as poor drivers." According to Officer Andrew Cohen, the editor of the video, the scene with the bicycle officer was another private joke: "The officer had failed a bicycle training test and had struck the captain's car before, and the video was a mock retest in which the officer pledged not to hit the car again."[53] Hardly social commentary on the skills of Asian drivers.

Cohen shot and edited the videos. Perhaps his greatest error in judgment was in posting his handiwork on his personal Web site for a few days, much to the shock and disappointment of others who had participated in what was supposed to be a private, admittedly, sophomoric joke. Instead, he should have pulled a Rosemary Woods.

According to the *Examiner*, "In one skit that is a takeoff on the TV show 'Charlie's Angels,' former Bayview Captain Rick Bruce suggestively sticks his tongue out at several female police officers and a transgender woman. They do the same gesture in return."[54] And, out came the so-called experts, for example, Noreen Farrell, a civil rights lawyer with Equal Rights Advocates, saying the *Charlie's Angels* skit was "really degrading to female officers who fought for decades to be respected for their hard work."[55] Not surprisingly, Ms. Farrell ignored several facts in her interpretation. First of all, the three female police officers playing the Angels are not dressed in uniform. Furthermore, the clips of Captain Bruce were shot years earlier for a video shot under department auspices and were revived in the *Charlie's Angels* sequence to make fun of his nervous habit of sticking out his tongue in conversation.[56] Once again, merely an inside joke in a portion of a video meant to honor Captain Bruce's retirement later this year. Bruce, despite his lack of knowledge of the entire video process, was the highest-ranking officer suspended.[57]

Critics of the video do not appreciate the humor and claim that portions of the video highlight unacceptable behavior by the officers. However, when you consider the context of the humor, the officers are actually mocking those behaviors precisely because they know they are unwarranted criticism of the department. For example, a portion of the video shows officers accidentally running over a homeless person and in another scene the officers portray themselves as playing video games while waiving overtime cards. Cohen's attorney, Daniel Horowitz, stated it best: "They are raw and emotionally honest. . . . We are talking about officers poking fun at themselves, stereotypes and the absurdity of their job."[58]

"There is no slander here, no racism, no nothing. . . . I don't have a racist, prejudiced bone in my body," says DVD creator Cohen. "We do a lot of stuff to let off steam, have fun."[59] The mayor and police chief do not share Cohen's sentiment. The San Francisco Police Department formally suspended approximately twenty officers for their part in the video.[60] Furthermore, the mayor appointed a panel to investigate the matter, and he has asked the city Human Rights Commission and the city Commission on the Status of Women to conduct their own investigations.[61]

At least the president of the San Francisco Police Officers Association, Gary Delagnes, came to the defense of the officers—*sort of.* "We are absolutely certain that none of the officers involved participated in the making of these comic parodies with the intent to disparage any individual or group," he said. "Anyone who has seen these skits knows the actors themselves include officers who are female, black, Hispanic, officers of rank and officers of the rank-and-file."[62] He also called the mayor's response a "conventional political ploy."[63] But he still felt the need to preface all of his remarks by stating that the officers were "100 percent wrong" in making the video.[64]

All of the attention on the video deflected the attention away from the real problem within the SFPD. "The suspensions come as San Francisco's murder rate has hit its highest level in a decade and the department faces an officer shortage."[65] "We're outgunned. We're outmanned," Cohen said. "The fact of the matter is that [Chief Fong] has an out-of-control department. She lives in the Bayview and has never stopped by the station to see her own officers."[66]

"The guys on the streets have only one tool to relieve the stress," said Cohen, "and it's humor."[67] The editorial in the *Examiner* states that there is a big difference between the officer's video skits and those seen on comedy shows on television: "Police officers must be held to a higher standard of behavior than what is acceptable for average citizens."[68]

I agree. Next year I hope they are able to shoot on a digital camera and have a better soundtrack.

One wonders if the Minnesota Vikings wish they'd hired Kirk Reynolds after his firing by the 49ers. The season after Reynolds's departure from San Francisco, more than a dozen Vikings were reportedly among an estimated ninety people who were part of an ill-fated two-boat cruise on Lake Minnetonka. Arrangements for the cruise were made by one or more of the first-year players as part of a tradition of their entertaining the veterans. In this case, the October 6, 2005, cruise was cut short by the bad behavior of those onboard. It was reported that crew members on the two yachts were offered money for sex and grew fearful for their safety. An attorney for the yachts' owner said the behavior on the cruise included oral sex, masturbation, and playing with sex toys.[69] The lawyer said that almost immediately after boarding, crew members noticed partially disrobed women walking around. One employee opened a galley and three nude women popped out. Then the players started to become more aggressive, demanding to pour their own drinks and screaming at the bartenders. Players were also reportedly approaching the wait staff and telling them they would be tipped if they danced.[70] Quarterback Daunte Culpepper, offensive tackle Bryant McKinnie, running back Moe Williams, and cornerback Fred Smoot were charged with indecent, disorderly, and lewd and lascivious conduct. Culpepper told ESPN that he was shocked and angry when he learned of the charges and said he didn't touch anybody and nobody touched him during the cruise. Among the offenses, Smoot was charged with using a sex toy on a woman, McKinnie with participating in oral sex, and Williams and Culpepper with receiving lap dances and fondling women.[71]

If only they had seen Kirk Reynolds's video.

3

Sorry We Got It Correct

Apologies will always follow violations of political correctness; the truth may not. Want proof? Just look at what happened to Larry Summers, the president of Harvard.

Summers was invited to be a luncheon speaker at an academic conference exploring the lack of women in certain professions. He obliged, and in an effort to stimulate debate, or "to provoke," as he put it, he offered three reasons why women are under-represented in math and science professions. One of his theories relied upon innate differences between men and women. In his comments, he said there were other examples of under-representation of groups in activities. "To take a set of diverse examples, the data will, I am confident, reveal that Catholics are substantially under-represented in investment banking, which is an enormously high paying profession in our society; that white men are very substantially under-represented in the National Basketball Association; and that Jews are very substantially under-represented in farming and in agriculture."[1]

So how'd it go over? Like the proverbial lead balloon. And what happened? One month later, he apologized. Said Summers: "If I could turn back the clock, I would have spoken differently on matters so complex . . . the issue of gender difference is far more complex than comes through in my comments. . . ."[2]

Political correctness cares about apologies, not the truth. The best example of all involves my own newspaper, the *Philadelphia Daily News*, where I write a weekly column. The newspaper retracted a true story. A cover story, no less!

I remember where I was when I first saw that cover. That's how startling it was. As we like to say in Philadelphia, I was "down the shore" in Ocean City, New Jersey, on vacation. On a humid, early-August morning, while en route to a workout with my friend, the fitness guru and former president of the 76ers, Pat Croce, I stopped at Wawa for a newspaper and cup of coffee.

It was a Thursday, the day my own weekly column runs in the *Daily News*, and I was anxious to see what headline my editor, Michael Schefer, had put on a column I had filed before going away with my family. Coincidentally, my opinion piece concerned my embracing of educational opportunities as the only legitimate form of slavery reparations. Schefer's headline was "Reparations: Ending the Guilt Trip,"[3] but that's not what was memorable about that morning's paper. In fact, I don't even think I got to my column that day. I couldn't take my eyes off the front cover.

"Fugitives Among Us" was the headline, and it was splashed across the photographs of some tough-looking dudes. Eighteen of them, to be exact. Mug shots actually. And every one of them had a look that said "don't f**k with me." The story that accompanied the piece spelled out why they were featured in the newspaper:

> Ten years ago, police believe, Lester Lambert stabbed his elderly boss through the head with a flat-blade screwdriver. Detectives say they quickly solved the crime. A murder warrant went out for Lester Lambert. But, as the years ticked by, the killing of 68-year-old Christian Ludwig went unavenged. Lester Lambert was never caught, even though he probably never left Philadelphia. Lambert, now 48, is one of dozens of people who are wanted by Philadelphia police on murder charges and who are living among the law-abiding. The cops know who they are. They have their pictures. They know something about their movements. They just can't catch them.[4]

I took one look and knew right away that this was going to be trouble. See, Philadelphia is a two-newspaper town, the *Daily News* and the *Inquirer*. Both newspapers are owned by Knight-Ridder Inc., but they maintain separate identities. The *Inquirer* customer base lies in the lilly-white suburbs while the *Daily News*, the self-described "People Paper," is the urban newspaper of choice.

I immediately foresaw a major problem with the cover story as it related to the *Daily News* readership—every person pictured as wanted for murder was a minority. I knew, standing there sipping Wawa coffee, there'd be hell to pay. But not because of any inaccuracy in the reporting. I was right.

It didn't take long for the controversy to erupt. The *Daily News* itself felt compelled to publish a follow-up the next day titled "Strong Reaction to People Paper Fugitive Cover."[5] In the story, Sharif Street, the son of the city's African American mayor, John Street, said the front-page story the day before would make life tougher for every young African American in Philadelphia.

The follow-up story also confirmed that the eighteen mug shots from the day before were all of fugitives wanted for murder by Philadelphia police, and that all were African American, Hispanic, or Asian. Most importantly, the story said, "The front page is representative of the latest available listing of suspected murder fugitives, which lists 41 African Americans, 12 Hispanics and 3 Asians."[6]

"There are plenty of white guys in jail for murder, but those guys are locked up," said Police Sgt. Bill Britt.[7]

Nevertheless, the story contained an apology from *Daily News* Managing Editor Ellen Foley: "We apologize if the graphic treatment offended black Philadelphians. We were trying to explore and provide accurate information about an issue of great concern to our community."

But the *Daily News*'s apology on behalf of the newspaper didn't end there. On August 30, eight days after the cover story, Ellen Foley issued a formal apology on behalf of the newspaper. "Would we do a story again about 41 fugitives wanted for murder by the Philadelphia Police Department? Absolutely. Would we do it differently? Absolutely. The front-page photos from last Thursday sent the message to some readers that only black men commit murder. That was a mistake."[8]

I thought that all of this kvetching was ridiculous. The message that was sent in the cover photos was the message the police department intended to send when providing the photographs to the newspaper—please help us find these miscreants wanted for murder, regardless of whether they are pink, purple, or Indian chief! I wanted to say something about it, but this was my newspaper, even though my relationship goes no deeper than a once-a-week column.

I was reminded of a political legend. Philadelphia Republican boss Billy Meehan was fond of telling candidates seeking his blessing that he could be for them or against them, whichever would help them more. I was thinking of these words as I deliberated whether to write in support of the initial decision by the *Daily News* to print the pictures. Perhaps they would be better served by my opposition. And, I wondered, to the extent I write a column and say the apology was unwarranted, will they print it?

Well, they did.

Atop what I wrote, which was published exactly two weeks after the now infamous cover story, Schefer's headline was "That Apology—It's Bunk."[9] I said that any criticism of the newspaper's leadership in connection with the August 21 cover was off base, and that the *Daily News's* recent apology was unwarranted and probably counterproductive. I wished the newspaper had responded to the criticism of a few with a demand for dialogue about the very real problem highlighted in photos and print that day. Instead, the capitulation of the *Daily News* did nothing but prove that, as a society, we remain unwilling to broach any subject that involves substantive dialogue about race.

I also said I wasn't surprised by this outcome. I had learned my lesson by my piece on slavery reparations. What did I say? First, that there exists a real disparity between the races; second, that slavery played a role in the origin of the disparity; third, that we, as a society, need to do something to level the playing field; and fourth, that a new commitment to minority education was the best answer. What did it get me? Hate mail.

Nowhere in the criticism was anybody saying the *Daily News* got anything wrong. The police homicide unit had identified fifty-six individuals wanted in the city for murder. The *Daily News* then profiled twenty-seven of them in its pages—which I consider to have been a public service. They put as many as they could fit on the cover. That happened to be eighteen of the fifty-six.

None of the forty-one individuals identified was white, and that was the rub. Of course, it wasn't the *Daily News's* fault that forty-one nonwhites were being sought for murder, but, in the twisted racial world in which we live, that was perceived by a few to be the fault of the *Daily News*. And, to appease them, the *Daily News* capitulated.

So there we went again. Instead of discussing why black-on-black crime threatened the city—minority victims in particular—we got caught up in a bogus debate as to whether the *Daily News* should have run accurate information. Meanwhile, crime continued and energy that should have been dedicated to that end was usurped by debate on the propriety of the *Daily News'* telling it like it is. Heaven forbid we should let facts get in the way.

Not long before this flap, the William Penn Foundation, based in Philadelphia, had funded a study by Public/Private Ventures, which was published in the spring of 2001 and titled *Murder is No Mystery*. It was an analysis of Philadelphia homicides between 1996 and 1999. Then Philadelphia (and now Miami) police commissioner John Timoney wrote the Foreword. The Introduction summed up the study as follows:

> And the tragedy of all is that murder, in this city at least, is not exactly a mystery. A look at the homicides committed between 1996 and 1999 reveals a pattern: 9 out of 10 victims were men, and over half were young men between 18 and 34 years old. Three victims out of four were African American. Four victims out of five were shot to death with handguns. Virtually all alleged murderers were the same race as their victims, with over 90 percent of African Americans dying at the hands of another African American.[10]

Further along, the study reported that Caucasians made up over half of the city's population but represented only five percent of its alleged murders, whereas African Americans made up less than half the city's population but represented over three-quarters of its alleged murderers.

In the August 21 cover, the pictures told that story. But *shhhhhhh*. It's politically incorrect to talk about it.

No wonder nothing ever changes.

It only gets worse. Unfortunately, there is an even more egregious and timely example of politically correct sanitizing of the news media at the very same *Daily News*. It involves a crime spree in 2005, in Philadelphia's toney Chestnut Hill section of town. A radio listener of mine who resides in Chestnut Hill brought to my attention the way in which the *Daily News* covered a crime wave in comparison to the way the neighborhood newspaper, the *Chestnut Hill Local*, did the same. The difference in the coverage was remarkable.

On the exact same day, both papers covered the same issue. Headline in the *Daily News*: "Teen Thuggery in Chestnut Hill." Headline in the *Local*: "New Wave of Assaults Hits Hill." So far, so good. The *Daily News*, in a news story written by G. W. Miller III, then published a twenty-two-paragraph story. It began:

A band of teenagers has been terrorizing ritzy Chestnut Hill, robbing residents at random including a 42-year-old mentally impaired man.

Over the past two months, starting June 19, there have been at least eight muggings and assaults by adolescents traveling in packs of up to seven youths, police said.

Police Inspector Joseph Sullivan, of the Northwest Detectives, said the teens don't target a specific group.

It's basically targets of opportunity: male, female, black, white . . . they're not picky.[11]

The *Local* coverage began as follows:

Four men fell victim to brutal assaults in separate incidents last week as they walked the streets of Chestnut Hill. The attacks, perpetrated by a roving group of teenagers, bear similarities to a recent spate of muggings reported on by the *Local* last month.[12]

While the leads of the two stories may sound similar, there was something dramatically different about the coverage. The *Daily News* made no mention of what the perpetrators looked like. None. The *Local*, on the other hand, said this:

The most recent series of assaults began on July 31 when a man in his early 40's was beaten by a group of three to four black males near the intersection of Winston Road and Mermaid Lane around 5 p.m. . . . Two days later, another man was attacked by a group of seven black males while walking in the 8200 block of Ardleigh street around 11 p.m. . . . On August 5, a group fitting a similar description jumped a man in the unit block of E. Mermaid Lane while he was walking to a video store. . . .

The radio listener who pointed out the disparity told me he felt the *Daily News* left him vulnerable by not giving him the description of those wreaking havoc on his neighborhood streets. He wanted to know if it was deliberate or an oversight. So did I.

So I tracked down George Miller, the author of the story. He shocked me with his admission: "The police made me aware of the race and the background of the suspects, and I left that particular part out for two reasons. The police think they know the group behind it—they think they know who these kids are—they think an arrest will be coming along very soon—so with that in mind, it's pretty much run its course. The cops know who these kids are. They're watching them. They have an idea where these kids live—so they've got them—they're on top of them."[13]

I said to him, wait a minute, you thought that you did not need to solicit public involvement in helping to catch the bad guys because "it's pretty much run its course"?

"Well, quite frankly I didn't think—there wasn't any reason to scare, you know, an upper-class neighborhood from African American kids," he said. "It's sufficient enough if you see a bunch of kids out there—you know if you see seven or eight kids regardless of what their race, what their ethnicity is, depending on what the kids look like, you should have your radar on. . . . I don't think you necessarily need to know that it's bunch of black kids or a bunch of Hispanic kids. You know, a group of kids is a group of kids."

In other words, let's sanitize the news so as to spare readers the truth. Sorta like not printing the Phillies' box score unless they win. I mean, by that logic, I wondered, why print the newspaper at all?

4

Dressing for
Political Correctness

You've heard of dressing for success? How about dressing for political correctness? And I'm not talking about the trend toward banning hobos and pirates at Halloween parties, although those developments are worthy of discussion.

Instead, I have in mind the recent, true story of a sales manager who cost his company more than a half million dollars because he had the audacity to distribute a best-selling business book. The manager, troubled by the appearance of a female account executive, had a colleague purchase a book about business dress which he then distributed to his staff. The how-to book had sold millions without incident over three decades. But in the New Millennium, an African American account executive was so offended by the content of the book that he quit his job. And when he filed a discrimination claim based on receiving the offending book on how to dress for work, he was awarded more than $600,000.

Here is how it happened.

Philadelphia Eagles' football games are broadcast on radio station WYSP, 94.1-FM. WYSP is owned by Infinity Broadcasting, which, in turn, is owned by Viacom. (That's the same ownership as the radio station where I do morning drive, but far be it for me to do my employer's bidding.)

Shawn Brooks was an account executive selling commercial time for Eagles' games on WYSP. His boss, Joe Zurzolo, was the sales manager. Zurzolo was frustrated with the manner of dress of one of Brooks' colleagues, a female named Heather Peterson. At a sales meeting for account executives on Wednesday, May 9, 2001, Zurzolo gave his staff copies of the latest version of the well-known and widely read book called *(New) Dress for Success*, written by John T. Molloy. Zurzolo, who had never read the book, relied upon the recommendation of a colleague and purchased copies for the staff.

Shawn Brooks took the book home that night and read it. He was appalled by what he saw in a chapter that gave advice to minorities in sales. Interestingly, Brooks never took his complaints to Zurzolo or Zurzolo's supervisor. (He later said he didn't trust Zurzolo, and was offended by other behavior of Zurzolo unrelated to the book.) Instead, the day after the books were distributed, Brooks called the company's human resources director and complained. When told of Brooks' complaints, the human resources director immediately collected the books from the other account executives.

Meanwhile, Brooks never returned to the office, other than to resign and pick up his possessions, which he did nineteen days after being handed the book. In the interim, Brooks was called many times by Zurzolo and by Zurzolo's supervisor, presumably so that they could offer an explanation and apology. (Zurzolo would later say that he "absolutely overstepped his bounds by distributing the book.")

Brooks never returned their calls. And, by the time he returned to the office to resign and clean out his office, he had already filed a complaint with the Pennsylvania Human Relations Commission (PHRC), something he did seven days after the book's distribution. Zurzolo was never punished for the incident, other than having his boss call him a "f**king idiot."[1]

The incident soon grew legs. When Brooks's legal complaint became news in Philadelphia, the NAACP promptly announced its intention to get involved. "We want to take this national," announced J. Whyatt Mondesire, the president of the Philadelphia chapter. Charles Bowser, a Philadelphian long involved in civil rights battles, would enlist the help of the Congressional Black Caucus.[2] Even the Philadelphia Eagles issued a statement saying they were deeply offended by the described activities.[3]

Just as all of this was hitting the fan, I was invited to appear on a Sunday morning television program carried by Philadelphia's ABC affiliate, WPVI-TV. The host, Wally Kennedy, had invited me to join him for a discussion about a column I'd written about problems in the Catholic Church. Before my live shot, I was seated in the "green room" next to (you guessed it) Shawn Brooks, who was a guest on the same program for a segment on his departure from WYSP.

Brooks struck me as a handsome guy in his early thirties. From the coverage of his case, I was aware he had been a linebacker at Delaware State and had once tried out for both the Eagles and St. Louis Rams before he began work as an account executive selling Eagles airtime. What took me by surprise was his appearance. After all of the hullabaloo, I half expected to see him in a kofi or some other form of traditional African American dress. Instead, the only thing ethnic about Brooks was that he looked like one of the Brooks Brothers: dark suit, pin-striped Oxford-cloth shirt, and a maroon tie.

He didn't look like he needed the advice of a dress book; he appeared as if he could have written one. I began to wonder what all the fuss was about and decided to track down a copy of the *(New) Dress for Success*. How, I wondered, could the book be on the shelf for many years of robust sales without any controversy? My suspicions were confirmed as I read it.

Mein Kampf meets Saville Row it is not. *Dress* is about four hundred mind-numbing pages of fashion tips. A chapter called "Some Advice for Minorities" is a total of four pages, and there you can find this advice:

It is an undeniable fact that the typical upper-middle-class American looks white, Anglo-Saxon and Protestant. He is of medium build, fair complexion, with almost no pronounced physical characteristics. He is the model of success; that is, if you run a test, most people of all socio-economic, racial and ethnic backgrounds will identify him as such. Like it or not, his appearance will normally elicit a positive response from someone viewing him. Anyone not possessing his characteristics will elicit a negative response to some degree, regardless of whether that response is conscious or subconscious. . . .

The two groups who have the most problems with their appearance are black men and Hispanic men. It is unfortunate but true that our society has conditioned us to look upon members of both groups as belonging to the lower classes, and no matter how high a minority individual rises in status or achievement, he is going to have some difficulty being identified by his success rather than by his background. But clothing can help. For sixteen years I have been giving the following advice to my black and Hispanic clients: Dress conservatively; wear those garments that are considered upper-middle-class symbols—pinstripe suites, end-on-end blue shirts, Ivy League ties; wear and carry only those accessories that convey the same message.[4]

It is also here that Molloy says he's been criticized for attempting to make "Uncle Toms" out of his clients: "My only answer is that my black clients include officers of several of America's major corporations and representatives of foreign governments. They are hardly Uncle Toms. I stick to my advice. If you are black or Spanish in America, and if you are moving up the rungs of corporate success, you should adhere to the dress code of the corporation and of the country, even going somewhat overboard in the direction of being conservative."[5]

Pretty tame stuff and pretty sound advice, at least if you ask me. To the extent controversy can be found within the pages of Molloy's book it comes in a chapter called "How to Use Clothes to Sell Yourself," where one can find a four-page discussion headed "When Blacks and Hispanics Sell to Whites (and Vice Versa)." There, Molloy offers tidbits, which the PHRC found to be discriminatory—such as advice to avoid loud colors and doff a 'fro haircut: "Men who [wear Afros] are less highly thought of by whites and blacks." No doubt some of the advice is a bit dated; other parts are simply ridiculous.

But the question is whether a manager who distributes a four-hundred-page book with this buried inside has used race as a motivating factor in creating a hostile work environment?

Said differently, did Shawn Brooks suffer intentional discrimination because of his race when Joe Zurzolo handed Brooks and his colleagues copies of John Molloy's book *(New) Dress for Success*?

To these questions, which are the heart of Brooks' legal action, the PHRC said yes. It found that Brooks suffered intentional discrimination in being handed the book. In fact, the PHRC said, the racial harassment was severe and pervasive.

And so the PHRC awarded Brooks $286,262 for back pay and $328,000 in front pay. Commission Chairman Stephen A. Glassman said, "This is the most egregious case of published documentation on stereotyping and bias toward race, gender, and religion in the workplace the commissioners have seen in a long time."[6]

I disagree. First, I think it's the equivalent of saying the *Encyclopedia Britannica* is pornographic because somewhere buried inside of volumes A-Z there is a depiction of a penis.

Second, Brooks confuses crass salesmanship with racism. I don't think dressing to establish a common ground with a business counterpart carries any racial animus. It's just a cheap sales trick. It goes on all the time, and I suspect it's been around since the days of Willy Loman. If it's discriminatory to tailor one's dress to your audience, including from a racial, ethnic, or socio-economic perspective, then I am in the same boat as Zurzolo. And I know I am not alone.

In April of 2005, on the heels of the PHRC award to Shawn Brooks, I tracked down John T. Molloy to get his reaction. First, I asked him what he made of the recent Philadelphia case. "It's the nuttiest thing I have ever heard of," he told me. "I thought they were crazy. My first reaction was to laugh. Then I said, 'My God, look at the implications of what they said.' They said, if I or anyone else takes any of the protected groups, and that's women and minorities and who else I'm not sure in your state, but any of the protected groups, and study them, then I've broken the law. And any individual who has been studied deserves to be rewarded. Now, every politician in your state does surveys of how African Americans will vote, how Hispanics will vote, how women will vote—so you have to sue every one of them!"[7]

In other words, he argues, if a politician looks at demographic breakdowns in a campaign poll, he is similarly acting in a discriminatory fashion. I like his logic. He also thinks the net effect of the recent case will be to hurt the people seemingly being protected by the PHRC ruling.

"The reason I put information on minorities in the book was to try to help minorities in business by giving them concrete information. This [ruling] says that minorities can't be separated and must be treated like everyone else. It's an official statement that prejudice no longer exists," Molloy further argued.

"If this stands up, I will have to leave that information [about race] out, and it will become untenable. It is a book aimed at corporate America and the first rule in corporate America is 'watch your rear end.' Even if thrown out, it may impact sales of the book. I will have to give a politically correct version which is terrible for minorities, who I am seeking to help. And it is not just me, but everybody else too. The arguments against affirmative action are the same as this Commission, you can't single out race.

"We've become so politically correct we're going to get ourselves blown up," Molloy told me. I told him that had already happened, on September 11.

The Philadelphia case is the first he's ever heard of where someone brought a discrimination case based on his advice. My own independent review of a nationwide court database bears this out.

So why now, after all these years, is Molloy's advice actionable?

Well, I think the answer lies in one of the many ironies of the case. Shawn Brooks, who cried racism, was not the intended target of the book distribution. The sales manager was concerned about the dress of a female salesperson. His solution: to distribute the book to the entire sales group. Doesn't this say something about who we've become?

My suspicion? He was probably worried that if he took the matter up with her alone, she'd have cried sexual discrimination! Come to think of it, had the guy been gay, it would have been all about lifestyle choice. And so it goes.

I keep coming back to the fact that the sales manager, Joe Zurzolo, never read the book before distributing it and was unaware of the content later objected to by Brooks. That, and the fact that when Zurzolo and his supervisor tried to call Brooks after the fact to ameliorate the situation, he didn't return their calls.

I can think of 600,000 reasons why he didn't answer the phone.

5

Oh, Yes, It's Ladies' Night

If you hear any noise
It ain't the boys, it's ladies' night, uh huh[1]
—KOOL AND THE GANG

I suspect that David R. Gillespie never liked that song by Kool and The Gang.

I know for sure David didn't like what he saw when he walked into the Coastline Restaurant in Cherry Hill, New Jersey. It wasn't the food or the drink that caused him angst. Gillespie was unhappy with the promotion that charged men a five-dollar cover while women were offered free admission and discounted drinks on ladies' night.

Not that there was anything new about the promotion. It's a time-honored tradition to boost the attendance of men who are the big spenders in bar trade. Men go where there are women. Attract the women, and you will have a packed house of guys paying full price for drinks. (Kinda like Tony Montana, a.k.a. Al Pacino in *Scarface,* telling Manny: "First you get da money, den you get the power, den you get the women.")

Well, Gillespie raised a fuss and found a willing ear in New Jersey's Division of Civil Rights when its director, J. Frank Vespa-Papaleo, issued a ruling in which he concluded that ladies' nights are discriminatory. And just like that, the twenty-six-year-old Wednesday night tradition ended at this nightspot, leaving owner Christos Mourtos angered and bewildered.

"For the past 25 years we have been doing a ladies' night on Wednesday night. There is a five-dollar cover for men, no cover for ladies," he told me. "And ladies were also getting their drinks for a reduced price . . . it's a common thing in the nightclub business . . . Well, 75 percent of customers on any given ladies' night are male . . . absolutely . . . but in 25 years that we've been doing this promotion, we've had one complaint."[2]

Even Governor Jim McGreevey (a man who would soon thereafter be outed as one more interested in a bar full of men than women) called the ruling "bureaucratic nonsense." "It is an overreaction that reflects a complete lack of common sense and good judgment," said the then governor of the Garden State.[3]

Gillespie was identified in the press as a forty-two-year-old teetotaler who worked as a massage therapist and attended nursing school. He said he had been to the Coastline twice. The first time he paid the cover charge and it gnawed at him. The second time he spoke out. He said he wasn't there to "get women drunk," and that he objected to the idea that women would drink cheaper than men and that men would accept it.

"It dawned on me that this is wrong, this is really wrong," said Gillespie, who claimed he had not been back to the bar. "Unfortunately, a lot of men don't think with their head. They just lose their logic when they're around women."[4]

The decision was greeted with controversy. Vespa-Papleo defended his order by saying that ladies' night was the equivalent of saying, "Christians can have free drinks but Jews can't."[5]

Which is ridiculous. One is driven by racial animus, the other by amour.

And besides, Coastline owner Chris Mourtos wondered where that left discounts for seniors and kids.

"Every business across the country uses some kind of promotion to attract a specific segment of the population. By doing so, according to this ruling, you're automatically discriminating against a different segment," he told me. "Well, we also do senior citizen discounts, and somehow they manage to say that the senior citizen discounts are legal. I can't understand how you can give a discount to one group and its legal, but you give it to another group and it's illegal."

His solution during the period of uncertainty? "We converted the night into what we called equal gender night. It started out as a joke. It has worked somewhat . . ."[6]

Perhaps most surprising is that New Jersey is not some aberration in the ladies' night controversy. Oh no—the legions of the politically correct abound—from sea to (not so) shining sea. Here's just a sampling of the cases from across the country that our vigilant bureaucrat took note of in his decision.

In Iowa, the Bluff's Run Racetrack ran a Ladies' Day promotion in the grandstand area of the track on Wednesday afternoons from June 17, 1987, to September 9, 1987. Women received free admission into the grandstand and discounted prices on food, drinks, and souvenirs. In overruling the trial court, which had essentially laughed the case out of court, the august justices of the Iowa Supreme Court wrote to complain that they couldn't see how this was any different from any other discrimination: "We can conceive of no way to differentiate between an accidentally discriminatory promotional scheme and a prohibited discriminatory practice . . ."[7]

A chain of Orange County car washes offering a Ladies' Day discount was found to have violated California's antidiscrimination laws when (you guessed it) a male patron complained about the two-dollar price difference and demanded the women's rate. Indeed, in this particular case, Dennis Koire filed suit against *seven* different car washes and, for good measure, a club named Jezebel's. Of course, the California Supreme Court sided with our champion. Citing cases of race-based discrimination from the civil rights era, the court easily made the comparison to dollar-drink night at a college bar.[8]

Now I may not have been out there with civil rights leaders in the sixties, but I hope everyone getting a high-school education in this country learns something of the terrible injustices suffered by African Americans in this country and the tremendous sacrifices millions of concerned Americans made to abolish horrors like the Jim Crow laws. To suggest that an eighteen-year-old kid from the LA 'burbs suffered the same sort of oppression by being denied a three-dollar soap and rinse for his jalopy cheapens the accomplishments of that time.

On nights where the entertainment included "go-go" girls, the Flintlock Inn in Dauphin County, Pennsylvania, allowed women patrons in without the normal one-dollar cover. Once again, the trial court judge laughed the overly officious state bureaucrats out of his courtroom. Given the Pennsylvania Liquor Control Board's tendency to miss the forest through the trees, Judge John Dowling observed that the Board's charges were "a little like stomping on a mouse in the kitchen when there's a tiger at the door."[9] Sadly, the panel of judges on the Commonwealth Court overturned the good Judge Dowling, finding the promotion a clear cut case: "as a matter of law there is a violation of the Human Relations Act's prohibition against discrimination on the basis of sex."[10]

Fortunately, political correctness hasn't prevented some states from recognizing the obvious—that Ladies' Night is more about evening the odds for singles (male and female) than singling out evenings as opportunities for sexual discrimination. The following examples showcase sanity and the triumph of common sense.

The Dock Club in Sangamon County, Illinois, offered a reduced cover charge to female patrons on its Ladies' Nights. Instead of mechanically applying the law, the court recognized that the bar could hardly have intended to exclude its male clientele. In a decision notable not just as plain sense but as plain spoken, Judge Green of the Illinois Appeals Court wrote: "Here . . . the price charged males on ladies' night was the regular established price and obviously not a price established for the purpose of discouraging their patronage. That charged females was a price reduced to a nominal sum and one obviously set for the purpose of encouraging their patronage."[11]

The Supreme Court of Washington also found the establishment's intentions important in applying the law sensibly. In a case alleging sexual discrimination brought by a male fan of the Seattle Sonics, the court noted that the team's Ladies' Night promotion was part of a larger scheme of promotions, including discounts for military personnel, children, and senior citizens. No one was about to suggest that a discount for servicemen (and women!) somehow discriminated against civilians. Nor could anyone suggest that males were excluded from these other promotions since males and females could be senior citizens, children, or members of the armed forces. The Sonics' intent was clearly to boost fan attendance and not to exclude or even stigmatize anyone.[12]

Political correctness succeeds so often because it assumes people are either too afraid or too lazy to think for themselves. In many instances, it just takes a quick look to see that the emperor has no clothes—and that no one is trying to keep him out of a bar on ladies' night.

As for New Jersey, within weeks of the publicity garnered by the decision, the New Jersey Assembly, by a vote of 78-0, approved a bill that would make it legal for promotions such as Ladies' Night.[13] A state Senate commission then voted to approve the bill and send it on to the full body, where it awaits a final determination.[14]

Coincidentally, I am putting the finishing touches on this chapter on a day that I attended a Phillies game (beat the Reds, 4-3). Today was Women's Fleece Phillies Blanket Day, meaning that women fifteen and older got a nice red blanket. Me, with my three young sons, got bupkus.

Next time I may take David Gillespie to the game with me. I'm sure he'll get me a blanket.

6

It's All about Me

Overreactions to the slightest hint of religion are well documented and abundant.

One of my favorites involves the celebration of "Me Week" in Mrs. Riley's kindergarten class at the Culbertson Elementary School in Newtown Square, Pennsylvania. The teaching concept didn't sound controversial. "Me Week" was intended to afford students the opportunity to learn about one another—their personal characteristics, preferences, and personalities. And that included having students identify their favorite books and then having one of their parents come read from it to the class. Like his classmates, six-year-old Wesley Busch was invited to select his favorite, and his mom was pleased to come to school and share it with the class.

But Wesley's choice caused quite a stir. And his mom never did get to share it with the class.

That's because Wesley's favorite book is the "Good Book," a.k.a. the Bible. Donna Kay Busch came to school prepared to participate on October 18, 2005, but she was barred from reading Psalm 118 at the school in suburban Philadelphia.

According to mom, the Busch family attends a local Baptist church, and Wesley is known to carry copies of the Bible in his knapsack. The family reads the Bible before bed and over breakfast, which helps explain why this six-year-old would have made what might seem to others as an unusual selection.[1]

When Wesley's teacher, Mrs. Riley, learned of Wesley's choice and Donna Busch's planned reading, she took the matter to the Culbertson Elementary Principal, Thomas Cook. "He said that I could not read the Bible in school, and that it was against the law, and the law he quoted was separation of church and state, and he said that he could not allow that kind of thing to go on in school. So I was forbidden to read from it," explained Donna Busch.[2]

It's a funny thing, that "separation of church and state." *Funny* in that it is fiction, which, nevertheless, doesn't stop it from being raised in these controversies, that, by the way, always seem to involve Christianity and not other religions! C'mon. Do you think that if young Wesley were instead young Ahmed or Mohammad anybody would have stood in front of his Burka-clad mom when she began to read from the Koran? No way.

What does exist is something known as the Establishment Clause within the First Amendment which states the following: "Congress shall make no law respecting an establishment of religion, or prohibiting the free exercise thereof, or abridging the freedom of speech, or of the press, or the right of the people to peaceably assemble, and to petition the Government for a redress of grievances."[3]

Would the school in this case have been "establishing" a religion if Donna Busch had stood in front of a room of kindergarten students and read from the Bible? Or would the children have simply learned a little more about their classmate and his favorite book, which happens to be about the religion practiced by his family?

Donna Busch didn't let it pass. She ended up in the hands of the Rutherford Institute, a conservative version of the ACLU, headed by attorney John Whitehead, who is best known for his representation of Clinton-accuser Paula Jones.

A civil suit was filed in federal court on May 2, 2005, claiming a violation of the Buschs' right to religious expression. The lawsuit pointed out that, while Donna Busch could not read to Wesley's class from a book connected to his Christianity, other students were allowed to read a book about Judaism, teach the class the dreidel game, place the Star of David on the monthly calendar sent to every child in the school, and participate in making decorations to remember the Jewish celebration of Hanukkah by creating Star of David and Menorah decorations.

The complaint also stated kindergartners and first graders at the Culbertson Elementary School once placed a witch's finger on their fingers when they were reading.[4] At the same time, they were barred from making Christmas decorations.[5] Speaking of which, Donna Busch told me the days of Christmas trees were over in the Marple Newtown School District. "They have to call it a giving tree," she told me.[6]

Ugh.

Back to Wesley's travails. School district superintendent Robert A. Mesaros didn't take the lawsuit lying down. Instead of the usual "we can't comment on a matter that is in litigation" that you often hear from parties that have been sued, he distributed a letter to the school community in which he said:

> We respect the practice of religion and the important place it holds in our community. However, the law says that place is not in the classroom of a taxpayer-funded public school.
>
> Because a public school teacher cannot read aloud from a religious text in a classroom setting, a parent can't do it in that setting either.
>
> The suit is baseless and is nothing more than an attempt to make headlines. . . . Sadly the defense of this suit will ultimately take away valuable financial resources that would normally be used to buy computers, musical equipment and books.[7]

When interviewed, School Board President Edward Partridge said:

> Our policy states that Marple Newtown School District cannot advocate any particular religion and that's consistent with the law that says you cannot teach religion in the elementary schools. Actually the state law, under public school code 1515, clearly states that, "Reading of religious literature including the Bible as literature in public schools is only permissible in secondary schools as part of an elected study of literature and must be pre-approved by the state as part of the curriculum." And obviously the curriculum would also have to be approved by the school board.[8]

The Rutherford Institute responded in kind: "The U.S. Supreme Court has recognized that public schools may include instruction on religion in various classroom settings, and that this practice does not violate the so-called separation of church and state required by the Constitution."[9]

John Whitehead insists, "There is no church here. It is an individual believer against the state. There is no church involved. What you have here is free speech, equal treatment. Donna Busch should be treated equally like everyone else. So it's really not a question of separation of church and state."[10]

Whitehead has seen it all before. "Well this last Christmas we were totally bombarded. They were doing away with Christmas trees. Kids were coming in during Christmas with red and green on and they were being sent home saying those were the Christmas colors, they were illegal to be worn in school."[11]

Whitehead continued, "Here you have an imitation of the school bringing parents in and I think that makes this case different. It opens up what we call a limited forum which, the Supreme Court says, once you do that and let other parents speak, you can't discriminate against religious viewpoints."[12]

Mark A. Sereni is the solicitor for the school district. In an opinion piece on the controversy that he later published, he pointed out that principal Thomas Cook was himself an assisting minister at a local church. Sereni said classmates of Wesley Busch would have viewed his mother as an authority figure had she read from the Bible.

He also noted that mandatory Bible reading had been declared unconstitutional by the Supreme Court more than forty years ago, and that a 2000 decision from the governing federal appellate court held that a school lawfully prohibited a Bible reading by a first-grade pupil during a mandatory classroom exercise.

"Had Donna Busch been permitted to read aloud Psalm 118 to the pupils at Culbertson Elementary School, the Marple Newtown School District would not only have violated the law, but in doing so also would have infringed upon the rights of every parent and student in the school district—including those of Busch and her son," he wrote.[13]

In the midst of the war of words, perhaps former school board member Linda Houldin said it best to a local newspaper: "How do you teach children tolerance and diversity if the subject can't be discussed in the classroom? I was exposed to and learned about many religions and cultures."[14]

As for Wesley, Mrs. Busch says, "He could be doing better. I don't know how to explain it to him because now he says the Bible is bad to read, and I said no, the Bible is not bad to read; so, we're going to have to continue to work with him and continue to reinforce our love for him and our love for Jesus. If it continues with time to go on throughout public school systems in our country, then it can be so much more damaging to him and other children."[15]

What a hassle for a reading that would have taken thirty seconds and harmed no one.

7

God Bless Patrick Cubbage

Patrick Cubbage—proud Vietnam veteran—decided, thirty years after he completed his service, to reenlist and join the New Jersey National Guard. At age forty-nine, he had a twofold purpose: first, to experience the privilege of again serving his country in uniform (as he did in 1969 when he saw combat as a sergeant in the Army's 173rd Airborne Brigade), but more importantly, he wanted to be the first enlisted man to salute his son, Adam, when Adam Cubbage graduated from the ROTC program at Penn State University as a second lieutenant. "I wanted the silver dollar," Patrick Cubbage later told me with a smile, referring to the military tradition that is said to require such payment to the first enlisted man to acknowledge a new officer.

On May 29, 1998, father and son got their wish. Adam graduated, Patrick saluted, and Adam proudly gave his father the traditional silver dollar, minted in 1998.

No one who knew Patrick Cubbage, nor any member of his large family, was surprised by his show of loyalty to his son and his nation. Cubbage is known for his government service, patriotism, and commitment to family. Cubbage is a former Philadelphia cop, a district attorney's prosecuting detective, a chief inspector sheriff, and a former city bail commissioner. He was proud to serve his country at a time when some ran to Canada and was equally pleased when his son followed in his footsteps. There are three Cubbage brothers and six (male) Cubbage cousins. All are working people. The Cubbages are the kind of fellows for whom the expression "good people" is often repeated.

In 2000, a few years after joining the New Jersey National Guard, Patrick Cubbage found himself performing active duty "special work." His primary mission was as a liaison between local, state, and military authorities where he assisted in military parades and presented military honors. Then came the events of 9/11. On that day, Patrick Cubbage worked the Emergency Operations Center at Fort Dix, outside Pemberton, New Jersey. He assisted in getting

National Guard airplanes off the ground at a time when not even the military could comprehend the nature of the attack.

Thereafter, he was requested to go to the largest veteran's cemetery in New Jersey, the Brigadier General William C. Doyle Veterans Memorial Cemetery in Burlington County, near McGuire Air Force Base. His assignment was now that of military honor guardsman. It was Cubbage's responsibility to either fold the American flag or to present a folded American flag to the next-of-kin of deceased veterans during the burial of those vets in the cemetery. It was a task he took very seriously.

"I accepted that position with respect, especially after 9/11. I considered it my privilege to honor those who served us. I believe it is an honor to serve their families. The flag is to be considered a living thing, and to give that to the family of someone who served our country was a responsibility I took seriously. Nothing offends me like those who would allow the flag to even touch the ground," Cubbage would later explain to me in a quiet voice full of emotion.

For his work at the military cemetery, Cubbage was paid $16 per hour without benefits. The compensation was important—Patrick Cubbage is not a man of wealth—but the experience of participating in the ceremonies gave him a sense of fulfillment beyond the pay. "When you look into the eyes of grieving people," he said, "knowing that the flag represents their past memories of their loved ones, they now have something in their hands that shows them that our country really cared about their spouse. It is a very important feeling."

Cubbage began work as an honor guard within a month of 9/11, and found himself working between twenty-five and thirty-five hours a week. By his estimate, he participated in roughly 2,000 burials up until Halloween Day, October 31, 2002. It was on that date, in a move that could only be described as ghoulish, Patrick Cubbage was fired as a military honor guard.

Why was he canned?

Because Cubbage had the nerve to say, "God bless you and this family, and God bless the United States of America" as he presented an American flag to the grieving family members of American veterans being buried in the cemetery, even when a family member of the deceased veteran expressly requested it be said. Indeed, it is true. He was fired for invoking God at the graveside of someone who served his country. (Meaning, someone who would have probably taken an oath under God when first joining the military.) Yes, in America.

The incident got some national press. And under the media glare, his superiors initially quibbled over the public explanation of his discharge. They said he was fired for departing from protocol, not for offering the blessing, even when their version was contradicted by the written protocol itself.

Just before he was fired, on October 16, 2002, Patrick Cubbage's superior, Iven Dumas, told him to stop offering the blessing after two of Cubbage's fellow honor guardsman complained. As Cubbage explained to me, "Dumas told me it could be offensive. So I asked how. He said it might be offensive to Jews and Muslims. I told him Jews and Muslims believe in God, also." This exchange caused Dumas to hand Cubbage a New Jersey regulation prohibiting "harassment or hostile environments" in the workplace.

The following week, on October 24, 2002, the affirmative action officer of the New Jersey Department of Military and Veterans Affairs wrote to Dumas to clarify the policy. In that correspondence, Joan L. Edwards said that government employees "must not engage in activities or expression that a reasonable observer would interpret as government endorsement . . . of religion. The policy is very clear in that the only time you would add: 'God bless . . .' in the presentation is when the next-of-kin has expressed a religious preference. If the next-of-kin does not express a religious preference, one way or another, then the protocol would be to omit saying the 'God bless . . .' portion of the presentation. This is not optional."[1]

But according to Cubbage, when he was initially hired as a military honor guardsman, he was provided with training literature and a video that was somewhat different. He kept in his possession that pamphlet, titled "Military Funeral Honors: Honoring Those Who Served." The multicolor brochure bears the insignia of the Department of Defense and says: "The Department of Defense pledges to make every effort to work with you to ensure that each valid request for military funeral honors is handled immediately and with the dignity, sensitivity and respect it deserves."[2]

Inside, there is a page headed "Flag Presentation Protocol."[3] The protocol explains that "Taps" is to be played, followed by the folding of the American flag into a triangle by the honor guard, who then presents it to a family member. ("Stand facing the flag recipient and hold the folded flag waist high with the straight edge facing the recipient.") The presenter, in handing the flag to the veteran's kin, is supposed to say something dependent upon the branch of the service of the deceased. For example, in the case of an Army veteran: "This flag is presented on behalf of a grateful nation and the United States Army as a token of appreciation for your loved one's honorable and faithful service." The protocol then states: "*If* the next of kin has expressed a religious preference or belief . . . add God bless you and this family and God bless the United States of America" (emphasis added).

Patrick Cubbage did not, as requested by Ms. Edwards, treat that language in a passive manner. In other words, whereas she had instructed "*unless* the next of kin expresses a religious preference one way or the other, then the protocol would be to omit the saying, 'God bless . . .'" Cubbage would assess the situation to determine whether the service was religious in nature. After all, the language in the DOD brochure on which he was relying said he could offer the blessing "*if*" there was an expression of religious preference. In those rare instances where he saw no indication of religion, he would offer no blessing.

Cubbage explained, "When I was doing the funerals, I always sized up the situation. If I saw clergy, or religious artifacts like a Christian cross or a Jewish Star of David, I gave the blessing. Some requested no flag presentation. I respected their wishes whatever they were. I never asked. Most often, 99.9 percent of the time, a clergy person would be there, and there was no question."

Nevertheless, after his mid-October dressing-down, Cubbage was limited to only folding the flag or playing musical tapes. He wasn't permitted to present the flag. Then came Halloween. On that day, Cubbage was working a veteran's funeral when a procession arrived. Cubbage told me that he noted a symbol on an automobile in the procession that he recognized as a symbol of Christianity— a fish—and he conversed with one of the funeral car drivers who was a member of a church affiliated with his own. (Patrick Cubbage is an evangelical Christian but, according to him, "not one who proselytizes.")

The driver, according to Cubbage, told him the family was deeply religious and would welcome the blessing. Cubbage told him the family needed to make a request for the blessing; family members told him they did so. The funeral director and the son of the deceased veteran approached Cubbage and stated that they had talked to the internment supervisor and asked to receive the blessing, and asked that Cubbage present the flag and say the blessing.

Cubbage's partner was present, and he gladly stepped aside so the blessing could be said. Cubbage offered the blessing to the wheelchair-bound widow who bowed her head in reverence as he said, "God bless you and this family, and God bless the United States of America."

That was it. Without complaint from the grieving family, and after having delivered the blessing an estimated "500 times," during which absolutely not a single participant complained, he was fired.

What brought it on? Political correctness. Or military rigidity. Maybe bureaucratic idiocy. Or all of the above. Whatever the reason, Cubbage wasn't about to be MUZZLED without a fight.

He quickly retained the Rutherford Institute, the same counsel retained by Wesley Busch's mom. John Whitehead told Cubbage that he was not only familiar with constitutional law, but he was also an Army officer with the Honor Guard.

After some saber rattling by Rutherford and a spate of bad press for the military surrounding the firing of Cubbage, in August of 2003, he was reinstated with back pay. But confusion reigned. He believed he was now permitted to offer the blessing that got him into trouble, but things were not so simple.

Lt. Col. Roberta Niedt, a spokeswoman for the New Jersey Department of Military and Veteran's Affairs, told the *Philadelphia Inquirer* at the time that she did not believe the return of Cubbage was so sweeping.[4] Her words were a sign of more trouble to come. Niedt said funeral protocol was dependent upon each branch of the service, and only the Air Force had adopted the "God bless you . . ." standard.

For his part, Cubbage again pointed to the pamphlet he'd been given when hired which said, in the case of an Army veteran, these words were to apply: "This flag is presented on behalf of a grateful nation and the United States Army as a token of appreciation for your loved one's honorable and faithful service." Additionally, according to the training pamphlet, the other branches of the service—Air Force, Coast Guard, Marines—permitted him, when the next-of-kin had expressed a preference, to say, "God bless you . . ."

In this state of confusion, on August 11, 2003, Cubbage went back to work. The newspapers continued to follow the controversy, and in their coverage, different military representatives involved were quoted as saying contradictory things.

In a memo dated October 20, 2003, Retired Colonel Stephen G. Abel, director of veterans' services in the New Jersey Department of Military and Veterans' Affairs, said, "all additional blessings will be offered by the clergy or funeral home staff."[5]

Abel maintained that the "God bless you . . ." phrase remained reserved for Air Force veterans. Meanwhile, Lieutenant Colonel Cynthia Colin was quoted as saying the blessing "is optional for every military service." She cited the same

DOD pamphlet, "Honoring Those Who Served," on which Cubbage had been relying.

The bureaucracy became too much for Patrick Cubbage. He found that his work was vastly reduced. Now, he was only permitted to play "Taps" and fold the flag, not present it. This caused numerous funeral directors to complain to Cubbage that the blessing had been requested, but it was not given.

"I went in and spoke to Dumas, and he said this is what the regulations will now be—only the clergy can give the blessing," Cubbage said. While the Rutherford Institute wanted to continue the battle by pressuring congressional action, Patrick Cubbage was ready for a change.

The financial burden of the limited role forced him to seek other employment. So on May 15, 2005, he resigned and accepted a job in plant security for Sunoco. Today, Patrick Cubbage looks at his experience through historical lenses: "People have to realize that our forefathers came here and fought for freedom of religion, not for repression of religion. You can worship with whomever you choose. We have to respect one another.

"I feel sorry for the families of the deceased veterans who want and deserve that blessing. When the veterans take an allegiance, they take it for God and country. But now, when they die, God gets left out. They deserve better. Maybe it's because I was an enlisted man and the politically correct people can't face reality, or maybe it's because of what the Bible says, God will put blinders on the unbelievers."

Meanwhile, Adam Cubbage, after graduating from the ROTC Program at Penn State, joined the Army's 82nd Airborne Division and moved from second to first lieutenant. He was the boxing champion for the 1st Battalion.

When his commitment to the 82nd Airborne was completed, he extended his military obligation and joined the 173rd Airborne Brigade—just like his dad—(one of only a handful of second generation Sky Soldiers) where he made captain and became company commander. He also got married.

And when the war in Iraq broke out, Adam Cubbage was called upon for the invasion. On March 26, 2003, the anniversary of the 173rd, Captain Adam Cubbage parachuted into Northern Iraq, and his boots were among the first the United States put on the ground. Adam Cubbage was part of a force that captured Bashur Airfield.

And no one was more pleased than his father who prayed to God for the safety of his son and our military. Cubbage remembered:

I felt proud and also very concerned because of the dangers involved. I knew he was going when he called and said that he wouldn't be able to talk to us for a while, and that I wasn't to be concerned. I told him that I couldn't think of anyone else that I would want to protect my country and my family other than my own son. And my concern was for Adam and his soldiers because all I could do was to compare it with the soldiers on D-Day.

As it was, the parachute jump into Northern Iraq was the biggest airborne exercise since WWII. I knew the risks. In Vietnam, I was a paratrooper in the 173rd Airborne Brigade and, although I never parachuted into combat, I saw plenty of guys get hurt from jumping out of the airplanes.

As a father, I was proud and worried. Every day I watched the news looking for information. One day he sent me an e-mail: "Dad, everything is okay. . . . Keep me in your prayers. Your son Adam."

Patrick Cubbage is still praying for all military personnel, chief among them his own son who, as of this writing, is now serving with the 173rd Airborne Brigade in Afghanistan.

God bless Patrick Cubbage.

8

Political Correctness
in Full Bloom

Maybe it's something about cemeteries: the only thing alive in them seems to be pervasive political correctness.

If you were shocked that in New Jersey, Patrick Cubbage was fired for saying, "God bless you" when presenting an American flag, you will be equally stunned when you hear about Collin Kelly, a young boy from New England, who was told to stop putting flowers on dead soldiers' graves. Chalk this one up to rigidity over common sense, more than political correctness.

Collin is a nine-year-old boy from Framingham, Massachusetts. In his community, he and his mother, Lynn, make it a habit to visit Edgel Grove Cemetery because that is where his grandparents are buried.

One day, Collin noticed that "everybody's lot in this place has flowers but in the soldiers' lot, no one does."[1] The soldiers' lot to which he referred is the final resting place of 156 veterans who served in every war with American involvement from the American Revolution through the Vietnam era. So Collin, whose young dream is "to be a soldier or a policeman," and who said, "Anytime he sees a soldier in uniform in public, he goes up and shakes their hand," decided to change that.[2]

His idea, as he told me, was simply to "put flowers there."[3] In fact, when I asked him what kind of flowers he wanted to plant in the veterans' lot, he told me, "Any kind, as long as I get to plant them."[4] At some point this young fellow next decided he was going to try to raise enough money to plant two flowers on each of the 156 graves in the Veterans' section of the cemetery. Like many of us did back in the days when it was still relatively safe to walk in your own neighborhood, Collin went door to door to raise money for the flowers and asked friends at school for donations. In his orange Kleenex box, he soon collected twenty-four dollars.[5]

Soon, Collin's efforts caught the eye of his hometown paper, the *MetroWest*

Daily News, and his idea to put flowers on the veterans' graves spread. His mother said that, after the story was printed, the Kelly's received many phone messages, even one from Sarasota, Florida.[6] Then Collin started receiving donations from people approaching the Kelly's house, knocking on the door and handing them $5 to $10 donations. On one occasion, a Korean War veteran stopped by Collin's house, in tears, wanting to shake his hand.[7]

Collin received much praise from people around his community. Initially, everyone was on board. Kevin Devlin, the Edgel Grove Cemetery's superintendent, said: "For a kid that age, this is unbelievable," noting, "there should be more kids like that."[8] Mal Schulze, president of the Framingham Veterans' Council, had a similar response to Collin's plan. "That's an absolutely, incredible . . . I don't know what verbiage. . . . That's just amazing . . . that breaks me down."[9]

But, apparently, there is something wrong with wanting to plant flowers on some of your heroes' gravesites.

After getting the "okay" from Devlin, Collin and his family planted twenty-two marigolds in front of eleven gravesites. When the family returned the next day, Devlin told them that the five-member elected cemetery board trustees had met and said they couldn't plant any more.[10]

It seems these rocket scientists decided Collin was breaking the cemetery's policy, which forbids anyone other than family members from placing flowers on graves. Kevin Devlin, who had shown strong support for Collin in his effort, said, "This was a decision that they made, and I just did what I was told."[11] Barbara Ford, vice chairman of the trustees, said, "No matter how thoughtful and charitable, evidently this wasn't handled properly."[12] Ford went on to say, "You don't just go into a cemetery and place flowers on graves that belong to somebody else. Those are private lots."[13]

But we are talking about gravesites where no one is doing anything. Think about it. If a loved one died, and you were caring for the grave, it would be upsetting to think that a stranger was coming and placing items near the headstone. But in the case of military veterans, most of whom left this earth a long time ago and have no one surviving them, and nobody visiting their graves on a regular basis, common sense should have prevailed. It didn't. Our man Collin was placing flowers on graves of not only Vietnam and Korean War vets but, also, honoring veterans of the Revolutionary War, the Civil War, the Spanish-American War, and World Wars I and II because no one else was doing so.

His mom, Lynn Kelly, told me that when she heard this, she "called the *News* and told them we couldn't do it, and they put a bit in the paper to say drop the donations. When the veterans heard that, they were up in arms. So there was an enormous galvanizing catalyst that brought these veterans out in arms; veterans, normal citizens in arms, saying that they were very upset that Collin couldn't decorate veterans' graves. A nine-year-old boy wanted to honor their heroes, and he wasn't allowed to do it."[14]

Belinda Adams, whose parents were the last veterans to be buried in the lot, said that she was "kind of perturbed,"[15] and that her parents would not be pleased about the situation. She said her father "would be upset. He'd be right there with the young man planting the flowers. Both of my parents would be there."[16] Adams said she respects that the trustees had to deny Collin the right to plant flowers on the graves but asked, "For a town that says it honors its veterans, what does this say to nine year olds?"[17]

Collin was disappointed, but he decided not to call off the entire plan. "If I don't get to plant the flowers at the graves, I want to give the money and the flowers to the veterans that are still alive."[18]

His story attracted national headlines. It even got Collin an appearance on the *Today* show[19] and in the *National Enquirer*.[20]

It took the Marines to restore order in Framingham.

Finally, Marine Corporal John Grigg stepped in with a proposal that would potentially allow Collin to carry out his wish. Grigg was in combat in Iraq and had just returned when he heard about Collin's idea and the later rejection that cancelled his plans. Corporal Grigg contacted Lynn Kelly and told her he would go with Collin to place flowers. When he heard about the case, he said, "It inflamed me."[21] Grigg said that he "thought it would be cool for him to have a Marine go with him. Here's a little boy who, I don't know if he fully understands it or not, but the fact that he wants to honor veterans is an amazing thing."[22]

After what Lynn Kelly said was "a bit of pressure from a number of veterans' groups and the media,"[23] the trustees met again and decided to allow Marine Corporal John Grigg to accompany Collin to place geraniums on the veterans' graves, which they did in the midst of a Memorial Day weekend.

On Memorial Day itself, when Lynn Kelly went to the cemetery to remove the flowers, she said, "Someone planted them all."[24] Some of her neighbors have taken credit for this,[25] and it is believed to have been a collection of local veterans in Framingham, Massachusetts. Along with the planted flowers was a note that read, "Thank You Collin. Planted by the Sisters and Brothers of the Brothers Lying Here."[26]

Lynn Kelly said Collin "was thrilled"[27] and said it made him "very happy that someone else did what I couldn't do."[28]

On that Memorial Day, Collin was presented and accepted an award from the Framingham Veterans' Council for "patriotic service rendered to the community." In the ceremony held on the Framingham Memorial steps, Collin received even more praise for his amazing effort.

Eddy Cutler, an eighty-year-old World War II veteran, said, "Without that kind of person, this country would go down the tubes." After receiving the award, Collin announced, "Thank you everybody for this day. See you at school tomorrow."[29]

Collin and his father, Gerry Kelly, were given the honor of riding in the lead vehicle at the annual Veterans of Foreign Wars Parade on June 18. Greg Strojny, commander of one of the group's posts, said that it was a no-brainer to have Collin as their guest-of-honor. Strojny said that Collin "showed his true patriotism and stamina to put flags on fellow veterans' graves."[30] Collin received a few citations and was made an honorary sergeant-at-arms and, according to Lynn Kelly, only one of seven in the country."[31]

When the dust finally settled, Collin formed an informal club with five of his friends at St. Bridget's School. The club planned to meet twice a month and at least once a month to do such things with veterans as "give them flowers, take them to breakfast, visit them."[32]

Lynn Kelly reports, "The flowers are still there."[33]

As for the future, Lynn said that a children's book is in the works. As for the whole experience, Collin says, "It's cool. I never thought it'd go this far, but I guess that I was wrong."[34]

9

Seeing Purple

I'm seeing red, uh, purple, actually, over something taking place in our schools. When it comes to grading papers, the color red is out. Now in vogue: the very Barneyesque shade of purple.

Consider the Daniels Farm Elementary School in Trumbull, Connecticut, where "teachers grade papers by giving examples of better answers for those students who make mistakes." Makes sense. But this became a source of controversy, not owing to the content of the teachers' remarks but, instead, their appearance: "Kids often found their work covered in red, the color that teachers long have used to grade work."

Outraged parents objected—tagging red as a "stressful" hue. The school's principal tried to step in, saying that "teachers were just giving constructive advice, and the color of ink used to convey that message should not matter." But parents insisted that red be blacklisted.[1]

An aberration, you're thinking. Some nutty incident unique to Connecticut? Nope. A short time in front of the computer and a few interviews told me the Daniels Farm Elementary is by no means the only school to witness the rising tide of kinder, gentler shades: blue, green, and, above all, purple pens.

In fact, a story in *NEA Today* claims, "Purple may be the new red." Why? Well, Sharon Carlson, a health and education teacher in Northampton, Massachusetts—ah, Massachusetts!—switched a few years ago, and seems to speak for many: "Purple stands out, but it's not as scary as red," she explained.[2]

Scary? (Somebody please tell these folks that it's the "F" that's scary, not the shade in which it's written. There's nothing scary about an "A" or "B," even if etched in the color of blood!) So pronounced is the trend that, guess who is taking note? Pen makers, of course. All of the major manufacturers of pens and markers, including Bic, Pilot Pen, and Sanford (which makes Paper Mate and Sharpie) are increasing output to match rising sales.[3]

Educators are "trying to be positive and reinforcing rather than being harsh," explained Pilot Pen's VP of marketing, Robert Silberman.[4] Paper Mate Public Relations Manager Michael Finn agreed: "This is a kinder, more gentle education system."[5] In 2005, Paper Mate raised production of purple pens by an estimated 10 percent.[6]

When I first caught wind of the trend toward purple, I was anxious to spark a conversation on the radio. This raised an interesting question: whom do you book as a guest on a matter like this? Well, a color expert, or "color consultant," of course. (In this Internet Age in which we live, there is always an expert for everything.) For me, the person who fit the bill was Leatrice Eiseman, director of something called the Pantone Color Institute. Eiseman has a background in psychology and has written several books on the importance of color to human communication.

She didn't disappoint. She confirmed what I'd been reading, and defended it:

> We find that a lot of teachers are starting to use purple pens for grading papers which, by the way, I feel is a very clever idea because, first of all, red has been traditionally the color that is used as the warning signal. The human eye is always tweaked by novelty and if you start to see red— particularly kids who have a problem with papers—they'll either secret the papers away or they simply don't pay that much attention because red becomes commonplace, so there are times when you have to change the color of ink so that you do get their attention. . . . I don't want to put this as a trend but I do want to say that teachers are taking notice of this and are beginning to change the color of the warning signal.[7]

Wait a minute, I say. Maybe I'm about to reveal that I was once on the receiving end of too much red ink, but what's wrong with a "warning signal"? Isn't that what we want? For a student who is not making the grade, or as a parent concerned about my son or daughter's education, isn't a warning signal appropriate? And to the extent that red becomes "commonplace," that's not a reflection of the color of the pen. It's a warning signal that a serious problem is not getting corrected.

Apparently I'm missing something.

The anti-red mind-set shows up even in the hardscrabble town of Pittsburgh, Pennsylvania. You know. Mean Joe Green. The Steel Curtain *et al.* Well, it's also where you can find Joseph Foriska, the principal of Thaddeus Stevens

Elementary, and he has instructed his teachers to grade with colors featuring more "pleasant-feeling tones" so their instructional messages do not come across as derogatory or demeaning. "The color is everything," said Foriska, an educator for thirty-one years.[8]

And then there is twenty-five-year-old teacher Justin Kazmark at Public School 188 in Manhattan. "My generation," says Kazmark, "was brought up on right or wrong with no in-between, and red was always in your face. . . . It's abrasive to me. Purple is just a little bit more gentle. Part of my job is to be attuned to what kids respond to, and red is not one of those colors."[9]

Ms. Eiseman, my "color consultant," agrees: "Purple is less aggressive than red, there's no question about that . . . and some teachers may choose to use it for that purpose, but I think in general it's because it's different. As I mentioned before, there is that inherent aggression that is present in red which could be precisely the reason not to do it if a kid's going to put a paper away and not show their parents, it's that red ink that they see on it. Perhaps if it was a little friendlier, they wouldn't have to do that."[10]

Friendlier?

There is nothing friendly about failing, nor should there be. And what about the storied history of red in education?

Editorialist Karl Zinsmeister explains, "[F]or generations, teachers have corrected answers and offered suggestions in red ink."[11] And, in fact, red ink has a much longer history. According to *NEA Today*, "red has been the preferred shade for corrections since the 1700s, when clerks and accountants dipped quills into red ink to fix ledgers."[12]

Ms. Eiseman maintains that the red is really still there beneath the surface: "I wouldn't say that purple is softer, necessarily. I don't want to give the wrong idea here—purple is really a combination, if you remember your grade-school color-wheel, of red and blue. So you still have that warning signal that's implicit in purple—that's what the red brings. But the blue makes it not quite as aggressive; makes it a little friendlier, makes it the kind of thing that [says], 'pay attention now,' the color is different but it still has the same inherent qualities as the mother color, which is red."[13]

Afraid to ask exactly what a "mother color" was, I asked Ms. Eiseman whether she wouldn't agree that students in our increasingly politically correct culture are being given too many carrots and not enough of the stick. She responded, "I can see your point where you think that kids are getting mollycoddled too much." But she, nevertheless, defended purple pens, saying: "The kids aren't getting a trophy by any manner of means; they're getting something that's going to catch their attention even more because it's different. As I said, the human eye, and most particularly kids' [eyes], are drawn by anything that's unusual, so it's going to make them sit up and pay attention, I think, even more. I think it's a good idea. . . . That's my case, that purple will get more attention than the red will."[14]

Ms. Eiseman attributed purple's current vogue not to political correctness but to simple market place trends: "I'm also a color forecaster, meaning that I'm one of those people who studies what's happening in the world around us and, therefore, what colors will be prominent in the next couple of years and the next season. When you study people's reaction to color, it's really quite interesting—this need for color forecasting. People are always saying to me, 'Why even bother with trends? Just put the same old colors out there.' But think what would happen in the market place if you had same old, same old all the time—nobody would buy anything."[15]

Okay, enough already. My head feels like it's spinning around the color wheel because of this debate, and it's time to spell out the bottom line. This rising tide of purple ink represents a trend, all right, a trend toward sparing our kids from the unpleasantness of life. This would be great if there were no unpleasantness ahead, but there is. And the sooner they begin to prepare for life's adversity, so says me, the better able they will be to cope with it when it arrives. Some day these kids will wake up with eyes that are bloodshot, not the shade of violets!

I see the purple issue as nothing but a continuation of the mind-set that says we need to get away from the clear delineation of letter grades because we don't want to hurt the feelings of the students who will attain something less than the gentleman's C. The same limp-wristed philosophy outlawed score-keeping at youth sports and, as we will soon explore, decided that everybody should be given a trophy for his or her athletic prowess, even if they have none. It's part of a preparatory process for a fantasy world, not the real world.

Forget ink. It has gotten so bad that in many school districts across the nation, kids are getting a mulligan when they bomb a test. In fact, that same public school district where I was a student from kindergarten to twelfth grade has just made regular retesting available to 4,700 students in its five middle schools and has plans for its three high schools to also join in.[16]

Students who pull Fs or Ds are now eligible to try again, as long as they attend a review session with their teacher. The second exam is not the same as the first, and they cannot obtain a better grade than a C.

Things are even looser in Cherry Hill, New Jersey. There, individual teachers make many of their own rules for the next round, meaning, who will get a shot at a retest, the work required beforehand, and the reward. Depending on the class, a student with a B may try again for an A.[17]

Down in Florida, schools are getting rid of letter grades. Instead, starting in the 2005-06 school year, Palm Beach County elementary students will get report cards where the numbers 1, 2, and 3 will appear next to different subjects and skills within those subjects.[18] A "1" means the student is working a year or more below grade level, a "2" indicates the student is working less than a year below grade level, and a "3" means they are working at or above grade level. Elementary principals voted for the change this year, saying the letter-grade system can be an obsession with students and parents and doesn't reflect how well a student is really learning.

"Somehow, people believe that when they see an A, B, C, D, or F they have all kinds of information about a child's progress," claimed Bill Thompson, principal of Forest Park Elementary. "When As, Bs, and Cs were chosen decades ago to rate students' work, there was no such thing as grade-level expectations, the Sunshine State Standards, or No Child Left Behind. An A is not the same in one class as in another class, but, prior to the adoption of standards, it was a way of measuring how kids did. Now we have a way of aligning ourselves class to class, school to school, even district to district," Thompson said.[19]

Elementary report cards were changed a few years ago to add the 1, 2, and 3 markings next to subjects, but the grades stayed. The result meant a child could earn an A even though he or she earned a 2 in the same subject. That means a child is doing well with his or her work, even though he or she is behind in the lessons. "That's where the confusion comes in," Thompson said. "There's somehow an assumption that that A means all is well."

Here's an even more incredible example of what I'm talking about. At a high school in Gloucester County, New Jersey, school administrators have cancelled final exams. It's true. At Delsea Regional High School in Franklinville, they have dispensed with the old two-hour finals as well as midterms.[20] Principal Joseph Sottosanti explained, "We were seeing GPAs decline, and we wondered what we could do about it." (Hey, Joe, you could just get rid of grading, period! Maybe I shouldn't give him any ideas.)

"Not everyone tests well, and everyone can have a bad day," Sottosanti explained. He and his staff debated how fair it was to base a big part of a final grade on how well a student does on a single day and concluded that students would be served best if final exams were ended.

Talk about MUZZLED. That's just not the way the world works. Employers don't permit a mulligan for a bad interview. If you fail the bar exam, we make you take it until you pass. Same with Realtors. And CPAs. And if you screw up in the market place, you pay a price, you don't get coddled as students do at the Delsea Regional High School.

Across the country, other school districts, including Detroit, are doing away with grades, too. And in Lee County, on the west coast of Florida, standard-based numbering was added to the middle- and high-school report cards, although it kept the letter grades.

This trend away from grades as we knew them is apparently not just an American phenomenon. Believe it or not, in the UK, if a group of teachers gets its wishes, the word "fail" will be banned from use in classrooms and replaced with the phrase "deferred success" to avoid demoralizing pupils. Members of the Professional Association of Teachers argue that telling pupils that they have failed can put them off learning for life.[21]

Real life is a series of highs and lows, and, unfortunately, plenty of the latter. Few will excel in education, and few will flunk. But there will be individuals who fall into the extremes, and they need to know who they are.

In any color you like, the handwriting is on the wall: darn few are headed to the major leagues of any particular sport. And the sooner students realize that, the earlier they can prepare for a more realistic career. None of us are going to get "The Girl." Sorry to report, guys, but that woman in the beer commercials is never coming home with you. Or me. Our waists will be larger than those in the magazines. And we're not going to live in the 90210 zip code, either. Even if you have your name on a Fifth Avenue tower, you may not be spared a lousy comb-over. That's how life works.

But political correctness ignores reality as it tries desperately to enforce a utopian equality of results—guaranteed "Happiness for all!" rather than the opportunity to pursue happiness. And its disciples grow shrill when those with common sense point out that sometimes our failures are our most precious possessions; they're often the crucibles of our character development. There are no failures—and therefore no true successes—in a carefree world of purple mediocrity.

No, this trend away from red ink, as one columnist opined, is "just one more layer in the self-esteem lasagna of public education, the kind of protectiveness that led to a decision at some elementary schools in Rhode Island earlier this year that spelling bees were dangerous to children's emotional health because all but one of the contestants would lose. Or, more correctly, be 'nonwinners.'

"It's also the kind of thing that probably tempts schoolteachers to leave education and search for more satisfying careers, such as pizza delivery. As the schoolteacher to whom I am married wondered when I mentioned this subject, 'Do you think the kids would mind if they got an A in red ink?'"[22] My guess is that it doesn't make much difference to them if their F comes in red or in mauve.

Another wag observed, "Maybe the little scholars are onto something. Perhaps the soaring federal deficit wouldn't be so alarming if we referred to 'drowning in a sea of purple ink.'"[23]

Former university philosophy professor Christina Hoff Sommers, coauthor of *One Nation Under Therapy: How the Helping Culture Is Eroding Self-Reliance*, did a beautiful job with an op-ed she wrote on this subject recently for *USA Today* entitled "Enough Already with Kid Gloves." Sommers believes that purple pens are just one instance of a disturbing trend of political correctness that is crippling the mental health of the next generation.

"Is the kind of over-protectiveness these educators counsel really such a bad thing?" she asks. The answer is yes: "children need challenge, excitement and competition to flourish. To treat them as combustible bundles of frayed nerves does them no favors."

"Solicitudes such as purple pens short-change today's students as they prepare to compete in tomorrow's global economy," she writes. Ironically, parents, educators, and counselors obsessively strive to boost children's self-esteem—often without merit.

Yet, "two decades of research have failed to show a significant connection between high self-esteem and achievement, kindness or good personal relationships." To the contrary, "unmerited self-esteem," writes Sommers, "is known to be associated with antisocial behavior—even criminality. Nevertheless, most of our national institutions and organizations that deal with children remain fixated on self-esteem."[24]

Her thinking deserves an A. In any color you'd like.

10

Trophy Mania

I'm grateful to Steve Rosenberg. He denied my son a trophy.

Don't get me wrong, my nine-year-old, Michael Jr., is a terrific boy. He's smart. He's ambitious. He has a hunger for knowledge, and he plays athletics with a pretty high level of intensity and concentration. But when it comes to his most recent Little League baseball season, his team's efforts weren't worthy of statutory recognition. Under the leadership of coach Joe Katz, a good guy who volunteers to teach the kids the basics even though he doesn't have a son playing, the Rattlers showed improvement every week, but they didn't win a regular season game and finished in last place.

Enter Steve Rosenberg. I know Steve well, as he was Michael's coach last season and the season before that. Steve is not only a coach (whose son, Jake, is a "ringer," by the way), but also doubles as the president of the Lower Merion Little League headquartered in Gladwyne, Pennsylvania. The league represents a very successful program for boys playing baseball.

This past season, 950 boys played Little League in Lower Merion, which is great to see in a world gone mad over video games and x-sports. Like many other places in the country, for several years now, boys in Lower Merion have grown accustomed to receiving trophies just for showing up. They even have a name for these statues: "participation trophies."

Over some initial opposition, Rosenberg put an end to the participation trophy system in his league for kids nine years old and above. And for that, I salute him. As a matter of fact, so did the *Wall Street Journal* in a major spread.[1] From now on, boys of that age will need to do something to get a trophy: win!

What a novel concept.

"When I brought it up in our league meeting, you would have thought I asked for the kids to have to walk across hot coals to get to first base," he explained to me.[2]

And Rosenberg did it in a community of Type-A personality parents who often take more than a passing interest in their kids' lives in general, and their activities in particular. I know. I am one of them.

Lower Merion is synonymous with Philadelphia's Main Line, a prosperous suburb given its moniker for the way in which it aligned itself with the stops along the once burgeoning Pennsylvania Railroad System. In 2005, *Advertising Age* magazine's American Demographics studied the richest zip codes in the nation and Lower Merion was credited as having two of them: Gladwyne (19035) and Villanova (19085).[3]

"Lower Merion: it's a wealthy community and it's sort of a very politically-correct community. Pretty much, I would say there were initially twenty-four guys in the room and, while one stood up behind me and said, 'I agree with you,' the rest felt like little Johnny should get a trophy just for showing up, and my response was . . . 'you had five trophies; I had six trophies my whole life growing up,'" explained Rosenberg, who was able to overcome that initial level of opposition.

He's so right about the number of trophies. I, myself, was a decent athlete back in "the day." I played Little League for years, lettered in baseball and football in junior high school on two championship teams, and lettered in high school on a football team ranked No. 1 in Pennsylvania.

Now forty-three, with an expanding waistline and diminished hairline, I can glance fondly at a bookcase in my office that houses the recognition of my youthful exploits. From my desk, I can see exactly four trophies.

As of this writing, my sons are four, seven, and nine. My seven- and nine-year-old sons have already outpaced me in the trophy category. Most significant, while mine are on display, theirs are already broken or gathering dust under their beds. No way will they have them on their shelves in their mid-forties.

My trophies meant something to me. They were awarded for merit. I either won a competition or my team came in first place. They were something I savored when they were awarded and items I still treasure today.

My kids, on the other hand, place no value on their trophies because they were awarded for simply showing up.

This is really about much more than trophies. It's part of a larger issue in youth athletics and the raising of children. It's symptomatic of the same mind-set that says we should not keep score in youth athletics or we should turn out the lights on the scoreboard if a game becomes a rout. We'll get to that in a minute.

Steve Rosenberg noticed the same thing at his house. "I walk into my nine-year-old's room now and I need sunglasses from all the bling from all the trophies in the place," he told me. Maybe that's why he decided to draw the line at age nine. Rosenberg knows the younger kids keep score even if their parents and coaches refuse to; but, technically, the games are not competitive and nobody wins or loses.

"But at nine, the games become competitive, there are winners and losers. There were ten teams in our nine-year-olds level this year; one will be the champion, nine won't be the champion. It doesn't matter whether you came in second or tenth, you're not the winner," Rosenberg said.

When Rosenberg took the matter to his board, he told them, "Do you understand that even a twelve-year-old kid who is on the worst team, and his team could lose every game, is going to walk away with a trophy? We don't want to hurt his feelings. But what if my son couldn't sing, and he wanted to be in the school play? He wouldn't get to be in the school play. They would make him the stage manager."

Rosenberg had experience with the coddling of his own son on a different type of athletic field. "It's unbelievable. You know my son who plays travel soccer, and he's on a very elite team, the same thing starts to happen; once they start to win by four or five goals, they have to stop scoring and they just have to pass the ball and play keep away from the other team which, I think, is even more demoralizing to another team."

Not everyone in the league agreed with Rosenberg's assessment. There were those who believed that rewarding mediocrity would engender a love of the game, to which I would argue that would be a fondness based on false pretenses because, in the "real" game, only winners get the rewards.

But an enormous splash in the *Wall Street Journal* offering his point of view gave Rosenberg encouragement. The *Journal* looked at Rosenberg as part of a trophy backlash that runs contrary to the "culture of coddling": "Some educators and psychologists argue that recent moves designed in part to build kids' self-esteem—giving partial credit for incorrect math answers at school, for instance, or overlooking misspellings—removes kids' incentives to push themselves."[4]

It sounds to me like the *Journal* was in the loop about the trend toward purple ink and away from letter grades in school that actually mean something.

Back in Lower Merion, Rosenberg was bucking this trend. Eventually, Rosenberg received his board's approval and, from now on, only the top finishers in the league's playoffs will get trophies. He credits the publicity he received.

"As soon as the *Wall Street Journal* came out, I received literally hundreds of e-mails and phone calls from people all over the country, and every single one of them said they stand behind me."

Right across town from Steve Rosenberg's Lower Merion Little League is an equally successful basketball program for girls, albeit run with a different philosophy. The Main Line Girls Basketball Association, or MLGBA, has been in existence for a dozen years and enjoys the participation of over 750 girls from grades two to eleven.

After Rosenberg's efforts to reduce trophy mania were written about in the *Wall Street Journal,* MLGBA officials wrote a letter to the editor and said they had never given out participation trophies and noted: "Kids expect trophies for showing up in a community sports league only if the grown-ups in charge create that expectation."[5]

So far, so good.

But, according to a friend of mine who is a coach in the league, this esteemed youth league is heavy on the coddling. According to him, "If a girl fouls out, she is to be replaced by someone with similar or lesser abilities."[6] And coaches are to keep the score within 10 points at all times. My coaching friend told me if the score gets to 15, or even a 20-point spread, "I have been subject to the following: (1) the score clock is frozen, and (2) we go into an offense that shuts down the 'scorers,' and we limit shooting to designated players (code for those that will not score)."[7]

Philadelphia is a big small town. One day on the radio, I decided to air-out the differences between these crosstown mind-sets—Rosenberg's cutting down on trophies with the boys and my friend's relating how the score clock sometimes gets frozen for the girls.

Our discussion about participation trophies segued into the related scoring issue, and I shared the information I had learned from my friend with my radio audience, specifically, his having told me that in a game he had coached, the scoreboard lights had been turned off when the point spread between the girls' basketball teams reached ten points.

Well, as fate would have it, one of the founders of the basketball league who was listening took umbrage with what I'd said and sent me an e-mail. I had TC, my producer, call him to come on the air during the same program where I was praising Steve Rosenberg, but we never heard back. So I did something I should have done at the outset, I looked up the girls' basketball rules on-line.

The rules of this league are exactly what I am talking about. I list some of them here, not to single them out for embarrassment, but because I believe them to be typical of what is going on across the country and worthy of some discussion.

For example, for third graders: "There will be no official score-keeping and no winners or losers. The girls always seem to know the score, however. If they ask you, tell them you think it's a tie."[8]

Huh? Lie to the girls? I have a third grader of my own. He's the same boy that Steve Rosenberg denied a trophy. Michael Jr. knows the score, as do his team-mates, regardless of the league policy, so why hide the truth?

My son can handle it, and so can his buddies. So can the girls for whom these rules apply.

And why lie to them by saying you "think it's a tie" when you know it isn't? What kind of message does that send?

Then there is this:

If one team is clearly trouncing the other team, please be sure to imple-ment some or all of the following to keep the "perceived score" close:

1. No fast breaks

2. Players take four passes before shooting the ball

3. No stealing or double teaming

4. Have the stronger players feed the ball to the weaker players

5. Pull the defense back into the lane

6. Have the whole team work toward having someone score who hasn't scored yet this year

7. If you have less than 10 for a game, play the less strong players more than the stronger ones

8. Use this time to try new combinations of players

9. No tears in the MLGBA!!!

(Quick, arguably an irrelevant quiz question, but: what movie comes to mind when you read that last line? And, by the way, they added the emphasis, not me. Answer: I know, he said it about baseball, but we were all thinking the same thing.)

If no score is being kept, why is there a problem with running up the score? The answer is that it's a charade. The coaches know the score and so do the kids. Heck, it even says "perceived score."

My friend, who coaches in this league and has done so at various age levels, tells me they certainly keep track. Moreover, I could have said in one rule what they have said in nine: Don't Run Up the Score! Which is entirely reasonable.

In a word, it's called sportsmanship.

11

Getting Maid on Campus

There's something about Harvard which provides endless fodder for a collection of stories about political correctness. Consider the plight of a student who wants to get a maid on campus. (I know, in your era it was something a bit different, but hey, things have changed. Read on.)

This is a story with a motivated and determined protagonist who almost drowned in a sea of obfuscation. The young entrepreneur, Michael Kopko, is a twenty-year-old economics major from Nyack, New York, enrolled in Harvard's class of 2007. Together with brother Matt (also an economics major at Princeton, 2008), he conceived a student-run business for which no one could possibly doubt the need—maid service for the dormitories—which the brothers Kopko creatively call DormAid. Actually, they had a better name when they started the venture.

It wasn't supposed to be DormAid; it originated as "DorMaid." But the Harvard brass told Michael Kopko that the chosen name for his Horatio Alger dream was both "sexist and demeaning" because of his loose use of the word "maid." That is why he was forced to agree to change DorMaid to DormAid.[1] Apparently, in that rare air of Harvard, maids have gone the way of garbage men (sanitation workers) and stewardesses (flight attendants). In the end, however, the thought police did him a favor.

"I think it's ridiculous that the university [Harvard] could have such a great influence over the name of our business, but it actually was a blessing in disguise. We're now expanding our business plan beyond simply cleaning rooms and are delving more into service-oriented areas. For this reason alone, the name DormAid better expresses the full range of opportunities available to our customers," explained Kopko.[2]

The partners' original idea was simple, and the outlook seemed favorable to all. They would hire people from the surrounding Cambridge area to clean dormitory rooms for about twenty bucks per cleaning, thus supplementing the existing Dorm Crew, which focuses solely on bathrooms.

"Win-Win," thought the brothers Kopko. They planned to employ local willing workers, while assisting students who weren't inclined to maintain their rooms as they appeared on parents' weekends.

Anyone who spends a few minutes perusing the DormAid Web site will see that this venture is no freshman lark. Students can select from a menu of options and determine their choice of time for the cleaning(s). The actual price is determined by the number of roommates, room size, and whether bathroom and kitchen are involved.

Michael Kopko launched the enterprise at Harvard by first writing a letter to the parents of sophomores, then by parading around in a sandwich board the first few days of class. (How do I buy stock in this guy?)

But Harvard stopped him. The grounds? Not only was the name of his business "sexist and demeaning," but there were concerns about insurance, security, the Fair Labor Standards Act, and elitism, according to Judith H. Kidd, an associate dean.[3] This, despite the fact that similar efforts at Boston University and Princeton were met with no such flack.

Kopko began exploring other service-oriented areas at more receptive universities. "Instead of getting hung up on seemingly obvious questions such as, 'Should students have the ability to hire a professional cleaning service,' [the other universities] have only asked that we take care of the technical areas of starting a business such as getting the proper insurance, etc."[4]

Kopko went on to explain how he plans to expand beyond simple dormitory cleaning: "At Rutgers, we are gaining expertise on laundry services, and at Princeton we've been gaining experience at grocery delivery."[5]

But Harvard was different. Harvard's student newspaper weighed in with an editorial entitled "Maid for Harvard?" The *Crimson* cried:

By creating yet another differential between the have's and have-not's on campus, DormAid threatens our student unity. There are already plenty of services at Harvard that sharpen the differences between socioeconomic classes. Harvard Student Agency Cleaners, for example, lets some students pick up cleaned and neatly-folded clothes in crackling plastic bags. The less well-off among us, however, make semi-weekly journeys to the basement with bulging mesh laundry bags and quarters in hand. These differences extend to the social sphere, as well, to clubs composed predominately of wealthy young men, or to basic activities like eating out that some students cannot afford to enjoy. [Are some really on their uppers?] But while class differences are a fact of life—yes, there are both rich and poor people at Harvard—there is no reason to exacerbate these differences further with a room-cleaning service.[6]

But the *Crimson* did not stop there. Their editorial staff went so far as to call for a campus-wide boycott of DormAid's services. Thankfully, not everyone saw it the *Crimson*'s way. While the paper bemoaned the fact that college life "is an egalitarian society that should level the playing field to foster respect for all backgrounds," other voices were raised in support of DormAid, believing that campus life should be a veritable "microcosm of society."[7] Not everyone will be able to afford maid service post-Harvard, either, observes this more grounded and reasonable school of thought.

And, according to a survey taken by Kopko, Harvard students were largely on his side. A campus-wide survey he conducted shattered the *Crimson*'s argument, citing that "74 percent of respondents supported the idea [of a professional cleaning service] and 26 percent would use the service. Of those who would not use it, only 25 percent said the reason was its cost."[8] This survey, according to Associate Dean Judith H. Kidd, "convinced Harvard officials that a class clash was not a big issue."[9]

Kopko came to learn that even an overwhelmingly positive response from the student community would not be enough to assuage the concerns of campus administrators. In the spring of 2005, Kopko sought and received Harvard's approval for the initiation of his business after lengthy deliberation.

That this required lengthy deliberation was telling. Perhaps only at America's most elite university would Kopko's entrepreneurial venture get tagged as "sexist" and "elitist."

I couldn't believe this controversy was for real when I first heard about it. (Gotta be some *National Lampoon* sort of thing, I surmised. Or maybe the Harvard Pudding.) But, in our initial conversation one morning when I roused him from bed, Kopko told my listening audience that Harvard is "trying to take choice away from people," and that "it's essentially against creating wealth for society."[10]

"We're creating jobs. We're having kids live in cleaner conditions. . . . All of our cleaning professionals have been criminal-background checked. . . . We're paying higher wages to the cleaning professionals that we bring in from the

Cambridge area, and we're teaching kids business experience and helping them get jobs to supplement their income. . . . Student managers help make [the hired cleaning professionals] efficient, help sell the business, and help advertise. . . . Students are not cleaning other students' rooms."[11]

It seems to me that DormAid has everything in order. It's time for the *Crimson* to learn to relax.

Kopko has even encouraged other enterprising young people to begin their own versions of DormAid at their respective colleges. Jason Reuben, an undergraduate at Babson College, has been in close contact with Kopko. With the full cooperation of the faculty and student communities, Reuben has taken it upon himself to begin a division of DormAid.

According to Kopko, "Babson College demonstrates how a great relationship with a business such as DormAid can benefit both colleges and entrepreneurs alike."[12] As long as DormAid gains approval from local law-enforcement officials, it should be fully integrated into Babson College life by the fall of 2005.

So, despite the initial objections of Harvard, DormAid—I mean DormAid— is up and running and, in the fall of 2005, began operations at NYU, Dickinson, Rutgers, Babson, UPENN, Princeton, and BU.

Who said there's nothing new under the sun?

12

Naked Tigers

It's a sunny April day in Princeton, New Jersey, at the Woodrow Wilson School of Public and International Affairs located on the esteemed university campus.

Enjoying the sunshine splashing against ivy walls that day was Dr. Chang, the public health expert from Taiwan, standing in close proximity to the famed economist, Mr. Loo. I can't confirm this, but I suspect Abdul and Mohammed were able to take time off their busy schedules at the Palestinian Peace Institute to be in attendance as well. They were all walking around, shaking hands, eating cheese, admiring the facility and the campus rites, nodding and smiling a lot. You can picture the scene. It had to be one of those "It's So Good To Be Alive!" moments, and where better than on an Ivy League campus in the springtime?

And then, all of a sudden—HEY! What's that? Did you just see? . . . What?

Oh, it's just a couple of guys, buck-naked except for their clown wigs and kamikaze headbands, running by the visitors with their own personal rendition of the Red Hot Chili Peppers' sock dance.

Just who were those guys in the festive headgear? you ask. It was the Princeton University Varsity Streaking Team. What else?

Unfortunately, that April 8, 2005, er, "Meet" (as they like to call it) may have been their last chance to go for the gold. The "team" was forced to disband under threat from the locals that they would be prosecuted if their behavior continued. Which is a damned shame.

The streaking team, a group of roughly 30 students whose competitions consist of seeing how big of a group they can get to go unclothed in public areas, gained attention for streaking an Abnormal Psychology lecture in December. Wearing nothing but shoes, wool hats and belts, the students slowly walked down the stairs, handed the professor a note, then walked back up the stairs. "We regretfully apologize that we will be unable to streak your lecture today," the note read. "Due to inclement weather we were not able to get sufficient numbers to field a full team. We had hoped to streak for the cause of legalizing streaking. Apologetically, the Princeton University Varsity Streaking Team.[1]

Allow me to introduce Scott Welfel, one of the founders and a co-captain of the varsity squad. Scott is a twenty-one-year-old junior majoring in philosophy, hailing from Roseland, New Jersey. I tracked him down after I heard about his exploits because I wanted first-hand confirmation that the future of the free world remains secure against a backdrop of political correctness, particularly in the Ivy League.

My thesis: If they can streak at Princeton, how bad can things really be?

He told me that he and senior Danny Brome founded the thirty-member group—fairly evenly comprised of both men and women, by the way—after being inspired by a similar team at Hamilton University.[2] For good reason, the Hamilton club, which not only has a Web site but, also, an on-line store at www.hamiltonstreaks.com, has been featured on *Fox News* and in the *New York Times*. And the two teams have actually competed against each other.

You're probably wondering how the winner of such an event is determined. "Streakers consider themselves victorious when people applaud or join in. Another sign of success is avoiding campus safety officials," the newspaper reported.[3]

Though the Princeton team was only recently founded, these brave streakers have already pulled off about ten successful runs, including one at a campus party where they "streaked across the dance floor down into the tap room, and then just decided to hang out for a little while on the dance floor—naked." Sounds like some party.

I asked Scott the obvious question: did he create the club to hook up? He surprised me by saying that he doesn't streak to see women naked but "because it's fun" and, if it wasn't coed, it "just wouldn't be as funny." Truly a budding young philosopher.[4]

He told me, "I streak mainly to make people laugh, to break up the monotony that can sometimes infect the routines of Princeton students. I love seeing anything out of the ordinary or talking to anyone who interacts a bit strangely or differently—it makes the day more exciting. Seeing a practical joke or someone just being goofy in public makes me smile and puts me in a good mood, and I try to share this feeling with others by streaking. I mean, it's not every day you see a herd of nude bodies trampling past the food court, making stork and bear noises. We just try to mix it up a bit."[5]

I was surprised to learn that Carolyn Hawkins, a spokeswoman for the American Association for Nude Recreation based in Kissimmee, Florida, had criticized the Princeton team: "It's great that students feel comfortable with their bodies," she said, but "we always go with 'Nude when possible and clothes when practical.' If you're in college, the logical thing would be clothes."

Yet Princeton film student Janine Jaffe, who made a documentary of the streaking team, disagrees. "The fact is, a lot of people at Princeton have sticks up their asses. It's the truth. I think a lot of this activity is geared towards loosening people up, making people more comfortable with things that are fun and free," she said.

One of the female team members, senior Eileen Hwang, said, "I'm just there for fun." Not surprisingly, it took the persuasion of "several male friends" before Eileen learned just how much fun streaking can be.[6]

But what did the Princeton administration think of the new campus fad *before* that final incident at the Woodrow Wilson School? Scott told me, "They were really pretty chill about it. We got called in to talk to one of the deans, but all she did was basically warn Danny and me that, if we were to get caught, we would likely get probation. She said the university 'is not trying to censor you guys.'"

Funny how everything becomes a free-speech matter.

Scott continued, "The dean didn't tell us not to streak. She just warned us what would happen if we did get caught. She said, 'This is not a big priority, we're not trying to stop you guys.'"[7] But the laissez-faire attitude changed shortly thereafter. The school administration says it had nothing to do with it; they blame the campus police.

Investigator Charles Peters at the campus Public Safety Office told Scott and his teammates that the foreign dignitaries had called the Borough Police. Peters made the team promise never to streak again or the Borough would press charges.

"Investigator Peters told us the Borough was pretty pissed and had hired a detective to investigate the incident. He wanted to be able to give the Borough assurance that we would promise to discontinue our streaking, which we were compelled to do," Scott said.

Borough Police Lieutenant Dennis McManimon disputed some of the details of the story. "There seems to have been some kind of function that day with school officials but not with foreign dignitaries. . . . I don't know why people said that," he told the student newspaper.[8]

The associate dean of undergraduate students, Hilary Herbold, declined to comment on the streaking incident but did tell the campus newspaper, "What I can say is that, regardless of dignitaries, we are not going to change the disciplinary response [based] on who was there to witness [the event]. Were specific students identified and were [it] to be acknowledged that they had been in a state of undress, then we would place them on probation."[9]

I think she was supposed to say *double-secret* probation? I mean the fact that Dean Herbold can't even say the word "naked" tells me she's probably Princeton's equivalent of Dean Vernon Wormer.

"The university will not go out of its way to search for the streakers if no reports are made to Public Safety and no students are identified. We basically rely on Public Safety to apprehend the students. If they don't, we won't actively pursue it," Herbold said.[10]

Entrepreneurs at Harvard creating a maid service. Streakers at Princeton. The future is looking bright! Then again, you haven't heard about the climate at Penn.

13

A Behemoth of an Incident

Okay. Now you've heard about the maid situation at Harvard and the lack of appreciation for streaking at Princeton. But prepare thyself. For, in the annals of political correctness, there is recorded the most unbelievable of incidents at yet another Ivy League institution.

I speak of the nightmarish freshman-year experience of a student at the University of Pennsylvania in the fall of 1993. It was a horror story that lasted nearly his entire college career and garnered the attention of the national media. If there were ever a timeline created of the most significant events of political correctness in United States history, surely Eden Jacobowitz's name would be chiseled in granite.

Eden Jacobowitz grew up in an Orthodox Jewish household in Lawrence, Long Island. Like most teenagers, he claimed to have found his religious high school "restricting." Graduating in 1992, he "was just dying to get to college and experience real life." A member of the college class of 1996, he eagerly looked forward to the best years—or what *ought to have been* the best years—of his life. "I came to campus really naïve," he says. "I was so idealistic. I was such a baby. I really hadn't experienced much."[1]

He was about to experience much more than he bargained for.

On January 13, 1993, Eden was up late at night struggling to overcome a case of writer's block and finish an English paper.[2] It was the start of the second semester of his freshman year. Outside of his high-rise dormitory, a group of young women from the African American Delta Sigma Theta sorority were celebrating—apparently rather boisterously—the anniversary of their founding, "which included traditional songs performed in a circle and choreographed against a rhythmic bass."[3] Sounds a bit like a Lawrence Welk routine, except that, according to some reports, the women were "screaming and making real loud 'Woo! Woo!' noises."[4]

The Deltas have a rich history beginning with their formation at Howard

University in 1913 and their participation in the Women's Suffrage movement shortly thereafter. This night, however, was not to be a high point in the sorority's history. The women's celebration, which they chose to perform late at night in a courtyard surrounded by dormitories, was met with curses as well as numerous demands to be quiet or "Shut the f*** up." Admittedly agitated by their disruptive behavior, but not one to yell curses out windows, Eden chimed in with a statement he deemed innocuous in comparison. First he simply yelled at them to "Shut up!" When the noise continued he added: "Shut up, you water buffalo! If you want a party, there's a zoo a mile from here."[5] He was referring to the Philadelphia Zoo, located approx 1.4 miles from the University of Pennsylvania's campus.

From the outset, Eden admitted he knew the race of the women but insisted it was no factor in his choice of words. "I heard students responding the way they always do to loud noise late at night, and I reacted the way I would to any group causing a late night ruckus. If I had heard other students yelling racial epithets or using language with racial overtones, I would not have yelled at all because I would not have wanted to take any part in that kind of ugly behavior."[6] He later told a reporter, "I basically said something that sounded ridiculous. I don't even know where it came from, but it had absolutely no racial implications."[7]

"I looked out my window and saw these women who were making noise and being disruptive," he told me. "They were making noises like cattle and stomping their feet, and I guess it struck up certain imagery. And the way my brain works, I was thinking to myself, what could I say in response? I was an immature college freshman with arguably a strange sense of humor. . . . I had called people water buffalo and aardvark in the past. It was something different. It had a lot to do with my personality. Where others would curse or use bad language, I went to the window and said something that I think no one could consider coarse, much less racist."[8]

Eden's freshman-year roommate was Christopher Pryor. After Eden called the women "water buffalo," an amused Pryor approached the window to throw in his two cents, yelling, "And get your fat asses out of here." After the noise subsided, Eden left his dorm room to visit a friend in a nearby apartment, having no idea that his headache had just begun.

Meanwhile, at the completion of their celebration, the offended women stampeded (I couldn't resist the word choice) Eden's dormitory searching for the "white boys" who had yelled at them from above.

When the herd (sorry again!) got to the Jacobowitz/Pryor lair, Christopher Pryor answered the door. According to Jacobowitz, Pryor denied yelling anything, telling the women Eden had done all the shouting. As he sees it, Pryor's "dishonest" actions in the initial stages of the investigation that ensued took the focus off of Pryor and placed the blame squarely on Eden's shoulders. Now armed with a name to pin their wrath upon, the women filed a complaint with the campus police.

They claimed that during their celebration they heard students call them "nigger, bitch, fat asses, and *black* water buffalo." They also added that they had found a witness, Christopher Pryor, who implicated his roommate, Eden Jacobowitz.

University police were quickly dispatched to the dorm to investigate what had quickly become a case of alleged racial harassment. "Functioning under the presumption that I hadn't done anything wrong and that there was nothing to hide," Eden says he matter-of-factly told police exactly what he had yelled.[9] This admission to uttering two sentences was about to shatter his freshman naïveté and threaten his entire college career.

Eden said, "I told them everything that had happened, not knowing that the women had brought race into it by alleging the words 'nigger' and 'bitch' were used nor that Chris had said I was the one who yelled everything. So I'm sure they thought that if I was admitting to calling them water buffalo, I must have used the other words, too, but that just wasn't the case. When I finally saw the complaint, it had the racial epithets, including 'black water buffalo,' and it said, 'roommate said Eden said everything,' and I was shocked."[10]

Eden avows, and the university's Judicial Inquiry Office later stipulated, that he did not say, "*black* water buffalo." He continued, "When I yelled out the window the last thing on my mind was that they were black."[11]

Ironically, it was Chris who could more easily be said to have crossed the line. He yelled "and get your fat asses out of here." I would never have yelled that. And you could say he stereotyped. If you look only at content, he should have been prosecuted more than me. But the school had a political agenda. I was a naïve freshman, and I had no support. When you get charged, the school sends a letter and tells you that you are entitled to have an advisor, and if you don't know anyone, there is a list of willing people made available. Well, I didn't know anyone. My roommate had someone with whom he had bonded and who worked on his case. The charges against him were dropped. But in my case, I spent months going to meetings with the inquiry officer, and she had the viewpoint that women were hurt and something needed to be done. That was it. It was insane. I said, "Look, if I wanted to harass them racially, there was no shortage of words that I could have used." The fact that I used water buffalo should mean something to you.[12]

After the case against Christopher Pryor had been dropped, and nine full months after the incident, it seemed like the one-time roommate of Eden Jacobowitz was sorry that he missed the limelight. Christopher Pryor wrote a column he titled "The Other Water Buffalo" for the campus newspaper in which he admitted to yelling what Jacobowitz had heard that night:

> What George Will, Rush Limbaugh and Gary Trudeau don't know is that there were many people who yelled out of the High Rise East windows at approximately 11:45 on the night of January 13, 1993. At least a dozen people were accused of screaming epithets that night, and some of them had complaints filed against them for racial harassment by the Judicial Inquiry Officer. The JIO formally investigated two of those accused. Eden Jacobowitz was one of those two. I was the other. . . .
>
> I will admit that yelling "get your fat asses out of here" just moments after Eden uttered the now nationally famous water buffalo comment was not the right thing for me to do. . . .
>
> The women of Delta Sigma Theta sorority mishandled what they perceived as racial hatred. . . .[13]

But back at the time of the incident, Eden was the only student to come forward and admit to yelling anything.[14] In return for his honesty, Eden soon found himself under prosecution for hate speech.

His offers to simply apologize for being rude were rejected by the university, and he was told that his overture might be possible "later in the process." As Eden wondered, "What process?" the five sorority women involved, Nikki Taylor, Ayanna Taylor, Colleen Bonnicklewis, Suzanne Jenkins, and Denita Thomas, filed a complaint against Jacobowitz, claiming "to have been barraged by racial slurs and epithets with sexual overtones."[15]

He told me, "I came to realize I was already locked into a process. PC stood in the way of regular civility and interaction. And it was all bulls**t. They said that by my calling them water buffalo I was saying they were unfit for Penn and were animals, ignoring that they were noisy, disruptive, and had acted like animals."[16]

Several weeks into the "process," Eden was informed by the university's Judicial Inquiry officer that he "would be prosecuted under the university's racial harassment code on the grounds that water buffalo referred to an African animal."[17] (Never mind that the animal in question, a species name *Bubalus bubalis*, is native to Nepal, India, Vietnam, Malaysia, and other parts of South Asia—not Africa.)

After initial proceedings, he received a plea bargain which he considered "a blow." He rejected it, outwardly telling the university to "shove it up your ass," but secretly returning to his dorm to cry in solitude.[18]

Eden said he "couldn't find anyone who was willing to take on the university" and felt "completely alone."[19]

He had made a decision not to tell his own family, although that would have to change when the *Wall Street Journal* caught wind of the spectacle playing itself out in University City, Philadelphia.

"My parents didn't know anyone at Penn. When I had been offered a settlement of the disciplinary procedures, I still had not told them. I didn't want to worry them. It was only the day before the *Journal* hit that I said, you might read this, but don't worry, I have it handled. I didn't. Not yet."[20]

But that was about to change—big time. Jacobowitz soon noticed the man who was to become his adviser and champion, history professor Alan Kors, in an article in which Kors criticized the administration's policies about another burgeoning campus controversy. Jacobowitz picked up his phone and called him, the "turning point" in his ordeal.[21] That other campus controversy is worthy of a quick mention here.

It involves the April 15, 1993, theft of nearly 14,000 copies of the University of Pennsylvania campus newspaper, the *Daily Pennsylvanian*. The newspapers were all gone. The *Daily Pennsylvanian* reported, "A sign posted at all of the sites identified the students responsible as the 'Black Community' and said the students are not willing to accept 'the blatant and voluntary perpetuation of institutional racism against the Black Community by the DP' and by the University. 'Sometimes inconvenience is worth the price,' the sign read. 'Think about it. . . .'"[22]

So what sparked the theft of the entire press run of the campus newspaper at this Ivy League institution?

The campus newspaper reported that "Judicial Inquiry Officer Catherine Schifter said . . . one 'could speculate' that yesterday's incident was connected to recent complaints about the controversial content of DP columnist Gregory Pavlik's columns."[23]

Pavlik, then a senior engineering major and founder of the Edmund Burke Society on campus, wrote a biweekly column entitled "The Idols of the Theater" after the phrase from British empiricist and philosopher, Francis Bacon. Pavlik's heady columns often reflected on provocative issues.

Take, for example, this rebuttal of political correctness from his November 1993 review of Jean Raspail's *The Camp of the Saints* (1973): "In the name of some abstract and non-existent equality among various peoples, Americans have decided to turn their civilization over to whichever group is smart enough to grab the reigns of power. Of course, no other group is going to be stupid enough to believe in this equality so when they do take power, out goes the West and in comes the expression of their own culture. Snoop Doggy Dogg for Mozart. Menchu for Hawthorne. 'It only seems right that we should make allowances for past inequities,' the argument goes. Except maybe things are going a little too far. What if we can't hold on?"[24]

Pavlik clearly pulled no punches. On another occasion, he urged readers to "buy an assault rifle to improve your stay in West Philly. If not, you're a sheep, and don't be terribly surprised when you are sheared."[25] Not exactly the most sensitive way to advocate gun ownership—he sounds like my kind of guy!

What sort of punishment do you suppose the thieves received from the university? Something at least comparable to the pain and anguish that Eden experienced, surely. Wanna bet? Try: *none*.

"While DP editors and even the University Trustees spoke out forcefully against the theft, explaining that the only legitimate way to counter disagreeable speech is with opposing speech, the offenders were not disciplined by the university. In fact, the only people punished in the whole affair were a university police officer and a University Museum security guard who scuffled with a student trying to remove papers from the University Museum."[26]

Watching the Pavlick/*Daily Pennsylvanian* controversy from the sidelines was Eden Jacobowitz: "In my case, it was PC to go after a white person who yelled at group of blacks. That is because of the other racial issues occurring and the concern about the conservative columnist and what happened with the *Daily Pennsylvanian*. Talk about suppressing speech. When the entire press run was stolen, the university didn't press charges against the thieves and did come down on the columnist."[27]

Who among the liberal Penn faculty defended Pavlik? Professor Alan Kors, soon to come to the defense of Eden Jacobowitz.

At about the same time the entire press run of the *Daily Pennsylvanian* was being trashed in response to columns by Gregory Pavlick, Eden Jacobowitz was meeting with the university's assistant Judicial Inquiry officer, Robin Read, who "initially offered him a three-part settlement, which included formally apologizing to the complainants, organizing a diversity seminar, and being placed on residential probation."

Later, however, "Read added a fourth stipulation—a racial harassment notation on his transcript for the next two years which would be seen by graduate school admissions offices—after telling him she did 'some soul searching' and evaluated her 'responsibility to the University.'"

This was unacceptable, and Eden told the JI Office so: "You interpreted my phrase 'water buffalo,' referring to people making loud noise beneath my window, to quote your words, as a reference to 'primitive, dark animals that live in Africa.' [As stated earlier, water buffalo are indigenous to South Asia.] That was the farthest meaning from my mind. Those are your words not mine. That is your meaning, not mine."[28] A formal hearing then ensued.

Professor Kors first tried to reason with his former history department colleague, University President Sheldon Hackney, one-on-one. Jacobowitz made a personal appeal to Hackney that fell on deaf ears: "Within a week of the incident, I went to the Hilell Society on campus for a kosher meal, and President Hackney was speaking. It was the Friday night on the week that it happened. I had just received the first letter. So I waited until the crowd left, and I went over to him and said, 'I have to tell you what is going on.' That is how naïve I was. I told him I called these women 'water buffalo' and just got charged. And he looked at me and gave me very noncommittal answer like 'I hope it all works out okay.'"[29]

Hackney claimed his hands were tied by university policy. To this day, John Leo of *U.S. News and World Report* bestows an annual "Sheldon Award" to the "college president who looks the other way the most in cases of freedom of speech and media." An Oscar parody, the trophy shows a spineless man looking the other way. "There were a whole bunch of college presidents behaving like weasels even before . . . but Hackney was the epitome of 'a president with no backbone.'"[33] In any case, Kors kept up the pressure, and when he saw that the university was digging in, he called for reinforcements. Numerous Penn faculty members responded including noted black sociologist Elijah Anderson, and linguistics professor Dan Ben-Amos. Eden's defenders maintained "there are no racial connotations associated with 'water buffalo.'"[30]

Eden said, "If you look at the speech code, you will see that it was twisted in a ridiculous way against me. And yet, if you look at the statement of 'where's that white boy,' they were violating the policy. In my case the words I used were not some racial epithet. I was just trying to get them to be quiet."[31]

Beyond campus support, Kors unleashed the attack hounds of the Fourth Estate. Soon Eden's "water buffalo" cry was receiving immeasurable attention nationwide. Articles and editorials from the *Wall Street Journal*, the *Washington Post*, and other major newspapers were read on nationally syndicated talk-radio programs. Even *Rolling Stone* magazine eventually wrote a several-page story.[32]

Nine months after that fateful January night, as Eden was starting the first day of his sophomore year classes, a CNN camera crew was there to capture it.

"There's a very good reason that the story reached so wide a press," said the *Wall Street Journal*'s Dorothy Rabinowitz, who wrote the first editorial lambasting Penn's administration. "The charges were ludicrous. . . . Mr. Hackney was ludicrous."[34]

Without question, the media impacted the outcome of the case. After the hearings but before the panel had delivered its decision, the five women complainants suddenly *dropped* their charges, citing "biased media coverage and the politically charged atmosphere" which made it "impossible to get a fair hearing." "The primary reason we withdrew our case was not because we were wrong or Eden didn't say what he said, but because we had a system working against us," they said.[35]

The university nevertheless reviewed its judicial procedures and racial harassment codes to determine whether they were "too ambiguous or contributed to problems in the case."[36] In the end, those reviews resulted in a *new* code of student conduct at Penn, one that eliminated speech codes.

Jacobowitz had prevailed, but his success came at a high price.

The now famous water buffalo incident happened in the beginning of the second semester of Jacobowitz's freshman year. It did not become news until the end of that semester, in which he dropped two classes and, as a result, had to take five classes each semester for the rest of his college career in order to graduate on time.[37]

The incident did not die a slow death until his sophomore year. During that year, Jacobowitz ran for the undergraduate assembly and got the highest number of votes. "There were thousands of students on campus, but people knew if I was in their class or not. Every once in while there would be someone who couldn't accept the fact that I was not trying to racially harass. I felt bad about that."[38]

"When it was over, I was dead-set on trying to make everybody realize that I was no racist. I would go out of my way to try to be a positive example of community," he told me. "One day, I ran into several of the woman involved in the incident. It was in my sophomore year. I was willing to discuss the incident. They just wanted to shout me down. And one of them turned to me and whispered, 'Christ killer.' I said, 'What did you say to me?' And she repeated it."[39]

Eden not only graduated on time, but a semester early. Yet he didn't go quietly. "The university figured it could blame all of the school's racial tension on one white Jewish kid," he said. "What they didn't realize was, if they pushed me too hard, I would start fighting back."[40]

In early 1996, amid accusations of greed and self-interest, Eden and his attorney, Edward Rubenstone, filed a lawsuit citing "gross negligence, breach of contract, infliction of emotional distress, invasion of privacy and defamation."[41] They eventually settled out of court with the university admitting no wrongdoing but agreeing to pay under $10,000 in legal fees and expenses.[42]

By now, Jacobowitz was himself in law school at Fordham and decided it was time to move on. After passing the bar, he "bounced around, trying new things" and recently settled into a job in real estate.

It's been more than ten years since the water buffalo incident—why bring it up again? Quite simply, there are still too many thin-skinned people thumping their PC bibles and claiming to be offended at every turn.

More specifically, the issue of free speech on college campuses remains urgent. "Do you have a map of the United States?" Thor Halvorssen, CEO of the Foundation for Individual Rights in Education (FIRE), likes to ask, his way of saying this crap goes on all overy the country. "It's the entire thing . . . at Harvard, it's called the Statement of Community Values," he said. "At some [universities], it's called the Tolerance Statement."[43]

FIRE, co-founded by Eden's advisor, Dr. Kors, itself came into being because of the water buffalo blow-up. And even though Penn may have eliminated their speech code, the folks at FIRE still have their work cut out for them: plenty of universities still ban hate speech. In their 1998 book, *The Shadow University: The Betrayal of Liberty on American Campuses*, Professor Kors and ACLU attorney

Harvey Silvergate have some harsh words to characterize any university that institutes a speech code: "This University believes that your sons and daughters are the racist, sexist, homophobic progeny—or the innocent victims—of a racist, sexist, homophobic, oppressive America. For $30,000 per year, we shall assign them rights on an unequal and compensatory basis and undertake by coercion their moral and political enlightenment."[44]

It took just over a decade after his graduation until there was reason for the name of Eden Jacobowitz to be invoked yet again on Penn campus. And when it was recalled, it was in the context of his faculty-patron saint, Professor Kors, yet again riding to the rescue of a student caught in the throes of a battle over political correctness. In December 2005, Kors was quoted as saying, "Penn students have the right to free speech and free expression. The University appeared to have remembered that lesson for a long time, and now it appears to have forgotten it."[45] Only this time, the debate didn't focus on a student's comments, but rather, his camera.

According to confidential University of Pennsylvania documents obtained by the *Daily Pennsylvanian*, an engineering junior "posted naked pictures of another University of Pennsylvania student on [his] personal Web site through the University's servers, without that student's authorization and in a manner highly invasive of the student's privacy."[46]

What kind of naked pictures?

Well, we're not talking about a peephole in the women's locker room. Nor that the Tri-Lambs put a hidden camera in the Omega Mu sorority house. The "naked pictures" were actually photographs taken from between two highrise dormitories on the Penn campus. In the photos, one can see the backside of a naked man "pressing ham"[47] against a large window with wide open drapes in broad daylight.

It appears as though a woman is in front of the man and that the two seem to be engaged in a sexual encounter.[48] One of the pictures was panned far enough back to make identification of the particular dorm room possible. In other words, students viewing the photograph could (and surely did) count the dormitory windows and figure out in just whose room the sex caper had taken place.

In late September 2005, the engineering student published the photos on his password-protected Web site on the University servers.[49] One month later, his graduate student advisor, Andrew Geier, received a letter from the Office of Student Conduct notifying Geier that a complaint had been filed against the student who took the photo.

In other words, a campus couple choose to get it on, in broad (no pun intended . . . okay, yeah, pun intended) daylight, in front of a big window with no drapes, in full view of countless other dormitory rooms, and then, when somebody took these exhibitionists' photograph and posted it online, the person who took the picture was the one disciplined. Only at Penn!

Geier was amazed by the complaint regarding the photo and told me, "It's not only broad daylight, but a number of people took pictures. The couple did this three days in a row . . . at about 3 p.m. The photographs . . . are not that great, you certainly cannot identify anyone that is in them."[50] How unexpected: a college junior saw two people naked in front of a wide open window three straight days and took their photo. Remarkable. According to Geier, "The spectacle couldn't be any more public than if they were at the fifty yard line at Franklin Field at halftime of the Penn v. Princeton game"[51]

In a maneuver that immediately had people invoking the name of Eden Jacobowitz, the University Office of Student Conduct proposed official sanctions against the photographer under the University's sexual harassment policy. According to the *Daily Pennsylvanian*, the official sanctions "would have required him to undergo disciplinary probation until graduation, admit to violating University policies regarding sexual harassment, student conduct and use of electronic resources, write an essay discussing the inappropriate nature of his conduct and write a letter of apology to one subject of his photograph."[52] The university defended the sanctions by stating that the ability to identify the particular dorm room "caused one of the pictured students 'serious distress' and created 'an intimidating living environment for her.'"[53]

Not surprisingly, the university's position had little support. Professor Kors, who said that "the absurd nature" of the charges led to his involvement, stated: "If a student at Penn does not have the right to take a photograph of what is in plain sight . . . then you have no rights. And I don't want to teach at a university where students have no rights."[54] According to Geier, the student body certainly sided with the photographer: "the overwhelming pervasive sentiment on campus is that he is in the right and that what the University is doing is unjust."[55]

The *Philadelphia Daily News* ran the story and featured the picture on its front page. The headline? Try this on for size: "Ivy League Grind: It's the Naked Truth."[56] It was soon picked up nationwide from the *Los Angeles Times* to the *Washington Post.*[57] Within hours, Geier and his advisee had received interview requests from a number of nationally known newspapers as well as offers to appear on Fox News' *The O'Reilly Factor* and MSNBC's *Rita Cosby Live & Direct* and *Scarborough Country.*[58] By the time the student appeared on the afternoon of December 1 for his conduct hearing, the school decided to drop all charges. No university officials would comment on the matter, but instead "officials issued a brief statement saying that though they had decided to drop the issue, they were still disturbed by the photographer's behavior."[59]

Ultimately, even the editors of the *Daily Pennsylvanian*, a group that is traditionally left of those that are left of the left, editorialized about the situation, connecting the dots to Eden Jacobowitz: "It is worth noting the black eye Penn received nationally when it took action against a student for speech it disagreed with a dozen years ago. The so-called 'Water Buffalo' incident reminded all of academia of the importance of free expression—whether that expression is politically correct or not."[60] Perhaps some University officials need to take a course in history.

Call it the lesson of Eden Jacobowitz.

14

Cops and Dancers

(Some People Just Shouldn't Be Either)

Like many Americans, I sat transfixed by my television set on March 11, 2005. It wasn't quite an OJ-White-Ford-Bronco moment, but it was compelling television, nonetheless. You'll remember the incident.

An Atlanta man on trial for rape escaped and went on a courthouse rampage; he shot and killed the presiding judge, a court reporter, and a deputy sheriff. The crime spree paralyzed downtown Atlanta for the day as the authorities unsuccessfully tried to hunt him down. During his getaway, the suspect hijacked a series of cars and set off a manhunt that expanded to several surrounding states by nightfall. He was finally apprehended with the assistance of a woman who calmed the man by reading to him from a religious bestseller.

The bad guy was Brian Nichols, a thirty-three-year-old former college football linebacker. His rampage began when he wrestled a gun from sheriff's deputy Cynthia Ann Hall. Unassisted, she was leading him to a holding cell where he was to change from prison garb into street clothes so he could face the jury looking like a civilian. But commoner he was not.

Captured on videotape—but not released to the public—was his overpowering of Mrs. Hall after she removed his handcuffs. Nichols slammed her against the cell wall, pushing her out of the camera's view before taking the key to a lockbox that secured her gun. As a result of her struggle with Nichols, she suffered a severe bruising of her brain and fractures to her face requiring hospitalization. She was classified in critical condition.[1]

Nichols, meanwhile, retrieved the gun, changed clothes, and headed toward the courtrooms, bent on vengeance. He entered the private chambers of Judge Rowland Barnes where he tore out the telephone lines and began taking hostages. One was a colleague of Mrs. Hall, another sheriff's deputy, whose gun he seized.

He then entered the courtroom from behind the bench and fired a single shot into Judge Barnes' head before shooting and killing Barnes' court reporter, Julie Brandau. Upon leaving the courthouse, Nichols shot and killed another sheriff's deputy, Hoyt Teasley.

Cable TV covered the Nichols case nonstop. Most of the post-incident conjecture focused on the way in which he was finally apprehended with the unlikely assistance of a twenty-six-year-old woman, Ashley Smith, who was held hostage by the spent but still desperate murderer at her apartment in Duluth, northeast of Atlanta. Smith, it was widely reported, had read to him from Rick Warren's hit book, *The Purpose Driven Life: What on Earth Am I Here For?*

While television pundits were focused on the failure of the police search or on the message of Rev. Warren's book, Yours Truly—in a Barcalounger in Philadelphia—was more interested in the physical dynamics of the crime spree itself; specifically, the way in which it all began, with a black-belt linebacker's overpowering of his petite female guard.

Nichols stands six feet one and weighs two hundred pounds. He'd been caught with two handmade knives in his shoe just two days earlier, yet was escorted by a lone deputy.[2] Hall, on the other hand, is a five-feet-tall, fifty-one-year-old grandmother.[3] That had to be the ultimate mismatch, and it never should have happened.

I'm sure suggesting a five-feet-nothing woman should never be charged with guarding a six-foot-one linebacker might be considered politically incorrect in some quarters (their PC, my common sense). Yet, the question begs to be asked: what in all justice was she doing in that job?

I ask honestly and with nothing but respect for law enforcement in general, and Mrs. Hall in particular. By all accounts, she is a hard-working and dedicated deputy, willing to put her life on the line, having to deal with some real scumbags. Clearly, she has guts. But we owe it to Judge Rowland Barnes, Julie Ann Brandau, Sgt. Hoyt Teasley, and Nichols' fourth easy victim, customs agent David Wilhelm, to pursue the inquiry.

Here are some telling facts. The average height of a man aged twenty to seventy-four years old increased from just over five feet eight inches in 1960, to five feet nine inches in 2002, while the average height of a woman the same age increased from slightly over five feet three inches in 1960 to five feet four inches in 2002.[4] Men, quite simply, are larger.

They are also stronger. A comparison of male and female public safety officers found that female officers had 32-56 percent less upper-body strength and 18-45 percent less lower-body strength than male officers.[5]

So, it should come as no surprise that increasing the number of female officers under these reduced strength and size standards consistently and significantly increases the number of assaults on police officers.[6] In general, every one percent increase in the number of women in a police force results in a 15-19 percent increase in the number of assaults on the police, simply because women tend to be smaller and weaker than men.[7]

So why then are individuals like Mrs. Hall, her obvious courage notwithstanding, dealing with hardened criminals the size of small buildings? Could police forces across the country have abandoned common sense in favor of political correctness and in the interests of "diversity"?

The short answer is that *police departments* didn't change their hiring policies in a vacuum. Like so many other stories I have shared thus far, this is yet another case of a simple truth's becoming the victim of political correctness. It doesn't happen all at once, but the tide seems almost irresistible.

I have a hunch that the origin of this movement can be found in 1964, with Willie Griggs, an African American janitor at Duke Power's steam station on the banks of the Dan River in what was then Draper, North Carolina. Willie was one of fourteen African Americans working at the plant, all of whom were janitors. Indeed, the eighty-one other employees—technicians, machine operators, and managers—were, without exception, white.

The plant's bathrooms, water fountains, and locker rooms were all segregated. A black employee's salary capped out at $1.65 while a white employee began his career at a minimum of $1.81.[8]

When the Civil Rights Act of 1964 became law, Willie and his fellow janitors went to management and asked to be eligible for promotion like their white counterparts. While Duke Power insisted they either have a high-school diploma or pass a written test, only fifteen of the plant's white workers had high-school degrees and *none* of the white employees who took the exam passed it.[9]

Fast forward some three years to the first hearing of the case called *Griggs v. Duke Power Company* before U.S. District Court Judge Eugene A. Gordon. At this time, it was essential to any successful claim for discrimination that the plaintiff show a discriminatory intent on the part of the employer. In denying Willie Griggs' claim, Judge Gordon emphasized that the testing requirement was, superficially at least, completely neutral.[10]

Eventually, the case made its way to the Supreme Court, which essentially developed a whole new standard. Where the requirement appeared to be even-handed in the books but quite the opposite when applied, the courts could disregard the need for a showing of discriminatory intent. Writing for the Court to describe the Civil Rights Act of 1964, Chief Justice Warren Burger noted: "The Act proscribes not only overt discrimination but also practices that are fair in form but discriminatory in operation."[11] Thus was born the disparate impact theory of discrimination.

It is a well-worn maxim that the road to hell is paved with good intentions. I think it applies here. The court had left a "business necessity" exception, clearly trying to define the limits of the government's power to intrude, but the precise shape of the exception would itself become the subject of intense controversy as the Supreme Court, Congress, and the executive branch each became intimately involved in defining it over the next two decades.

At one point, the Supreme Court attempted to ease restrictions on employers only to have Congress restore the more demanding set a couple of years afterward.[12] This is where the life of Willie Griggs, the janitor, intersects with Cynthia Ann Hall, the sheriff's deputy.

Freed from the requirement to show a discriminatory purpose, plaintiffs could challenge virtually any employer to prove his screening procedures were valid. Of course, that's precisely what happened. Nowhere was the absurdity of the battle more obvious than in the context of hiring and promoting law enforcement officers. Commonly held beliefs in the need for superior height and reasonable physical fitness among law enforcement types were no longer common sense.

Whatever you might hear today, height and weight standards *were* at one time quite obviously necessary. Federal Judge Robert Carter of the Southern District of New York noted the prevalence of height standards among local law enforcement agencies almost three decades ago. "The use of height requirements is a well-established practice among law enforcement agencies throughout the country. In a large sample of the nation's police departments, *97 percent* had some minimum height requirements for male officers in 1973, with the average minimum requirement being 68 inches."[13]

In an opinion that would earn poor Judge Carter a one-way ticket to retirement today, he went on to cite the most common reasons for minimum height requirements in peace officers: (1) strength is related to height; (2) taller officers have a psychological advantage; (3) the visibility of taller officers is an asset in crowd control; (4) many adult males find small body size a threat to self-esteem and tend to depreciate their own personal worth as a result of this perception; and (5) shorter officers are more likely to be assaulted.[14]

Unfortunately, the pressure to ease physical standards, including height, had already begun to show. Two years before Judge Carter's opinion in *Guardians Association of the New York City Police Department*, Judge Weber of the Western District of Pennsylvania sounded a warning. Observing that a local police academy had waived physical restrictions for protesting female applicants, he wrote: "We do not agree with the rationale of these decisions because we have a strong feeling that physical size, strength and agility are important elements to consider in the selection of one who is to be a guardian of the public safety."[15]

And although Federal District Court Judge Thomas Lambro of the Northern District of Ohio "lost the battle" when his decision overturning height and weight standards for police was itself reversed, he noted the trend in eliminating such requirements. In 1973, the Law Enforcement Assistance Administration, a federal agency, refused grants to local agencies that didn't prove the need for such standards through "professionally validated studies." That same year, the Iowa Civil Rights Commission ordered the Des Moines police to stop using them, as did the Pennsylvania attorney general.

Surveying the battlefield a quarter of a century later, it seems the forces of political correctness have won the war. The heavy burden on employers to prove that their screening procedures are not discriminatory, developed by the Supreme Court in *Griggs,* is now enshrined in law.[16] More specifically, the Equal Employment Opportunity Commission (EEOC) has all but written the prohibition on height and weight requirements into the Code of Federal Regulations, which, in turn, has the force of law.

No longer can you expect a Judge Carter or a Judge Weber to restore sanity; in the decade since the legislators turned back the Supreme Court's attempt to give some bite to the business necessity exception, the courts have followed Congress's lead. Unfortunately, the bar is now so high as to make it almost impossible to demonstrate necessity. Let me give you an example.

The Southeastern Pennsylvania Transit Authority (SEPTA) runs the buses and trains for the Philadelphia area and employs its own cops for policing the system. In an attempt to revamp its police force about a decade ago, it hired Dr. Paul Davis to recommend physical fitness requirements for its officers. An exercise physiologist, he rode the trains and buses, and he conducted an in-depth study with twenty seasoned officers to get a sense of the physical demands of patrol duty. What stuck out in his experience was the overwhelming amount of jogging that the officers did on a daily basis.

He recommended, and SEPTA instituted, a 1 1/2-mile run with a twelve-minute time limit. The data showed what most of us would expect—women did much worse than men because of natural physical differences.[17]

Judge Carol Mansmann, writing for a three-judge federal court panel hearing the case on appeal, wrote that "a discriminatory cutoff score is impermissible unless shown to measure the minimum qualifications necessary for successful performance of the job in question."[18]

I need to take a moment here because this is the point at which the train goes completely off the rails. The late Judge Mansmann, in a decision that the Supreme Court refused to review let alone overturn,[19] demanded that SEPTA show why the passing time was twelve minutes and not twelve minutes and two seconds (or twenty minutes and thirty seconds for that matter).

So, unless the Atlanta Sheriff's Department can conclusively show that Sheriff's Deputy Cynthia Hall really should be sixty-eight inches, and not sixty inches tall, they must get rid of any height requirement.

I can't speak for the politically correct, but I think Brian Nichols demonstrated that to my satisfaction.

Although no information can be found regarding the exact reason why cities such as Atlanta and Philadelphia changed or eliminated their height requirements, I have a hunch, which is confirmed in a Pennsylvania attorney general's opinion addressing this issue. The opinion found that a state minimum police requirement of five feet six inches unjustifiably discriminates against applicants of Spanish descent and women, and was therefore illegal.[20]

And there you have it. Somebody's idea of discrimination translates into the hiring of small cops. Women and Hispanics are typically shorter than Caucasian males; so, unless you lessen the height requirements, women and Hispanics will be underrepresented in police departments.

We can't have that. So we throw out the height requirements. That is how people with the physical characteristics of Mrs. Hall get hired and are ultimately required to guard an ox like Nichols.

This, of course, overlooks that we are not all created equal in mortal form and that some of us are just not equipped to perform certain tasks, hummingbirds notwithstanding.

I, for example, am finally coming to terms with the fact that I will not end up in the Phillies bullpen. Nor in *GQ*. Or playing in Toby Keith's band. That isn't the hand I was dealt. I'm also not suited to be a cocktail waitress at Atlantic City's hottest new hotel and casino. Some, however, might disagree.

Consider the controversy at the Borgata Hotel and Casino, Atlantic City's hottest spot, which first opened its doors to the public and began doing business on July 3, 2003.[21] The Borgata was the first new casino to open in Atlantic City in thirteen years.[22]

Despite casino gambling's having lured the minions to AC, the place never developed a reputation as being an "in" town. The Borgata set out to change that. It's a showpiece, which markets itself to a younger, hipper crowd. Located at Renaissance Point in Atlantic City, the property features 2,002 guest rooms and suites, 125,000 square feet of gaming, 11 destination restaurants, 11 retail boutiques, a 50,000 square foot spa, 70,000 square feet of event space, and parking for 7,100 cars.[23]

The Borgata is a trendy place in a dated town. I stayed there with my wife soon after it opened and took note of the sign on the doorknob that you post when you want privacy. Forget the customary "Do No Disturb." At the Borgata, it reads "Tied Up" on one side and "Tidy Up" on the other. (We did neither.)

I should not have been surprised. The Borgata opened amid an advertising campaign that intoned: "Go to your happy place." And the Borgata raised eyebrows when it refused to put the customary Bibles in hotel rooms.

Atlantic City is taking a lead from the Borgata. The town that used to bill itself as "America's Playground" is now marketing itself as "Always turned on" (no doubt in response to Las Vegas's claim that "What happens here stays here"). In other words, consumers know, or should know, what they are getting in the Borgata.

No big surprise then, at least not to me, that the Borgata wants cocktail waitresses who look hot.

On February 21, 2005, the Borgata instituted a policy limiting the amount of weight their costumed cocktail waitresses, so-called "Borgata Babes," and their male bartender counterparts can gain.[24] Under the new policy, the Borgata Babes cocktail servers and the casino's costumed bartenders will be fired if they gain more than 7 percent of their body weight and fail to lose the extra pounds.[25] The Borgata began weighing "each worker to establish a base weight, and those who fail to stay within the prescribed percentage are given unpaid suspension up to 90 days, during which they have access to a company-sponsored weight-loss program."[26] However, if employees fail to lose the required weight, they will be terminated.[27]

There are exceptions to the new policy. For example, employees who gain weight due to a pregnancy are exempt from this policy and may wear "transitional" uniforms while working.[28] Additionally, employees who gain weight as the result of a medical condition are also exempt.[29]

A Borgata vice president, Cassie Fireman, was quoted as saying that the policy clarifies existing appearance standards: that female servers have "natural hourglass figures" and men "V-shaped torsos, broad shoulders and slim waists."[30] According to Fireman, "Our costumed beverage servers are a huge part of our marketing and our branding image . . . [w]e feel it's fair, we feel it's legal, we feel it's what our customers have come to expect at Borgata."[31]

Not everyone was pleased with the new Borgata Babe standards. One union is openly hostile. As a result of this new weight-limit policy, Local 54 of the Hotel Employees and Restaurant Employees Union filed a grievance.[32] The Borgata rejected the grievance, prompting union officials to seek arbitration before the American Arbitration Association.[33]

Additionally, James McNally of Manahawkin filed a lawsuit against the Borgata (after applying for a bartending job), contending the policy violates both New Jersey antidiscrimination law and the federal Americans with Disabilities Act.[34] McNally said the policy discouraged him from applying for a job as a bartender. Only a dozen Borgata Babes were men at the time. "I believe that the Borgata's weight-gain-policy embarrasses, degrades and humiliates me in that it assumes that I cannot perform the job duties attendant to being a cocktail server in the event I gain weight," he said in his complaint.[35]

Hey, maybe I should introduce him to David Gillespie, who filed the lawsuit to stop the Coastline Restaurant from having a Ladies' Night.

The Borgata situation has yet to wind its way completely through the legal system. But I asked Professor Maryellen Motman from the Widener School of Law what the law says in this area. She explained: "The Borgata has an interesting way of putting it. They say that they have a performing arts profession and have certain images to maintain. Some employers have tried this before, most have not tried it in quite the way Borgata has. You have employers who have a history of trying to hire women only. Borgata has tried to craft its policy to apply to both women and men and I think they are paying attention to those prior cases that were problematic. There have been two notable suits brought by the EEOC against airlines that have weight restrictions and both of those suits ended up settling."

She said the law holds that "you can't discriminate based on gender, based on age, or based on disability. And I think those are the three things that are at play here."[36]

The Borgata, according to Professor Motman, is vulnerable in two areas: older employees and the disability area. Professor Motman told me that the defense position, "Well, don't apply for the job in the first place," doesn't cut it.

Too bad. It should. The Borgata can be forgiven if they think otherwise, if they see their serving sylphs in the realm of the performing arts—twisting, turning, stretching, rushing—like dancers. It's an unwritten law: there are no mooses in Las Vegas, unions or not. Some people are not meant to be street cops, other people are not meant to be Borgata Babes, and, ultimately, some people are not meant to be either.

That individuals are created in many different ways is a benefit, not a problem. While people are always crying "diversity" with respect to culture, they should be just as aware that there is physical diversity, as well. Those inevitable demarcation lines give us everything from prize-winning jockeys to world-record-holding weight lifters.

As cops, Borgata Babes, bullpen pitchers, and talk-show hosts, we're all cut from different cloth, and the law needs to respect that.

The madness continues even as I write this, only now we're not talking eye candy but life and death. In Denver, "diversity alarms" are going off at the local fire department. "It's absolutely embarrassing that we haven't hired an African American in five years," Denver Fire Chief Larry Trujillo said. "There's no excuse for it. We've done well with hiring Hispanics and others, but not as well as we would like."[37]

So, what are they doing to fix "the problem"? Besides hiring a "full-time recruiter to target women and minorities," would you believe that they're considering how—not *whether*, but how—to lower the bar: "The commission is overhauling the testing process in an attempt to fix the problem which, if not addressed, could get worse in the next few years as many minority firefighters become eligible for retirement. We are working co-operatively with the fire department. Our goal . . . is to make sure the Department reflects the diversity of the community."[38]

Um, has anybody told these guys that we're talking about Denver, Colorado, not North Philly? The 2000 census showed that the population of Denver County, Colorado, was 65 percent white and only 11 percent black.[39] That's not drastically different from the makeup of the fire department (reportedly 606 whites and 54 blacks out of 916 total members). And yet they insist, "We know there's a diversity issue, and it's been especially problematic among African Americans," said Chris Olson, president of the Civil Service Commission. "It's disturbing to us all."[40]

No, what is disturbing are their proposed measures to even the playing field. "One of those stumbling blocks was the testing process," Trujillo said. He laid blame at the foot of the Civil Service Commission, which instituted a computerized testing system five years ago that he believes was culturally biased and crafted in a way that largely benefited white applicants.[41]

We're not talking about rocket science here. Candidates are given "a battery of tests that includes written and suitability exams, a psychological profile, agility exam and background check. They also were given a video simulation test that was designed to gauge their on-the-job judgment abilities. What led to black applicants' failing to make the cut in the past five years? Most did not score high enough on the video exam to move forward. The one black applicant who did took a job with another fire department."[42]

Wait a second. You're telling me it's not the reading or math sections that's tripping these applicants up, but a video game? Granted, it's a lifelike simulator that tests split-second judgments and reflexes. In any case, I just don't see how such tests are culturally biased "stumbling blocks" to diversity.

Next, they claim that the fire department keeps moving the goalposts: "The Civil Service Commission set the passing score for each group of applicants, and it could change with each group. For example, the passing score for one group could be 85 and for the next it might be 86."

Olson, the commission president, said the cutoff score was adjusted to limit the applicant pool competing for a limited number of jobs and to contain testing and training costs. "The cutoff score was not moved so that it eliminated minorities," he said.

Trujillo and some employment experts disagree. "If you move the bar knowing the population you profess that you're trying to capture is not in the pool, then you make it harder to capture the people you say you're going after," said

Alton Scales, a human resource and recruiting expert at Edinboro University of Pennsylvania.[43]

They make it sound insidious, but think about it. If I'm a boss who's hiring only 5 people versus 50 people from a pool of 500, then it just got tougher for each applicant. 'Cause guess what? If I only need 5, there's no reason for me not to set the bar a little higher in order to make the hiring process that much easier and the outcome more favorable for my business. If you can't make the cut, too bad! That's like the Eagles telling TO to turn it down a couple of notches at spring training to give all the rookie tryouts a chance. Please!

And finally—you're not going to believe this—they want to dilute the security background check for minorities: "In many cases," Trujillo said, "potential black and Hispanic recruits grew up in tough northwest and northeast Denver neighborhoods where they had to do things society and the law frown upon. It sickens me that they're penalizing people for what they did in their past. . . . I grew up near Florida and Federal . . . a scrappy part of the city where you had to do things just to survive."[44]

I can picture it now: "Ah, yes, Mr. Atta, it says here you have prior experience with incendiary devices. That's excellent. We'll just overlook that silly 'red flag' inserted in your dossier by the Able Danger team. You're hired!"

Look, I'm all for common sense and I understand about adolescent run-ins with the law. But what are we doing? Why should the Denver Fire Department have to invest company time and taxpayer treasure weeding out candidates with (pardon the pun) "colorful" pasts, when they could simply hire people with no criminal records? Oh, that's right: diversity.

Here's the bottom line: if you want more blacks in the Denver Fire Department, then fix the schools and local communities. Don't lower your standards. Slavish attention to diversity over safety and aptitude will only result in people getting injured or killed.

Cops need to be big enough to fight the bad guys. And casinos should be able to hire curvaceous cocktail waitresses. It ain't rocket science; it is playing the hand that was dealt you.

More difficult perhaps is whether a cosmetics company should be able to favor the hiring of the good looking. The California Supreme Court recently dealt with the subject of whether some folks lack the physical attributes for certain careers in the context of analyzing what happened to a certain cosmetics manager.

Keep in mind that the California courts are often at odds with prevailing judicial sentiment on any given topic—witness the Supreme Court's frequent overturning of Ninth Circuit decisions. Maybe that's why I wasn't exactly shocked when I found that the California Supreme Court had short-circuited sexual harassment law in the case of a L'Oreal cosmetics manager from San Francisco.

The Court's majority found *for* Elysa Yanowitz, a regional sales manager for L'Oreal and chief of marketing for Ralph Lauren fragrances in Western states, when she bumped heads with her boss, Jack Wiswall.

Admittedly not the smoothest operator, Wiswall ordered Elysa to fire a sales clerk who was "not good looking enough" and to "get me somebody hot."[45] Unfortunately for Elysa, Jack actually meant for her to let the saleswoman go. When she didn't, she claims she was harassed by her superiors, given poor evaluations, and generally run out of the company. She took disability in July of 1998.[46]

Forget Elysa. What about the sales clerk? Should her physical attractiveness play any role in her hiring? Well, if you say not, what about a fashion model? If today the cosmetics counter can be filled with the not-so-hot, how far behind are the days when someone sues for the right to be a fashion model, despite lacking the looks?

Before I draw too much artillery fire from the arch feminist crowd, I should tell you that I am not citing this as some sort of hymn to the Jack Wiswalls of the world. Of course he acted insensitively, especially because the woman was *already working for L'Oreal.* If she didn't make the cut for her looks, then that should have been the policy from the get-go.

But that isn't really the point here, is it? The political correctness here is so obvious, so blatant, that you have to take a step back to see it in all its glory.

Why is there even a question about whether a makeup salesperson should be attractive?

Would you go to a dentist with bad teeth? Would you buy meat from the vegetarian butcher? How much stock do you put in the shop teacher's reputation for safety when he is missing his fingers (and maybe a few toes)?

These women are selling *beauty* products, and, more directly, they are pitching *themselves.* "Look at me," they say. "If you buy my makeup, you too can look this good." Why on earth isn't *that* the issue before the California Supreme Court?

For the same reason that we accept five-feet-tall sheriff's deputies escorting six-feet-one former football players, of course.

15

There She Isn't

In September of 2002, Erika Harold, a Phi Beta Kappa graduate of the University of Illinois and a member of *USA Today*'s 2000 All-USA College Academic Second Team, was crowned as Miss America 2003.[1] Said George Bauer, the Miss America Organization's CEO at the time, "You have a Miss America that absolutely personifies what this program is about and where we're going."[2]

Ugh. Unfortunately he was telling the truth, which is a shame for the future of the pageant, and will mean a continuation of the decline in its television ratings. Before I share with you those numbers, let me first give you some others. This is the scoring breakdown for the finals in the year Ms. Harold won the big prize:

- Composite attributes: 40 percent.

- Lifestyle and fitness in swimsuit: 10 percent.

- Presence and poise in evening wear: 10 percent.

- Artistic expression in talent: 20 percent.

- Peer respect and leadership: 10 percent.

- Top five knowledge and understanding quiz: 10 percent.

Wait a minute. Lifestyle and fitness in swimming suit is only worth 10 percent? Presence and poise in evening wear the same? Isn't this supposed to be a beauty pageant? Heaven forbid one of the contestants would have a shapely frame that looks good in both a bikini and a Vera Wang.

Clearly, as the scoring system indicates, someone has decided that more important are the competitors' platforms on issues, as if they were political candidates running for office. And by this tally, only the PC need apply. No longer does the armchair speculation focus on how well she'll look in a two-piece, now it's whether she'll feign interest in promoting antiviolence, or will it be literacy?

And they wonder why the ratings are in a free fall.

If we watch the Miss America Pageant, er, the "Miss America Scholarship Whatever Theycallit," we're tuning in to look at hot women. And I'm not just talking about guys.

Women love to check out other women. Just think about how they scrutinize one another in social settings. It's all about their figures, then the shoes, and finally, the handbag.

My mother is one of eleven children—eight sisters and three brothers. Growing up, I can remember my aunts commiserating while the competition was on, taking bets, and voting for the woman they thought *was the most beautiful.*

Both sexes appreciate outward beauty, and the pageant in its current incarnation doesn't acknowledge that. It dismisses the time-honored custom of Americans gathering in living rooms and voting among friends on which of several competing beauties, not brainies, should win.

Don't get me wrong, Erika Harold is an attractive woman with many fine attributes that are not skin deep. But she's no "ten."

(Editorial note: the author readily acknowledges and accepts his status as a six on the superficial beauty schedule, but asserts that were he to compete in similar fashion, he expects that he would be able to "clean up" in "peer respect and leadership.")

Even if we could reach a consensus that Erika Harold is a "seven," I'll bet that would suit the PC crowd who run the pageant just fine. The last thing they seem to want is a raving beauty whose academic well roundedness might be overshadowed by other well roundedness.

How things got this way will require a quick history lesson.

The Miss America pageant began as a beauty contest on Atlantic City's Boardwalk on September 7, 1921, "to entice summer tourists to stay in town past Labor Day." "The fall festival included a 'National Beauty Tournament' on the beach to select 'the most beautiful bathing beauty in America.'"[3] Back then, the pageant was what it should still be: a beauty pageant with no pretense of being anything else. Contestants were scored solely on their looks, and it worked. For example, in the 1920s, the official scorecard for the pageant included only physical features of the contestants such as head, eyes, hair, nose, mouth, facial expression, etc.[4] (Can you imagine if they returned to those roots?

Two things would happen: NOW would go crazy *and* ratings would go through the roof.)

The pageant took a dramatic shift in the 1930s due to several scandals involving contestants and charges of indecency by women's organizations.[5] These organizations claimed the bathing suits were "too revealing" and that the pageant portrayed women in a negative light.[6] These scandals and criticism from women's groups led pageant officials to change the format and style of the contest in an effort to attract a "better class of girls."[7] That's when the talent competition was added.

Additionally, the scorecard was changed to reflect other, nonphysical attributes of the contestants. For example, in the 1940s, the scorecard consisted of four categories, equally weighted.[8] Judges would assess the contestants based on their performance in the talent competition, their appearance in an evening gown and swimsuit, and their overall personality.[9] Still, you could say beauty reigned.

New rules were placed on the contestants as well, including a minimum age requirement, a requirement that the contestants be chaperoned at all times, and an outright ban on "visiting bars, smoking, or private visits with men."[10]

In 1945, "the pageant distinguished itself from other beauty contests by creating an innovative scholarship program. In its first year, the program awarded a $5,000 scholarship to Bess Myerson, the first and only Jewish Miss America."[11] (By my informal polling, which you could say has a margin of error of +/- 85 percent, she comes in as the second best known Miss America, behind my girl, Vanessa Williams.)

The pageant was first broadcast on television on September 11, 1954.[12] That first airing of the show attracted more than 27 million viewers. That figure represents *half* of the entire potential viewing audience at the time! The pageant peaked in the early 1960s when it was repeatedly the highest-rated program on American television. In fact, between 1955 and 1970, the television broadcast was consistently in the top ten, and was number one five times.[13] It had its best year in the ratings in 1960 when 85 million viewers tuned in to get a glimpse of the action at the shore.[14]

Trouble came in the 1980s, when the rocket scientists who ran the thing ushered in yet another change to the scoring system. Pageant, I mean, "scholarship" officials added an interview segment, which was worth 30 percent of the overall score.[15]

Additionally, the talent competition, which used to be worth only 25 percent, was now worth 40 percent.[16] But to add insult to injury, now the portions of the contest based on physical attributes, i.e., the swimsuit and evening gown segments, were worth only 15 percent each.[17] I would argue this marked the beginning of the end for the show.

By the 1990s, PC changes were aiding in the decline of the pageant's ratings. In 1995, just 25 million viewers tuned in to watch the broadcast.[18] Remember, that is roughly the same number as watched the 1954 premier, but by now the possible viewing audience was significantly larger. By the year 2004, the viewership had sunk to just 9.8 million.[19] No longer the hot commodity it had once been—even in an era where reality television had become all the rage—the pageant was finally dropped by network television altogether.[20] Currently the pageant is broadcast on CMT (Country Music Television) in limited form.[21]

Those associated with the pageant were confused by ABC's decision to drop its coverage. Miss America 1999, Nicole Johnson Baker, stated, "It sounds so ridiculous: We go from ABC to CMT, and there's nothing in between?"[22]

As I see it, the problem here does not lie with the execs at ABC. The problem is what the pageant has become. If I were ABC, I wouldn't want to air *Miss America* in its current form either. It's simply not entertaining.

I read an interesting, internet-based news article called "An Honest Look at Miss America (2005)." The *Pageant News Bureau* displayed a picture of Victoria Bechtold, a 2004 contestant, with a caption that read: "Victoria Bechtold of Pennsylvania looked almost scandalously sexy, but sexiness counted for little."[23] Therein lies the problem.

While I am not advocating for more trash TV, I am a believer that the pageant has gone too far to eradicate beauty, and, no matter what they may call it, to the rest of us, it remains a beauty pageant.

In other words, it's the product that is causing the low ratings—not the change in channel. In an effort to cave to the PC police, organizers forgot their purpose.

With the competition's attempt to be more than just a beauty pageant, those in charge have lost sight of the appeal of such a pageant. To them, just being a beauty pageant isn't enough anymore. If you don't have a better, higher purpose, you will be looked down on by others. Give me a break.

The problem is, in their quest for deeper meaning, pageant organizers have had an effect on the type of contestants that participate. According to the former CEO of the Miss America Organization, Leonard Horn, "The world has changed since the 1950s and 60s, but the pageant has not."[24] "By the time (the contestants) reach the national level, they no longer look like fresh girls or twenty-one-year-olds . . . they look like forty-year-old Stepford Wives. If they are going to relate to the women in the audience, they have to look and act like their peers."[25]

Horn also told me, "Political correctness is playing a role in the Miss America pageant."[26] He should know, as it was under his watch that the pageant began to include the idea of a platform. The idea that each contestant would choose a platform to run on began in 1989. Take a look at what the Miss America Web site has to say about platforms:

> In 1989, the Miss America Organization founded the platform concept, which requires each contestant to choose an issue about which she cares deeply and of relevance to our country. Once chosen, Miss America and the state title holders use their stature to address community service organizations, business and civic leaders, the media and others about their platform issues. Since 1989, Miss America title holders have appeared at thousands of public speaking engagements and charitable events to generate awareness for a variety of causes including homelessness, HIV/AIDS prevention, domestic violence, diabetes awareness, character education, literacy, etc.[27] [How far do you think a contestant would get if her platform were pro-life, or in support of reducing control on firearms, or in support of the death penalty?]

Platforms championed by Miss America winners have included everything from "Motivating Youth to Excellence" to "Education Is Everyone's Business."[28] Judges seem to base their decisions on what the contestants pledge to do after being crowned rather than on what they did during the competition.

This is lunacy!

Now, I may be naïve, but I don't think anyone actually cares what platforms individual candidates choose. The pageant was never supposed to be a brain trust event. No foreign policy decisions were ever meant to emanate from its proscenium arch. People don't particularly look to the pageant for guidance in their daily lives. Its appeal was that it was a place to watch beautiful women looking beautiful. Plain and simple.

The fate of the pageant is unknown at this point. However, it does appear, at least for now, that CMT will be the new home of the pageant as the contract provides for renewal options through 2011.[29]

"The concept of a beauty pageant . . . has lost its luster over the generations, and to some people it's a No-No,"[30] Leonard Horn told me. Well, maybe that's true for the PC crowd, but that doesn't seem to hold true for the viewers.

If the pageant wants to become a televised Mensa meeting, that's their choice. But if they want to make some headway in the ratings, they need to drop the act. It has become clear that they can be one or the other, but not both. When all is said and done, it is a beauty contest, not a humanitarian competition!

There is some reason for optimism that things can get turned around. As already mentioned, CMT has one pageant under its belt so far and the network, a unit of giant Viacom, is making some changes that appear headed in the right direction. First, the pageant was relocated, not to the country music capital of Nashville, but to Vegas, where Mayor Oscar Goodman is the embodiment of un-PC. CMT has bagged the casual-wear competition and the multiple-choice civics quiz that pitted five finalists against one another in a game show fashion. Also gone is the head-to-head talent contest between two remaining finalists. Reports the *New York Times*, "In place of stiff blue jeans and halter tops that made some onstage segments seem like a debutante's bad idea of casual Friday, CMT will emphasize event wear, with sashes bearing state names—little seen in recent years—again draped prominently across the contestants' long gown throughout the night so viewers can better chart their progress."[31] And guess who is returning? Miss Congeniality, after a quarter-century hiatus! Brian Philips, the forty-three-year-old executive vice president and general manager of CMT, said, "We want to get the pageant back to the one we most remember from the collective childhood of everyone involved." He has the right attitude. I'll bet his mom was calling his aunts and placing bets the way my mom did.

I have a hunch America wouldn't mind a little more of an old-fashioned beauty pageant. So let's bring back the busty baton twirler.

So how does my prescription for salvaging the Miss America Pageant blend with the thoughts of a woman who has actually taken the famous walk down the aisle in Atlantic City? I had the chance to get the thoughts of at least one former Miss America about the changes in the contest. Kate Shindle, Miss Illinois, was Miss America 1988. This graduate of Northwestern University is now a successful actress having appeared in, among other things, *The Stepford Wives*. We started out seeing eye-to-eye on the value of beauty in what I consider to be a contest about appearances:

"There's nothing wrong with being attractive or looking for a Miss America who is attractive," she told me. "Frankly, the assertion that looks have little to do with selecting a Miss America, though it has long been the party line of many affiliated with the Miss America Organization, is suspect precisely because it's untrue. If it looks like a beauty pageant and walks like a beauty pageant, well, hey, it's probably at least the first cousin of a beauty pageant."

Amen to that. I have been saying that the first part of my prescription for the pageant is to appreciate that it is a pageant.

She continued, "The reality, though, is that the Miss America program has always sought out representatives who offer more than T&A. Now, more than ever, this is essential if the pageant is to survive. Thanks largely to the proliferation and unexpected staying power of reality TV, American homes are filled with images of lithe young women wearing much less than your average pageant contestant (and quite often drunk and in hot tubs). Aside from preserving the dignity, which is a crucial part of the pageant's identity, the big problem is that the more conservative Miss America telecast will simply never compete with these images. I'm happy for that."

Well, I'm not so sure. I think there needs to be a proper balance somewhere between "T&A," to quote Miss America, and braniacs who have been winning of late. Frankly, that balance should tilt toward T&A but not by stripping women of their dignity. I am not advocating a move toward the raunchy that is all too popular in music video television. What men and women want to watch are good looking, All-American women, in bikinis. Not thongs. Not giant boobs. Just give me and everyone else fifty good looking women in swimsuits, and watch the ratings.

"I think that the pageant's lowest moments in the past decade have come when it tries to give reality TV a run for its money," she said. "These instances are not hard to spot: the language of the telecast becomes more negative; the microphone and provocative host go backstage to encourage the contestants to talk trash about each other. The swimsuits get skimpier. The quiz show shows up for no discernible reason. Substance is downplayed, allegedly because the public doesn't buy it, and the telecast attempts to hint that these girls could blend seamlessly with any *Real World* cast."

Guess what? They can't, and they don't need to. The Miss America

Organization is dying a slow death; first, because there's no clear sense of identity and, second, because many of those who do recognize its identity are ashamed to say that it's okay to aspire to be classy and inspirational.

"It's easy to mock a pageant where contestants claim they want to make the world a better place through activism. But as someone who's been there, I assure you that the opportunities to do so are real. And at least for me, that's much more of a reason for this program to exist than the opportunity to put a crown on the hottest chick on stage."

Hmmm. Here is where she loses me. While I applaud Kate Shindle for aggressively advocating better HIV/AIDS prevention and treatment during her year as Miss America, that is really not what I think the pageant is about, nor do I agree that activism is more of a reason for this program to exist than the opportunity to put a crown on the hottest chick on stage. In my mind, she's conjuring up visions of Mother Teresa taking a walk down the aisle, and nobody is tuning in for that. Frankly, that is the problem with the pageant of late; or, to use her words, it is the explanation as to why it's dying a slow death. HIV/AIDS advocacy is important, but it should not trump appearance in what is actually called a *beauty* pageant. I'm for maintaining both ingredients, but reversing their priority should be the priority.

16

Will the Real Rob Morris
Please Rise

"We apologize to all Americans, and especially to African Americans and people of African descent." Those words, spoken in 2005, came from the chairman of the nation's fourth largest bank in a statement concerning a bank officer who you could say is no longer associated with the firm.

This was Wachovia Corporation's chairman, Kennedy Thompson, apologizing for the supposed conduct of some of the bank's predecessors approximately 225 years ago. The subject? You guessed it: that surefire headline-grabber, slavery in America—the mother country's legacy of shame exported to its North American colonies, where it skillfully slipped them into the economic system then employed by what were the equivalent of the G-Countries of the seventeenth century.

But the bank's startling oral statement was gratifying to Blondell Reynolds-Brown, a Philadelphia City councilwoman, who sponsored a bill that was passed by her colleagues and signed into law by the city's second African American mayor, John Street. The law she initiated required the disclosure to be made by Wachovia because the bank does business with the City of Philadelphia. The City of Brotherly Love is not alone. Other cities, including Chicago and Los Angeles, have also initiated slavery disclosure laws.

Councilwoman Reynolds-Brown explained: "They are the first company in Philadelphia that has stepped forward, and I believe their acknowledgement and recognition goes to the intent of this bill which was to ask corporations that seek contracts with the City to disclose if they derived profits from slavery."[1]

Me, I wondered exactly what prompted that apology and just how much in "derived profits from slavery" the councilwoman was talking about. That answer is not so clear as the straightforward apology had led me to believe.

I started my inquiry by obtaining a copy of the research report that led to the corporation's request for forgiveness. Wachovia had hired an entity called the "History Factory," which Wachovia described as "a leading professional research company with extensive experience in corporate historical research."[2] (What a country! Even the trends toward political correctness create a cottage industry.)

According to Wachovia, the History Factory used a seven-member research team who expended 1,800 hours of effort, which included visiting twenty-four repositories housing information on Wachovia's predecessors. "The research began with an exhaustive effort to identify all predecessor institutions of Wachovia Corporation. This included predecessors of mergers and acquisitions throughout Wachovia's history as well as absorbed institutions. This yielded a list of approximately four hundred predecessor institutions dating back to Wachovia's earliest predecessor, the Bank of North America, founded in 1781."[3]

The list of four hundred predecessors was then pared to fifty-two that existed in 1865 (the year in which slavery was abolished) or earlier. Thirty-three of the fifty-two were then eliminated because their ties to Wachovia were deemed "too tenuous to pursue."[4] That left nineteen institutions that were then the focus of a 109-page report.

An impressive effort, to be sure. The bottom line? Two of Wachovia's predecessors, Georgia Railroad and Banking Company founded in 1833 (172 years ago) and the Bank of Charleston founded in 1834 (171 years ago), owned slaves.

In addition, nine predecessor companies of Wachovia were determined to have profited more indirectly from slavery, and this list included the earliest known predecessor of Wachovia, the Bank of North America. And that is where a gentleman named Robert Morris entered the picture.

According to the History Factory report, Morris was one of three founders of the Bank of North America. He was its first president and one of two founders (along with Thomas Willing) who amassed at least part of their personal fortunes from the slave trade. In 1781, the two formed Willing & Morris, a Philadelphia-based merchant business that dealt significantly in slave shipments and trading. According to the History Factory, both Willing and Morris used their profits from the slave trade to fund the establishment of the Bank of North America.[5]

Sounds compelling. Morris and Willing traded human flesh. Made a bundle. Parked the profits in the Bank of North America, which grew into the modern day Wachovia. But, as I would learn, not everyone agrees with that conclusion.

The Wachovia "revelations" grabbed headlines across the country. And, after digesting the coverage, many, like myself, were left wondering: Okay, now what? I had my suspicions, and it didn't take long for confirmation that I was correct.

Councilwoman Blondell Reynolds-Brown was a guest on my radio program within days of the Wachovia announcement. She explained her role and thought process in initiating the legislation that led to the Wachovia research: "The history of American slavery still does feel distant to some, but it doesn't seem distant at all to millions of African Americans who still struggle to build wealth while our descendants like those of Wachovia slave holders and bank directors are wealthy today. That *inequity* [she emphasized] if you will, is still at issue for many African Americans."[6] More importantly, she spilled the beans that her colleague, Councilman W. Wilson Goode Jr., was about to introduce a legislative follow-up using the R-word: reparations. Sure enough, soon came word from Councilman Goode, son of the former mayor of the same name, that he would introduce a "Financial Reparations Bill."

Goode's proposed law would "mandate that all depository banks provide the City with an annual certification with regard to financial ties to slavery by January 1 of each year. If the depository has disclosed such ties, it must also provide the City with a statement of financial reparations. The reparations statement shall include a description of any new financial products or programs developed by the depository to address racial disparity in its current lending and investment activities."[7]

So there you have it. Having undertaken the research effort that disclosed conduct many years ago (about which Wachovia is no doubt chagrined), the City of Philadelphia now intends to extract a "statement of financial reparations." Reparations are always a call generator for a radio program like mine. Predictably, the e-mail reaction to the Wachovia story was fast and furious. Most came from people who believed minority activists were holding Wachovia hostage. This particular e-mail from a Civil War descendant caught my eye.

Dan wrote:

I want to know where I can apply for my reparation for the injustices done to myself through my ancestors.

My great-grandfather enlisted in the 122st Pennsylvania Infantry in August of 1862 to fight for the Union in the Civil War. He fought in all the major battles from Fredricksburg, Gettysburg, the Wilderness battles, Petersburg, etc. He was captured in October, 1864, and sent to a

Confederate prison camp in Salisbury, North Carolina. While there, he came in contact with TB, which he unknowingly passed on to his children. He had 9 children of which 8 never made it to their teens, the exception being my grandfather who died from it at the age of 40.

Now what black organization do I contact for *my* family's pain and suffering in the fight for the Black Community's freedom? Wachovia?

On the other side of the argument came this. J. Edward Brown, Esq., wrote:

I listened to your show with Blondell Reyolds-Brown this morning and the comments by your listeners afterward. I noticed that neither you nor your listeners are informed or honest about slavery and the subsequent effects. There were some important elements that Ms. Brown overlooked in her interview. Slavery began more than three hundred years ago and the institution was abolished about one hundred forty years ago. However, you do not distinguish the chronology of the event from the effects and institutions that continued slavery's legacy. In other words, the event ended but the legacy continued. Slavery is the root. The current economic, social, political and governmental structures are the tree and fruit. The banking and financial institutions that exist now were financed through the trading of slaves. Slaves were a financial asset and used for collateral to finance transactions and other enterprises not related to slavery. The insurance policies written against the slave cargo financed the insurance giants we have in the present. All of the supporting documents were written and supported by the American legal system and government which also profited from these transactions. Then the actual labor the slaves performed jump-started the agricultural economy in the United States as well as the textile industry. Of course, the banks that lent the money to entrepreneurs who started these industries had the resources to lend from these collateralized proceeds of the slave trade. These industries and institutions facilitated the growth and creation of other institutions and the value and worth has recycled several times among their oppressors without benefiting the slave at all.

After slavery ended, African Americans were not permitted to participate in the aforementioned industries. They were shut out despite the fact their labor and flesh provided the foundation for this country's wealth and development. This period of Reconstruction and Jim Crow not only prevented participation economically but led to further brutality against African Americans. Ironically, African Americans post-slavery represented the largest body of skilled labor and craftsmen in the United States. In addition, they produced a large number of inventions that really pushed the United States forward on the world stage. Innovations include the railroad, telephone/now telecom, computers, military, automotive industries. Not to mention the design of our nation's capital and the regulation of our traffic and transportation as well as medical breakthroughs in plasma and the human circulatory system are all from African Americans. Unfortunately, the system did not permit African Americans to reap the windfall from these inventions. In fact, the inventors were often cheated, swindled or intimidated out of their ideas and concepts. Further, the towns where African Americans set up their own economies and social orders were burned down and destroyed. That is, their banks and insurance companies were destroyed and assets lost. These occurrences happened not only in the south but in the Midwest and northeast. (See massacres in New York in the turn of the 20th Century.) These things were done because the African Americans were still regarded as little more than slaves (see Badge of Slavery, 13th Amendment) without any rights.

Meanwhile, immigrants were able to establish themselves without the hardships that African Americans experienced. In fact, they came into the country at a higher status than African Americans. They had access to resources that African Americans did not. Immigrants that came from Europe during slavery could come here and own slaves. Additionally, after slavery, they were not shut out through fear, terror and murder the way African Americans were. Even now, those same immigrants and their descendants have access to resources that African Americans do not (see below). Imagine you are in line at a restaurant and you have waited a long time to eat. Someone jumps in front of you and eats your dinner. To compound the matter, you pay for their dinner and yours. That's what it is like. They benefit from the privilege of not being African American and shut out. They immediately have access and privileges you have never had.

If African Americans had been permitted to participate fully after slavery or had not been subject to continued brutality and interference, then there would be an African American version of GM, Microsoft, Chase Manhattan, etc. and no mention of reparations because African Americans would be full market participants.

Finally, the African Americans are still subject to a higher cost to do business and acquire resources. For example, African Americans pay a higher percentage rate on loans for homes and autos, and [are] turned down at a higher rate for business loans. In contrast, Whites get lower loan rates and are approved at a higher rate for business loans. The resources are more readily available to one group because the other group is systematically limited. Again, ironically, the same institutions doing the lending are the successors-in-interest to the institutions which financed and benefited from the slave trade. Unfortunately, those benefits have not trickled down to those who have paid the highest price.

Please be honest with your analysis and really research the full scope and effects of this matter before drawing conclusions.

J. Edward Brown, Esq.

I was so impressed with Mr. Brown's expression of his view—out of the mainstream of callers to my program—that I had him on the show as a guest in his own right. I was particularly taken with his argument that, but for slavery, there would be a black version of GM, Microsoft, or Chase Manhattan today.

From that same vantage point, I also spoke with Bruce Crawley, chairman of the Philadelphia African American Chamber of Commerce. He joined me in the studio to discuss a number of race issues that were making news (Philadelphia had just required the teaching of African history in its high schools). In the course of our conversation, he, too, weighed in on Wachovia. Once again, the name of Robert Morris was invoked.

The whole issue with Wachovia Bank is one that makes very clear that resources that were generated by slaves through the good work of people who were not paid were gathered by people who owned banks and people who started banks and people who use that slavery contingent as collateral for other business that they do. I have a business office for my own firm—I have a PR and ad agency—and it's at 510 Walnut Street, Michael. And I look out my window and I look into a park between 4th and 5th Streets, right off Walnut, and there's a big statue of Robert Morris and Robert Morris I remember in school—and I went to Catholic schools—St. Joe's Prep and SJU, and Temple—and I remember as a very young man reading that Robert Morris was the financier of the American Revolution. That he played a very important role. And I didn't realize until I saw the disclosure by Wachovia that he generated the revenue that he financed the revolution with and that he started the Bank of North America with, through the slave trade.[8]

At the same time, as people in Philadelphia were debating what was next for Wachovia, a columnist in Boston weighed in on the situation. Jeff Jacoby, writing for the *Boston Globe*, pulled no punches. His piece was titled, "The Slavery Shakedown." Here is a taste:

> In other words, Thompson's apology was for something Wachovia didn't do, in an era when it didn't exist, under laws it didn't break. And as an act of contrition for this wrong it never committed, it can now expect to pay millions of dollars to activists for a wrong they never suffered. . . .
>
> America long ago paid the price for slavery: a horrific Civil War that killed 620,000 soldiers, more than half of them from the North. It is as vile to insist that white Americans today owe a debt for slavery as it would be to insist that black Americans owe a debt for freedom.[9]

I read Jacoby's piece to my audience, and it received a strong and supportive reaction from callers. His arguments were not new, but the forceful style was a rarity.

And just when I thought I had heard from all sides in the reparations debate given life by the release of historical data came the reaction of one Rob Morris! That's Rob Morris, descendant of Robert Morris. Rob Morris is a fifty-one-year-old resident of the Philadelphia suburbs who is the great-great-great-great-grandson of Robert Morris.

Long before Wachovia took an interest in his family, Rob Morris spent a considerable amount of time studying his lineage. I asked him to respond to the Wachovia research conclusion that Revolutionary War financier Robert Morris and his partner "amassed at least a part of their personal fortunes from the slave trade." Like Jeff Jacoby, Rob Morris wasn't about to pull any punches, either.

"Basically, the report is completely wrong, and it's laughable," Morris told me. "It's as if Wachovia paid ransom in counterfeit bills and the city is happy about it. Morris was never the president of the bank, which was the first line of their report; so it starts off wrong. Then they try to pretend that somehow, by losing money, he *made* money."[10]

Rob Morris believes the slave trade was a net loser for Robert Morris and that Wachovia today—at least with regard to his forefather—apologized for conduct that was unprofitable. "Oh yeah," he said, "definitely, and they got out of it. And then he spent the next thirty years of his life trying to replace slavery with economic freedom. That was his whole life—creating economic freedom and opportunity and getting rid of a 5,000 year-old system."

Rob Morris also finds it objectionable that Robert Morris's distinguished career is being unfairly characterized with the slave-trader moniker:

> I've done a lot of reading into this, and it's been very eye-opening. He was a merchant, and he had real estate operations. He not only founded the first bank in U.S. history (Bank of North America) but was, also, a daring patriot who smuggled guns and powder for America before the Revolution. During the war, ships under his orders ran the British blockade with diplomats, supplies, silver, and intelligence. He signed the Declaration of Independence, the Articles of Confederation, and the United States Constitution. He was a member of the Continental Congress, the superintendent of finance, and a United States senator. You'd think he'd be a local hero instead of this.
>
> I mean this whole slavery thing happened because the king wanted his friends to make money sixteen years before the Revolution. Robert Morris supported the Non-Importation Agreement, and he then lead the charge to get rid of the importation of these things—slavery and other taxable items—and that stopped the importation of slaves years before the Revolution even happened.

When the Wachovia report hit the headlines, it caused him to summarize his own findings in writing and react to the notion that Robert Morris derived most of his wealth from the slave trade and then used the proceeds to finance a bank. Rob Morris calls that a "blood libel." In his written work, Rob Morris says this: "In fact, the financing for the Bank came from forty-eight different individuals and nearly half the money came from a French loan."

After proving that Morris was not even an operating officer or director, as the report claims, but founder and stockholder, he continues:

What they do not say is that Morris tried to tax slavery out of existence, or how many of the Bank of North America personnel acted against slavery and helped African Americans. For example, director James Wilson argued against slavery at the Constitutional Convention . . . and Bank president, Thomas Willing, provided a start-up loan to James Forten, an African-American entrepreneur and active abolitionist who became rich operating sail lofts on the Atlantic seaboard. Are we now to believe the abolition movement was financed with "the blood of slaves"? And who will be forced to apologize for that?[11]

According to Rob Morris, there were no profits to speak of for Robert Morris from the slave trade:

An analysis using a profit-and-loss table from an 18th century Report of the Liverpool Privy Council indicates that Willing and Morris *lost money* in the business because they shipped too few per voyage. . . . [Yet] we are told that "Both Willing and Morris used their profits from the slave trade to fund the establishment of the Bank of North America." There is no accounting to support this; not one bill of sale, not one tax receipt, not one expense report, nothing.

He goes on to show how what little is known is possibly based on the 1777 capture of two British slave ships in which Morris owned an interest and was due 9 percent of the profit.

At best, Morris could have bought two-thirds of one $500 bank share with the money he made if he had held on to the cash for another four years. Unfortunately for this assumption, by April of 1781 Morris had lost well over 50 of his own ships in the Revolutionary War, so it is likely that wicked slave money was lost with them and unavailable on May 17, 1781, when he proposed the Bank. In any case, these 1777 attacks on the slave trade were acts of war sanctioned by Congress and conducted under a Letter of Marque. These attacks and others like them resulted in a hiatus in the British slave trade and saved untold Africans from hardship.

Morris said he asked Wachovia to change its report to reflect the documented facts, and the bank declined. He now challenges Wachovia to prove its conclusions by presenting to an objective third party the accounting used to support the allegations found in this document. Without objective third-party verification, he says, "Wachovia owes a *huge* apology to one of America's Founding Fathers, Robert Morris."

Rob Morris's research into Robert Morris casts doubt on the argument that Morris and Willing traded human flesh, made a bundle, and parked the profits in the Bank of North America, which grew into the modern day Wachovia. It also makes Councilman Goode's plan for Wachovia and other businesses with similar backgrounds to develop a statement of reparations sound a bit ill-conceived.

My legal background tells me that by making Wachovia "confess" to its predecessors' sins, Philadelphia and other cities are opening the door for litigation and other dubious means of seeking remuneration from present businesses which can be tied, however loosely, to a slave-related past. And all of this combined makes me wonder whether other businesses who have a history as complicated as that of Wachovia might choose to bypass doing business in Philadelphia and other locales playing the reparations game. One wonders what would have happened if, for no other reason than to protect stockholders, Wachovia chairman Kennedy Thompson had told the City of Philadelphia to pound sand when required to delve into a two-hundred-plus-year-old history. The answer, of course, is that corporate America cannot tolerate the label of racism, which would surely have been thrown around if Wachovia had taken such a stand.

The living Rob Morris made one other point to me: "Two of the chief beneficiaries of the slave trade were the state of Pennsylvania and the city of Philadelphia, which was the capital of the state at the time. They collected a large tax on the sale of each slave brought into the state for sale. They had no expenses and the tax was very high. Granted, they had such a high price to discourage the trade, but while it continued they made more money than anyone. Is the city obliged to apologize to itself, and will Ed Rendell be forced to confess before the city will take any money from the state?"[12]

The truth is, I am all for reparations, just not in the form sought by Councilman Goode or Louis Farrakhan and others. My thinking is basically different. I agree there is a disparity in the standard of living between whites and blacks in America: infant mortality and long-term health care, education, income, crime. Take your pick. The truth is that blacks lag behind whites in all quantifiable respects, and while there has been progress, the playing field is nowhere close to level.

I accept the argument that the origin of the disparity lies in the slavery that ended 140 years ago. (I am less accepting of the idea that slavery is the reason that the disparity exists today.) Then I ask myself if I care. I quickly decide that I certainly do and will not penalize all blacks for the idiocy and racism of the knuckleheads who sold "Kill Whitey" T-shirts at Louis Farrakahn's 2002 march on Washington. Blacks must do likewise regarding whites on the fringe.

I question what we've done so far to redress this disparity. I reflect on the fact that a Republican president is owed credit for abolishing slavery and that many whites gave their lives in a civil war fought largely on this issue.

I conclude that we live in the most generous nation ever on the face of this earth, one in which there have been countless efforts to give opportunities for advancement to all, particularly minorities. This country has never stopped trying to level the playing field. But we have failed. Why is that? Probably because we have a simplistic solution to a complex problem: we throw money at it. White Professional Liberals can have the credit for that. It's a guilt thing. Writing checks makes them feel justified about their own status. Think public housing. We see squalor and decide that the answer is to spend more than $200Gs each for new units. But bricks and mortar aren't the problem. Which is also why the answer isn't "millions of acres of land that black people can build on," as Farrakhan tells the crowds. That is how I frame the problem and assess our attempts at a solution.

So what now? First, it's time to end the era where the only individuals touted as spokesmen for blacks are the Sharptons, Jacksons, Conyers, and Farrakhans. They lack any iota of credibility with whites, which is desperately needed to truly effect change. They are all about self-preservation.

Second, we need to end the handout mentality. Giveaways create dependence and the answer is not another check.

Third, our highest priority must be to fix the family, the black family. So much of what ails us is attributable to the lack of strong fathers in African American households: fathers free of addiction; fathers who impregnate only their wives; fathers who raise their sons to be solid citizens; fathers who work every day and pay taxes and stay out of jail. How do we do that? Through reparations? Not Louis Farrakhan's land-give-away kind.

The only way to really repair black America is through unprecedented educational opportunities for black youth, that black youth appreciate and take advantage of. The latter is not always the case, but that must be our chief focus on a local, state, and national level. Get serious about the blessing of education. Education is the stepping-stone to opportunity. Opportunity leads to employment. Jobs keep people's lives stable by giving them income and expenses. Making sure income exceeds expenses leaves less time to get into trouble. That's the formula. It was used by every indigent immigrant group fleeing to America from hunger and oppression during the past century and a half, yet never needed more than today as we attempt to compete in a global economy. Our solutions must fit the global economy and not the dubious wrongs of long dead generations whose world was so different from our own. It's a solution that can more easily be sold to white America than forty acres and a mule, because a hand up, not a hand-out, is a lasting thing.

Some among us are pushing for "reparations" because they were uprooted from their African "homeland." The black diaspora was a disgrace, to be sure, its victims brutally uprooted and ferried by heartless ignorance in the seventeenth century to far away, labor-intensive lands being lit by the sunrise of empire.

But can any among us doubt that the descendants of those long-ago slaves are better off, even having gone through the crucible of slavery, living in the United States today than the descendants of the unfortunate people who remained in Africa and are now so hopelessly ensnared? The African economy is in shambles, and the quality of life, outside of South Africa, is horrendous: famine, AIDS, disease, unemployment. You name it.

Think about that. Then think about why no elected official here would ever stand up and say so. It's the labeling thing, again.

17

It's All about the Wampum

I remember a great episode of the *Sopranos* in which Tony's guys were upset the New Jersey Council on Indian Affairs planned to disrupt the annual Columbus Day Parade. Tony needed help in mediating the dispute. So he hooked up with an Indian chief he believed had some clout. The chief's name was poetic—Doug Smith—and his connection to anything remotely Indian was tenuous at best. Still, he was the CEO of the Mohonk Casino, no doubt owing his position to the infinite wisdom of Congress.

Truth in jest. I was thinking about that episode recently when reflecting upon a few trends related to Indians, er, Native Americans—the quest for gaming rights and the fight over naming rights.

Not too long ago, a group of Oklahomans laid claim to 315 acres in Pennsylvania's Lehigh Valley. They said the land was stolen from them, and they want compensation. Specifically, they claim that acreage in Forks Township was conveyed in 1738 to Chief Tundy Tetamy, a Delaware Indian chief, only to be fraudulently taken away from his descendants in 1802. Their suit argues that to facilitate a "walking purchase," Thomas Penn, son of Pennsylvania namesake William Penn, falsely told the chiefs of the Lenni-Lenape tribe that their ancestors had agreed, decades earlier, to give the colonists title to as much Indian land as they could cover in a day-and-a-half walk. The chiefs agreed, thinking any such concession would be small. Penn then had workers clear paths through the forest and hired the fastest runners he could find to cover as much ground as possible. When the "walk" was over, the Lenni-Lenape, also known as the Delaware, had lost 1,200 square miles.[1]

To be fair, the fellows from Oklahoma look a lot more Indian than Chief Doug Smith. And it would seem that their ancestors were among the first in a long line of people in this country to get swindled in a real estate transaction. Trouble is, their beef occurred over two hundred years ago, and today there is a Crayola crayon plant on 200 of the acres (out of the 315 acres to which the

Indians now lay claim), while elsewhere there are about two-dozen homes. Not that the homeowners should worry. It's not really about the land. Nobody is looking to build a tepee reservation. Instead, it's all about the wampum that will flow from legalized gambling.

"If slots at racetracks or any other forms of gaming are coming to Pennsylvania, the Delawares demand a seat at the table," confirmed Bernard Kahrahrah, a so-called tribal planner.[2]

To advance their claim, the Delaware Indians have hired one of the best legal talents the white man has to offer. Steve Cozen is their Pennsylvania counsel. He explained to me that both the Delaware Nation and the Delaware Tribe are federally recognized with valid land claims under both federal statute and federal common law in Pennsylvania; therefore, they have federally protected rights to established Indian gaming in the Commonwealth. According to Cozen, there is a congressional mandate that allows Native Americans to utilize casinos to enable them to establish self-sufficiency.

I understand the underlying principle. The Indians got screwed long ago and the nation with a heart wants to make amends. It's how that got translated into gaming that I can't grasp.

And it may get worse. If the Indians pursue their federal rights all the way and win, they could not only obtain a gaming license in Pennsylvania but will pay *no* taxes to Pennsylvania, which puts the administration of Governor Ed Rendell in the position of either negotiating a better deal than that now, or taking its chances in court. So far, the state is taking its chances, and that strategy is working.

"The fact of the matter is that if we go the long route and win at great expense, there is no motivation on the part of our client to deal with the Commonwealth other than what the federal mandate says," Cozen told me one day on the radio.[3]

Pay me now, or pay me more later. So far, it is pay me later. In 2004, a U.S. federal judge ruled that the Delaware Nation is not legally entitled to get acreage even if its claims are true because Thomas Penn then had king-like powers and was free to take the Indian land as he saw fit.[4] The case is on appeal.

I don't doubt it happened as the Delawares say, but just as with the story of Rob Morris and Wachovia, an awful lot has happened since then. Like the War of 1812, the Victorian Age, the Civil War, World War I, World War II, the growth and fall of Communism, and September 11, to name a few.

When I told Cozen I thought the entire situation was a bit ridiculous, he invited me to rally several million Americans and change federal law, which he believes to be on the side of the Native Americans. I wish somebody would do just that and pass a new law with my solution. There ought to be a statute of limitations that runs with the lifespan of the oldest living human. If anybody walking the face of the earth at the time of an injustice like this is among the living, then they get redress. If not, forget it. Or maybe it's the second-generation rule. Your claim survives until the children of everyone alive at the time passes on, and then that's it. Take your pick. At some point, it's over. Congress needs to end the Indian gaming madness. After all, it's all about the wampum.

My aim is not to besmirch Native Americans. But this is yet another case of where we are MUZZLED as a society. No one is willing to stand up, except maybe Tony Soprano, and tell it like it is on this casino business. True, this land was their land. Also true, it was stolen from them. But they are not the only ones who, as a group, were taken advantage of by a superior economic or military force. Many segments of society have been taken advantage of in the history of the world, some in this country. At some point, the write-a-check mentality has to end.

There is something else I find morally repugnant: the role of gambling revenue in this debate. Don't get me wrong. As you can tell from the subject matter and language of this book, I am no prude. And when it comes to gambling, I enjoy throwing some of my money away on a blackjack table now and then in Atlantic City. But I do so knowing that gambling is a dirty business. I find it odd that in our bid to make amends for the theft of Native American land and eradication of their culture in this country, the prescription is to create an affirmative-action program for their entrée into an industry that carries with it the baggage of gambling.

Want proof that this Indian gaming thing is a boondoggle? Consider the case of Jack Abramoff. You know, the hot-shot Washington lobbyist who prepped for his guilty plea on charges of three felonies by dressing as a cross between James Cagney and Meyer Lansky? Well, Abramoff's plea deal spelled out a litany of indiscretions that he committed while representing Indian interests which showed just how flush with cash the industry has become as a result of the white man's redress. Abramoff's largest apparent kickback came from a Louisiana tribe that used his services. In the plea agreement, Abramoff said the tribe paid companies run by his associate $30,510,000![5] And wait until you hear how they rolled some other tribesman down in Texas. Abramoff was reportedly hired by a

Texas tribe in an effort to help them reopen its casino through legislation. While that tribe was paying them $4.2 million for lobbying to obtain gaming approval, a Louisiana tribe was paying him at the same time to *oppose* all gaming in the Texas legislature. Now, I'm not blaming Indians for Abramoff's shenanigans, but I do think the scandal that engulfed the man says something about the gravy-train Indian gaming has become for people other than Indians whose land was taken from them a long time ago.

I may as well get all of the Indian subject matter off my chest. While I can't fathom the mind-set behind throwing the bone of casino gambling to Indians for the theft of their land, I am equally perplexed by the perpetual battle over the naming of all things sounding Indian. The NCAA recently resolved a huge go-around with Florida State University over whether it could continue to be known as the Seminoles, complete with Chief Osceola as its mascot. After being on the warpath, the NCAA smoked the peace pipe with FSU and granted a waiver in the first challenge to a new policy, removing FSU from a list of colleges and universities whose sports teams, it said, use "hostile or abusive" Native American names and imagery.[6] But the resolution came only after things got a bit ugly, and other schools are still under the hatchet.

I've been thinking about my own experience in the world of mascots. I was first a Doyle "Eagle." Then, I became a Holicong "Colonial." After that, I was a C. B. West "Buck," then a Lehigh "Engineer," and finally a Penn "Quaker."

Doyle Elementary didn't select the eagle as a mascot because it was demeaning to birds. Presumably, Doyle wanted the same symbolism sought by the United States—the beautiful, symbolic, strong, American eagle. Holicong Junior High School was offering a tip of the hat to the colonial roots that lie in Philadelphia and its surrounding environs, where the school is located. I really can't offer much of an explanation for my high-school alma mater, C. B. West. The only relevance of the buck that I can determine has to do with the popularity of hunting. I doubt that is what they were thinking. Lehigh has always been known for its strong engineering program, hence that mascot (they have since changed to mountain hawks, a reflection of the topography of the campus), and the University of Pennsylvania "Quaker" is an acknowledgement of its own roots.

As a group, they are not exactly mascots that strike fear into opponents' hearts. But each had purpose. And to the extent any judgment was being passed in the name usage, it was all complimentary.

It's the same thing with naming our children. We gave our second son the middle name of Wilson because we admire, not castigate, the memory of Ronald Wilson Reagan. Which is why I just don't get the beef of the Indians, er, Native Americans, who complain about schools adopting their names for their teams. It'd be like Nancy Reagan telling me I have besmirched the memory of her late husband because I thought so much of him that I named my son for him. Which is crazy. (Apologies to the mental health community.) You have to agree, it is insane. (Damn.) Total blankin' lunacy! (I give up.)

Same thing with the Washington *Redskins*, the Atlanta *Braves*, the Dodge *Dakota*, and the Jeep *Cherokee*!

None of this common sense has stopped the NCAA, the United States Commission on Civil Rights (USCCR), the National Association for the Advancement of Colored People (NAACP), the National Organization for Women (NOW), or the National Congress of American Indians (NCAI).[7] All are currently pushing for an end to Native American names and symbols in American universities on the grounds that these names can be interpreted as racially/culturally offensive.

On August 5, 2005, the NCAA's Executive Committee declared a ban on all offensive nicknames of Native Americans. Eighteen colleges and universities were continuing to use Native American imagery or references and subject to the new policy, including (at that time) FSU:

- Alcorn State University (Braves)
- Central Michigan University (Chippewas)
- Catawba College (Indians)
- Florida State University (Seminoles)
- Midwestern State University (Indians)
- University of Utah (Utes)
- Indiana University-Pennsylvania (Indians)
- Carthage College (Redmen)
- Bradley University (Braves)
- Arkansas State University (Indians)
- Chowan College (Braves)

- University of Illinois-Champaign (Illini)

- University of Louisiana-Monroe (Indians)

- McMurry University (Indians)

- Mississippi College (Choctaws)

- Newberry College (Indians)

- University of North Dakota (Fighting Sioux)

- Southeastern Oklahoma State University (Savages)

Bradley University was the first to fight the NCAA in a situation where a school did not have a namesake tribe from which it could cite support, and lost its appeal to the NCAA. "Clearly, no Native American tribe 'owns' the word 'Braves' in the same way it owns the name of a tribe, and therefore [Bradley] cannot overcome the position that the use of such a name leads to a hostile or abusive environment," said a statement from NCAA vice president Bernard Franklin.[8]

One of the more interesting battles has been waged at the University of North Dakota. The North Dakota campus is home to the Ralph Engelstad Arena, a $104 million stadium where thousands of fans flock to watch the Fighting Sioux men's hockey team walk across the likeness of the handsome Sioux face in profile with its four eagle feathers attached to the crown of the head, which is spread like a welcome mat in front of a statute of Engelstad himself. Englestad was a North Dakota goalie who later made money in gaming. The fact that he donated $100 million for the arena didn't erase his controversial past and apparent fascination with Nazism in particular. The floor, walls, and furniture of the hockey arena are plastered with as many as three thousand of the Sioux Indian logos. It can be found on each row of seats, on frosted glass doors and pillars, and stitched into every two steps of carpeting ringing the luxury box floor.[9] North Dakota originally adopted the Fighting Sioux nickname in the 1930s. In 1969, a delegation from the Standing Rock Sioux tribe—including a grandson of Sitting Bull—gave the university permission to formally use the name. In fact, a large statute of Sitting Bull on horseback is in front of the main entrance to the arena. Apparently that doesn't matter now. *Stay tuned*: this could be the mother of all garage sales.

Already, fourteen schools have removed all references to Native American culture or were deemed not to have references to Native American culture as part of their athletics programs:

- California State-Stanislaus University (Warriors)

- Lycoming College (Warriors)

- Winona State University (Warriors)

- Hawaii-Manoa University (Rainbow Warriors)

- Eastern Connecticut State University (Warriors)

- East Stroudsburg University (Warriors)

- Husson College (Braves)

- Merrimack College (Warriors)

- Southeast Missouri State University (Indians)

- State University of West Georgia (Braves)

- Stonehill College (Chieftans)

- San Diego State University (Aztecs)

- Wisconsin Lutheran College (Warriors)

- University of North Carolina-Pembroke (Braves)

And the College of William and Mary has been given an extension to complete its self-study on the mascot issue.[10]

The committee's guidelines state, "Effective immediately, these nicknames are not to appear on any team paraphernalia or on any student athletes. Any college previously awarded the honor of hosting an NCAA championship tournament must take steps to cover up offensive material, effective February 1, 2006. All offensive mascots, cheerleaders, dance teams and bands are to do away with offensive uniforms by August 1, 2008. The new NCAA rules would only apply to NCAA sponsored tournaments since the organization's authority for this particular issue does not extend into regular season play."[11]

One has to wonder, why now? After all, the use of Indian nicknames and mascots by colleges and universities started in the early 1900s. Many of these names were generic—Braves, Chiefs, and Warriors—but some were the names of tribes like the Chippewas, the Hurons, the Sioux, and, of course, the Seminoles. Eventually, there were more than 100 colleges with Indian mascots and some 2,500 high schools. Professional sports teams joined in, too.[12]

I maintain that the issue has reached its pinnacle now because of the PC climate in this country, which, I argue, is compromising our ability to fight the war on terror. We're so damn afraid to offend anybody, even the members of radical Islam who threaten us. And to the list that we don't want to insult, you can add Indians. So to make amends, we give them a casino and tell them we will ditch the mascots that, ironically, were being utilized to honor, not disrespect them. It's become the American way.

The background on the FSU/Seminole situation is itself a great illustration of what lunacy this has become. The Seminoles are the only American Indian tribe to never sign a formal peace treaty with the United States. That's why FSU erected "Unconquered," a statue of the Chief Osceola mascot, outside its stadium.[13] They want their team to be like the Seminoles and remain unconquered. Unwavering. Brave. Defiant. Do I really need to go on? These Seminoles survived by selling otter pelts and alligator skins to white settlers in Fort Lauderdale and Miami. When South Florida tourism boomed in the 1920s, Seminoles capitalized by wrestling alligators for money.[14] Now doesn't that sound like a squad you don't want to tangle with, on the football field or anywhere else?

FSU has used the Seminole nickname since the school went coed in 1947.[15] For the last three decades, there has been dialogue between FSU and the Seminole Tribe of Florida since there was a first expression of concern about some university traditions and symbols associated with their tribal name.[16] The result of those talks was a slew of agreed-upon, time-honored FSU traditions still practiced even today.

According to Max B. Osceola Jr., one of the five members of the Seminole Tribal Council of Florida, "We have been in dialogue with the university since the early 1970s and we feel it's a reflection of the Seminole spirit. We have many Seminoles (tribe members) who are (FSU) alumni, many Seminoles who are FSU fans. We feel it's an association that reflects the spirit of the Seminoles and is not derogatory in any way."[17]

Despite this cooperation and support by the Seminoles themselves, the NCAA thinks it knows best. FSU's president, T. K. Wetherell, wrote a letter which was produced at an emergency meeting of FSU's Board of Trustees in the midst of the NCAA challenge, which attacked and successfully destroyed a good amount of the NCAA's credibility on the issue. The letter began by demonstrating the true origin of FSU's Seminole namesake:

> It is clear to us that the NCAA's process of adopting this new policy was seriously flawed and undemocratic. . . . "Florida State Seminoles" is not a nickname. It is, rather, a name that we use to identify not only our athletics teams but also many other internal and external groups because it represents traits of a heroic people whom we admire and would like to emulate.
>
> The name "Florida State Seminoles" was selected by vote of the university student body in 1947, when FSU became a co-educational institution. The name was selected to specifically honor the indomitable spirit of the Florida Seminoles—those people whom the Seminole Tribe of Florida's history refers to as the "few hundred unconquered Seminole men, women and children left—all hiding in the swamps and Everglades of South Florida." The name honors the bravery, courage, strength and determination of these people, who never surrendered and persevered to preserve their heritage and traditions, and who in 1842 were finally left at peace—free at last from government oppression.[18]

The letter made reference to a recent vote held by the Seminole Tribe of Oklahoma:

> Contrary to the NCAA's statements, the Seminole Nation of Oklahoma is on record as unopposed to the use of the Seminole name. This past July, the Seminole Nation General Council, the legislative body for the Seminole Nation of Oklahoma, resoundingly defeated a motion to denounce the use of Native American nicknames and images in sports and other events. The vote was 18-2.
>
> Moreover, Ken Chambers, principal chief of the Seminole Nation of Oklahoma, has said publicly that the name "gives the type of recognition that allows people to identify with the name Seminoles." He also said, "As far as the mascot itself, it is not degrading to us. It is not humiliating."[19]

FSU doesn't think of Chief Osceola as a mascot. "As for the NCAA's concern about 'mascots,' we do not have them at the university. We use imagery in a tradition of tribute to the Florida Seminoles—namely a horse, a rider and a flaming spear—all of which were created after consultation with and the concurrence of the leadership of the Seminole Tribe of Florida."[20] A pretty convincing argument overall, if I do say so myself.

FSU got some help along the way. Florida Governor Jeb Bush, upon hearing that the NCAA was meddling with the Seminole name, said, "These folks that make these decisions need to get out more often." He added that the NCAA campaign was itself offensive to the "Seminole Indian tribe who support the traditions of FSU."[21]

More support came from a U.S. representative from Florida, Republican Tom Feeney, who threatened to get Congress involved in the matter, if necessary, to protect the FSU Seminole heritage and the use of Chief Osceola. Feeney said, "Florida State University has historically had a contract with the Florida Seminoles. The Seminoles love the fact that they get royalties from FSU but, more important, FSU honors the Seminoles in Florida, using their name to pay their respects to the historic bravery, courage, and teamwork that the Seminoles of Florida are known for."[22]

The congressman went on to jest but raised an undeniably excellent point: "I happen to be an American of Irish descent. If anyone has a right to be upset, it's probably the people that are made the object of fun known as the 'Fighting Irish.' . . . There's really no end to this slippery slope."[23]

Thankfully, FSU has been removed from the McCarthy-like list of colleges and universities that have been singled out for usage of Indian names and mascots. "The executive Committee, which unveiled the restrictions, continues to believe the stereotyping of Native Americans is wrong," NCAA Senior Vice President Bernard Franklin said in a statement. "However, in its review of the particular circumstances regarding Florida State, the staff review committee noted the unique relationship between the University and the Seminole Tribe of Florida as a significant factor."[24]

Even after FSU won its battles, the NCAA continued with its crusade against mascots. First, it announced it will extend its prohibition of "hostile" or "abusive" use of American Indian nicknames, mascots, and logos to include bowl games. And it denied an appeal by the University of North Dakota that it be removed from a list of schools subject to the restriction that applies to those that have Indian mascots. (As of this writing, three of the eighteen schools that the NCAA cited for being in violation of its PC rules won appeals:

FSU, Central Michigan, and Utah.) At issue at UND is the "Fighting Sioux" name and logo.

Remaining universities on the list are hopeful of having their names removed. In the process, they're fighting like (dare I say it?) Utes, Sioux, and Chippewas!

Here's a closing example of where a compliment can get someone in trouble because of the MUZZLED environment in which we live. Legendary Air Force Academy football coach Fisher DeBerry got himself into a jam last season in the week after his team took a 48-10 drubbing at the hands of TCU. DeBerry, then a sixty-seven-year-old fellow with a terrific record and a reputation for folksy charm, attributed that particular loss, in part, to the fact that TCU "had a lot more Afro-American players than we did and they ran a lot faster than we did." The coach said, "It just seems to me to be that way. Afro-American kids can run very well. That doesn't mean that Caucasian kids and other descents can't run, but it's very obvious to me that they run extremely well."[25]

Who among us can argue with that logic? I'd say only those who have not recently watched the NBA.

And by the way, is he demeaning or complimenting African Americans? I think it is obvious.

Nevertheless, he found himself apologizing within days of these truthful statements. The point here is that just as Indian tribes mistakenly take umbrage when their identify is adopted by sports teams despite the fact that the name adoption is usually a compliment, so too was it felt necessary for Coach DeBerry to apologize for praising the black athlete.

Go figure.

18

Intelligently Designing
a Curriculum

MAS: *Caller, welcome to the Big Talker, 1210.*

Caller: *Yeah, Michael, I heard what you just said (fill in the blank on subject matter) and that violates the separation of church and state.*

MAS: *Oh really, what violation of separation of church and state might that be?*

Caller: *You know, the violation of separation of church and state in the United States.*

MAS: *Well, where can I find the "separation" to which you refer?*

Caller: *In the Constitution!*

MAS: *Where in the Constitution?!!*

Caller: *In the First Amendment!!!*

MAS: *What does it say in the First Amendment?!!!!*

Caller: *It says we have to separate church and state!!!!!*

MAS: *No, it says this: "Congress shall make no law respecting an establishment of religion; or prohibiting the free exercise thereof; or abridging the freedom of speech, or the press, or the right of the people peaceably to assemble, and to petition the Government for a redress of grievances."*

Caller: *. . . .*

MAS: *Caller . . . hello . . . caller???!!!!!!!*

Welcome to my world. I wish I had a nickel for every time that kind of call has played itself out in the decade-plus that I have been hosting a talk-radio program. The First Amendment could not be more straightforward; it says that the government is not going to establish a religion. The issue, then, in so many of these church-and-state controversies should simply be whether the action complained about is, in fact, representative of government's establishing a religion. Not tolerating religion, or its exercise, but establishing a religion. And under that review, much of what is often complained about should be permitted. The current debate on intelligent design is but the latest and perhaps clearest example of a manufactured debate.

Let's go back, eighty years.

It's 1925 all over again.

In that year, John Scopes, a twenty-four-year-old public high-school teacher in Dayton, Tennessee, decided to include Darwin's theory of evolution as part of the curriculum of his biology class. The only problem was, Tennessee had recently passed a law forbidding the teaching of "evolution or any other theory denying the biblical account of the creation of man" in public schools.

Defending Scopes in this "trial of the century" was the legendary ACLU attorney, Clarence Darrow. William Jennings Bryan, a former candidate for the U.S. presidency, headed the prosecution. As each side presented its case, it soon became clear that, rather than the validity of the law under which Scopes was being charged, the authority of the Bible versus the soundness of Darwin's theory became the focus of the arguments.

Scopes lost the fight and was fined $100, but it was widely believed that although Bryan had won the case, he had lost the argument.[1]

Now, eighty years later, we're repeating the debate.

Among the states, arguably the most heated battleground, the "Scopes trial of our day,"[2] took place in otherwise sleepy Dover, Pennsylvania. There, a debate raged as to the propriety of teaching the relatively new theory called "intelligent design" (or ID). The Dover case, *Kitzmiller et al. v. Dover Area School District et al.*, garnered wide attention and showcased this new theory to a nationwide audience.

Now that President Bush has recently entered the fray, the culture wars are rapidly escalating. The president, in response to a reporter's question about his "personal views" on the subject, said he "believed intelligent design should be taught in schools along with evolution theory so people can better understand the argument."[3] Amen to that, I mean, er, ah, yes sir.

But what is intelligent design theory, and is it the same as creationism?

ID says science and Darwin can't explain it all. ID is "a new and developing" hypothesis that "says certain features of living systems are best explained by an intelligent cause rather than an undirected mechanism. While ID does not reject evolution as change over time, or common ancestry, it does challenge the idea that life arose by undirected processes of natural selection."[4] Creationists, on the other hand, believe that the Genesis account should arbitrate, *a priori*, scientific views on creation. Or as *USA Today* explains, creationism is "the religious concept that a supernatural creator produced the universe and life directly. It's often based upon the Bible's Book of Genesis."[5]

The notion that the universe was created by an intelligent being is as old as Plato, but intelligent design theory as it is presently known began to be advanced in the 1980s—with the publication of the "supplemental biology textbook" *Of Pandas and People* in 1989, greatly contributing to widespread public awareness of ID.

I'm proud to say that the leading advocate of ID is from my alma mater, Lehigh University. His name is Michael Behe, and he acknowledges this theory may lead people to believe that the intelligent designer is God. However, Behe does not wish to be labeled a creationist. He says, rather, "Our starting point is from science, not from scripture."[6]

Salvador Cordova, another advocate for intelligent design, goes even further, saying, "Intelligent design doesn't have any theology to it."[7]

Behe is a biology professor at Lehigh. I was anxious to speak with him about his prominence and ask him to articulate for me ID for dummies. He obliged. He said he likes to explain it using a well-known national monument: "Suppose you were walking by [a] set of mountains and it turned out to be Mt. Rushmore, and somebody said, 'Well, how do you think these got here?' You'd say, 'Well, you know, plate tectonics and wind and erosion explain part of it, but they certainly don't explain all of it, and if you look at the faces of Washington and Jefferson and Roosevelt and Lincoln and so on there, you'd say that these were not caused by random forces, but these were caused by intelligent activity.'"[8]

Just in case you don't buy his analogy, Behe offered an example from biology. "Bacterial flagellum," he said, is like "an outboard motor that bacteria use to swim." In fact, "It's exactly like an outboard motor on a motor boat." And this is just one of hundreds of other "molecular machines" that scientists have discovered. Such complex—and seemingly "designed"—mechanisms are left out of Darwin's account, according to proponents of ID. To explain them, they propose the existence of a supernatural designing intelligence.

Critics of ID say it doesn't belong in a science class for a very simple reason—it's not science. Instead, some view it as a Trojan horse attempt by creationists to sneak religion into public schools. And, by the way, I'll bet that in some instances they are correct! But not in all instances, and, even so, it does not represent an establishment of religion under the First Amendment.

Nicholas Matzke is one of the critics. He's the project information specialist for the National Center for Science Education and calls intelligent design "creationism in a cheap tuxedo."[9]

Then there is Dr. Jerry Coyne, a professor in the Department of Ecology and Evolution at the University of Chicago, who offers: "Intelligent design is simply the third attempt of creationists to proselytize our children at the expense of good science and clear thinking. Having failed to ban evolution from schools and later to get equal classroom time for scientific creationism, they have made a few adjustments designed to sneak Christian cosmogony past the First Amendment. And these adjustments have given ID a popularity never enjoyed by earlier forms of creationism."[10]

Darwinists further respond that, if there are gaps in our current evolutionary picture, then those gaps are rapidly being closed as more and more discoveries are unearthed. "It should embarrass ID'ers that so many of the missing links cited by *Pandas* as evidence for supernatural intervention are no longer missing," writes Dr. Coyne, adding that creationists (as he mercilessly labels ID advocates) "make a serious mistake when using the absence of transitional forms as evidence for an intelligent designer. In the last decade, paleontologists have uncovered a fairly complete evolutionary series of whales, beginning with fully terrestrial animals that became more and more aquatic over time, with their front limbs evolving into flippers and their hind limbs and pelvis gradually reduced to tiny vestiges. When such fossils are found, as they often are, creationists must then punt and change their emphasis to other missing links, continually retreating before the advance of science."[11]

In other words, paleontology is slowly but surely completing the puzzle of evolution by natural selection as proposed by Darwin. Therefore, there's no need to invoke a designer whose existence is beyond the proof of science anyway.

The only problem is, when opponents of ID attack its lack of scientific rigor, critics often find themselves drifting outside the domain of science and into questions of philosophy and theology. Dr. Coyne's critique of ID is a perfect example. If he doesn't think ID qualifies as science, that's one thing, but then he asks: "Would an intelligent designer create millions of species and then make them go extinct, only to replace them with other species, repeating this process over and over again? . . . Why, about a million years ago, would the designer produce creatures that have an apelike cranium perched atop a humanlike skeleton? And why would he then successively replace these creatures with others having an ever-closer resemblance to modern humans?"[12]

At moments like this, the argument starts to sound like a philosophy debate more than a scientific one: Can God create a rock so heavy that He can't lift it? How many angels can stand on the head of a pin?

More importantly, lighten up, fellows! This debate is exactly the sort of exchange I want my four kids to experience. Please don't deny them the free exchange of such important ideas. That's why they are in school!

You've heard the saying that all politics is local? Well, it really extends to the debate on ID. Take what happened in Dover. On October 18, 2004, the Dover County School Board mandated by a 6-3 vote the teaching of intelligent design in all public schools. Carol and Jeff Brown, two of the three board members who opposed the mandate, resigned after the vote. When asked to describe the climate among members of the Dover School District, Jeff and Carol responded, "Split, very split."[13] Carol also added, "We have a vocal group within the community who feel very strongly, in an evangelical Christian way, that there is no separation of church and state."[14]

In Dover, most arguments arose over the fact that many people see ID as a new form of creationism. I asked Carol and Jeff Brown about that. Carol told me, "A lot of the experts in the field are viewing it in that way."[15] Witold Walczak (you've got to love a name like that; we're probably related!), the ACLU of Pennsylvania's legal director agrees: "There's a constant impetus by conservative evangelical Christians to bring religion back into the public schools. The end goal is to get rid of evolution. They view it as a threat to their religion."[16]

Aside from religious animosity, some believe that implementing ID into a school's curriculum could affect a student's college placement. As Jeff Brown explains, "There's another segment of the community that is extremely concerned as to what this [ID] is going to do to our students' chances of getting into better colleges."

The atmosphere of suspicion is best summed up in the words of Rev. Barry W. Lynn, the executive director of Americans United for Separation of Church and State. Lynn believes, "There is nothing random about this. You might say it's a planned evolution of an attack on the science of evolution."[17]

Clearly, ID is making a lot of people nervous. So I put the question to the Lehigh biologist and ID advocate, Michael Behe: should ninth graders be taught about ID? And I was surprised to hear a person in this debate who didn't get shrill. He simply said, "Yeah sure, I mean one doesn't have to dwell on it. There's lots of things to talk about in biology."[18]

Too bad eleven Dover high-school parents apparently didn't share Behe's nonchalance. They joined the ACLU of Pennsylvania, Americans United for Separation of Church and State, and attorneys at Pepper Hamilton LLP in filing a lawsuit against the Dover County schools. The lawsuit argued that presenting intelligent design in public school science classrooms violates their religious liberty by promoting particular religious beliefs to their children under the guise of science education.[19]

"Public schools are not Sunday schools, and we must resist any efforts to make them so. There is an evolving attack under way on sound science education, and the school board's action in Dover is part of that misguided crusade. 'Intelligent design' has about as much to do with science as reality television has to do with reality," said Reverend Lynn.[20] One of the parents involved in the lawsuit, Bryan Rehm, added: "As a parent and a person of faith, I want to share my religious beliefs with my own children, but as a teacher, it would be a great disservice and fallacy to teach students that a perfectly valid faith constitutes scientific knowledge."

Despite the lawsuit, Dover still planned on teaching ID to its ninth grade class. Originally, because of their lack of textbooks covering the topic, science teachers in Dover were only required to mention ID briefly as a competing theory. That almost changed, however, when fifty copies of *Pandas* were donated to the school anonymously.

After reading the book, Carol Brown stated, "The problem is, the text is not ninth-grade level to begin with. It was never written for high school, it was written for college-level classes. Ninth graders are going to begin to read this, and they're going to be clueless when they do." She told me, "When I read the text I said, 'This is bad science and even worse religion.'"[21]

To me, what is most remarkable about the Dover controversy is all the hullabaloo is over a simple 159-word statement. If Dover folks get what they want, here is what it will take a teacher about one minute to read to students at the start of a ninth-grade biology lesson on evolution:

The Pennsylvania Academic Standards require students to learn about Darwin's theory of evolution and eventually to take a standardized test of which evolution is a part.

Because Darwin's theory is a theory, it continues to be tested as new evidence is discovered. The theory is not a fact. Gaps in the theory exist for which there is no evidence. A theory is defined as a well-tested explanation that unifies a broad range of observations.

Intelligent design is an explanation of the origin of life that differs from Darwin's view. The reference book, *Of Pandas and People*, is available for students who might be interested in gaining an understanding of what intelligent design actually involves.

With respect to any theory, students are encouraged to keep an open mind. The school leaves the discussion of the origins of life to individual students and their families. As a standards driven district, class instruction focuses on preparing students to achieve proficiency on standards based assessments.

If I may attempt the wisdom of Solomon here (uh oh, there I go again, "establishing a religion"), I think both sides in this debate need to step back and take some deep breaths.

First of all, to the ID'ers, one word: patience. Your theory is practically brand new and has not yet gained wide acceptance. Don't expect ninth graders all over the country to be carrying around *Of Pandas and People* instead of *The Origin of Species* quite yet. I highly doubt that high-school students were being taught Einstein's theory of relativity until decades after its publication. (As a matter of fact, I seem to recall it barely receiving more than a cursory mention in my high-school science class!) Expect the same to be true *if* your theory is able to stand on its own over time.

Many ID advocates understand this. "The Discovery Institute in Seattle, which is regarded as a leader in intelligent design theory, also opposes the Dover school board's policy, in part because it seems to take three steps into old-fashioned creationism. 'This theory needs to be debated in the scientific sphere,' said Paul West, a senior fellow. 'It's much too soon to require anyone to teach it in high school.'"[22]

To the Darwinists: don't become that which you despise. In other words, keep in mind that Darwin's theory is just that, a theory. The word "dogma" is unthinkable to scientists, who are not "men in white coats" handing down capital "T" Truth etched in stone, but people who "argue about how best to interpret evidence."[23] The best science can do is propose verifiable hypotheses to explain observed phenomenon; a model may contain fact but it remains a model, nonetheless. As one opponent of ID himself admits, "A theory that cannot be rejected is not a scientific theory."[24]

Ideally, what we need in the field of biology is something along the lines of what physicists have going for them: they teach both Newton's classical approach to the universe as well as Einstein's modern innovations. If you ask them, "Does light consist of particles or waves?" They'll answer yes to both, because it depends on the model that a physicist chooses to adopt when studying a particular problem. Chemists do the same.

Part of the reason this biology debate has become so heated, perhaps, is that it is so binary: either you accept "Bible-thumping" creationism or you buy into mechanistic Darwinism. Wouldn't it be more helpful—and more rigorously scientific—if we considered other proposed models to explain the origin and variation of species? Certainly, Darwinism (or one of its later "neo-Darwinist" formulations) ought to command center stage in the classroom. It's been with us a long time and still remains the reigning theory, whatever its problems or gaps.

But why not free ourselves from this animosity by exposing our kids to other models as well so that they learn that science is as much about evidence and arguments as a law court? Surely the widely acclaimed theory of Stephen Jay Gould and Niles Eldredge called "punctuated equilibrium," whereby biological adaptation occurs in rapid spurts during brief periods of environmental stress (rather than Darwin's notion of tiny, incremental changes over long stretches of time) deserves attention.[25]

Besides the "punctuationists" (hey, how'd that get through spellcheck?), there are those who toss out Darwin altogether. It's not the Bible that leads cladists to reject Darwin's assumption that adaptations are based on ancestry; with their theory of "convergent evolution," they believe environment and function alone dictate change, even in widely different types of animals. That's why birds, bats, and insects all have wings, they say.[26]

Do you get it? "Rather than teaching evolution as an incontrovertible 'truth,' teachers should present the arguments for modern neo-Darwinism and encourage students to evaluate these arguments critically. In short, students should learn the scientific arguments for and against contemporary evolutionary theory."[27] It's much more difficult to be a staunch, unbending fundamentalist—toward the Genesis account *or* Darwin's—if you have to contend with more than one other position. In fact, Darwin himself "addressed every competing argument he could in *The Origin of Species*. When evolution is taught as Darwin presented it—as 'one long argument' resting on a large and diverse body of facts, but nevertheless as an argument from which thoughtful people (and scientists) can dissent—fewer parents will object to their children learning about it." As John Scopes said during his trial nearly a century ago, "If you limit a teacher to only one side of anything, the whole country will eventually have only one thought. . . . I believe in teaching every aspect of every problem or theory."[28]

If we break out of the either/or mind-set of Darwin vs. the Bible and see that this scientific issue is, like most, a complex field of competing theories and models—then I suspect that this particular battle of the culture war will subside. And our children's education will be the better for it. Not that breaking out will be easy.

Just days before Christmas 2005, Judge John E. Jones III of the U.S. District Court for the Middle District of Pennsylvania put a lump of coal in the stocking of supporters of ID, or at least those who were behind the ID movement in Dover. Judge Jones ruled that it was unconstitutional for the district to present ID as an alternative to evolution in high-school biology courses because it is a religious viewpoint that advances "a particular view of Christianity."[29] By the time his opinion was issued, Dover voters had themselves already voted out of office the ID proponents on the board. And, after his opinion was issued, the new Dover board itself voted unanimously to remove ID from the curriculum and not to appeal the federal court decision.

I know Judge Jones and have been in his company socially. (I think we took in a ballgame with our mutual friend Jonathan Newman.) He's no judicial activist. He is a Tom Ridge protégée who was appointed to the federal bench by President George W. Bush. Still, I was a bit surprised by the outcome of the case—that is, until I read his 139-page opinion. Judge Jones was clearly put off by revelations in the trial over which he presided which indicated that some of the ID proponents on the Dover board had lied in their sworn deposition testimony. That's why he said in his opinion that "The citizens of the Dover area were poorly served by the members of the Board who voted for the ID policy. It is ironic that several of these individuals, who staunchly and proudly touted their religious convictions in public, would time and again lie to cover their tracks and disguise the real purpose behind ID Policy."[30] He was referring to evidence suggesting that two school board members lied about how they raised money in a church to buy copies of the intelligent design textbook, *Of Pandas and People*. Judge Jones' opinion states that one member "actually made a plea for donations to purchase *Pandas* at his church, the Harmony Grove Community Church, on a Sunday before services and a total of $850 was raised."[31] That's not right. I have long said that people misunderstand what the Constitution does and does not say about church and state, but I think we can all agree that you shouldn't have public school texts paid for by a passing of the basket at church.

So now I have a new solution to the ID debate. Put aside Darwin, *Pandas*, and the Bible. Let's copy Judge Jones' 139-page tome and distribute it to the students and teach them about what went on in Dover—the competing theories, the science, the religious conviction, the politics, the judicial review. They'd be well served by what they would learn about life, regardless of how it began.

19

I Wish I Were Joking

On November 5, 2005, best-selling author Dean Koontz was the keynote speaker at the sixth annual Men of Mystery gathering at the Irvine Marriot in Orange County, California.[1] Koontz is author of such bestsellers as *Intensity*, *Sole Survivor*, and his most recent novel, *Forever Odd*. He is one of only twelve writers to have nine different novels reach number one on the *New York Times* hardcover bestseller list.[2] Therefore, it is not a surprise that he often makes the rounds on the speaking circuit. It is even less of a surprise that Koontz recycles anecdotes in his speeches—a common technique among speakers.

During his November 5 appearance in front of about five hundred mystery novel fans—and forty to fifty mystery writing colleagues—Koontz launched into a story of his real-life recent battle with a Japanese company that owned a movie studio in the process of making a film version of one of his books.[3] Koontz wanted his name removed from the project, but his requests fell on deaf ears. After making a written plea for the movie studio to delete his name and getting no response, he changed tactics.[4] The man known for his work with a pen wanted to ensure that his next letter garnered some attention.

As Koontz later told me, "I've learned that sometimes humor . . . can get a response when nothing else can."[5] Koontz's invocation of humor in this case included addressing his Japanese counterpart as "Mr. Teriyaki," and in the midst of his speech to mystery writers in Orange County, California, he regaled the crowd by quoting from his letters to "Mr. Teriyaki." For example: "My letter of 10 November has not been answered," it read. "As I am certain you are an honorable and courteous man, I would assume your silence results from the mistaken belief that World War II is still in progress and that the citizens of your country and mine are forbidden to communicate. Enclosed is a copy of the front page of The New York Times from 1945, with the headline, JAPAN SURRENDERS." As they had for years, the letters were a hit with the crowd and "many in the audience laughed and applauded during his speech."[6]

By all accounts, the great majority of the crowd roared as Koontz recounted the story. Of course, there were a few who wanted to throw Koontz on the Hibachi for his comments. One was author Lee Goldberg, who was present at the event and wrote about it on his blog. "I was astonished that people were laughing when they should have shunned him with silence," wrote Goldberg. Other bloggers started posting opinions immediately after the speech, and Koontz's publisher, Bantam Dell, began receiving feedback "from people who weren't even there, people who were calling [Koontz] names."[7]

Despite some criticism, Koontz did not back down from defending the letters. "I'll stand by the letters" to the Japanese executive, he said. "They're George Carlin-esque. There's some political incorrectness in it, but nothing mean."[8] In an interview with me, he said, "We live in a world where people are offended way too easily. I'm sorry if I offended anyone, but I don't apologize for what I said."[9]

To be sure, not all of the authors turned on him. J. A. Konrath, author of *Whiskey Sour*, wrote in an e-mail to the *Los Angeles Times*, "My writing peers need to spend more time writing and less time defending the free world from the menace of Dean Koontz."[10] Perhaps the best judge of Koontz's comments would be the host of the event. "It was not racist," said Joan Hansen, founder and chairwoman of the Men of Mystery event. "He first asked politely that his name be removed from the movie, and never heard back. So he wanted to do something to get their attention."[11]

As I read about Teriyakigate, I saw that author Charles Fleming was one of the authors who had been present and was now publicly objecting to Koontz's behavior. I'd read where Fleming had been quoted as saying, "I gasped from the moment he said, Dear Mr. Teriyaki. I thought okay, this is not going in the right direction."[12] Fleming was particularly enraged by a Koontz backhanded compliment to Mr. Teriyaki: "I admire the Japanese resilience . . . after all we bombed the s**t out of Tokyo several times and you guys kept rebuilding it."[13]

So I decided to track down Fleming to speak with him about the incident. I asked him if he felt the Mr. Teriyaki letters were offensive and racist or, alternatively, if they were offensive, but not necessarily racist. He told me, "I certainly wouldn't be willing to go out on a limb and say that Mr. Koontz is a racist, because I don't know. But, I'd be willing to go out far enough to say this kind of talk is racist. It is racist in its nature, it draws its humor from the idea that we can laugh at somebody because of his ethnicity, because of the place he lived, because of the color of his skin, because his culture, because of his habits, because of the language he speaks." Fleming continued, "Anytime we are doing this it is inappropriate . . . especially when it is not in the context of out and out comedy."[14]

These are remarkable words coming from Fleming, considering that his claim to fame is his role as the coauthor of *The Goomba's Guide to Life*, *The Goomba's Book of Love*, and the work-in-progress *The Goomba's Diet*.[15] Fleming has written these books with Steven R. Schirripa, a.k.a. Bobby Baccala of the *Sopranos*. Think about that. The guy paying his mortgage by preaching the goomba philosophy doesn't like it when Koontz writes to Mr. Teriyaki? When I called him on this contradiction he responded, "If I'm an Italian American and I'm calling myself and my chums a bunch of goombas that is different from someone calling me a goomba and making fun of me."[16] Which would be a great defense . . . if only Fleming weren't Irish.

Shortly after I interviewed Dean Koontz on my radio program, he sent me a note that said, "Thanks for a great interview . . . and for the support in regards to the neo-McCarthyite, Orwellian crowd." Love this guy. But as Koontz found out, comedy today is sticky stuff—even for the professionals.

When I was in the eighth grade, our family of four took a winter vacation that I will never forget. At Christmas time, we flew from Philadelphia to Las Vegas and stayed at the MGM Grand. This was prefire. I was awestruck by the town. I remember peering out of my hotel room, staring into the lights of the Vegas skyline, wondering which building housed Howard Hughes in his hermetically sealed apartment. The plan was to stay in the desert for two nights and then drive a rental car to my uncle's home in Southern California. Then, while in LA, we were to go to the Rose Bowl Parade and the football game. Like I said, it was an extraordinary vacation.

One thing that made it great was that, while in Vegas, we saw a show. Don Rickles was playing in one of the big showrooms, and my dad obtained the necessary four seats. Actually, what he purchased was access to a banquet table, and the location of the banquet table he purchased was to be determined by the size of the tip he would hand the maître d'. My parents pointed all of this out so my brother and I could watch and learn. We did. Dad handed the guy twenty dollars, and we went to the back of the room. Viva Las Vegas!

As memorable as the seating lesson was, the show itself, Don Rickles, was even more so. I can't claim to have understood all of his humor as an eighth grader, but I was sufficiently savvy to be impressed by his command of the room. And what I remember most about the jokes themselves was the ethnic brand of humor that he used so well. Rickles incorporated people in the front row into his act (we were at no risk for those insults), then made fun of whatever hand he'd been dealt with the seating. No one was off limits. Whites, blacks, Asians, Catholics, Jews, men, women. He was an equal opportunity offender. And everybody loved it, including our family from Pennsylvania. Of course, this was 1976 and, sadly, things have changed.

Nowadays, it's hard to find a place where you can hear a good joke, and it's risky to try to tell one in mixed company. Our litigious society and the age of sexual harassment videos at work have seen to that. Talk about MUZZLED. We've rendered obsolete all the best material.

Penn Jillette, the side of the comedy/magic duo Penn and Teller who talks, and a great talk-radio guest by the way, recently said, "You used to feel safer telling jokes. . . . Since all your best material is mean-spirited, you feel less safe. You're worried some might think that you really have this point of view."[17] The need to be politically correct has affected some of the biggest names in Hollywood, including on what is arguably television's biggest night: the Academy Awards.

Robin Williams performed at the 2005 Oscar ceremony, but was dissuaded from doing a song which itself was intended to ridicule the increase in broadcast censorship post-Janet Jackson's wardrobe malfunction. The proposed editing was so severe that the writers of the song, Marc Shaiman and Scott Wittman, refused to let it be performed. That's why Williams ended up taking the stage with a piece of tape over his mouth.[18] Robin Williams didn't let it end there. Soon thereafter, he appeared on *The Tonight Show* with Jay Leno and revealed some of the banned original lyrics to the public.

Williams was later interviewed on the controversy and said he was disappointed. "For a while you get mad, then you get over it," he said. "They're afraid of saying Olive Oyl is anorexic. It tells you about the state of humor. It's strange to think: how afraid are you?"[19]

This was not the first time Marc Shaiman's work has been censored at the Oscars. It was his collaboration with Trey Parker on the song "Blame Canada" from the soundtrack to *South Park: Bigger Longer and Uncut,* which received a nomination for best song at the 2000 Oscar ceremonies, but they ran into a problem when deciding how to actually perform the song on Oscar night. The song comes at a point in the film where the mothers of South Park wage war on Canada for releasing a film that turned their children into foul-mouthed brats. The satirical nature of the movie strikes a jab at censorship in general. This is why when it came time to perform the song at the Oscars, Parker and Shaiman would not budge on the issue of censoring the song. "It would be ironic to have to change the words in a song in a movie about censorship," Shaiman told the *Hollywood Reporter*. "We won't tolerate changing the lyrics," Parker said to the *Washington Post*. "That's the wrong way to go—the song got nominated for what it is."[20]

This trend toward joke censorship has been underway for a while. In the early 1990s, comedian Bill Hicks's stand-up set he did for David Letterman's *Late Show* was canned by higher-ups at the network, making him the first comedy act to be censored at CBS's Ed Sullivan Theatre. What got him in trouble was this:

> You know who's really bugging me these days? These pro-lifers . . . [Smattering of applause.] You ever look at their faces? . . . "I'm pro-life!" [Here Hicks made a pinched face of hate and fear, his lips were pursed as though he'd just sucked on a lemon.] "I'm pro-life!" Boy, they look it, don't they? They just exude *joie de vivre*. You just want to hang with them and play Trivial Pursuit all night long. [Audience chuckles.] You know what bugs me about them? If you're so pro-life, do me a favor— don't lock arms and block medical clinics. If you're so pro-life, lock arms and block cemeteries. [Audience laughs.] . . . I want to see pro-lifers at funerals, opening caskets. "Get out!" Then I'd really be impressed by their mission. [Audience laughs and applauds.]

Not my brand of humor, but nor is it something that I think should have been banned. And there was this:

> I've been traveling a lot lately. I was over in Australia during Easter. It was interesting to note they celebrate Easter the same way we do— commemorating the death and resurrection of Jesus by telling our children a giant bunny rabbit . . . left chocolate eggs in the night. [Audience laughs.]
>
> Gee, I wonder why we're so messed up as a race. You know, I've read the Bible. Can't find the words "bunny" or "chocolate" in the whole book. [Audience laughs.]
>
> I think it's interesting how people act on their beliefs. A lot of

Christians, for instance, wear crosses around their necks. Nice sentiment, but do you think when Jesus comes back, he's really going to want to look at a cross? [Audience laughs. Bill makes a face of pain and horror.]

Ow! Maybe that's why he hasn't shown up yet. [As Jesus, looking down from heaven] "I'm not going, Dad. No, they're still wearing crosses—they've totally missed the point. When they start wearing fishes, I might go back again. . . . No, I'm not going. . . . O.K., I'll tell you what—I'll go back as a bunny."[21]

After his performance, he believed everything had gone smoothly. Even the word in the Green Room after the set was good. But a few hours later, Bill Hicks received a phone call in his hotel room from Letterman executive producer Robert Morton, telling him he'd been cut. According to Hicks, here are some key quotes from that conversation: "You killed out there," Morton said, but went on to tell Hicks that the CBS office of standards and practices felt that some of the material was unsuitable for broadcast.

"Ah, which material exactly did they find . . ."

"Well, almost all of it."

"Bob, they're just jokes. I don't want to be edited by you or anyone else. Why are people so afraid of jokes?"

Hicks summed up the experience as follows:

Comedy in the States has been totally gutted. It's commercialized. They don't have people on TV who have points of view because that defies the status quo, and we can't have that in the totalitarian mind-control government that runs the f***ing airwaves. I can't get a shot there. I get David Letterman a lot. I love Letterman, but every time I go on, we have tiffs over material. They love me, but his people have this fictitious mainstream audience they think they play to. It's untrue. It doesn't exist. I like doing the show, but it's almost like working a puzzle: How can I be me in the context of doing this material?[22]

One more example: Rob Lotterstein, former writer for *Will and Grace* and *Ellen*, has recently come under scrutiny for his current project *War at Home*, which received criticism because of some lines in the pilot that some deemed offensive to gays. A storyline in the show involved the possibility of one of the sons being gay. At one point, his sister remarks, "He's not gay, he's just a fag."

Lotterstein said, "Politically correct humor ain't that funny. The only way to make it funny on TV is to make fun of it, in my opinion. . . . I believe if no one gets nervous, it's probably not that interesting."[23]

Beyond the television studio, the workplace has arguably suffered the most in the PC backlash against fun and frivolity. I just read about a lawsuit filed in California in 1999, which epitomizes how crazy things have become in the workplace. It, too, involves the television world, but an aspect of TV land that I maintain should be a litigation-free zone when it comes to inappropriate speech. Amaani Lyle is a former writer's assistant on the NBC series *Friends*. It had been Lyle's job to record anything that any of the writers said in skull sessions. Given that the show deals with sex, the writers talk about—you guessed it, sex. So what did Lyle do? She sued for—yes, sexual harassment.

"Sometimes, typically at 2 or 3 in the morning, comedy writers make jokes they never expect anyone else to hear. These are trotted out exclusively for the pleasure of punchy, bleary-eyed co-workers whose senses of humor have been hardened by years of professional wear-and-tear. One writer might start with the story of a humiliating colonic, which might trigger speculation about what a particular network executive would look like dressed in bondage gear, which could inspire a poem composed entirely of venereal diseases. 'If someone put out a transcript of what goes on in a writers' room, it would be very, very hard to explain,' explains Diane English, creator of the CBS sitcom *Murphy Brown*. 'I can remember some nights lying on the floor screaming with laughter, thinking if anyone was here with a tape recorder, my God, how horrible.'"[24] Well, Lyle had a pen, not a tape recorder, but the net effect was the same.

In her suit, which began with a complaint of racial discrimination, Lyle says that, while recording anything the writers said, she was subjected to her bosses' dirty, personal, and just plain weird banter. (This, to me, is akin to a sanitation worker complaining that he had been exposed to trash.) Lyle said that one writer passed around a "dirty little coloring book that would allow a person to make the pictures anatomically correct, and another enjoyed blacking out the letters on scripts to change the word *Friends* to the word 'penis.'" What I love about this litigation is the Warner Brothers defense, which is, essentially, "Yeah, and your point is what?" In other words, Warner Brothers doesn't dispute that the *Friends* writers were often lewd, crude, and extraordinarily vulgar. The excuse/defense is that they are comedy writers.[25]

While this won't come as welcome news to my employer, Infinity Broadcasting, the climate around my morning radio program is one of total mockery of the PC trends. I am a believer in the need for maintaining a creative environment, even for a talk-radio program that is mostly front-page news driven. And part of that environment demands a free flow of ideas including, and especially, humor. So in the wee hours of the morning, as I am preparing my program for broadcast surrounded by TC, my producer; Greg Stocker, our technical producer; and Joan Jones, who does the news; we let it all fly. And if somebody makes a particularly politically incorrect statement, or tells an off-color joke, the common response is "somebody go type that up for the complaint." (By now the complaints could fill a law library.)

My point here is that work environments (not mine, obviously) have become breeding grounds for intolerance—intolerance of a laugh here and there. I am not condoning pinching fannies at work. Or maliciously making fun of people. Nor discrimination. I support no glass ceilings. I am just embracing some common sense, some levity, and some lightening up in general.

We live in such an increasingly humorless society that I have wondered whether someone whose humor is ethnically based, meaning politically incorrect, could become successful if launching a career today. Not minorities. White guys. In other words, while it is acceptable for a guy like Chris Rock to utilize racial and ethnic humor in his act, and I happen to think he is gifted with his craft, I doubt a white guy could successfully launch a career today doing the same thing.

And who better to ask about that than the greatest practitioner of ethnic humor in our time, Jackie Mason. Jackie Mason is the master. I love his humor. I have seen him many, many times on Broadway and elsewhere, and I think his humor is actually healthy. He brings to the surface those things we're all thinking but are afraid to say, and better there be some kind of airing than to allow some sentiments to go unexpressed.

I remember a few years ago, my wife and I went to see Jackie Mason on Broadway and, as luck would have it, we sat two seats away from Barbara Walters. After the show, we went backstage to pay our respects to Jackie. I think a recent appearance on my radio program had enabled me to do that. Anyway, it was just the three of us for forty-five minutes, and Jackie was aware of the fact that

Barbara Walters had been in the house. When we told him she was two seats away, he wanted to know how she reacted to the show.

Well, the truth was that she was a deer in headlights. All night long, as Jackie Mason told jokes about Jews, Wasps, Arabs, Asians, men, women, gays, and just about every other way society can be broken down, she looked shell-shocked. Too bad. I think his humor is medicinal, and she missed the healing. He makes light of that which separates us, and in the process draws us together.

And I will say something else—that old adage about truth in jest is itself truthful. When I caught up with him, Mason told me the chilling effect kicks in only in one particular circumstance. Remember, he didn't write his reply. I hit him cold with the subject, and he delivered his response rapid fire:

> It's just an imaginary problem because, periodically, if you say something about blacks, a white audience gets panicky and nervous because whites are guilt-ridden people when it comes to blacks. Every time you see people at a dinner table, any white people at a dinner table, mention the word black, everybody suddenly becomes a detective and their heads starts spinning all around the building because they're panicky that a black person may have heard the word "black" some place, and they'll misinterpret, they'll reinterpret, they'll accuse, or they'll be disturbed, and people are so frightened, helpless, and nervous about the possibility of a black person hearing any word from a white person about anything with reference to a black human being. This is a sickness of the white people who are nervous in general, walking around panicky.[26]

Of course, now that I'd opened the door, Mason could not help using my question to do a little comedy himself. "It happens to me, I get nervous myself. I went to get into a taxi, and I saw a black driver, and I got scared, so I said, 'Listen, do me a favor, take me wherever you want, it's up to you.'"

Jackie Mason, the king of the borscht belt, is truly a deep thinker who offered me an explanation for what drives the reticence of whites to be any part of humor that uses blacks as a punch line.

Time for more a little more shtick.

> A Jew gets mad, he'll sue. A black person gets mad, he might rap you in the mouth or who knows what he might do to you. White people are

basically just sick with guilt, with complexes about it, so they overcompensate every time a black person is involved. If a black person hits somebody over the head with a pipe, everybody's afraid to mention that he was actually black. They remember there was a pipe; they remember the person. If they remember the person they remember he was colored, not necessarily a black person, maybe it was a Jew with a tan."

(I love this guy! If you're not laughing, close my book, now.)

But when you reverse it, you notice that there are no ethnic fears in this country because when black people are talking they'll call whites pigs every day in every show and you know what happens? The white people applaud it! Whenever black people call them names, they want to pay penance to the blacks. As soon as the blacks say, "White people are lowlifes, racist pigs, and degenerates," the white people applaud and applaud as if to say "call me names for a few hours, maybe I'll feel a little bit better that I'm such a low-life all my life and I've hurt you so much and I'm so responsible for every problem you got. Maybe if I laugh loud enough I can prove to you that I'm pleading for your forgiveness."

The fact of the matter is, the worst prejudice right now exists from the black people who are calling you a racist, because there are very few white racists left in this country. There's nothing more disgusting than calling me a racist without knowing whether I'm a racist or not because I'm a different color.

Mason told me there is no dearth of this kind of humor. What is significant is who is making the delivery. "There's all kinds of racist humor today, more than ever before. You hear nothing but ethnic jokes all the time about Polish people, Irish people, all kinds of people, and you never hear anything about political correctness. You only hear the words political correctness when the word 'black' is mentioned and all of a sudden all the white people go into a state of shock."[27]

Joe Piscopo of *Saturday Night Live* fame is yet another comedian with whom I had the chance to kick this subject around. Piscopo was a part of SNL's first major overhaul of the cast in 1980. The original cast members—John Belushi, Dan Aykroyd, Jane Curtin, and Gilda Radner—had left. Most of the new members were busts: forgotten names like Tony Rosato, Mitchell Kriefman, Yvonne

Hudson, Charles Rocket, and Patrick Weathers. Of that group, only Eddie Murphy and Piscopo had long runs on the show.[28]

More recently, Piscopo has successfully launched a variety show of sorts at the Copa Lounge at the Sands Atlantic City Hotel and Casino. I wanted to know from him whether, in 2005, he had to be mindful of the PC police.

"It is very, very difficult, and when we go to the Copa Room I'm careful because I really take the high road," he told me. "I just try to keep it politically correct. However . . . last week it was a *Saturday Night Live* weekend. Victoria Jackson was in . . . and Don Novella came in. We walk the line and we became politically incorrect because that's what *Saturday Night Live* is, but I make sure I tell the audience that. I ask the audience—in essence, I'll say, 'Can I tell a joke?' I make it fun because, lemme tell you something, 100 percent of the time the audience goes, 'Yeah, tell the joke, tell the joke!' and then I'll tell the politically incorrect joke and of course they love it but, absolutely, in a room, in a comedy room, it's not so bad, but out there it's very, very difficult. You're right, Jackie Mason would have trouble if he were starting out today."[29]

That's a shame.

20

Stamps of Disapproval

One of the big lies of political correctness is its tendency to reduce everything to a black-and-white issue. On the one hand, European descendents are lumped together into a plain, stale, old Wonder Bread patriarchal culture that is supposedly riddled with bigotry, racism, and a dozen forms of xenophobia. And on the other is the wonderfully rich, diverse, burgeoning, open-minded, culturally valuable contribution of _____ (fill in favorite ethnic minority or oppressed group here). In reality, however, intolerance is not restricted to whites only, and it can be highly educational (not to mention, entertaining) to watch what happens when things get a bit more complicated than the promoters of political correctness would lead us to believe.

A recent coincidence of news stories exposed this oversimplification rather nicely. In the first instance, the same tired, black-and-white template of political correctness was applied to the activities of a U.S. corporation. Go figure. It went something like this: Philadelphia-based retailer Urban Outfitters came under fire for selling a T-shirt that read: "New Mexico, Cleaner than Regular Mexico."

The Anti-Defamation League was (surprise, surprise) not amused. "This is saying that the country of Mexico is a dirty place," said Barry Morrison, regional director of the civil rights group. "Dirty can be interpreted figuratively and literally."[1]

Incidentally, this T-shirt controversy should not be confused with previous scandals involving the retailer. Two years ago, it stopped selling a game called "Ghettopoly" after protests by black civil rights leaders. Last year, it halted sales of a T-shirt that read: "Everyone Loves A Jewish Girl" surrounded by dollar signs after the Anti-Defamation League objected. A "Voting Is for Old People" T-shirt similarly angered pro-voting groups."[2]

Hmm, do you think Urban Outfitters might be enjoying the free publicity?! PC disciples may find the shirts outrageous, but Outfitters clearly realizes that teens will rush to buy something edgy and taboo.

I invited José Quiñonez, the founder of BlueLatinos.org, an "internet-based organization of progressive Latinos throughout the country," to discuss the latest T-shirt controversy. José described the purpose of Blue Latinos saying, "Basically, what we do is we organize ourselves online so that we can have our voices heard. You know, in cases like this, we can mobilize and put pressure on companies that are kind of being anti-immigrant or anti-Latino, so that way they can feel our pressure."

José called the T-shirt "soft racism" and urged people to visit his Web site and sign a petition asking the president of Urban Outfitters to discontinue sales and discard its inventory.[3]

I suggested to José that the T-shirt simply expresses a perception of Mexico shared by many, like me, who have visited Tijuana or have witnessed the blight across the border from El Paso or some other border town. In that sense, New Mexico is certainly cleaner than regular Mexico, and so there's truth in jest.

José responded, saying, "Well, you can think about that in many different ways. I mean I am looking at it from the perspective about conjuring up this racist idea of the dirty Mexican and that, in fact, is what a lot of Latinos, progressive Latinos, sort of think about when we read that message. Now, of course you can talk about the environment; you can talk about the water; you can talk about all those things; those might be all true, but that is not the point. The point is that here is a shirt that is actually demeaning of a certain segment of the population of our country, and right now is not the time to actually be dividing us in such a way. So, we object to it because it does conjure up this idea of the 'dirty Mexican' and I don't think that is fair."[4]

"That's not fair!" It's the constant refrain of the PC crowd, and I firmly believe it jeopardizes genuine instances of discrimination. Consider a hypothetical situation involving what I call the "saturation effect." Suppose someone is denied a position, or denied a promotion, or denied an apartment lease because they are Hispanic. They go to the legal system and seek redress but then they come in front of jurors who have been saturated with stories of political correctness; that is, they have become so conditioned to so many complaints about so many different things that they don't take the person seriously, or as seriously as they should, who is denied the job, or denied the housing. After all, they heard that boy-who-cried-wolf complaint about the T-shirt and what was the big deal about that?

Well, I think we have reached that saturation point. You see, political correctness is an all-or-nothing proposition. Rather than say, "It's wrong, but you've got to pick and choose your battles and, in the bigger scheme of life, this T-shirt is just not worth working yourself into a lather about," political correctness stomps its foot and insists, "That's not fair!"—no matter how small the stakes are in the matter.

"A fanatic," according to Winston Churchill, "is one who can't change his mind and won't change the subject." That pretty much describes the preachers of PC, if you ask me.

Well, maybe it isn't fair—or then again, maybe it is if you consider that what comes around, goes around.

I'm referring to the other news story to cross my desk at about the same time as the Mexico T-shirt controversy—only this one turned PC's black vs. white template inside out.

The fiftieth anniversary of Memín Pinguín, a Mexican comic book character, was not a joyous occasion, even though his half-century in print was recently celebrated with a commemorative postage stamp series. In PC terms, Memín could be described as an economically disadvantaged, mentally challenged, Afro-Mexican boy.

Yet he is much more offensive to some than that description would suggest. His offensiveness is due to his thick lips, protruding ears, and bulging eyes—all of which, critics say, are reminiscent of the Little Black Sambo of the postbellum South. It doesn't help, either, that Memín's washerwoman mother looks like Aunt Jemima. As a result, the outrage over the commemorative stamps was swift, vocal, and given the PC climate we live in, rather predictable.

For starters, the NAACP called the stamps "injurious to black people who live in the United States and Mexico."[5] Still, the Mexican government stood behind their decision to release the stamps and, at their unveiling, the comic's publisher, Manelick De La Parra Vargas, said that the character helped many Mexicans learn to read in the '50s and '60s. Civil rights advocates countered that while Memín may be well intentioned yet hapless, he nevertheless reinforces stereotypes of blacks as lazy, devious, and uneducated.[6] Sergio Penalosa, an activist in Mexico's small black community, said, "One would hope the Mexican government would be a little more careful and avoid continually opening wounds." Penalosa added: "But we've learned to expect anything from this government, just anything."[7]

Right on cue, Reverend Jesse Jackson spoke out on the issue, saying the stamps "insult people around the world" and urged President Bush to push Mexico to take the stamps off of the market. It was Jackson's second clash in as many months with the Mexican government.

In May of 2005, President Vicente Fox shocked many by stating that Mexican migrants in the U.S. were taking jobs that "not even blacks want." Fox later apologized for any offense caused by the remarks and insisted his comments were misinterpreted.[8]

Jackson said that "the impact of [the Memín stamps] is worse than what the president said," referring to the comments Fox made in May.[9] The National Legal and Policy Center (NLPC) refuted Jackson's comments, saying that they rang hollow. They accused him of "selective outrage" with regard to his protests of the stamps since Jackson had previously hosted a speech by the blatantly anti-Semitic Louis Farrakhan in June—accepting money from Toyota to underwrite the event.[10]

The Mexican government continues to maintain that the comic book character is simply misunderstood by people outside of their culture—that Memín "had, in fact, done a lot to fight racism."[11] A spokesman for President Fox said that the comic has promoted family values and understanding for decades and that the comic was "not racist, it's exactly the opposite."[12]

In addition to Mexico, Memín remains a popular magazine in Puerto Rico, Venezuela, Peru, Argentina, Chile, Panama, Colombia, the Philippines, and other countries. At its peak, it had a weekly circulation of one and a half million issues in Mexico; as of mid-2005, it sells over 100,000 issues a week. There's even been discussion about bringing Memín to television and the big screen.[13] It should not be surprising, therefore, that by mid-July, 2005, "the 750,000 Memín postage stamps that had sparked the criticism were sold out."[14] And though they have a face value of about $3.50, they were going for $30 to $40 dollars on eBay.[15]

The debate has sparked some, including columnist Gregory Kane, to question which image actually does more damage to black people: the image of Memín Pinguín or the images of rappers such as 50 Cent promoting crime and violence. Kane describes an issue of the *XXL* magazine dubbed "The Jail Issue" which pays homage to "hip hop's incarcerated soldiers" and features 50 Cent and Tony Yayo seemingly in handcuffs on the cover.

NAACP spokesman John White said comparing the stamps to the magazine cover was like "apples to oranges" but did say that the NAACP hopes rappers "would portray more positive role models than they do."[16]

Others refuse to consider comparisons; they believe the "monkey boy" is an unparalleled "degradation and mockery of the very Black race that flows through most Mexicans' veins."[17]

I'm more inclined to agree with those who look beyond the black face. Hector Ayala, an English teacher at the Cholla High Magnet School in Tucson, Arizona, is one such person. His recent opinion piece, so refreshingly thoughtful, spoke of a Mexican comic character named Memín Pinguín: "It was a funny, entertaining, poignant comic about a small African-Mexican kid, drawn in black face . . . who had three close friends: street-wise Carlos; the well-off Ricardo and intelligent, motherless Ernesto."

Ayala describes the powerful, positive impact this "culturally aware" comic book, which dealt with tough, mature issues such as poverty, alcoholism, and death, had on his young mind, as well as others:

> Memín Pinguín became to me, my family and friends, as well as to Mexico, as important a cultural icon as Mickey Mouse and Bugs Bunny were in America. . . .
>
> Never did I or anyone I know feel he was anyone to laugh at, to ridicule, and as kids, we all secretly wished we could have become part of his group of friends. He was a likable, mischievous, affable character that, like it or not, is and has been part of the Mexican culture and has meant a great deal to many children.

And though recognizing how the black-faced caricature could be misrepresented by today's sensibilities, Ayala concludes by contrasting the positive influence this character had on his culture—teaching Mexican children "how to love our mothers, how to be loyal to friends, how to apologize for mistakes and how to hug everyone lovingly and unabashedly"—with the negative influence of today's outspoken critics.

> This is much ado about nothing. Like citizens in the Stalinist Soviet Union, people are now expected to rewrite history so as to appeal to the sensibilities of certain oversensitive people.
>
> As a cultural icon, Memín Pinguín should indeed be commemorated in a stamp. Maybe this makes [Jesse] Jackson jealous.[18]

So there you have it. Hector is right—this whole thing is way overblown. Blacks complain about Mexicans; meanwhile, Mexicans complain about the New Mexicans. We are all walking around on eggshells, and I wish we would all just lighten up a bit.

I would much rather live in a society relaxed enough to enjoy occasional light-hearted jokes about ethnic stereotypes than live among thin-skinned, hand-wringing schoolmarms looking to MUZZLE anyone or anything they deem "unfair."

21

Can't We All Just Get Along?

Yeah, I know, it was Rodney King who famously delivered that line.[1] And ever since, I have been repeating him, usually in jest. But this time I mean it.

The fact that we've become MUZZLED is not only the fault of the Left. There are plenty of conservative-initiated actions, overreactions more specifically, that have similarly had the effect of stifling words and actions. The failure to permit those with debilitating illnesses who get relief from smoking pot to do so is but one example. The refusal of the Bush administration to take down Fidel Castro by trading with him, and unleashing the economic power of capitalism on Cuba, instead of perpetuating the failed embargo is another. Treating that which exists in a Petri dish the same as a fetus viable outside a womb, and therefore limiting medical advance, is one more example of what I consider to be overreaction on the Right, which, like the instances I have been describing, has the effect of keeping us a bit too buttoned up.

Here is one more. Intolerance of gays and lesbians. I consider this to be a form of right-wing political correctness. It is the product of a political system where, too often, people suit up in the jersey of their usual party or ideological affiliation without giving consideration to opposing points of view.

That happens on the Left and on the Right. The conservative who rails against gay relationships because that's what conservatives do is no better than the liberal who opposes Indian mascots or hands out trophies to the kids just for showing up lest someone's feelings get hurt.

Some conservatives need to *relax* when it comes to gays and lesbians. And so, too, do some liberals. Nothing seems to bring out the extremes as does any debate on gay rights.

Let me get a few things out of the way.

I'm all for the nuclear family. I belong to one. A man. A woman. A couple of kids. Usually, it works.

And I agree with those who suggest that, when all else is equal, the intact traditional family unit fosters the best environment for its members from a variety of standpoints. Chief among those benefits is child rearing. Kids, I think, are best served when raised in a two-parent, heterosexual household. (So far, this doesn't seem like much of a condemnation of the Right, does it?)

Senator Rick Santorum is a friend and weekly guest on my radio program. We agree more often than not, but we have areas of sharp differences. Even in those circumstances where I think he is wrong, such as his role in the attempt at federal intervention in the case of Terry Schiavo, I find myself admiring his principled positions. He's like the late Frank L. Rizzo in this regard. Both stand for something in an age of blow-dried, poll-dependent politicians.

Senator Santorum recently wrote a book called *It Takes a Family*, a retort of sorts to Hillary's *It Takes a Village*. In the book, Santorum writes: "Marriage matters because children matter. Without marriage, children suffer. There is simply no better investment parents can make in their children's future than a healthy marriage."[2]

It's hard to argue with that assertion, particularly in the face of the data he cites which suggests that kids living in single-parent households are more likely to suffer physical, emotional, or educational neglect; are at greater risk as teens to use drugs; are more likely to receive poorer grades, have attendance problems, and experience higher drop-out rates; and are more likely to have behavior or emotional problems.

You could probably carry those arguments even further than Senator Santorum would approve. The data he cites is the same sort of information that caused Steven Levitt and Stephen Dubner, in their bestseller called *Freakonomics*, to conclude that abortion fights crime, a finding I am sure Senator Santorum shudders to hear![3] But Levitt and Dubner make logical sense.

Levitt, a University of Chicago economics professor, recently received the John Bates Clark Medal, which is awarded every two years to the best American economist under forty. Dubner is his writing companion. Levitt studied why crime dropped in America in the 1990s.

Levitt debunked the usual explanations: innovative police strategies, more prisons, bursting of the crack bubble, aging, gun laws, the economy, more cops, and various other rationales.

Instead, Levitt offered legalized abortion as a more likely explanation. It is indeed a freaky notion but one which, upon reflection, makes total sense.

He notes that, by 1970, five states had made abortion entirely legal and widely available while the rest of the nation followed in 1973 after *Roe v. Wade*. That means that the early 1990s were when those born immediately after *Roe* would have reached late teens, a criminal's prime.

"What sort of woman was most likely to take advantage of *Roe v. Wade*? Very often she was unmarried or in her teens or poor, and sometimes all three. What sort of future might her child have had? One study has shown that the typical child who went unborn in the earliest years of abortion would have been 50 percent more likely than average to live in poverty; he would also have been 60 percent more likely to grow up with just one parent. These two factors— childhood poverty and single-parent households—are among the strongest predictors that a child will have a criminal future," writes Levitt.[4]

Levitt claims that the five states that had legal abortion before *Roe v. Wade* saw their crime drop before the other forty-five states. Levitt is a number-cruncher extraordinaire who does not want his work to affect abortion policy. Having spent time with him, I can attest to the fact that he offers those findings not with a political agenda, but with the dispassionate analysis befitting the extraordinary number-cruncher that he is.

His findings are not about abortion policy. They are about families and the crime-stopping value of intact families. The bottom line here is that abortion is a manifestation of fatherless homes and so, too, is crime.

My goal here is not to examine abortion in depth. I simply start with the premise that traditional families function best and create the most conducive environment to sound child-rearing. Where I differ from my very conservative counterparts is the belief that, as a result of this reality, efforts to somehow bond same-sex couples must be opposed.

One has nothing to do with the other.

Show me the heterosexual man leading a life as a husband and father who would, given the legalization of same-sex marriage, abandon his family and get together with another man? He does not exist. No lack of license is inhibiting someone who would otherwise turn to a gay lifestyle.

So while I appreciate the societal value of intact families headed by heterosexuals and think government needs to focus on what it can do to create more of them, it's my view that the increasing number of divorces in this country has nothing to do with a rise in gay rights. Half of American families are not divorcing because Daddy has run off with a guy from the office. C'mon already.

I'll tell you something else. There aren't enough gay guys out there to disrupt American families. The proof came on 9/11. (Prepare for another tangent!)

In 1948, Alfred Kinsey did some research and concluded that 10 percent of the population was gay. Ever since, there has been great debate about that figure. It's not just cocktail chatter either. There is power at stake because gays draw political support from politicians' perception of their numbers. It's all about the votes. But information from the 9/11 tragedy cast doubt on Kinsey's number.

Kenneth R. Feinberg was the special master of the fund created by Congress to compensate the victims of 9/11. He made headlines when he cleared the way for the compensation of surviving gay partners.[5] Feinberg's decision could have enabled gay survivors to lay claim to the average of $1.85 million that the government gave to families of survivors. That's a big incentive to come out of the closet. The wishes of next-of-kin were to be considered as part of the funding decision.

So, if we assume Kinsey to be correct, 10 percent or so of the victims of 9/11 would have been gay or lesbian. Assuming a total of 3,000 victims, that would equate to 300 gay victims. Now, not all of the 300 could be expected to be in committed relationships. Line up any 300 people who are straight or gay and many will not be in such relationships. So, let's cut it in half and take the number down to 150. In fact, let's be cautious and cut it by another third. Say that 100 of the 300, or one-third were in committed relationships.

But here is the rub: there are only twenty-two known surviving gay partners![6]

That suggests that the gay population among the victims of 9/11 was less than one percent! Some may say we'll never get an accurate picture because of a lingering social stigma that is attached to being gay. I can think of 1.85 million reasons that no surviving partner would remain in the closet.

Others may say gays were underrepresented in the tragedy. I think the victims were a pretty random cross-section. Men, women, blacks, whites, Americans, foreigners, cops, firefighters, busboys, brokers, the young, and the old. Obviously none of them volunteered for this fate.

By contrast, Professor Kinsey relied entirely on volunteers. And 25 percent of his survey sample was made up of prisoners who, arguably, had a higher proportionate share of individuals who had engaged in homosexual behavior. So this just might be the most accurate assessment of the percentage of gay population ever.

Don't get me wrong; even if the gay population is closer to 1 percent than 10 percent, it should not alter the debate about compensation. Despite opposing gay marriage, I think we should compensate surviving gay partners as long as there is evidence of a committed relationship.

William Randolph and Wesley Mercer are one case. They were together for twenty-six years until Mercer died on 9/11. Mercer, who was vice president of corporate security at Morgan Stanley, has been credited with saving all but two of the company's employees. Mercer never divorced his wife, so she will be getting his Army pension, Social Security, and worker's compensation.[7] I think Randolph should share in the fund created by Congress.

In the summer of 2002, child abductions grabbed all the headlines. Then, in 2003, it was gay rights that became the topic *du jour*.

Canada sanctioned gay marriage. Even Senator Santorum got in hot water by saying something that was interpreted as his having equated homosexuality with incest, which I don't think is what he was saying. Then the Supreme Court threw out the Texas sodomy statute, which is what Santorum had been anticipating, and in my hometown, the Philly Boy Scouts tried to institute a "don't ask, don't tell" policy. (More about them in a moment.)

Episcopalians elevated their first gay bishop. *Queer Eye for the Straight Guy* became a TV rage. And the University of Michigan put a course in the curriculum called "How to Be Gay."

It was a lot to process, and Americans remain conflicted as to how to react. But, sitting in my back yard in the middle of that summer, smoking a cigar on a hot Sunday afternoon, I think I sorted it out.

I had an epiphany while reading the wedding announcements in the *New York Times*. It was not the usual Buffy is marrying Chet but, rather, a photo of two guys caught my attention. "Gregory Krzyminski, Raymond Konz" it said above a picture of two men in tuxes. Gregory is the son of a steelworker from Chicago, and Raymond is the son of a Milwaukee detective.[8]

Wait a minute.

That doesn't fit the stereotype. Sounds way too macho an upbringing for a couple of guys with sugar in their pockets. I was expecting a career in the theater. Or a hairstylist.

Here's why that's relevant.

If sexual orientation is a part of someone's wiring and not a matter of choice, then there should be no debate as to whether we afford the full protection of the law to homosexuals. Common decency dictates that, if a person is born with some characteristic that separates them from the norm, we must take measures to assist with their assimilation and ensure that whatever separates them from the mainstream is not used to hinder their attainment of a full and prosperous life.

That's why I was interested to learn about the backgrounds of Raymond and Gregory, so I called them up. At the time, Raymond told me they've been together for twenty-three years and are both Roman Catholics from "strong Polish backgrounds." Not surprisingly, both men said there was nothing in their upbringing that prompted or promoted a gay lifestyle, and that their sexual orientation comes down to their wiring.

"Sending our announcement to the *New York Times* was a choice. Sexual orientation is not," Raymond said.[9] I think he's right.

While I remain uncomfortable in calling a same-sex union a "marriage," my afternoon in the back yard shed some light on the way things should be.

Apply their example to your own childhood. I'll bet you can identify someone with whom you grew up who turned out gay even though their environment was remarkably similar to your own. I know I can.

One of the guys with whom I grew up has left this earth due to AIDS. He was a terrific guy growing up. You wouldn't see anything in our school-days photographs that would lead you to believe he was any different than the other guys on the block. But looking back, I now see so clearly the signs that he was headed for a gay lifestyle. Don't get me wrong, there were no incidents, no compromising situations, nothing said, and nothing acted upon. But in a way that is hard to articulate, things were different with him.

I think about him when callers phone my radio program and suggest homosexuality is a choice. Because you could never convince me that he chose homosexuality. The lifestyle chose him, not the other way around.

And if the lifestyle chose him, who am I, or who are we, to somehow penalize him for fulfilling his destiny? I know some will respond that I am laying the predicate for some kind of disability claim on behalf of those with an alternative lifestyle. That's not my aim, nor do I believe that to be warranted. I'm just offering my own limited life experience on the choice question.

The bottom line is that the knee-jerk intolerance to a lifestyle for which no one volunteers and which does not itself jeopardize the foundation of a heterosexual marriage has got to end. But tolerance has to be a two-way street. Live and let live has to apply to all. While gays and lesbians wish to be left alone to pursue their interests, so, too, must be those who disapprove of the lifestyle.

I'm not supporting denial of a job, or housing, or some other life essential to someone on the basis of sexuality, but I am supporting denial of admission to a club. Not just any club. I am thinking of the Boy Scouts.

The Boy Scouts of America, I'm talking nationally, require Scout leaders, not members, to be straight.[10] This leadership requirement has withstood the scrutiny of the United States Supreme Court.[11]

Nevertheless, some local scouting branches have expressed their dissenting opinions regarding the decision to be antigay. The Philadelphia scouting organization, known as the Cradle of Liberty Council, was one of these dissenting chapters. They disagreed with the national policy and tried to distinguish themselves by not discriminating against homosexuals. However, when they put their plan into action, they realized they were not as autonomous as they had hoped. Once the national BSA got wind of the local chapter's intentions, it vowed to revoke the Philly charter. Therefore, the Cradle of Liberty Council was left with no choice but to go back on their pledge not to discriminate. In doing so, they forced Gregory Lattera, an adult volunteer leader from South Philly, to leave the organization.[12]

This reversal of the Cradle of Liberty Council's decision angered one of the group's donors, The United Way, and caused them to cancel the second half of a $400,862 grant, targeted to a program called "Learning for Life."[13] According to an article in the *Philadelphia Inquirer* soon after the decision, "The United Way has a policy of non-discrimination based on sexual orientation and does not provide funds to organizations that discriminate."[14]

In the process of the United Way's being PC, guess who got hurt? Not some modern incarnation of Hitler youth but, rather, 35,000 urban kids in grades K-12 who participate in the program. The values-based life skills program was run in collaboration with the Philadelphia School District.[15] David H. Lipson Jr., chairman of the Cradle of Liberty Council's board, described the Learning for Living program as follows: "It's character-building training for kids. The program cost $600,000 a year and the United Way gave us $400,000."[16]

"We developed Learning for Living to reach areas not traditionally served by scouting," said Patrick Coviello, then the chief operating officer for the local scouts, when I interviewed him. "For many kids this is the first and only time that they learn about different careers, how to get ready for their first job interview and how to prevent drug abuse."[17]

This is precisely my point. The program was providing a beneficial service to the youth of the city of Philadelphia. It was absolutely nondiscriminatory! It had absolutely nothing to do with traditional scouting. And it had nothing to do with homosexuality. The schools, companies, and organizations who partner with the scouts in Learning for Life select the leaders based on their standards, not the standards of the Boy Scouts of America.

But that wasn't good enough for the United Way of Southeastern Pennsylvania, which had an antidiscrimination policy and a wad of cash. It was this local United Way that had a problem with the national scout membership rules, and so they cut off the funding for the Philadelphia Scouts.

Gutless. That's what the United Way decision was.

And harmful too, to some who can ill afford the loss.

"Urban scouting is on life support and, if we do not reach an accommodation with the United Way, no one can guarantee its survival," Lipson explained to me on my radio program.[18]

At the time of the defunding by the United Way, they posted an explanation on their Web site. The United Way acknowledged the efforts of the local scouts to disassociate themselves from the national scout membership policy but decided to cut their funding nonetheless: "There was not sufficient organizational separation between Learning for Life and the overall Boy Scouts organizations" to be assured that United Way of Southeastern Pennsylvania dollars would only be issued for Learning for Life.[19]

Thereafter, in order for the United Way to be a funding conduit to Scouts, supporters would need to specifically designate that their donation go to the Cradle of Liberty Council and the United Way will be obligated to pass these funds onto the Scouts, despite their PC views.

By the way, the specific code for such contributions was number 00076. The hell with the United Way. If you agree that the Boy Scouts are deserving of support, then send a check. Their address is: Cradle of Liberty Council, 22nd and Winter Streets, Philadelphia PA 19103.

I have already sent the first $100.

22

Up in Smoke

Marijuana, Medicine, and the Myopic

Quick quiz. Read the following two columns of information. One of these lists gives just a few of the nasty consequences associated with one of the most lethal killers, by sheer numbers, on the planet. The other is Alberto Gonzales's list of the perils of smoking marijuana. See if you can figure out which one is legal in all fifty states and which one drove heavily armed federal agents in bullet-proof vests and Kevlar helmets into a standoff with a handful of wheelchair-bound invalids. (Take a peek at the end of the chapter to see if you guessed correctly).

COLUMN A

- contains about 4,000 chemical agents, including over 60 carcinogens[1]
- those under 40 have a five times higher chance of having a myocardial infarction (heart attack) than nonsmokers[2]
- creates immune system impairment[3]
- recognized by the World Health Organization (WHO) as a drug that provokes dependence[4]

COLUMN B

- contains more than 400 chemicals
- increases the risk of a heart attack by a factor of five for an hour after smoking
- weakens the immune system and raises the risk of lung infections
- is considered an addictive drug[5]

Before you get too far ahead of me here, let me draw your attention to the title of this chapter. I am *not* going to spill ink making common cause with Woody Harrelson or Willie Nelson. No, I am *not* going to sit back with a bong after finishing this piece. *I do not advocate the wholesale legalization of marijuana.* Nor do I believe in casting tobacco users off the cliffs of political correctness onto the rocks of hypersensitivity. After all, I am one of them. Tobacco user, that is.

Since college, I have enjoyed the pleasure of smoking cigars. Usually one per day. Never more than two. Yes, I know that this is not in the best interest of my health. It also happens to be a high point of my day when I get the chance to sit and smoke, read something that requires concentration, and do so in a quiet house with my dog at my feet. But I do not intend to advocate cigar smokers' rights, either.

What I want to address is the way that the rights of individuals with debilitating illnesses to smoke pot have been MUZZLED, as have the cancer research interests of those who have smoked cigarettes. There are some facts about *medical* marijuana—marijuana prescribed as a last resort by medical doctors to patients with chronic and often excruciating conditions—that have not been afforded sufficient attention and discussion. And I would suggest that, in its zeal to prosecute the War on Drugs, the federal government is just a few feet shy of a fair ball, perhaps a couple of inches outside the strike zone as well. If we really want to do something about tobacco use, we should stop ignoring the problem and get moving on some real honest-to-God *answers.*

What is the connection to the war on terror, you wonder? As I have tried to explain through true stories, in my view of the world, we're on the verge of banning the sort of rugged individualism that once defined this nation, in favor of rewarding the behavior of automatons. Andrew Susser was fired from Banc of America because he dared be different. He acted outside the box and was fired for it, despite that he'd committed no true indiscretion. Ditto for Kirk Reynolds. Patrick Cubbage lost his job, too, simply because he thought it appropriate to say "God Bless You" when presenting American flags to the families of dead soldiers. We hire men and women who lack the physical attributes to work in law enforcement because we're afraid to tell them they are too short for the job. So afraid to offend are we that red ink is now banned in many a school because it might upset the psyche of young students. Instead, we'll give you a trophy for mediocrity—happy now? There was a time when telling an inappropriate joke might get you slapped. Today it gets you fired, and sued. We want everybody happy. Everybody equal. Everybody looking, acting, and talking the same, and those who dare to be different will be damned. In short, we have become a society that is trigger-happy to be offended and unyielding in opposition to anyone who, at any time, says or does something that might be commonsensical, but runs contrary to these new, touchy-feely norms. That mind-set has extended to the war on terror.

We don't implement the commonsensical means of fighting the bad guys. Instead, we execute plans that we hope will get the job done without causing offense. We put our tails between our legs on Abu Ghraib instead of simply saying, "Hey, it was a half-dozen dopes out of 140,000; we're sorry, now give it a rest."

We search eighty-year-old blue-haired ladies the same way as Habib and Mohammed at airports, because no one has the stones to say, "Sorry fellows, but you resemble people trying to murder us—again—so we have to take a few precautions." We're gutless. We are yielding to forces at work in society who not only think they know what is best for themselves, but for all of us, and they seek to impose their utopian, "I'm OK, you're OK" view on everyone.

People need to be freed from this bondage and lead their lives as individuals. That means speaking out, acting out, joking aloud, and smoking pot if it makes their debilitating illness a little more bearable. And if you're one of those unlucky souls who has cancer because you defied the rules of good health, we extend our sympathies and promise not to be judgmental when whacking up the research money. After all, there are more of you dying of the Big C than all of the top-funded forms of cancer combined.

Let me try to convince you by relating an incredible, *true* story.

Our story begins a year shy of the Bicentennial in our nation's capital. Robert Randall, almost totally blinded by glaucoma and frustrated by the failure of conventional treatments, smoked joints rolled from homegrown marijuana plants. Arrested on August 27, 1975, Randall explained to Judge Washington of the D.C. Superior Court that he needs the relief that only marijuana provided him.

This "necessity" defense is actually a pretty specific and rather narrow defense rolled out by criminal defendants when: (1) the defendant did not intentionally bring about the circumstances that precipitated the unlawful act; (2) the defendant could not accomplish the same objective using a less offensive alternative; and (3) the evil sought to be avoided was more heinous than the unlawful act perpetrated to avoid it.[6]

Think of the guy who burns down a field to stop a larger forest fire. Judge

Washington of the D.C. Superior Court found for Robert, failing to find any harm substantial enough to outweigh losing his eyesight.

At the same time, Robert successfully petitioned the federal government to expand the Compassionate Investigational New Drug (IND) program, administered by the Food and Drug Administration. Today, the regulations allow the FDA to green light an IND for emergencies if "(i) The drug is intended to treat a serious or immediately life-threatening disease; (ii) There is no comparable or satisfactory alternative drug or other therapy available to treat that stage of the disease in the intended patient population."[7] Thirty years ago, however, the phrase "politically correct" hadn't even been coined, and our guy actually got the federal government to supply him with marijuana cigarettes—three hundred a month.[8]

Randall didn't stop there. He advocated *expanding* the IND program so others might benefit. Others did get into the program. But shortly after AIDS patients began enrolling in significant numbers in the 1980s, the federal government realized it couldn't "just say no" and dispense pot.

Today, seven people remain, grandfathered in when the program closed down in March of 1992.[9] Peter Guither, a blogger picked up by Salon.com, describes the process for the seven participants:

> They continue to get their marijuana on a fairly regular basis. They have to work with a pharmacy that's been approved by NIDA [the National Institute on Drug Abuse] and that has a secure safe. Then usually a five month supply is shipped at once, and the patient is informed so they can pick it up. The marijuana is grown on a farm at the University of Mississippi, mostly from seeds of Mexican origin, rolled and packaged at the Research Triangle Institute in North Carolina under the supervision of the National Institute on Drug Abuse.[10]

Remember that passage from the book of Job, "The Lord gave, and the Lord has taken away"?[11] Well, the federal government apparently took a page from the long-suffering Job and put it in the playbook for the Drug Enforcement Administration. Here's how Christopher Krohn, the mayor of Santa Cruz, California, described the events of September 5, 2002:

> My story begins on the morning of Sept. 5 when approximately 30 men, dressed in military fatigues and carrying automatic weapons, descended

on a small cooperative farm run by the Wo/Men's Alliance for Medical Marijuana in northern Santa Cruz County, about 65 miles south of San Francisco. They were pulling up organically grown marijuana plants.

When the Santa Cruz County Sheriff's Office learned what was going on, it was at a loss to explain who the intruders were or what type of response was in order. I didn't hear about the raid until 10 A.M., when I was called by members of the collective. I then telephoned the Santa Cruz police chief and other local officials. The chief hadn't heard anything either.

Later it became clear that the D.E.A. was making a raid. Agents collected more than 130 plants and arrested the founders of the medical marijuana collective, Valerie and Mike Corral.[12]

Now perhaps the good mayor was trying for a diplomatic tone in his piece for the *New York Times* three weeks after the raid, or perhaps things had just calmed down a bit since then. Regardless of his reasons, he neglected to mention precisely how the raid ended for the DEA. After chopping down all 130 plants (a quantity usually considered small potatoes by local law enforcement officials), but before making their way off the hospice grounds, the DEA agents were brought to a standstill.

In a real public relations disaster for the DEA, they were blocked by a small group of cancer and AIDS patients, some apparently in wheelchairs and others walking only with the assistance of a cane. It may not bring to mind the lone Chinese youth blocking a tank in Tiananmen Square, but the gross display of brute force by the DEA isn't exactly terribly reassuring either. One paraplegic polio patient at the facility woke up to see DEA agents, in full combat gear, pointing automatic guns at her and demanding that she get out of the bed pronto. They continued to insist even after noting her crutches and leg braces by her bed.[13]

Thus it seems you and I have been following Alice through Wonderland—a world where marijuana can be distributed for a quarter of a century by the federal government because of its medicinal value and yet confiscated from seriously ill patients in raids by men armed for close combat against insurgents in Fallujah. A world where the Supreme Court can uphold the government's right to prosecute medical marijuana users while expressing sympathy for them.

Straight down the rabbit hole to June of 2005. The Supreme Court has heard arguments in the case of two chronically ill women busted by DEA agents for smoking marijuana. Of course, Diane Monson and Angel Raich were doing so under doctors' supervision in California, where such use was sanctioned by the voters under Proposition 215 in 1996.

Diane Monson has suffered from back spasms since 1989. A forty-nine-year-old accountant living in the small Northern California town of Oroville,[14] she wrote in her brief to the Ninth Circuit Court of Appeals, "I use medical *cannabis* with the recommendation of my physicians for the treatment of my severe chronic back pain and spasms. . . . Without *cannabis*, these spasms would be tortuous and unbearable, no matter whatever other medications were available."[15]

With the help of marijuana, she owns and manages several rental properties, keeps an orchard full of apple, pear, peach, apricot, cherry, and peach trees, and volunteers teaching people to read.[16] Not exactly a hardened career-criminal.

And I swear I didn't make up her codefendant, "Angel" McClary Raich. You can't make up stuff this good. Angel is a thirty-nine-year-old mother of two teenagers who smokes medical marijuana to cope with an inoperable brain tumor, wasting syndrome, uterine tumors, endometriosis, and various other illnesses. And still, the decision to smoke did not come easy for her. In a *Washington Post* piece early this year, the reporter described the long road for Angel, who was partially paralyzed and in constant pain. In 1997, a nurse suggested medical marijuana.

> "I was really offended at the suggestion," said Raich, who is a pale 98 pounds on a 5-foot-4 frame. "I was very conservative. I was taught that drugs are bad. And I followed the law. I've never even gotten a speeding ticket."

When Raich's daughter approached her, though, asking her why she couldn't do the things "other mommies do," Raich made the decision to take drastic measures to get better.

> "I faced my own conservative ways and my own moral judgments and I realized that because I loved my children so much and so deeply—they are my world—that I would do everything I possibly could for them."[17]

So how did the Supreme Court rule? Did it abolish the medical marijuana laws in the twelve states that now have them? Did it condemn medical marijuana as the Justice Department has over the last few years?

Actually, nothing big happened at all. Nada.

In a 6-3 decision, conservative court members William Rehnquist and Clarence Thomas voted *in favor* of state-sanctioned medicinal use of marijuana and typically *liberal* justices John Paul Stevens and Ruth Bader Ginsburg were in the majority against it. However, the justices limited themselves to the narrow question of whether the federal government had the authority to prosecute people like Angel Raich and Diane Monson. The decision stated, "The question before us, however, is not whether it is wise to enforce the statute in these circumstances; rather, it is whether Congress' power to regulate interstate markets for medicinal substances encompasses the portions of those markets that are supplied with drugs produced and consumed locally."[18]

Obviously sympathetic to the plight of medical marijuana users, the justices' ruling does nothing to medical marijuana laws in the twelve states that allow supervised and controlled use.[19] Indeed, local and state officials are still not obligated to help federal agents with prosecutions. And when Ed Kubo, the U.S. attorney for Hawaii, indicated that doctors might get into trouble for prescribing marijuana, a firestorm of criticism forced him to retract his statement. Of course, he had already said that medical marijuana patients had nothing to fear so long as they observed the state restrictions.[20]

So where are we exactly? Here's what I know: This *isn't* about Cheech and Chong's lighting up a few in one of their forgettable, if funny, movies. There is nothing laughable about the suffering of Diane Monson or Angel Raich. Nor is this about the War on Drugs in which countless lives have been lost. I refer to the law-enforcement agents who lost their lives battling the spread of destructive poisons in our society and to the souls lost to addiction.

What this *is* about is the obvious benefit people with AIDS, people with cancer, and people with glaucoma (chronic diseases all)—get from a drug with side-effects not much different from tobacco.[21] And even if you don't agree with the Institute of Medicine, the American Academy of HIV Medicine, the American Academy of Family Physicians, the American Nurses Association, the American Public Health Association, the California Medical Association, the Lymphoma Foundation of America, the New York State Association of County Health Officials, and the Medical Society of the State of New York about the good that marijuana can do, you must at least concede that there just isn't the corrosive effect on society that one can easily associate with cocaine, heroin, or methamphetamines.[22]

Besides—if grown correctly—you can play thirty-six holes on the right hybrid cross between "Kentucky Bluegrass, Featherbed Bent, and Northern California Sensemilia" grass, then "take it home and just get stoned to the bejeezus-belt that night."[23] (If you need to look at the endnote to source that quote, close the book, find your receipt, and try to return it. You are not worthy!)

I know I have taken a couple of shots at tobacco thus far, suggesting that marijuana is arguably no worse for you than the stuff that Joe Camel or the Marlboro cowboy hawk legally every day. In truth, cigarette smoking is pretty damn bad for this country, and as we will see in a minute, politicians are falling over themselves to tell people where they can and cannot smoke.

Instead of shaving a few amendments off the Bill of Rights for the sake of some good press, however, let's get the smart types thinking about ways to cut the body count—namely, education and awareness—as well as medical research. We aren't doing nearly as much as we should to get the word out and to advance the medical options for dealing with its effects. And I believe that political correctness is partly to blame for our reluctance.

In 2004, for example, the National Cancer Institute spent twice as much on breast cancer as on lung cancer, even though lung cancer killed more than four times as many Americans.[24] No doubt women and those who have lost loved ones to breast cancer won't want to hear this, but the numbers don't lie. They show our priorities are way out of line. Put the PC-driven arguments aside for a moment and consider: the roughly 160,000 deaths anticipated from lung cancer this year are more than the total fatalities from the next four most deadly forms of the disease *combined*: colon cancer, pancreatic cancer, prostate cancer, and, yes, even breast cancer.[25]

What's the problem? Why the enormous difference? I buy the "shame on you" argument that most of us (rightly) associate lung cancer with cigarettes. As *Newsweek* noted recently, 87 percent of all cases of lung cancer result directly from smoking.[26] So we blame smokers for bringing it on themselves, while we pity the poor mother with breast cancer. "There's been a blame-the-victim mentality for lung cancer," says Dr. Margaret Spitz.[27]

Is this true? How, exactly, do we as a nation treat smokers?

I googled the phrase "smoking ban" and chose articles at random from *just the last seven days* (the first week of September) and found no less than four concerted government efforts to draw the noose just a little tighter around smokers.

Wisconsin: Advocates of the current ban on smoking in restaurants and bars in Madison are gearing up to fight desperate owners who have mounted their own campaign to save their businesses. Says Lisa Davidson, speaking for the Tobacco Free Dan County Coalition, "When you talk to different people, the numbers vary, one person says business is down 10 percent, another 20, another 33."[28] Never mind that all the statistics point the same way—down!

Pennsylvania: State legislators are considering a bill that would greatly expand the list of public places under the ban to include *all* commercial and retail stores, sports arenas, shopping malls, exhibition halls, and bars or taverns.[29] One frustrated restaurateur asked why the state doesn't just ban smoking in people's homes, since many people employ housekeepers: "The housewife or house-husband needs to put out a cigarette when Molly Maids shows up, but nobody talks about Molly Maids."[30]

Washington: In Novemeber 2005, voters passed Initiative 901. The measure extends smoking bans to all public buildings *and vehicles*, as well as restaurants, bars, bowling alleys, skating rinks (has this really even been an issue at your local skating rink?), card rooms, and mini-casinos. For good measure, the ban extends twenty-five feet beyond the doors and windows of these buildings, forcing most smokers out somewhere by either the dumpster out back or in the middle of the oncoming traffic. Violators can look forward to a fine of $100.[31]

Arizona: In one of the most oppressive efforts, a coalition of antismoking advocates has put together their own ballot initiative to limit smokers to "their homes, certain hotel rooms, on outdoor patios, and at other designated places"! Strictly taboo would be "all public places, including workplaces, office buildings, banks, bars, health care facilities, hotel and motel common areas, restaurants, sports arenas, and licensed child-care centers."[32]

At the end of 2005, *USA Today*, in a page one, above-the-fold story, reported that 39 percent of Americans are now living in areas covered by statewide or local laws limiting smoking. Whereas in 1985 there were fewer than two hundred such state and local laws in the USA, today there are more than two thousand, according to the Americans for Nonsmokers' Rights. And which is the most stringent law in the land? That Washington state ban I just mentioned. Vermont also went all the way, extending a ban in restaurants to bars and other workplaces. Rhode

Island enacted a comprehensive ban on smoking in all three places, too. Montana did the same but gave bars until 2009 to comply.[33]

Is it really any wonder that lung cancer is the Rodney Dangerfield of cancers when smokers have become convenient whipping-boys? You can say that they bring it on themselves, whereas other cancer patients are true victims. But think about it: smokers fall prey to an addictive habit that ultimately leads to an excruciating fatal malignancy—yet they aren't given fuzzy pink ribbons and no major cities are lighting up (so to speak) their skyline as a reminder "to protect themselves against this disease."[34] In fact, smokers are open to abuse that would be considered positively Neanderthal if directed at any politically correct group.

Exhibit "A" comes to us by way of my interview with Jack McKeon, a New Jersey state assemblyman from Essex County, with a *very* interesting idea. Just wait until you hear what he wants to do. He wants to ban smoking in cars!

When I spoke to him, he told me it was the distraction effect of a lit cigarette that troubled him more than the health effects. I told him if that was his aim, he might as well get rid of the radio and CD players as well. I asked him if his legislation addressed those other distractions, or just smoking. He told me only smoking because someone else's pending bill "looks to an overall category of distraction versus listing things in a category. I put the smoking bill in and fully expect that it would be soon merged into an overall bill dealing with any distraction in a vehicle."

MAS: I get it, so let me just—Assemblyman John McKeon— make sure I understand. There is a separate piece of legislation that has been introduced; it's not yet law that would address, in New Jersey, distraction generally, right?

Mr. McKeon: That is correct.

MAS: And it does not enumerate lipstick verses radio verses Wawa hoagie?

Mr. McKeon: That is absolutely correct, and you can understand why I didn't try to get into all those different categories.[35]

John McKeon is correct when he says smoking is a distraction to drivers. But so is lipstick. And the CD player. And the kids in the backseat. The windshield wipers. The heat. And the billboard for Hooters.

I'm sure he is well intentioned, but we could render him and his colleagues obsolete by simply making it unlawful to ignore common sense.

Let's admit it. As a country, we have not handled either medical marijuana or the issue of tobacco very well. In both instances, we have been told, "Here is something 'bad,'" and the knee-jerk reaction has been exactly wrong. Instead of tackling the problems, we pass laws that MUZZLE us.

To see what I mean, look back at the "Chinese Menu" with which we began this chapter. Did you guess correctly? When you get past all of the World Health Organization rhetoric and look at the two substances closely, the drug in Column A (tobacco) is said to have the same effects as the drug in Column B (pot).

And, while I am not suggesting that Mary Jane and the Marlboro Man are completely interchangeable, I do want to underscore the irony of our laws and public policies: we tell helpless patients they are not allowed to use medical *cannabis* even as our government is hooked on tobacco—or at least the tax revenue that rolls in because of our use of it—even when they know it's bad for us. It makes no sense.

Marijuana does, despite all protestations to the contrary, have some redeeming value in limited situations. Tobacco is bad for you, but bringing government *into my car* doesn't make as much sense as getting doctors cracking on lung cancer and getting us all smarter on the subject.

If we're going to cure our national myopia, conservatives need to lighten up about medical marijuana, and liberals need to start advocating for cancer research based on statistically proven, urgent need rather than gender, ethnicity, or other irrelevant factors.

23

Mumidiots

Every element of the tragic story I will spell out in the following extended paragraph is supported by sworn, trial testimony:

On December 9, 1981, a twenty-five-year-old Philadelphia police officer named Daniel Faulkner was working the midnight shift when he pulled over a Volkswagen going the wrong way on a one-way street (Locust Street) in Center City.[1] The neighborhood was dicey at best, and it was the middle of the night. Think hookers and druggies, not priests and choirboys. The driver of the Volkswagen was a guy named William Cook. Witnesses report that William Cook had opened the door of the Volkswagen and stepped out before Officer Faulkner was able to approach.[2] A witness testified that Cook was directed by Officer Faulkner to stand spread-eagle up against the Volkswagen. With Officer Faulkner behind him, Cook turned around and punched Officer Faulkner in the face.[3] Across the street, a taxi driver took interest. The taxi driver was William Cook's brother, Wesley Cook. Wesley Cook was a wannabe journalist and sometimes Blank Panther activist who had glorified violence toward police officers in some of his writings.[4] Wesley Cook was armed with a weapon he had lawfully purchased from a Philadelphia sporting goods store.[5] Wesley Cook ran across Locust Street, pulled out a pistol, and started shooting at the officer.[6] Cook fired his gun as he approached the curb where Officer Faulkner was standing, striking Faulkner in the back.[7] Wounded as he fell to the ground, the young cop was nevertheless able to get off a shot of his own. The bullet, which struck Wesley Cook in the stomach, was determined to have been shot from Officer Faulkner's .38-caliber gun.[8] With that bullet, Danny told the world exactly who had shot him. Wesley Cook then stood over the fallen officer and finished him off by shooting him in the head.[9] The ballistics of the case pointed to the bullets in Officer Faulkner's body as matching Cook's gun that was found at the scene.[10] Ballistics evidence also revealed that the attack occurred at close range.[11] There were four eyewitnesses called by the prosecution to testify against the defendant. And

Wesley Cook confessed to the crime when, in an odd twist of fate, both Officer Faulkner and his murderer were taken to Jefferson Hospital, just blocks from the shooting location. In the emergency room, Wesley Cook proclaimed, "I shot the motherf***er, and I hope the motherf***er dies."[12] The only thing William Cook ever said to authorities was, "I didn't have anything to do with it."[13] Wesley Cook had a two-week trial for first degree murder in Philadelphia, in 1982, in front of a jury he personally helped select and which included people of color. They deliberated for just under six hours and returned a conviction. The same jury then deliberated another two hours before returning a sentence of death.

It was really that simple. And as Paul Harvey might say, now you know the rest of the story about a man named Wesley Cook, a.k.a., Mumia Abu-Jamal.

I'm talking about the same Mumia Abu-Jamal who has nevertheless received support from the likes of: Ed Asner; Whoopie Goldberg; the Yale Law Journal; National Public Radio; Antioch College; Paris, France; Spike Lee; Pacifica Radio; Addison Wesley Publishers; Jim Hightower; Maya Angelou; Alec Baldwin; the City of Santa Cruz; David Byrne; Tim Robbins; Rage Against the Machine; Naomi Campbell; Noam Chomsky; David Dinkins; E. L. Doctorow; Roger Ebert; Mayor Willie Brown Jr.; Mike Farrell; Gloria Steinem; Molly Ivins; Evergreen State College; Casey Kasem; John Landis; Norman Mailer; Danny Glover; Bobby McFerrin; Ben Cohen; Salman Rushdie; Susan Sarandon; Michael Stipe; Oliver Stone; Alice Walker; Paul Newman; Joanne Woodward; the Beastie Boys; and Peter Yarrow.

This is a crew who should be MUZZLED. They have been sold a bill of goods. This is not the injustice it has been made out to be, and, if they are truly committed to ridding the country of the death penalty, they would be well served by concentrating their attention on another case where, arguably, an innocent person stands accused of a crime he did not commit. Collectively they tried to muzzle the widow of Danny Faulkner, Maureen.

They are a group who facilitate the sort of political correctness that I have been describing and which I believe creates an impediment to a successful fight against the war on terror. While many books have been written about the excesses of the Hollywood Left, never has there been a thorough examination of how they have done so in the context of supporting this cop killer. I can't do the entire subject justice here, but some things need to be said, now.

Mumia Abu-Jamal became a one-man tidal wave of political correctness that seems to have rolled out of the Pacific and over Hollywood, educational institutions, and the nation's self-described cultural elite. The ways in which Abu-Jamal's story has been spun out of control are as disgusting as they are numerous. Keep in mind that this is all *after* he was convicted of murdering a policeman: The *Yale Law Journal* published his musings; National Public Radio signed him to do radio commentaries from behind bars; Addison Wesley published a book of his writings, penned while on death row; students at Evergreen State College in Olympia, Washington, and Antioch College, in Yellow Springs, Ohio, hosted Abu-Jamal via audiotape as a commencement speaker; thousands marched in his honor in cities around the world; hundreds of Web sites have been maintained in his support; a full-page ad ran in the *New York Times* embracing his cause, signed by many of the individuals identified in the paragraph above; Rage Against the Machine and the Beastie Boys played in an Abu-Jamal benefit in New Jersey; the City of San Francisco named a day in his honor; the City of Oakland, birthplace of Ebonics, closed their city schools for a day to teach children who can barely read and write about the "travesty" of Abu-Jamal's conviction; the City of Paris named him an honorary citizen; and, when a group of French communists came to Philadelphia to protest his conviction and sentence, the mayor's office allowed them to use an official City Hall room for their denunciation of the American system of justice, and then saw to it that they were presented with Liberty Bells!

I wish I were kidding. I have always found it telling that the further you get from Philadelphia, the more support that Wesley Cook, a.k.a. Mumia Abu-Jamal, seems to garner. I can remember being with my father in London several years ago and walking into Piccadilly Circus with a cigar in hand, feeling no pain, when a woman associated with the Communist Party's *Daily Worker* tried to sign us up for something. I asked her if she was familiar with Abu-Jamal. She said, "Oh, yes, he's a political prisoner in the United States." Give me a freakin' break.

This was a case of a cop murdered for doing his job. Period. End of story. Or so it should have been. Instead, this straightforward story has been subject to more politically correct manipulation than any other murder in the United States. Without foundation, it has nevertheless been spun into a tale of persecution and injustice.

I personally know a great deal about the Mumia Abu-Jamal spectacle. For more than a decade, I have been honored to serve as *pro bono* legal counsel to Maureen Faulkner, Officer Danny Faulkner's widow. Maureen is an amazing individual and source of inspiration to all of us who have closely followed the case.

After Danny's murder, Maureen Faulkner left Philadelphia to escape the countless threats and near-constant reminders of her husband's murder. She settled in southern California and set about rebuilding her life. First, she co-owned a deli, and then joined a start-up OB/GYN practice as a receptionist. Today, two decades later, that same practice encompasses several offices which she manages. She has a man in her life, but has never stopped loving Danny Faulkner or defending his memory from attack. And, despite having traveled three thousand miles from the murder scene to live anew, she has been constantly reminded of what happened at 1234 Locust Street on December 9, 1981. Any respite she received was short-lived.

Consider how Mumia Mania first reached Maureen as she was trying to rebuild her life. In the tenth year after Danny's murder by Abu-Jamal, she received one of those "you're not gonna believe this" phone calls; the *Yale Law Journal* was publishing an essay by Abu-Jamal on life behind bars for death-row inmates. Not long thereafter came news that National Public Radio had hired Abu-Jamal to do radio commentaries for a national audience. Abu-Jamal was contracted by NPR to record and broadcast radio essays describing his perceptions of life on death row, and his first commentary was to describe the interactions between prisoners and guards when a thunderstorm cut short recreation time. These were scheduled to be aired during the "All Things Considered" program beginning on May 16, 1994.[14] NPR planned to broadcast one commentary, each about three to four minutes long, each month for at least six months.[15] As of the first airing, NPR had compiled ten such recordings which were taped in the visitors' area of the state prison in Huntington, Pennsylvania, where Abu-Jamal is incarcerated. NPR planned to pay the convicted cop killer its standard rate of $150 per segment.[16]

The proposed employment of Abu-Jamal by NPR came to a halt, however, after Maureen Faulkner waged almost continuous protests against the broadcasting giant.

Just a short time after NPR backed out, Pacifica Radio stepped up to the plate to pinch-hit. Pacifica had already been airing Abu-Jamal's commentaries since 1992 and offered to air the commentaries which NPR had planned to use. Maureen had no idea this offer was being made and learned of Abu-Jamal's new deal while driving to work.

Maureen told me, "I was on the 101 one morning on my way to work. All of a sudden, I heard Jamal's voice coming from the radio. When I heard his voice, I started to shake; I mean, my whole body started shaking. I literally had to pull off the side of the freeway, and I just sat there with my head in my hands thinking: 'I can't believe it—after all I tried to do to keep him voiceless because of what he did to Danny.' At the time, I felt defeated. I felt that, when he murdered Danny and was put behind bars, he lost his freedom of speech."[17]

On another occasion, Maureen Faulkner was again driving to work and was startled to see fresh graffiti sprayed on the side of a retaining wall in the name of Abu-Jamal. A freshly painted mural, some two hundred yards in length and nearly twenty yards above the roadway, read, "Free Mumia." It was more of a billboard than innocent graffiti.

"I saw the mural on the 405," she said. "I remember calling the Los Angeles transportation section of the highway department and speaking to them about it, telling them that I wanted it removed. At first, they were quite confused about what I was talking about, and who I was, and they didn't know anything about the case. They did take notes. It was up there for about three weeks before they painted over it, but they did take care of it; they removed it."[18]

These events were the first signs of the groundswell that was then beginning to ferment for the cop killer. The culmination would come in the mid-1990s, at about the time that hundreds of Hollywood phonies and uninformed academic eggheads would lend their names to his petitions and advertisements, and Rage Against the Machine would headline a sold-out Abu-Jamal benefit concert in front of 16,000 fans at the Continental Airlines Arena in New Jersey.

So how did this happen? How did the conviction of a cop killer in Philadelphia grow, arguably, into the largest crusade against common sense of modern time? I think I can answer that by giving a concrete example of how the Abu-Jamal supporters were overly accepting of his legal team's mischaracterization of the evidence in their stampede to climb aboard his defense. They wanted to believe anything that would indicate the innocence of this man to whom they refer as "a former distinguished journalist," not the ne'er-do-well cabbie who had once written about killing cops.

Their zest for this to be a case of a minority journalist wrongly accused by the system blinded them to the real evidence in the case. Consider just one instance. Celebrities and activists across the country and world routinely claim either that no ballistics research was ever done in terms of linking the bullets in Officer Faulkner's body to the gun owned by Abu-Jamal, or that the ballistics evidence proves Abu-Jamal is innocent. In the efforts of full disclosure, it might be interesting to see what the players leading Team Mumia have to say about the ballistics evidence.

Jeff Mackler leads the San Francisco Bay area's movement to support Abu-Jamal. When asked why he supports Abu-Jamal, he frequently cites the following: "There was no ballistics evidence ever presented in court."[19]

Then there is actor Ed Asner, who put forth a similar complaint when questioned by ABC News' Sam Donaldson during a *20/20* story on the case in 1998: "The fact that no ballistics tests were done, which is pretty stupid."[20]

Or how about French professor, Claude Pujol, who put forth another assertion that is common among Abu-Jamal supporters—that the bullet in Danny Faulkner's body did not match Abu-Jamal's gun: "The bullet is not the size of the gun, first thing. They never did any tests."[21]

How Professor Pujol could make a claim that the bullets and gun don't match, while also asserting that there were never any ballistics tests done, makes no sense. If he knows the bullets and gun do not match, it seems quite obvious that belief came from the knowledge that some sort of ballistics tests were done. Which is correct. Extensive ballistics tests were done. Where Pujol and countless other Mumidiots go wrong is in their claim that the bullets found in Officer Faulkner's body and the gun owned by Abu-Jamal which was found at the scene do not match. As it turns out, the bullets and gun do match.

You would never know this if you read the literature emanating from Team Mumia. This is because anti-death-penalty activists see a savior in Mumia Abu-Jamal. To them, he is a vessel who can carry their message to the masses by use of sympathy for his "just" cause.

The problem is, the sympathy and anger surrounding Abu-Jamal's supposed innocence are based on an unbelievably loose understanding of the actual facts of the case. You know the old saying: if you tell a lie and tell it often enough, it soon becomes truth. This is exactly what has happened here.

Leonard Weinglass, one of Abu-Jamal's attorneys during the 1990s, responded to the claim that many Abu-Jamal supporters lack a clear command of the facts of the case during an interview with KGO-TV in San Francisco in 1998: "I don't think that happens at all. I think there are people who don't know every detail that's in 10,000 pages of transcripts, but I think they do understand very well the substantive issues and the essence of this case. And I think what they say is entirely accurate."[22]

Consider the following excerpt from Sam Donaldson's *20/20* report on the

Abu-Jamal case which aired on ABC in 1998. It's telling in regards to what it shows about the fundamental lack of understanding of the basics of the case on the part of Abu-Jamal supporters.

Sam Donaldson:	But ballistics tests were done and proved the bullet was fired by a .38-caliber revolver. The claim that the bullet was a .44 rests solely on a hasty note scribbled by a pathologist at the autopsy. However, the pathologist later testified that he had no expertise in ballistics, that he had only been guessing. But Weinglass refuses to believe that. You don't think it was a guess?
Leonard Weinglass:	I don't think he would guess.
Sam Donaldson:	The police say that that slug has the lands and grooves consistent with being a .38 slug.
Leonard Weinglass:	It does.
Sam Donaldson:	But if it's a .38, then your contention that it was a .44 is wrong.
Leonard Weinglass:	Well, I think that issue is very much something that should be played out in front of a jury.[23]

That's the Abu-Jamal spin machine at its very best. When confronted with the real facts of the case, which prove with near absolute certainty that Abu-Jamal was rightly convicted of murder, his supporters routinely ignore the truth in an effort to deceive the public.

Here is the truth. Assistant Medical Examiner Dr. Paul Hoyer made a note on a piece of scrap paper during a preliminary examination of the wounds on Officer Faulkner's body prior to the time the official autopsy began. This note was not a part of the official autopsy record and was never intended to be a part of Dr. Hoyer's professional opinion. It was merely his own preliminary speculation and was not included in the final autopsy report. Therefore, there was absolutely no reason for the notation to have been entered into the record. Had the notation been presented to the jury, Dr. Hoyer no doubt would have been called to testify. Dr. Hoyer did later testify about his notation, in the 1995 Post-Conviction Relief Act (PCRA) Hearing for Abu-Jamal, in which he rejected the claims by Abu-Jamal's defense team that his notation should be regarded as authoritative.

Here is Dr. Hoyer's response to Leonard Weinglass, who was holding up the paper that the .44 caliber notation was written on:

Weinglass: What is it doctor?
Dr. Hoyer: It's a notation I made on a piece of paper that was normally, normally discarded.[24]

This next excerpt from the 1995 PCRA hearing exposes the fact that Dr. Hoyer had never received formal ballistics training and that his notation was merely speculative:

Fisk: Am I correct, sir, that you've never had training in the field of ballistics and firearms identification?
Hoyer: I've never had formal training in that, that is correct.
Fisk: And am I correct that in 1981 you were by no means an expert in that field?
Hoyer: That is correct.
Fisk: Would I be correct that any statement by you as to the caliber of any projectile would merely be a lay guess and not that, not the valuation of an expert in the field of ballistics?
Hoyer: Correct.[25]

Dr. Hoyer's responses explain why his notation was never submitted in the final autopsy report and why it was never shown to the jury. He had no ballistics training, and his speculation as to the caliber of the bullet in Officer Faulkner's brain is just that, speculation.

In the 1982 trial, firearms expert Anthony Paul presented official ballistics evidence to the jury. This evidence confirmed the bullets in Officer Faulkner's body, although mangled, were consistent with bullets that would have been fired from a .38 caliber Charter Arms revolver.

It's possible to say that it [the bullet which killed Officer Faulkner] was fired from a revolver with that type of rifling, with the Charter Arms type of rifling.[26]

The general characteristics being part of the eight lands and grooves and a right hand direction of twist, you have a part of that [bullet] still exposed with sufficient quantity to be able to say that a firearm rifled with eight lands and grooves with a right hand direction of twist discharged that projectile.[27]

Even Abu-Jamal's own ballistics expert from the 1982 trial and 1995 hearing, George Fassnacht, agreed with the prosecution's assertion that the bullets in Officer Faulkner's body were not .44 caliber.

> ADA Grant: "In any event, no matter whether that explains it or not, you know from your own expertise that this is in no way close to being a .44 caliber bullet, don't you?"
> Mr. Fassnacht replies, "Yes."[28]

There is absolutely no question that the bullets in Officer Faulkner's body were not .44 caliber. Even Abu-Jamal's own expert agreed to this. There is absolutely no question that they came from a Charter Arms .38 caliber revolver. Conveniently, the only such weapon found at the crime scene was one purchased by Mr. Mumia Abu-Jamal. Case closed.

Sadly, the act of presenting this factual information to the Mumidiots does nothing to slow their quest to prove the innocence of Mumia Abu-Jamal. Keep in mind that, during the *20/20* interview in 1998, Leonard Weinglass had already seen Dr. Hoyer's testimony play out in court during the 1995 hearing. He had also seen it do absolutely nothing to prove the innocence of his client in the eyes of the court. Nevertheless, he continued to obfuscate and ignore the truth. This is telling. Those who support Mumia Abu-Jamal are overwhelmingly not in favor of finding the truth of the case but, rather, are most interested in furthering their anti-death penalty goals.

The caliber of the bullets found in Officer Faulkner's body is not the only ballistics evidence that Abu-Jamal's supporters routinely put forth as evidence of an unfair trial. They continue to assert that the ballistics testing throughout the trial was mistake-filled and contend more should have been done to ensure that ballistics tests were comprehensively and accurately completed. The only problem with this assertion is that comprehensive and accurate ballistics tests were done throughout the investigation and were subsequently admitted as evidence to the jury.

There are two quotes that are quite telling about the Mumia Abu-Jamal case itself and the supporters who have flocked to his cause. The first quote is from Assistant Philadelphia District Attorney Arnold H. Gordon to NPR in regard to the strength of the city's case against Mumia in 1982: "From an evidentiary standpoint, the case against Mumia Abu-Jamal was . . . one of the strongest I have seen in twenty-four years as a prosecutor. Abu-Jamal was identified . . . by three eyewitnesses who had never lost sight of him during the entire incident."

The last is a response from actor Ed Asner, one of the most vocal of supporters over the past decade, to a question from Buzz Bissinger asking whether he (Asner) had ever bothered to read the transcripts from the case he so frequently pontificates about: "Could I stay awake?"[29]

As recently as last year, the governor of Maureen Faulkner's home state has just shown appropriate support for the memory of her deceased Philadelphia police officer husband who was murdered more than twenty-four years ago by Mumia Abu-Jamal.

I refer not to Pennsylvania Governor Ed Rendell, but to California's Arnold Schwarzenegger—one of the few good guys in Hollywood. In denying clemency for Crips gang founder and convicted murderer Stanley "Tookie" Williams, Schwarzenegger cited Williams's support of Abu-Jamal, among others, as an indication of Williams's lack of repentance while behind bars.

Three hours after Williams's death by lethal injection, I broke that news to Maureen Faulkner who was shocked but grateful to hear that Schwarzenegger had acknowledged Williams's support for the man who killed her husband in the line of duty on a cold December night nearly a quarter-century ago.

"These weeks have been very emotional for me because people have been bringing up Danny's case out here in California," she told me. "Last week I was driving home from work and a talk radio station was discussing Williams and Abu-Jamal, and there was Mike Farrell, saying many of the same things he has said in Danny's case. I just pulled over and started crying. It's been twenty-four years, and I am a strong woman, but it was emotional to hear it once again."

Schwarzenegger's denial of clemency for Williams is a must read. The five-page document starts by recounting the facts of that case.

During the early morning hours of February 28, 1979, Williams and three others went on a robbery spree. Around 4 a.m., they entered a 7-Eleven store where Albert Owens was working by himself. Here, Williams, armed with his pump action shotgun, ordered Owens to a backroom and shot him twice in the back while he lay face down on the floor. Williams and his accomplices made off with about $120 from the store's cash register. After leaving the 7-Eleven store, Williams told the others that he killed Albert Owens because he did not want any witnesses. Later that morning, Williams recounted shooting Albert Owens, saying "You should have heard the way he sounded when I shot him." Williams then made a growling noise and laughed for five to six minutes.

On March 11, 1979, less than two weeks later, Williams, again armed with his shotgun, robbed a family-operated motel and shot and killed three members of the family: (1) the father, Yen-I Yang, who was shot once in the torso and once in the arm while he was laying on a sofa; (2) the mother, Tsai-Shai Lin, who was shot once in the abdomen and once in the back; and (3) the daughter, Yee-Chen Lin, who was shot once in her face. For these murders, Williams made away with approximately $100 in cash. Williams also told others about the details of these murders and referred to the victims as "Buddha-heads."[30]

Schwarzenegger noted that the basis of Williams's clemency request was not innocence, but rather, the "personal redemption Stanley Williams has experienced and the positive impact of the message he sends." A message, his supporters have been quick to point out, that he had offered in writing in the form of books written behind bars.

What Williams did not count on was that the governor, or members of his staff, would take the time to read the books. And when they did, they found that in his 1998 *Life in Prison*, Williams dedicated the book to "Nelson Mandela, Angela Davis, Malcolm X, Assata Shakur, Geronimo Ji Jaga Pratt, Ramona Africa, John Africa, Leonard Peltier, Dhoruba Al-Mujahid, George Jackson, Mumia Abu-Jamal, and the countless other men, women, and youths who have to endure the hellish oppression of living behind bars."

Wrote the governor: "The mix of individuals on this list is curious. Most have violent pasts and some have been convicted of committing heinous murders, including the killing of law enforcement," a reference, no doubt, to Abu-Jamal's execution of Faulkner. Schwarzenegger found this list to be a "significant indicator that Williams is not reformed and that he still sees violence and lawlessness as a legitimate means to address societal problems."

George Jackson, who along with Abu-Jamal, was one of Williams's role models, warranted a footnote of his own in Schwarzenegger's statement. There he was identified as a

> militant activist and prison inmate who founded the violent Black Guerilla Family prison gang. Jackson was charged with the murder of a San Quentin correctional officer. In 1970, when Jackson was out to court in Marin County on the murder case, his brother stormed the courtroom with a machine gun, and along with Jackson and two other inmates, took a judge, the prosecutor and three others hostage in an escape attempt. Shooting broke out. The prosecutor was paralyzed from a police bullet, and the judge was killed by a close-range blast to his head when the shotgun taped to his throat was fired by one of Jackson's accomplices. Jackson's brother was also killed. Then, three days before trial was to begin in the correctional officer murder case, Jackson was gunned down in the upper yard at San Quentin Prison in another foiled escape attempt on a day of unparalleled violence in the prison that left three officers and three inmates dead in an earlier riot that reports indicate also involved Jackson.[31]

I shared all of this with Maureen Faulkner. "I feel as though justice was done to this man who has never actually said he murdered these individuals, he denied it, he never apologized and it's a sad thing for the families, but at least they have peace,"[32] she said.

She was referring to the sort of peace she still seeks.

24

The Parade at PC and Main Streets

So far, we've covered lots of ground, geographically speaking. Speech and actions are being MUZZLED on Wall Street. At the *Philadelphia Daily News*. In corporate America. Inside the San Francisco 49ers. On T-ball fields across the nation. In the Miss America Pageant. At Harvard. Princeton. And Penn.

Worse, domestic political correctness has now spilled into the war on terror, whether we're talking about the hysterics generated over five or six bad actors out of 140,000 troops deployed in Iraq who did some stupid things at Abu Ghraib, or the disproportionate attention heaped on whomever may have flushed a Koran down at Guantanamo, or the failure to control our borders and airports by keeping an eye out for those who resemble the nineteen on 9/11. This trend has hit even middle America. Proof can be found in Chesterson, Indiana.

> **WARNING!** This chapter may offend those who are p**riotically challenged or hate America insofar as (but not limited to the fact that) it describes, references, or alludes to acts of duty, loyalty, and p**riotism. It discusses (*ex proprio motu*) persons who consider themselves p**riotic and have made statements or exhibited behaviors conducive to that of individuals with loyalties to the United States and its armed forces, e.g., flag waving, prayers for military personnel (living and fallen), recognition of veterans, and uncouth expletives prefixed to the name Osama Bin Laden, *inter alia*.
>
> Any commentary rendered herein may therefore (*res ipsa loquitur*) also lend itself to p**riotism or p**riotic tendencies.

The author is not aware of the views of said persons regarding the Second Amendment (though he can guess), yet does know, acknowledge, and approve of the dog ownership subsequently referenced. The names have been preserved to recognize the aforementioned individuals for their fealty to family, community, and country (God bless 'em!) and to heap shame on those who have ridiculed them.[1]

Quietly tucked away in the northwestern corner of Indiana, the town of Chesterton (population, 10,000) is not known for controversy and turmoil. We're talking the home of the Indiana Dunes National Lakeshore, a gorgeous stretch of beach that fronts Lake Michigan. People come to Chesterton to get away from problems, not find them. Yet this Heartland town would find itself embroiled in the culture wars on, of all days, the Fourth of July, not even four years removed from 9/11.

This story began as many controversies do, at the bar. David Kozinski and a friend were "having a couple of drinks one night" when they came up with an idea for the Chesterton annual Fourth of July parade.[2] In Chesterton, this parade is a big deal, as David explained to one of my guys. As a matter of fact, the two young men really get into every holiday celebration by dressing up and spreading the cheer. This time it would be a bit more serious.

The plan was for David to dress up as Uncle Sam while his buddy would don an Osama bin Laden costume. As they marched with the parade, they were "going to have Uncle Sam lead Osama down the road"—acting-out, in other words, the capture of Osama bin Laden.[3] The Osama costume, recycled clothing from previous Halloween costumes, were thought to be sufficient to present an obvious Osama bin Laden.

David told his mom, Penny Kozinski, about the idea. She's a member of an organization called "Supporters of the Military." SOM, as it is more frequently known, is a support group for military families. Given her dedication and patriotism, she agreed to pass along the idea to her fellow group members at SOM as they met to discuss their float preparation for the parade. When she did, no one objected. To parade the capture of the mastermind of 9/11 fit well with SOM's overarching theme: Support Our Troops.[4]

Peggy offers this parade color commentary:

We were on the back of a truck and the whole entire truck was decorated with different military magnets, which was supporting all of our troops. And in the back of that truck was sitting a man that was in World War II and then I was sitting on the tailgate. Another girl was sitting on the tailgate, and we were handing to the people who were walking to the float, candy and balloons, different gifts, and stuff. . . . On the float, we had a wooden statue and a soldier kneeling down by a grave, with a cross [Uh-oh! Not a cross!], and he's holding his gun and his helmet. We had an [inflatable] Uncle Sam on the float. . . . We had boxes that said: "Thank you to our community, we have sent a little over 300 packages to our military." A lady was sitting on the float because she couldn't walk due to illness. So she was sitting on the float, with a flag that her son flew over in Iraq. On the back part of the float was a [quilt pinned with the pictures of] all of the people that belong to the SOM, their loved ones, whatever branch of the military they were in. . . . There was a black ribbon for the ones that we lost. There was a huge flag that said: "Supporters of Military." We flew a flag with all of the branches of serv-ice that said: "Iraqi Freedom" on it.[5]

I don't know about you, but to me it sounds downright Norman Rockwellian. Not so offensive, right? I mean, clearly, the SOM float got its message across in every possible way: support our troops and the mission they're carrying out.

In front of the float, David, dressed as Uncle Sam, was leading his buddy, dressed up as Osama bin Laden. David said he had a hunch that "there were going to be some people that didn't think that it was very nice" but, aside from that, he felt good.[6] The crowd of a few hundred was overwhelmingly supportive. There were, he said, "probably only seven or eight people at most that we heard say, 'That's wrong; that's disgusting; they're being un-American.'" Busting Osama is un-American? Thankfully, most didn't see it that way. "I'd say 90 percent of the people were like, 'Yay! We got him! We got Osama!'" David said.[7] How outra-geous is it that—wanting to capture Osama is "un-American"?! How easily they toss around this word, and yet we're *never* to question their patriotism.

At one point David said there were "veteran guys sitting on the side of the road yelling: 'Where's the hanging? Where we gonna store him at?'" (This was clearly someone whose conscience is not bothering him about Gitmo!) "The majority of the people thought it was really cool and they were cheering for it," he added.

Penny agrees: "People kept tapping [David and his friend] to stop long enough for them to take their picture" and "kept cheering them on." David added, "I wouldn't change it. I'd do it again, and so would my friend."[8]

The SOM float won "Most Patriotic Unit" in the parade—something that did not go unnoticed by critics. Neither David nor Penny thought news about their award-winning float would get too far.

David recalled, "[Over the following weeks] we were actually more popular in the papers around here than the [7/7] London bombings." The local media coverage was as negative as the crowd reaction had been positive. The press was incapable of finding anything good to say about SOM or the float, and seemed to be interested in interviewing only detractors who, according to David, were in the distinct minority.

A typical headline read: "'Osama' Parade Float Draws Negative Image in Chesterton."[9] The article went on to say, "In the wake of criticism about a Fourth of July float that depicted a bloody, dog-leashed Osama bin Laden being pulled along by Uncle Sam, many local residents expressed their concern." This newspaper, Northwest Indiana's *Post Tribune,* could only find one person who wasn't offended by the float, though they did interview several (four to be exact) who wanted to express their "concern." An editorialist named Dave Rutter sneered: "At its most benign, Osama-on-a-rope was shallow. At its worst, it was racism. Real patriotism is not mindless, mean-spirited devotion. It's a spiritual celebration. It's the light. Not the dark. Patriotism is smart, not stupid."[10]

Cries of racism in Chesterton? For the capture of Osama Bin Laden by Uncle Sam? Talk about MUZZLED.

Penny explained how much the newspaper articles on the float frustrated and angered her: "When the newspaper reporter called me and did an interview on me, he was an Iraqi. But when it came out in the paper, another guy wrote the story. When they took my interview, they twisted it so much, so I was like, 'Okay, I'm not doing any more.' I've been called by a lot of newspapers and I tell them, 'I'm not doing any more interviews because you guys can't get s**t straight.'"

The AP quoted a Chesterton resident as saying, "If the Founding Fathers saw that, they'd freak out. . . . It was just hate, pure and simple."[11] Interestingly, the article also read: "Maybe they didn't mean anything racist, but if I saw that coming down the street, I would have been offended," said Tarek Shahbandar, who was shown a photo of the float Tuesday at the Northwest Indiana Islamic Center in Crown Point.[12] It's worth noting that Mr. Shahbandar was apparently not at the parade at all. Sounds to me like the AP went fishing for negative opinions to support a preconceived bias on the story. (Arguably, the only thing worse is for me to now weigh in on the side of pranksters, given that I wasn't there, either!)

"They didn't want to publish the positive things. And there were positive people writing things to the newspaper, but they weren't getting publicized. It was maybe just one short [story] here and one short [article] there," Penny protested.

The Osama likeness "did not have feet shackled, he had a pair of sandals on. He doesn't usually walk in a long dress and he was having trouble walking in his dress, but nothing was tied."[13] The dress they used was from a previous Halloween, and Penny explained that was the reason for the blood.[14] Reading of a "dog-leashed Osama bin Laden," one might assume the leash was around his neck; but it was "loosely wrapped around his [Osama's] wrist."[15]

People claimed it was not apparent that it was Osama and, therefore, it could be interpreted that the float's message was that all Muslims should be captured. Penny responded, "Everybody says that it was wrong because we didn't have a sign around his neck. You know what, those people over there that are walking around [with] bombs and everything else, they don't have signs on them that say 'Good Guy' or 'Bad Guy.' He looked like Osama Bin Laden."[16]

So shrill was the outcry that Penny, David, and other members of SOM received threats. In fact, a fellow SOM member's truck had the screens ripped out and received calls from people yelling accusations of racism.[17]

So when the dust had settled, what is it Penny wanted to say to the people of Chesterton? She responded: "We are supporting our guys. If the people in this town think it's wrong to have Osama tied up and leading him down the street, then what are those guys over there doing to our people?" Penny then added, "If they think it's so right, then they ought to live in their country, and don't be here."[18]

David was unapologetic in his message. "I come from a patriotic family and I'm patriotic myself, and a lot of my family has been in wars, my dad and my brother are both overseas. I didn't see the problem with it. I don't have a problem with Muslim people, or any race of people or anything. I have friends of all nationalities and races," David said.

He also maintains the belief that the people who trash-talked his mother and his family are "ignorant people that I guess don't care about the 9/11 bombings." He went on, "They're telling us that we're racist bigots and bad people for wanting to capture Saddam Hussein, or be in his land, or doing what we did in the float, and they miss the main message of supporting our troops and getting the bad guys, getting the terrorists to stop killing people, and I often wonder if people who have family in the military, or friends, or if they had anybody in the 9/11 bombings, that they care about that something happened to, would they be saying this stuff about us or would they actually be supporting that we're trying to get the bad guys, and that we're supporting our troops."[19]

Penny and David have two family members fighting the war on terrorism. Their message is clear, and we should stop wringing our hands about it: Support the Troops. That entails capturing or killing terrorists like Osama bin Laden. He's the only one who needs to be MUZZLED.

25

24 and There's So Much More

I was late in climbing on the *24* bandwagon. Friends and radio listeners were quick to recommend the Fox television show starring Kiefer Sutherland as an anti-terrorist special agent Jack Bauer, but for whatever reason, it wasn't until season four that I gave it a look-see.

When I finally checked it out, I loved it. If you don't know, the premise is that every episode is but one hour of a single day in the life of Bauer; the programming season itself comprises a full twenty-four hours, hence the title. It sounds like that would be impossible to pull off, but they get it done.

The series premiered on November 5, 2001, not two months after the attack on the World Trade Center. Jack Bauer starts off as a field operative for the Los Angeles division of the Counter Terrorist Unit, or CTU. The plotlines are as creative as they are ambitious. In season one Jack Bauer saved his daughter, in season two he saved a city, and in season three he saved the USA. As season four would develop, Jack Bauer was trying to save the world from nuclear annihilation.

For a while, I have been noticing that Hollywood seems to go out of its way to cast characters who don't look real-life when it comes to crime. The urban car-jacker looks like the suburban carpooler. This has permeated commercials, too.

Well, in *24*'s first few episodes of season four, the terrorists looked like the real ones. The Araz family was the focal point. A husband and wife and teenage son. They were up to no good. They were Middle Eastern. How novel. How un-MUZZLED.

But would it last?

Just as I was setting the TiVo for *24*, I had the pleasure of interviewing both Roger Cross and Shohreh Aghdashloo, two of the show's stars. Roger Cross plays Curtis Manning, who works with Jack Bauer at the CTU. Shohreh Aghdashloo plays Dina Araz.

I was particularly interested in speaking with Shohreh Aghdashloo, a gifted actress of Iranian descent. I wanted to learn whether Ms. Aghdashloo had any qualms about playing a Middle Eastern terrorist. She revealed to me that she had to think long and hard before committing to the show.

> My issues were different. I was told that I could not have a screenplay to read. And I said that I couldn't get myself involved with a project that I have no idea of. I can't go around saying, "Oh I'm sorry, I didn't know what I was doing or what I was getting involved with." Therefore, after two weeks, our producers decided to give me the screenplay and tell me what the story is about. And then I found out what a strong woman (Dina Araz) is, and what a complex character I'd be playing. As an actress I realized that it's a great opportunity to play a variety of roles represented in one character only.[1]

She went on to say that, "People tell me my role is a stereotype, which I do not believe at all."

Roger Cross's words were even more profound. When I asked to explain the show's success, he said, "They pay attention to all of the details. They give you a quality script. Then they give you people who deliver on that script. . . . They're not afraid to work with you and say, 'You know what, this isn't quite right.' They're all about getting it right."[2]

Early on in season four, I believed *24* was getting it right. Specifically, the Araz family looked to be a terrorist sleeper cell based in Los Angeles at a time in the United States where people were wondering whether such things truly existed. One had been exposed in Buffalo post-9/11, and it seemed like a plausible premise for action television.

Those qualities most appealing about *24* soon raised hackles in the Arab community. The Council for American-Islamic Relations (CAIR)—which has seen three of its former employees indicted on federal terrorism charges—sent representatives to meet with Fox network officials on January 12, 2005, due to concerns that the series portrayed American-Muslim families as "sleeper cells."[3] They feared such a portrayal might "cast a shadow of suspicion over ordinary American Muslims and could increase Islamophobic stereotyping and bias."[4] CAIR spokeswoman Rabiah Ahmed said the way in which *24*'s Araz family is portrayed casts an unwanted "cloud of suspicion over every American-Muslim family out there."[5]

I naïvely hoped Fox would hold the line. In fact, I was initially so psyched that I wrote about the series in the *Philadelphia Daily News*, expressing my hope that airport screeners would take a page out of Jack Bauer's book and hunt for terrorists who look like the real ones.

It became clear that CAIR was MUZZLING *24* when, just before the eighth episode, meaning the 2:00–3:00 PM hour of the season, Kiefer Sutherland appeared on camera (as himself) and said this:

> Hi, my name is Keifer Sutherland, and I play counterterrorist agent Jack Bauer on Fox's *24*. I would like to take a moment to talk to you about something that I think is very important. Now, while terrorism is obviously one of the most critical challenges facing our nation and the world, it is important to recognize that the American Muslim community stands firmly beside their fellow Americans in denouncing and resisting all forms of terrorism. So when watching *24*, please, bear that in mind.[6]

At home, my stomach turned. While no doubt I wasn't the only one offended, few spoke. I did see an on-line columnist named Robert Spencer, who wrote: "It is astounding that anyone would be offended by a fictionalized portrayal of the terrorist group that actually has perpetrated the largest terror attack, or attack of any kind, on American soil, but these are confused times."[7] *Allah Akbar*, er, amen to that.

It took just a few episodes before the Kiefer Sutherland disclaimer began to show up in the script. The plot took a turn. Now things were out of control, and I had given up on the show. No longer does it appear that the real culprits are Middle Eastern terrorists—now it's a bunch of suburban white guys affiliated with some kind of Halliburton knock-off. The tipping point came in the thirteenth episode, the 7:00–8:00 PM hour.

Jack Bauer finds himself pinned down in a sporting goods store owned by Arab Americans. After the executives at McLennan-Forester decide to detonate an electromagnetic pulse bomb (which knocks out every type of electrical instrument) at their building in the middle of Los Angeles, half of the city was placed in total darkness. Looters run rampant in the streets. The corporate army hired by McLennan-Forester close in on Jack, Paul, and the two Arab Americans in the sporting goods store. After Jack tells the store owners to flee the scene, they decide to tell Bauer exactly why they want to stay and help:

Arab Male 1:	We were the first to be hit [by looters] because everyone knows we're Arabs. And we're good citizens. We had nothing to do with what happened today.
Arab Male 2:	Look he doesn't care. Take what you need, but leave us two guns. We chased looters off once before, but they'll be back.
Male 2:	What are you guys doing here?
Jack:	We needed to take cover.
Male 2:	What do you mean? Who's after you?
Jack:	It has to do with the terrorist attacks. I have critical evidence that I need to get to the authorities. The men that are chasing us are responsible for this blackout. They detonated a device called an electromagnetic pulse bomb which destroys all electrical activity within an eight-mile radius.
Male 1:	So everything that's happened to us tonight . . . the looting . . . the blackout . . . it's all because of the terrorists?
Jack:	Yes, and the evidence that I have will prevent further attacks from happening.
Paul:	Jack, the commandos will be here any minute.
Male 2:	Commandos?
Jack:	He's right. You boys need to leave this store. Right now. We're their target. You're not safe here with us.
Male 2:	Why don't you leave? This is our store.
Jack:	I would, but right now there's no other place to be. You have weapons and shelter.
Male 1:	Can I talk to my brother for a second?
Jack:	Stay where I can see you. (Paul and Jack talk for a little while)
Male 2:	My brother and I talked about this. We're staying.
Jack:	I can't force you to leave your own property. But this is not just a bunch of looters. This is a very dangerous situation. I cannot guarantee your safety.
Male 1:	You don't understand. For years we've been blamed for these attacks by these terrorists. We grew up in this neighborhood. This country is our home. If you're fighting

the people who caused today's bloodshed, then we'll
help you.

Click. And so ended my watching of season four of *24*. What began as a fast-
paced crime story about terrorism had degenerated into a CAIR commercial.
The first half of season four focused on a Middle Eastern terrorist plot to detonate nuclear power plants and nuclear warheads in select cities across the United
States. But by the midway point, the plot began to involve rich white businessmen as the facilitators of the terrorist scheme. The only mystery in my mind was
in determining which was to be Dick Cheney. What a shame.

24 was no longer a realistic program willing to portray terrorists the way we
know them to be; it had become a soapbox for angry Arab Americans. After I
tuned out, I'm told that the show continued to move away from what had
attracted me to it in the beginning, namely, a realistic portrayal of terrorists.

After seeing all of the twists and turns in this show, it is clear it was
MUZZLED halfway through the season. Too bad. While I could sufficiently sus-
pend reality to deal with Jack Bauer's heroic exploits, I simply could not stomach the sanitization of what a terrorist looks like in 2005.

I know that many a hardcore *24* fan will have a problem with my analysis.
I myself recently met one such individual, a college student named Geoff Brock,
and after I shared with him some of my thinking, he told me:

> The show takes a complete 180 at least once an episode. Every single sea-
> son of *24* contains several unlikely connections, in which unexpected
> parties become somehow involved in the conflict, sometimes even inad-
> vertently, which was the case here. The main villain still remained
> Middle Eastern and still Muslim. His name was Habib Marwan. This
> never changed, nor did the fact that Navi & Dina Araz and the rest of
> the terror cell network shown were Middle Eastern Muslims. Even up to
> the final episodes of the season, well after CAIR's complaints, Marwan
> remained the main threat and he even allowed himself to die without
> leaking any info. I'm sure CAIR did not appreciate this, nor do I see how
> the show can be viewed as going soft. Even so, it would not be fair, and
> would be extremely uninteresting, to make every criminal be a Middle
> Eastern Muslim. The reason why the show is so intense is because peo-
> ple that you wouldn't expect end up having hidden agendas, usually dis-

cordant with civilian safety, and usually in an effort to make money or gain power. These twists are scattered all throughout each and every season. Most terrorists may be Middle Eastern but most Middle Easterners certainly are not terrorists. One more point to add is that the nature and ethnicity of the villains in *24* have been diverse since season one. So far, villains have come from just about every continent, from drug peddlers to corporate power-mongers, the terror is always connected to some unexpected party. The truth is, the villain network in season four was just as complicated, surprising, and intriguing as it has been in the previous three seasons, and I am expecting nothing less for season five.[8]

While it is certainly the prerogative of *24*'s creative forces to take the plot in whatever direction they choose—this is not some news reporting/bias charge I am making—I just found it profoundly disappointing that the one program on television that seemed willing to cut its own path against the tide of political correctness, in the end, succumbed to the MUZZLED mentality.

I shudder to think about television's depiction of 9/11, when it is ten, or twenty years in the future. Already, the footage of the airplanes striking the Twin Towers is relegated to the dustbin, worthy of airing only on the anniversary, and then, not as often as it should. I've grown so tired of this refusal to confront reality that I end all of my radio programs with a one-minute montage of 9/11 sound, with a music bed supplied by Toby Keith's "American Soldier." It doesn't have the same effect as showing those airplanes, but it's radio, and it's the best I can do.

26

The T-Word, Shhhh!

Time for some definitions:

Terrorist: One who engages in an act of terrorism.

Terrorism: The unlawful use or threatened use of force or violence by a person or an organized group against people or property with the intention of intimidating or coercing societies or government, often for ideological or political reasons.[1]

The MUZZLED mentality is not an American phenomena. I really can't speak to whether it began here or over there, but the reality is that it exists on both sides of the Atlantic. Proof lies in the refusal of some media outlets to use the above words when they clearly apply.

The London terrorist attacks on July 7, 2005, which killed over fifty people and injured more than seven hundred innocent people,[2] were another attempt by Islamic extremists to disrupt the world. Soon after the attacks, speculation focused yet again on the hand of radical Islam. British Prime Minister Tony Blair, speaking soon after the attacks, said it was "reasonably clear there has been a series of terrorist attacks in London."[3]

Throughout the next week, the newspapers were riveted by this "terrorist bombing." As common sense would dictate, the newspaper coverage referred to the bombing of three subway lines and one double-decker bus as acts of terrorism. In fact, you could *not* go through an article without seeing the words "terrorist" or "terrorism." (Think of it as the American press writing about the World Series and mentioning the world "baseball.") By way of example, two days after the attacks, in the English newspaper the *Guardian*, the words "terrorism," "terrorist," or a word relating to terrorism appeared in *each* of the first eleven pages.[4]

Closer to home, coverage was similar. No less than the *New York Times* referred to what had occurred as a "coordinated terror attack." It was the same with the wire services. An AP headline read, "London Terror Bombings Kill 37, Wound 700."[5]

Meanwhile, the word "terrorist" was completely absent from one major United Kingdom media outlet, and it was deliberate. This news source was arguably the most prominent news source in the UK: the British Broadcasting Company, or BBC. "The BBC is much more influential than any other news organization, probably in the world . . . there is no equivalent in the United States," Tom Gross said to me.[6] Gross is with the *Jerusalem Post*. I spoke with him after reading an excellent analysis he wrote on the BBC's reluctance to use the T-word. He said, "If you took ABC, NBC, CNN, FOX and rolled them all into one, that's how powerful the BBC is."

Gross' analysis ran on July 11, four days after the attacks. He described how the BBC's initial report of the attack in the first couple of hours after the bombings was totally different from subsequent reports. He focused on two articles, both of them from BBC News. The first article was titled "Bus Man May Have Seen Terrorist" and was published on the July 7, the day of the attacks. The article begins, "A bus passenger says he may have seen one of those responsible for the terrorist bomb attacks in London." Gross reported that, at 10:14 AM GMT, on Friday, July 9, the Friday after the attacks, the article was changed. Suddenly, the article's title now read, "Passenger Believes He Saw Bomber," and the first line now was: "A bus passenger says he may have seen one of those responsible for the bomb attacks in London." In the span of a few hours, the BBC completely changed the article and deleted the word "terrorist" from their coverage.[7]

It doesn't stop with just one—Gross uncovered another BBC rewrite. Early on Friday morning, an article was put up on the BBC Web site titled "Testing the Underground Mood." In the article, the London attack was called "the worst terrorist atrocity Britain has seen." Within hours, at 12:08 GMT on that same Friday, this line was changed, the only one in the article that was altered. That same sentence declaring the London bombings as "the worst terrorist atrocities" was now labeled "the worst peacetime bomb attacks." Just like that, the "terrorist" attack that killed more than fifty people and injured another seven hundred was made to look like a peacetime bomb attack, not a terrorist attack!

Needless to say, Gross gets it. Speaking from London within days of the terror attacks, he told me that the BBC has, as the British say, "a stiff upper lip." He said that, in his opinion, "What they have done was quite inappropriate; this isn't correcting an error or something."[8] He told me that the mind-set of the BBC in not calling these attacks "terrorism" is "kind of like the mind style of the BBC news staff, and if you don't fall in with that mindset, you simply don't hold your job there."[9] He said BBC writers actually think avoiding the word "terrorists," and calling terrorists, such as suicide bombers in Israel, militants or activists "is glamorous somehow. They won't quite say this . . . some of them even have a sneaking admiration for Osama bin Laden."[10]

Soon after chatting with Gross and on the heels of yet another attack in London (the attack of July 21, 2005, in which four bombs failed to fully detonate), I spoke with James O'Brien, a radio talk-show host ("presenter") across the pond in London on LBC 97.3 FM. O'Brien is regarded as one of Britain's best young political broadcasters. I asked him about the BBC's refusal to use the T-word. "It's disgraceful that the BBC is avoiding using the term *terrorist* or anything connected. It makes me ashamed to be a British journalist," O'Brien stated. O'Brien told me that the BBC moves quickly to defend the rights of Muslim clerics in England to stand up and call for attacks upon the British society.[11]

In the face of this sort of criticism, the BBC nevertheless continued to sanitize the news. There were additional articles by the BBC that were changed within days, even hours of the London terrorist attacks. Two headlines on the BBC Web site on July 8, a day after the attack, contained the word "terror" in them. One read: "See Scenes Across London After the Terror Attacks," while the other read: "How the Key Incidents Unfolded on London's Day of Terror." By July 9, the two headlines were taken off the BBC Web site and replaced by a headline saying: "In Detail: What Happened: Four Explosions Ripped Across Central London on Thursday 7 July, Killing More Than 50 People and Injuring 700. This Guide Explains How the Key Incidents Unfolded." On the eighth, the lead to the article read, "Series of explosions has ripped across central London, killing at least 37 people and injuring many hundreds more. In what appears to have been a co-ordinated terrorist attack, there were blasts on three Underground trains and a bus, as the morning rush hour drew to a close." A day later, that was changed to "Four explosions ripped across central London on Thursday, killing more than 50 people and injuring 700. The co-ordinated attack hit three Underground trains and a bus, as the morning's rush hour drew to a close." In one day, the BBC switched from terror attacks to merely explosions and coordinated attacks.[12]

The question is why did they do it?

Why did they use *terrorist* and like terms, only to change them hours later? You won't believe this. It comes down to some warped notion of "even-handedness." The BBC's guidelines actually state: "The word 'terrorist' itself can be a barrier to understanding. . . . We should try to avoid the term, while we report the facts as we know them."[13] The BBC guidelines also state that its credibility is undermined by the "careless use of words which carry emotional or value judgments."[14] Despite the BBC's domestic news broadcasts still using the word "terrorist"[15] and a BBC spokesman saying, "The word terrorist is not banned from the BBC,"[16] within days after the attacks, the BBC World Service was, as Gross wrote, "slowly reverting to its old habits, both on air and on line."[17]

I raised these issues on my radio program. This caused one of my listeners to send an e-mail to the BBC, not really anticipating a reply. His message included this admonition: "TERRORISTS . . . they are TERRORISTS!!!!! Not your politically correct, saccharin-sounding 'bombers,' they are TERRORISTS!!!!!!!!!!!!!!"[18] (You gotta love my listeners!) A couple days later, he was surprised to receive a response, which made him even more upset, and caused that vein in my forehead to pop when I read it. The BBC News Web site, specifically a group in BBC called "NewsOnline" with the e-mail address newsonline@bbc.co.uk, responded:

> Thank you for getting in touch about our coverage of the London attacks. It is our policy generally to avoid describing organizations or individuals as "terrorist" in our stories unless we are quoting others. We recognize that the word "terrorist" can look like a reflection of editorial bias rather than a statement of fact. However the blasts which have hit London have been described as terrorist attacks by a wide range of prominent figures, including G8 and other leaders, London's police chief and the Pope, and we have reflected these statements and quoted from them in our coverage. In the context of these comments and the day's events we feel the language used in our reporting has been justified and accurate. Thank you for your interest in the BBC's coverage.[19]

Are they serious? "We recognize that the word 'terrorist' can look like a reflection of editorial bias rather than a statement of fact."

I say MUZZLED. A terrorist is one who engages in terror. In the dictionary definition for terror and terrorism, there should be a snapshot of the double-decker bus that got hit in London on 7/7!

Just how bad are things at the BBC? In September of 2005, Rupert Murdoch, the media tycoon who counts Fox News among his holdings, participated in a panel discussion for big wigs hosted by former President Bill Clinton. The conference coincided with a UN Summit in New York City. Murdoch reported that British Prime Minister Tony Blair had complained to him that the BBC's coverage of Hurricane Katrina was itself anti-American.

"Tony Blair—perhaps I shouldn't repeat this conversation—told me yesterday that he was in Delhi last week. And he turned on the BBC World Service to see what was happening in New Orleans," Murdoch was quoted as saying in a transcript posted on the Clinton Global Initiative Web site. "And he said it was just full of hate of America and gloating about our troubles. And that was his government; well, his government-owned-thing," he said of the publicly owned broadcaster.

Guess who supported this view? Bill Clinton.

"There was nothing factually inaccurate. But—it was designed to be almost exclusively a hit on the federal response without showing what anybody at any level was doing that was also miraculous, going on simultaneously in a positive way," Clinton said.[20]

What has me further concerned is a trend toward similar behavior by other media outlets. In my own hometown, just eleven days after the first London attack, the *Philadelphia Inquirer* posted a column under their "Public Access, Inquirer Policies" section on their Web site. Titled "Definition and Use of the Word Terrorist From The Inquirer's Stylebook," it stated the following: "These words are highly controversial. Groups and factions often wish the *Inquirer* to characterize their foes as terrorists in order to make them appear as enemies of the United States and its people."

Next, it listed five occasions in which, "with the approval, marked in notes mode, of an assigning editor," the words *terrorism* or *terrorist* can be used:

1. In direct quotations (no approval needed in this case).

2. Where an official, government or agency is characterizing an event even though a definite claim of responsibility or a clear explanation has yet to be established, such as: *The Belgian government said it believed the fire was not an accident but was an act of terrorism. Or President Bush reported on progress in the war on terrorism.*

3. To describe an individual or group that has credibly claimed responsibility for terrorist acts.

4. To describe an individual convicted of an act of terrorism.

5. In rare cases where the question of terrorism is not in dispute, such as the attacks of Sept. 11, 2001, or at the Munich Olympics, or historical events such as the attack on Archduke Francis Ferdinand in Sarajevo.[21]

And here is where the *Philadelphia Inquirer* started to sound somewhat like the BBC:

Instead, use words that specify the act or person, such as *hijacker, bomber, suicide bombing, attack. Militant* is not to be used in an attempt to avoid saying terrorist. To describe a group, use words that describe what it has done or what it is accused of doing. An example: *The group Hamas, which has admitted involvement in many suicide bombings, claimed responsibility for the attack.*

To describe in a general way seemingly related acts, use sentences such as *Bombings and other acts of political violence have been on the increase in Indonesia,* instead of saying *Acts of terrorism have been on the increase in Indonesia without attribution.*

Background: *Terrorist,* always an emotionally charged, politically loaded term, became a much more controversial word after September 11, 2001.

Merriam Webster's dictionary gives the political definition of terror this way: *violence (as bombing) committed by groups in order to intimidate a population or government into granting their demands. Terrorism* has come to mean the use of force or threats against civilians by a movement of some sort as a means of affecting the policy of one or more third parties.

Attacks by a recognized national armed service do not meet this definition; an army could be found guilty of war crimes, but not of terrorism. Attacks on military personnel also generally do not meet the definition, but an attack on, for example, a market where non-uniformed soldiers were among the shoppers.[22]

So, how did the *Inquirer* cover the London attacks?

I looked at articles in the *Philadelphia Inquirer* published in the days following the terror attack. The first article I looked at was titled "As Bomb Toll Reaches 50, Stoic Londoners Carry On." As you can tell by the headline, the *Inquirer* stuck to their policy by trying to call it what it was on the outside, a bombing.

In the article itself, in the first sentence, it reads, "Londoners went back to work yesterday, boarding buses, subways and taxis in defiance of terrorists as authorities pledged 'implacable resolve' to hunt down those responsible for the subway and bus bombings that killed at least 50 people." Although they call it a bombing in the headline, the *Philadelphia Inquirer* recognized that the bombers were terrorists. Later in the article, they refer to the attacks as specifically as possible, sticking to their policy, by calling them "bus bombing," "blasts," and "attacks," but only mention the T-word a few times, mainly when referring to the terrorists, but fail to mention the words "terrorist attacks."[23]

The next article I looked at was titled "London Awash in Worry for Missing" published on July 10, three days after the attacks. As their policy states, in the first sentence of the article, the *Inquirer* called the attacks as specifically as they could, "mass-transit bombings." They continued to use the word "attack" and call the people who carried out the attack "bombers." In this specific article, the attack was not called a terrorist attack and the word "terror" was only used when referring to what someone else stated.[24]

The last article I looked at was titled "Four Tied to London Bombings," published on July 13, just under a week after the attacks. As you can see by the headline, the *Philadelphia Inquirer* was sticking to calling this a "bombing," not a terrorist attack. In the first couple of lines, when referring to the terrorists, the *Inquirer* calls them "bombers." Interestingly enough, in this article, the word "terror" in reference to the attacks was not mentioned once.[25]

And just how did the English newspapers, such as the *Telegraph* or the *Guardian*, describe these horrible terrorist attacks? Did they deem the attacks merely "bombings," such as the BBC, or did they take the offensive to call this attack the way it is, "terrorist attacks"?

The *Telegraph* is the first on-line daily newspaper in the UK.[26] An article titled "Al Qa'eda Brings Terror to the Heart of London" is the article covering the attacks the day after. It starts off "Three terrorist bombs." Later the article stated "co-ordinated attacks" and "attacks."[27] I looked at one article written two days after the London attacks. In a *Telegraph* article titled "They Will Not

Change Our Way of Life, Says the Queen," the first line read, "The Queen issued a defiant message yesterday to the terrorists who bombed London." Throughout the rest of the article, the event is called "attack" a number of times, but once is referred to as "bombings."[28]

The *Guardian*, another English newspaper, described the attacks in the article following the attacks titled "Four Bombs in 50 Minutes—Britain Suffers Its Worst-ever Terror Attack." It was written that "terrorists struck at the heart of London" and obviously, by the headline, deemed this a terror attack. It was also referred to as a "series of coordinated strikes."[29] Although both of these news sources referred to the attacks as "bombings" or "coordinated strikes," both recognize, or at least mention, that this was a terrorist attack, or some form of terrorism.

This is a situation that has gone out of control. As Tom Gross told me, "It's like PC gone out of control."[30]

And it's not just terrorism.

The BBC's banning of "terrorist" is only the tip of the jagged iceberg. Our British friends are themselves becoming MUZZLED by the forces of political correctness.

In the aftermath of the attacks of 7/7, British tourism took a hit, particularly as a result of Americans who decided not to travel to see the London Eye or Big Ben. That's why I found myself invited by British tourism officials to do my morning radio show live from London. The hope was that as I talked up the sites, my radio listeners would be reminded that London remains very much open for business. A few years ago, in the midst of the Intifada, I did exactly the same thing when invited to Jerusalem by the Israelis. This time, I was again only too happy to oblige as London is my second most favorite city in the world. (*Need you ask?* Philadelphia, of course!) The trip was terrific. One day I did my show from the Churchill Museum and Cabinet War Rooms, the underground bunker where Winston Churchill rode out the Blitz. It is, by far, the best of any historical/tourist site I have ever seen, and I had been there on a number of previous occasions as a private tourist. On another morning, I was joined in studio by Nick Mason of Pink Floyd. A few days in London gave me the opportunity to get caught up on more than just the controversy over the banning of the T-word by the BBC. London is the greatest newspaper town in the world, and as I devoured five or six newspapers daily, I learned that just as our British friends are themselves defending against terrorism at home, there is an onslaught of political correctness affecting the Island.

Consider some recent examples:

- Halifax and Nat West banks are scrapping piggybanks, the time-honor symbol of savings for generations of school kids, because they fear that the image will offend some Muslims.[31]

- Prison officers were recently asked not to wear tie-pins featuring the St. George's Cross—the English national flag!—for fear that they might offend criminals, even where the tie-pins in question were purchased in support of a cancer charity.[32]

- A hit-and-run victim was told by a policeman that she could not use the word "fat" when providing a description of her assailant, for it is too offensive.[33]

- In an example of the Peter Principle run amok, a black police bodyguard who protected Camilla, wife of Prince Charles, won a $70,000 racial discrimination lawsuit against Scotland Yard for being—and I'm not making this up—"over-promoted."[34]

Anthony Browne is a British journalist who writes for the *Times* and who has recently published on the phenomena of PC movement in the UK. He had his own rather rude indoctrination into the subject matter. He was booked to appear on a BBC Radio 4 program to discuss the exponential rise in HIV since Labour was elected in Britain in 1997. The data showed a 25 percent rise in just one year. The conventional wisdom was that a new complacency among heterosexuals was to blame. But Browne had written otherwise. Relying on government information, he had pointed out that African immigration was the cause of the spike. His work was shunned, the interview scrapped. It took a full two years after his story before the Public Health Laboratory Service would come to terms with the real cause: African immigration. And as he describes, "even the left wing media are enabled to report it."

Browne offers one of the better definitions of PC that I have found: "Political correctness is an ideology that classifies certain groups of people as victims in need of protection from criticism, and which makes believers feel that no dissent should be tolerated."[35]

Perhaps in a further sign of the times, the weather forecasters were banned by the Meteorological Office from gloomy forecasts. They were told to look on the bright side and accentuate the positive. Instead of "chilly in areas" it is now "warm for most." No longer is there "heavy rain," now only "rain." "Isolated storms" are now "hot and sunny for most."[36] And I thought things had bottomed out over here.

Thankfully, at least when it comes to terrorism, there is one guy in the UK who gets it. He is the also the one guy who matters most. His name is Tony Blair.

Tony Blair had the right reaction on the days after the terrorist attacks on his country. Immediately following the attacks on July 7, Blair, while attending the G-8 summit in Gleneagles, Scotland, spoke to reporters. He was not scared to call it what it looked to be: "We condemn utterly these barbaric attacks," he said. He added how sure he is that it was a terrorist attack: "Just as it's recently clear this is a terrorist attack or series of terrorist attacks, it's also reasonably clear that it is designed and aimed to coincide with the opening of the G8." One more statement Prime Minister Blair made was that: "It's important, however, that those engaged in terrorism realize that our determination to defend our values and our way of life is greater than their determination to cause death and destruction to innocent people in a desire to impose extremism on the world."[37]

Blair spoke again an hour later, saying: "All of our countries have suffered from the impact of terrorism." Later in his statement, Blair warned that "The terrorists will not succeed. Today's bombings will not weaken in any way our resolve to uphold the most deeply held principles of our societies and to defeat those who impose their fanaticism and extremism on all of us."[38]

On July 7, after his meeting with the government's Emergency Committee, Blair made a statement concerning the Muslims who attacked: "We know that these people act in the name of Islam, but we also know that the vast and overwhelming majority of Muslims, here and abroad, are decent and law-abiding people who abhor this act of terrorism every bit as much as we do."[39]

Tony Blair addressed Parliament on July 11 concerning, as he said, the July 7 "terrorist attacks in London." He expressed Britain's "revulsion at this murderous carnage of the innocent," but said that all British "are united in our determination that our country will not be defeated by such terror but will defeat it and emerge from this horror with our values, our way of life, our tolerance and respect for others undiminished."

Through his whole speech, he repeatedly referred to the catastrophe as "terror striking," "terrorist attack," and an "act of terrorism." He said it "seems probable that the attack was carried out by Islamist extremist terrorists."

He also made a statement toward the end of his address directed at the Muslim community. He said, "People know full well that the overwhelming majority of Muslims stand four square with every other community in Britain. We were proud of your contribution to Britain before last Thursday. We remain proud of it today. Fanaticism is not a state of religion but a state of mind. We will work with you to make the moderate and true voice of Islam heard as it should be."[40]

Do I need to do the talk-show host rant here? Do I really need to waste the ink to say how out of control things have become if these sons of bitches can fly airplanes into office towers and kill innocent Americans, or detonate bombs on the London Underground and kill innocent Brits, and yet, some among us— those with control of the media—will not even call them terrorists?

I didn't think so. You get it.

27

Still Flying Blind

On the third anniversary of 9/11, my first book, *Flying Blind: How Political Correctness Continues to Compromise Airline Safety Post 9/11*, was published.[1] I never set out to write the book. It evolved from a personal flying experience and revelations about political correctness that came to light at a subsequent hearing of the 9/11 Commission. I became so incensed at what I learned after looking into the relationship between political correctness and airline safety that I felt compelled to write the book as a means of sounding the alarm that we remain vulnerable *post*-9/11, exactly where we were *on* 9/11. Thank goodness my book caused government officials to wake up and effectively change these policies, so now all is well. (Joking, of course, but I tried.)

The sad truth is that things are still screwed-up. If anything, I have only become more concerned about our politically correct manner of protecting the airways since writing the book. That is why I decided to write MUZZLED.

My hope is that by exposing some pretty incredible cases of domestic PC, and suggesting that therein lies the foundation for the way in which even our wartime battle against terrorism has been infected by this virus, I might better effectuate change. Call me crazy, but I think that the sooner we toughen up and stop handing trophies to all of our kids for everything, correcting their papers in purple, and permitting lawsuits for the distribution of a book that tells a salesman how to dress, the sooner we will be better equipped to handle al Qaeda.

Before I tell you about what is new on this front since *Flying Blind* was published, permit me a quick recap of that which is old.

In March of 2004, my family of six headed to our Florida home for spring break. That means: me—bald, forty-ish suburban white guy with expanding middle; beautiful wife of twenty-six (kidding, she was then in her early forties, too); daughter, sixteen (going on forty!); and three boys ages four, six, and eight. At the ticket counter at the Atlantic City Airport, our point of departure, my eight-year-old son was singled out for "secondary" or random screening. How absurd.

I didn't complain about the process. I believed that we all have an obligation to do our small part in the war on terror, and I figured this was mine. I did think it was a bit ridiculous and questioned whether the screening resources could be better spent but, under my breath, I blamed Osama bin Laden, not the United States government. We headed to Florida where we enjoyed a week's stay. The same thing happened with my son on the return flight. Again, I didn't whine about it. It was happening to many others.

About a week after the trip, Dr. Condoleezza Rice testified in front of the 9/11 Commission. While much of the media attention on the day of her testimony was on the title of the President's Daily Briefing (PDB), of August 6, 2001,[2] what caught my attention was a particular question put to her by John Lehman who, at age thirty-eight, had been appointed Ronald Reagan's secretary of the Navy and was now an individual who owed his 9/11 Commission status not to the White House, nor the Democratic leadership, but to Senator John McCain, who wanted an independent set of eyes and ears on this investigative body.

Secretary Lehman knocked me out of my Barcalounger when he asked Dr. Rice: "Before I go to Justice, were you aware that it was the policy, and I believe it remains the policy today, to fine airlines if they have more than two young Arab males in secondary questioning because that is discriminatory?"[3]

I found that to be a mind-boggling question. Dr. Rice had no knowledge of what he was talking about. But I wanted to know. So I tracked down Secretary Lehman who told me this:

> We had the testimony a couple of months ago from the president—past president of the United Airlines and the current president of American Airlines—that kind of shocked us all. They said under oath that indeed the Department of Transportation continued to fine any airline that was caught having more than two people of the same ethnic persuasion in a secondary line for questioning including, and especially, two Arabs. That is really the source because of this political correctness that became so entrenched during the nineties, and continues in the current administration, that no one approves of racial profiling. That is not the issue, but the fact is that Norwegian women are not, and 85-year-old ladies with aluminum walkers are not, the source of the terrorist threat. And the fact

is our enemy is violent Islamic extremism. And so the overwhelming number of people that one needs to worry about are young Arab males.[4]

Amen to that! I wrote up what I was told by Secretary Lehman for the *Philadelphia Daily News*, and what I penned got lots of play in cyberspace. It also led to television interview requests for me on the subject, and when I obliged, the Department of Transportation (DOT) reacted with a vehemence you would hope they'd reserve for Arab extremists. They called me "wildly incorrect" in my reporting when all I was doing was repeating what a 9/11 Commissioner had told me.[5]

So I decided to dig deeper. I might have stopped when the DOT trashed me had it not been for a chance encounter with Herb Kelleher, the legendary ballsy founder of Southwest Airlines who confirmed for me some of what Secretary Lehman had raised with Dr. Rice. I uncovered the fact that random screening is in existence so that when the guys we should be interested in, Abdul and Mohammed, see little suburban white kids like my eight-year-old getting screened, they can't claim they are being singled out when it's their turn. Worse, I learned that in the immediate aftermath of 9/11 there were four U.S. commercial carriers that were actually fined millions of dollars by our Department of Transportation because they were said to be involved in discriminatory conduct.

Let me be specific with you. United and American were the airlines victimized on that tragic day. They lost two airplanes apiece and a combined total of more than thirty of their own personnel. Yet, in the aftermath of 9/11, our Department of Transportation initiated discrimination complaints against both of them that were settled for $1.5 million apiece.

In those litigation files you will see scenarios like the following: a pilot is in the cockpit and ready to pull back from the gate. He's got a schedule to keep plus a statutory obligation to see to it that anyone who is perceived to be (and here are the magic words from the statute) "inimical to public safety" is removed from the aircraft.[6] Then comes the knock on the cockpit door, and the pilot is told, either by someone from the flight crew or in law enforcement, that "so-and-so in seat 3-C" is of Middle-Eastern descent, has been acting in a suspicious fashion, and has a name which is either on, or similar to a name which is on, a federal watch list. "What should we do, Captain?" And, to the extent the pilot agrees to have the passenger removed and questioned while he goes ahead and departs, our government perceives his actions to be discriminatory and initiates legal proceedings against his airline.

The airlines initially fought these "enforcement actions" but ultimately settled with the government. I wish they hadn't. American Airlines put up the best fight, but they, too, succumbed. As a lawyer, I can understand why they didn't want to incur the black eye that might go with fighting a discrimination lawsuit. Still, I wish they had hung tough.

By the way, the DOT hates it when I refer to the money paid as a "fine." It is money that the airline has to pay into a fund and use for sensitivity (or as I describe it, Kum-ba-yah) training of all personnel. What a disgrace.

Here is my thesis. The nineteen hijackers on 9/11 had a variety of commonalities: race, gender, religion, ethnicity, and appearance. To the extent we do not take that information into account as we seek to prevent a repeat of 9/11, we are Flying Blind.

I always tell those who disagree to please look at page seventeen of my book. That is where you can find the mug shots of the nineteen terrorists. I defy anybody to take a look at those photos next to one another and tell me that we should be pulling eight-year-old boys and eighty-five-year-old women with aluminum walkers out of airport security lines.

Truth be told, this mug-shot page was my choice for the cover of the book. You know the saying: "One picture is worth a thousand words." Well, Running Press, the publisher, refused on the basis that purchasers of the book might not want to walk around with the book under their arms, particularly at airport bookstores, if the mug shots were on the cover. (To which, I, of course, responded, "Now you're getting politically correct with me.")

Okay, so what's new since the book was published? Many things I believe to be worthy of mention. Let me tell you about ten developments that summarize our present state of affairs.

First, in *Flying Blind*, I tell what I call the real story of Flight 93. Remember, there were two things that distinguished Flight 93 from the other three flights on 9/11. First, due to a passenger revolt, it did not complete its mission, crashing instead into a field in Western Pennsylvania, and second, from a terrorist standpoint, Flight 93 was shorthanded.

Recall that Flight 93 had four terrorists on board while the other airplanes each had five. There has been a lot of conjecture as to whether there was to have been a twentieth hijacker, meaning a fifth person, on Flight 93. The 9/11

Commission believed the answer was yes and that the person who was to have been on Flight 93 is a man named Mohammed al-Kahtani. Why didn't he make it?

Mohammed al-Kahtani was stopped when he sought entrance to the United States on August 4 of 2001 at the Orlando International Airport. Kahtani was then a Saudi national who came before a very alert secondary inspections officer named Jose Melendez-Perez. Kahtani was sent to secondary screening simply because he had incorrectly filled out a Customs Declaration Form, and claimed not to speak English. Melendez put Kahtani's basic data into his computer, and it came up negative. His documents appeared genuine. And a check of his possessions was also unremarkable. But Melendez still didn't let him pass. To the consternation of his colleagues who were concerned about the political power of Saudi nationals, Melendez kept probing.

Why? "My job requires me to know the difference between legitimate travelers to the U.S. and those who are not," he told the 9/11 Commission. "This included potential terrorists." Keep in mind—this is a month *before* 9/11.

What caused Melendez-Perez to slow him down? As he told the 9/11 Commission about Kahtani, "He just gave me the creeps."[7]

I was never able to catch up with Melendez-Perez before going to press with *Flying Blind* to learn more about the incident. But I did interview him by telephone and met with him after the book came out; he confirmed all of my suspicions about the need to allow street smarts to play a role in securing our airports and our borders.

With regard to Kahtani, he told me "the reason that he got into screening was that, when I went to the secondary waiting room to pick him up to take him to the secondary interview office, he just gave me this scary look. He was staring in my eyes in a very scary way, and when he looked at me that way, I decided to look into more details on the documents he presented. At the same time I noticed that he didn't have a return ticket or an airline reservation, and it came to mind that the guy didn't speak English. I wondered how he was gonna get around to take care of his business. I was trying to put in place my training in military and interview techniques . . . what I thought was that he was a hit man."[8]

Now here is the kicker. What we now know is that, at precisely the moment that Mohammed al-Kahtani was being given his walking papers by Jose Melendez-Perez at the Orlando Airport on August 4, 2001, there to pick up the new arrival was 9/11 ringleader Mohammed Atta. That was one of the more interesting details to emerge from the work of the 9/11 Commission. And that is why Commissioner Richard Ben-Veniste, when Melendez-Perez testified in front of the 9/11 Commission, told him that his conduct had arguably spared the Capitol or White House an attack.[9] In other words, Ben-Veniste reasoned, with the added muscle of Kahtani on board Flight 93, the terrorists could have fended off the passenger revolt and continued toward Washington.

One more thing about the good work of Jose Melendez-Perez. Guess where the man he kept out of the United States, Mohammed al-Kahtani, next encountered Americans? How about on a battlefield in Afghanistan when he was fighting for al Qaeda post-9/11?

And here is something incredible. He is the individual referred to as "Detainee 063" in a *Time* magazine cover story that sought to engender sympathy for prisoners of war at Guantanamo, who were complaining that they were deprived or that we had played Christina Aguilera music too loudly. I kid you not. As if I give a damn if the man who wanted to be the twentieth hijacker, the fifth aboard Flight 93, got his feathers ruffled![10] (More about that in the next chapter.)

I was so moved with the unsung heroism of Jose Melendez-Perez, my radio station permitted me to host a luncheon in his honor in Philadelphia close to the fourth anniversary of 9/11. Five hundred of my listeners paid to attend the event in his honor.

Congressman Bob Brady, the head of the Philadelphia Democratic Party, arrived unannounced with a flag tucked under his arm that he had flown over the Capitol in Melendez-Perez's honor and thanked him for saving his life on 9/11. City Councilman Frank Rizzo gave him a proclamation from his colleagues. State Assemblyman Dennis O'Brien did likewise on behalf of the Commonwealth. Alice Hoglan, the mother of Flight 93's Mark Bingham, sent a video greeting from California. And both Debra Burlingame, the sister of Chic Burlingame, who was the pilot of American Flight 77 which crashed into the Pentagon, and Ellen Saracini, wife of Victor Saracini, the captain of United Flight 175 which hit the South Tower, both came to extend their gratitude. It was one of those life events that no matter how effective the prose, no written description will ever be able to fully describe. And when it was finally time for Melendez-Perez to address the crowd, he choked back tears and told the crowd, "I wish my father were here to see this." Jim Murray, the former general manager of the Philadelphia Eagles, in offering a benediction, told Melendez-Perez to rest assured his father had been watching. There was not a dry eye in the house.

What is the lesson from the good work of Melendez-Perez? He said it best: "I think that sometimes we just want to be politically correct and not harm anybody's feelings."[11] Too bad, I say.

For my second update, let me tell you about another good guy. Similar to my finally speaking with Jose Melendez-Perez, I also caught up with Michael Tuohey after publishing *Flying Blind.* You could say that Michael Tuohey stared the devil in the eyes and thought he recognized him. Now he kicks himself for not having acted, although, if he had, our government probably would have punished him for trying to take the devil down. I'll explain.

For many years Tuohey worked the ticket counter at the airport in Portland, Maine, first for Allegheny Airlines and then its successor, US Airways. He'll never forget one particular day of his thirty-four years of employment. It began like any other. This married Army vet had a routine. He'd awaken at 3:30 AM and walk to the kitchen to grab a cup of coffee. Then he'd flick on the television, watch some CNN, and check the weather forecast. After feeding his cat, he'd jump in his car for the fifteen-minute drive to work. On most days, the big rush would come between 6:00 and 7:30 AM That's when the tiny Maine airport would be abuzz with travelers heading for connecting flights in Philadelphia, Boston, and Pittsburgh. But it's what happened at 5:43 AM on a particular day that he replays in his mind over and over.

On a bright and beautiful Tuesday morning, two men wearing sport coats and ties approached his ticket counter with just seventeen minutes to spare before their flight to Boston. Tuohey now knows they had stayed the night before at the Comfort Inn down the road. And he suspects they arrived late to take advantage of an airline system that was then "more concerned about on-time departure than effective screening." He thought this pair was unusual, mostly because they each held a $2500 one-way first-class ticket to Los Angeles (via Boston). "You don't see many of those." The second reason is not so easy to explain. "It was just the look on the one man's face—his eyes," Tuohey told me.[12]

"By now, everyone in America has seen a picture of this man," he continued, "but there is more life in that photograph we've all seen than he had in the flesh and blood. He looked like a walking corpse. He looked so angry. And he wouldn't look directly at me."[13]

The man was Mohammed Atta. The other fellow ("he was young and had a goofy smile; I can't believe he knew he was going to die that day") was Abdul Aziz al Omari. In other words, Michael Tuohey is the individual who checked them in at the Portland Airport as they began their murderous journey! He said, "I looked up, and asked them the standard questions. The one guy was looking at me. It sent a chill through me. Something in my stomach churned. And, subconsciously, I said to myself, 'If they don't look like Arab terrorists, nothing does.' Then I gave myself a mental slap. In over thirty-four years, I had checked in thousands of Arab travelers and I never thought this before. I said to myself, 'That's not nice to think. They are just two Arab businessmen.'" And with that, Tuohey handed them their boarding passes.

As they walked through the metal detectors, out of his sight, the jackets and ties were gone. Now the two were wearing open neck dress shirts when they went through security. Atta and Omari arrived in Boston at 6:45 AM where they were joined by Satam al Suqami, Wail al Shehri, and Waleed al Shehri. The five checked in and boarded American Airlines Flight No. 11 bound for Los Angeles. At 8:46 AM, it hit the North Tower. Back in Portland, Tuohey got word of the crash.

"One of the agents from another airline said, 'Did you hear what happened in New York?' I said, 'Oh my God,' and I was sorry I had judged them. I thought it was an accident," he told me. But when United Airlines Flight 175 hit the South Tower at 9:03 AM, back in Portland, Tuohey knew his first instinct had been correct. "As soon as someone told me news of the second flight, I had a knot in my stomach."

Now here is the irony. While Michael Tuohey still second-guesses himself about his conduct on that day, the reality is that had he taken action, he would have been punished by our government! They would have fined US Airways in the same way they fined United, American, Continental, and Delta had Michael Tuohey used any of his intuition. Remember, in the aftermath of 9/11, each was fined amounts that added up to millions of dollars by the Department of Transportation for incidents where DOT believed airline employees had factored race, gender, ethnicity, religion, or appearance into security screening decisions. This, despite the fact that all nineteen hijackers on 9/11 had all those characteristics in common!

Tuohey didn't learn of the fines until he read my book, *Flying Blind.* Now he gets it. "Here you have an industry in mortal peril, and you are fining them for political correctness?" asks Tuohey.

One more thing about Michael Tuohey—and Jose Melendez-Perez, the astute screener who kept the twentieth hijacker out of the United States on

August 4, 2001. When *Flying Blind* came out, it was reviewed in the *Boston Herald*. The Department of Transportation's mouthpiece was asked for a statement on my book. He said that I possess "a woefully warped sense of American values."[14]

So, initially I was "wildly incorrect," and now I have a warped sense of American values. Well, with guys like Tuohey and Melendez-Perez, I'd say I am in damn good company.

Which brings me to update No. 3. Recall that my interest in airline safety was largely initiated by a single question posed by Secretary John Lehman to Dr. Condoleezza Rice in her public testimony before the 9/11 Commission. It was the quota question, implying airport security screeners could not pull more than a certain number of individuals of a particular ethnic stripe out of an airport security line at once as that would be discrimination.

Secretary Lehman asked that question because Edmond Soliday, former head of security for United Airlines, told that to the 9/11 Commission. ("[A] visitor from the Justice Department who told me that if I had more than three people of the same ethnic origin in line for additional screening, our system would be shut down as discriminatory."[15])

When I was able to get U.S. Senator Arlen Specter to hold a Senate hearing on the subject of political correctness and airline safety (held on June 24, 2004), Senator Specter was anxious to hear from Mr. Soliday. So was I. But Soliday requested that he not have to testify because the 9/11 Commission report was still in progress, and he did not want to speak until the report was final. My book *Flying Blind* went to press before the work of the 9/11 Commission concluded, meaning I never got to speak with Soliday.

But someone recently did. Investigative reporter Paul Sperry spoke to Soliday in support of his book *Infiltration*. Soliday reinforced what he told the 9/11 Commission, including identifying the individual who issued the quota warning and its context. It turns out it was not someone from the Justice Department but, rather, a visitor from the Department of Transportation. Sperry's interview with Soliday revealed that on September 16, 1997, Soliday was present for a meeting at United Airlines headquarters in Chicago with Sam Podberesky, the assistant general counsel of the DOT, and a civil rights' attorney, whose wife and son are Hispanic. Soliday says that Podberesky "told me that if I had more than three people of the same ethnic origin in line for additional screening, our system would be shut down as discriminatory."[16] Podberesky viewed any human profiling as discriminatory even if based on statistical probability. As a result, Soliday says United "loaded up the system with randoms to make it mathematically impossible to get three ethnics in line at the same time," including "soccer moms, Girl Scouts, and even little old ladies with walkers."[17] Soliday still regards that policy as a point of vulnerability for what occurred on 9/11: "Don't have your guy come down there and tell me we can't pull more than three Arab guys out of line for additional security screening, and then tell us after 9/11 that we should have thrown five guys like that off our planes."[18] And he knows the problems still remain. "PC is still tying our hands in fighting terrorism. I think the American people will lose their resolve, and we'll continue to waste billions of dollars on CTX [bomb-scanning] machines and other weapons-screening equipment rather than profiling passengers, and the political correctness will win."[19]

You can already guess update No. 4: we're still not profiling terrorists. The closest we have come is what was touted as a passenger-profiling system instituted at Logan International Airport in Boston (from which two of the four airlines involved on 9/11 departed). But it really doesn't profile, which hasn't stopped the program from drawing its first lawsuit.

The ACLU (surprise, surprise) has already filed a claim saying that the new system relies on race and ethnicity. I wish! Unfortunately, the architect of the new system, State Police Sgt. Peter DeDominica, has gone to great lengths to say that those factors which united the nineteen on 9/11—race, gender, religion, ethnicity, and appearance—will *not* be relied upon.

I interviewed DeDominica. He struck me as an earnest and bright guy, but I was disappointed when he told me the commonalities of the 9/11 hijackers will not be relied upon. His system is behavior based only. I told him that perhaps I should have known, when I read in *Time* magazine that his program would be "racially neutral," that it would not look for the characteristics of the nineteen hijackers on 9/11. DeDominca told me:

> It's clearly not going to use a person's appearance, race, or ethnic ancestry as a factor, and there are a couple a good reasons for that. Number one, it's illegal in this country, and, number two, it's not going to be effective. I think there are some misconceptions about the threat, about who's carrying it out; the fact is that people are being recruited from all races to carry out these attacks. If you look at the people, the most recent attempts in this country involve individuals of a wide broad array of

races—John Walker Lind, Jose Padilla, Richard Reid. We even had a sergeant in a National Guard Unit out in Washington State that was convicted by a military tribunal of attempting to provide information to al Qaeda, and they're actively recruiting people of all races.[20]

To which I respond that al Qaeda has been a failure in recruiting individuals of all races; instead, we are confronted with an enemy bearing many commonalities. Think about it. Every time there is an al Qaeda leader captured and presented on television, that individual resembles the nineteen on 9/11. To which DeDominica replied: "There are commonalities, but it is also easy to be deceived and get into stereotypes and lose focus. Potentially, anybody can be a terrorist. We are trying to do it intelligently and within laws of this country."[21]

I asked him if the P-word is a dirty word.

He answered, "No, it is a part of the fabric of this country. When I was a kid and tried out for Little League, I was profiled. When I went to college and took the SAT test, I was profiled. When I went to get life insurance, I was profiled. When you decide where to sit on train at night, you profile passengers. We all do it."

DeDominica and I agreed the Transportation Safety Administration (TSA) resources need to be reoriented and no one should get a free pass from passenger screening, including suburban white guys like me. But where we disagreed was on the issue of whether the commonalities of the 9/11 hijackers should be factors taken into consideration. And if they aren't prepared to do that at Logan Airport in Boston, rest assured it's not being done anywhere else in the nation. Go figure.

Fifth, the FBI agent who authored the famous pre-9/11 memo now known as the "Phoenix Memo," a recommendation that the State Department coordinate with the FBI so that flight students from Middle-Eastern countries could be investigated, made his first public remarks after 9/11 in which he stated that profiling concerns hurt the antiterrorism effort. Ken Williams is the FBI agent who wrote the memo dated July 10, 2001, and he offered those sentiments in his first ever interview given to the *Arizona Republic* as he was receiving an award from war veterans.

Prior to the attacks, Williams said, there was a deep concern over racial profiling—or targeting a class of people for investigation because of ethnicity—that stopped some from acting on his recommendations. "We are in a war with people who really want to hurt us. In my opinion, it is not over," Williams said.

"Intelligence is not an exact science. I tell people it is like drinking from a fire hydrant."[22]

Sixth, in the aftermath of the downing of two Russian airliners that killed nearly one hundred people on both planes, the TSA authorized pat-downs by screeners of passengers. This caused a ruckus when passengers began reporting that they felt violated in the process. In response to criticism, the TSA issued a seven-point customer-service pledge promising, among other things, that pat-downs would be done with screeners of the same gender as the passenger. At the same time, the TSA said it is hoping that "trace portal" machines that test of explosive residue would eliminate the need for most hand searches.[23]

What does this all mean? Quite simply that we are still looking for bombs, but not bombers. The answer, as anyone who has flown El Al to Israel can attest, is to take a page from the playbook of the Israelis and do both.

Seventh is the strange flight involving passenger Annie Jacobsen. She is a business writer for WomensWallStreet.com who was thrust into the airline security arena after an incredible flight on which she was a passenger, Northwest Flight 327 on June 29, 2004, from Detroit to Los Angeles.[24] According to Jacobsen, fourteen Middle-Eastern men between the ages of twenty and fifty acted in a strange and coordinated manner, scaring her and other passengers to death.

The men followed one another into the restrooms, and one walked into the bathroom with a full McDonald's bag and came out with it empty. Jacobson said, "Then another man from the group stood up and took something from his carry-on in the overhead bin. It was about a foot long and was rolled in cloth. He headed toward the back of the cabin with the object. Five minutes later, several more of the Middle-Eastern men began using the forward lavatory consecutively. In the back, several of the men stood up and used the back lavatory as well."

She reported the suspicious behavior to a flight attendant who told her that federal marshals on board were monitoring the situation. Then, just before landing, a half-dozen of the men got up in unison and went to the bathrooms yet again. No one asked them to take their seats. According to Jacobsen, the last man out then mouthed no to the others and ran his finger across his throat.

When the airplane landed, it was met by federal officials who detained and questioned the Middle-Eastern men. Supposedly, the feds determined that they were traveling musicians, although it was later reported they were traveling on expired visas.

After speaking to Jacobsen, I became convinced she was indeed the victim of terrorism. Either she was witness to a dry run, much like actor James Woods watched onboard a pre-9/11 airplane with Mohammad Atta, or she was victimized by some sick individuals having fun at the expense of a skittish American.

What I found most credible about Annie Jacobsen was her lack of an apparent agenda. This was a California mom traveling with her husband and young son, and no political baggage. But she gets it. "If you ask me, Michael, I think the secretary of the Department of Transportation, Norman Mineta, has way too much of his own agenda to remain objective about any of this . . . to separate his personal priorities . . . from those of the general flying public."

In the spring of 2005, Audrey Hudson, reporting for the *Washington Times*, revealed the Homeland Security Department's inspector general was investigating the incident.[25] Hudson reported that Ms. Jacobsen had recently been interviewed and that federal agents had confirmed to her the James Woods story, which, although widely reported, has never been substantiated by law enforcement. The federal interest in Annie Jacobsen and Flight 327 represents a turn for the better. Dave Adams, a spokesman for the Federal Air Marshal Service, initially dismissed Jacobsen's story as coming from "untrained civilian eyes."

Eight is the case of KLM Flight 875 on April 8, 2005, and what it says about yet another area of vulnerability. The initial report said that this flight from Amsterdam to Mexico City was blocked mid-flight by U.S. authorities for having two "undesirable" people on board.[26] The next report included more data. Specifically, the two individuals were Saudi pilots who had trained at the same flight school in Arizona as 9/11 hijacker Hani Hanjour.[27] The United States caused the airplane to turn around instead of flying over our airspace, no doubt causing discomfort to those who had already flown five hours, but a necessary result of the war on terror. I am sure you agree. But here is the kicker. I assumed from these reports of the flight's reversal that the United States is always provided with flight manifests of commercial airliners traveling through our airspace. Wrong.

Soon after the reports on KLM Flight 875 came the news that the Bush administration is considering requiring foreign airlines to check the names of passengers on all flights over the United States.[28] In other words, this is not presently required. Instead, only foreign airlines planning to land in the United States must submit passenger and crew lists to the government within fifteen minutes of departure. Turns out that in the case of KLM Flight 875, Mexican officials "tipped" the U.S. authorities to the presence of the two Saudis but apparently were not required to do so. Flying Blind, indeed. We need to see the flight manifesto of every commercial airplane flying over the United States regardless of whether or not they have a scheduled landing here.

Ninth should be self-evident; Norman Mineta needs to go. He was one of the few holdovers in the second Bush administration when, as the architect of much of the political correctness that still corrodes the system, he should have been sacked before anyone else. To be helpful, I've come up with a few questions that should be used at the Senate confirmation hearings for any prospective secretary who will play a role in the war on terror:

- Mr./Ms. Secretary Designate, do you acknowledge that the war on terror is a war against radical Islam?

- Mr./Ms. Secretary Designate, would you agree that the nineteen hijackers on 9/11 were all associated with radical Islam?

- And that they had their race, gender, religion, ethnicity, and appearance in common?

- And that in looking for those who would emulate the nineteen on 9/11, we should be mindful of that which those individuals had in common?

- Even if some call that profiling?

Only a "yes, yes, yes, yes, and yes" are acceptable.

Now on to update No. 10. It is only appropriate I now crown a winner. Of what, you ask? My competition for best horror story involving airport security screening in the post-9/11 world. I think I'm qualified to do the honors given that in the first six months since I published *Flying Blind: How Political Correctness Continues to Compromise Airline Safety*, I was overwhelmed with anecdotes from across the country about the ridiculous nature of present passenger screening. I've heard it all. Military personnel returning home from the front lines in the war on terror (in uniform and with papers) who take a commercial flight, only to get searched after being selected for random screening. Or people with pacemakers and documents that say metal detectors might cause a heart hiccup who are nevertheless "wanded" and then questioned as to what they are hiding in their chest!

I've heard from eyewitnesses to the full-scale screening of government leaders like Senator Joseph Lieberman and former Secretary of Defense William Cohen. Then there has been the full complement of seniors with walkers and young kids on whom we've wasted precious resources.

Yet none compare to the Yocum family from Boothwyn, Pennsylvania. They win. Their experience occurred on October 28, 2002, at the Phoenix Sky Harbor International Airport. Frank and Claire Yocum's visit to Arizona was due to her quadruple pregnancy. The pregnancy was high-risk. (What they never dreamed was our government would think that translates into high security risk!)

The plan was for Claire to deliver at the Good Samaritan Hospital, home to Dr. John P. Elliot who is nationally recognized for his delivery of quadruplets.

Claire's delivery was nine weeks premature. The babies then needed two months in the ICU. Their immune systems were severely compromised, and they needed to be kept free from germs. A common cold could have killed them.

The Yocums were eager to return to Pennsylvania. Their doctors were nervous about the travel. Airplanes, with their recycled air, are not exactly the most sanitary of environments. After consulting the physicians and America West Airlines, they decided to make the trip on a direct late-night flight when there would be few other passengers. America West was sympathetic to the difficulty of the traveling brood and offered to fly the entire family free of charge. So sensitive was the situation that the Yocums had to take CPR training before the hospital would permit the travel to take place. Frank Yocum, a cop's son, was meticulous about the planning for the journey.

On the morning before the flight, Frank actually made a test run so that he knew exactly where to go, minimizing the babies' contact with anyone. On the day of the flight, the nurses and doctors prepared the Yocums for their seven-hour journey. They organized all the babies' bottles, medicines, and other necessities. (Organization was extremely important because the babies were all on different formulas.) More importantly, each baby was on a heart monitor, and the darkness of the night flight was expected to make the necessary maneuvering quite a challenge. The travel from the hospital to the airport was smooth until it came to airport screening.

By now, I'm sure you've guessed, the newborn Yocum quadruplets were selected for additional screening! Nineteen Arab look-alikes had wreaked havoc on the United States on September 11, and four newborns from Philadelphia are the ones getting the hairy eyeball.

The babies, wrapped tight in blankets and with nets covering their car seats, were removed from their carriages and searched. All of their bags, which had been prepared and organized by the nurses, had to be removed. Worst of all, the screeners woke the four sleeping babies.

Frank and Claire never again got a handle on the situation and the flight home was chaotic. Everything was thrown back into bags to sort out later, which never happened. Unlike the screeners, the other passengers had common sense. They all voluntarily moved to the front of the plane and gave the Yocums about twenty aisles to themselves. Says Frank now, "Still, I can only imagine what it was like for the other passengers with four crying babies and heart monitors going off on a five-hour flight."

A member of Congress with whom I spoke recently told me the TSA has backed off the random screening of children. But when I tried to confirm this with the TSA, they reported no change in policy. Instead, the TSA says the policy of selecting passengers for secondary screening originates with the individual air carriers at the ticket counters in one of two ways, random selection by the airline or based on CAPPS (Computer Assisted Passenger Pre-screening System) screening which looks for "trends in travel." Children under the age of twelve who are randomly selected *may* be "de-selected" at the carrier's discretion, and a parent need not be screened in place of the child.

So, the stupidity can continue.

Here is a final thought. After my book came out, I received a vote of confidence from a very important person in the world of profiling. Roger Depue, the former head of the FBI Behavioral Science Unit and author of *Between Good and Evil*, was my guest on the radio. (We're talking the real deal as portrayed by Jodie Foster and Anthony Hopkins in *Silence of the Lambs*). I had provided him with a copy of *Flying Blind* in advance of his appearance, which was to promote his book. When we spoke on the air, he told me:

> I travel quite a bit as you know, and I'm constantly going through airports and have been singled out myself many times to go through a more intense screening and it's a very difficult problem for these airports. To me, common sense says that you have to look at the people who are most likely to present the danger, that's just common sense. That's balanced on the other side with this whole concept of racial profiling, and I think that a good airport security system ought to be able to justify looking at

the people who are most likely to present a danger to the airline industry or the passengers on a particular plane. So I'm in agreement with you, Michael. I have your book *Flying Blind*, and there's a common sense quotient that has to be put into the equation—and that is that if you have a declared enemy and you have people who represent or look like those people, then you have to pay more attention to them—it's foolish not to.[29]

28

Is That All There Is?

It is one thing to allow the forces of political correctness to MUZZLE our day-to-day lives here at home in the United States, but it's quite another when that same cancer metastasizes into the war on terror. Sadly, this is the case. We won't stop it over there unless we first stop it here. This is why you should be not only be engaged and entertained by the stories I have told, but outraged as well. Political correctness has invaded the heartland.

Airport screeners don't look for terrorists and television terrorists don't look like real terrorists. "Terrorism" itself is a banned word. We're four years post-9/11 and still vulnerable. Let's recognize that first responders don't have time for a crash course in irrelevancy before rescuing those in peril. And that all of this limp-wristed worrying over hurt feelings is compromising our ability to defeat radical Islam, and just might get us killed. There. All said.

What do I mean when I say that political correctness is a killer? It's not just our unwillingness to look for terrorists who look like terrorists in airport screening lines or border checkpoints, as described in the last chapter. I'm talking about what we do with terrorists when we do catch them. Whether it's Abu Ghraib or Guantanamo Bay, I find the way the civil libertarians and Amnesty International types have manufactured a debate about the rights of suspected terrorists to be absolutely appalling.

Abu Ghraib, the Iraqi equivalent of Stalin's Lubyenka prison when it was under the control of Saddam Hussein, has been used since his toppling by the U.S. military to house some insurgents. A handful of knuckleheads out of the approximately 140,000 U.S. soldiers then deployed in Iraq engaged in some stupid behavior that was tame by Saddam's standards. But you would think the United States was recreating the Holocaust by the way it was covered in the news.

Brigadier-General Janis Karpinski has had a long, distinguished career in the military: she received a Bronze Star for her service in the Gulf War, and most recently, served as the Commander of the Military Police Brigade and was the first and only female General Officer commanding troops in a combat zone in Iraq. But in the minds of many her military record will forever be known for only one thing: her command of Abu Ghraib.

The most notorious of the soldiers in her charge were a pair of Army reservists, Private First Class Lynndie England and Specialist Charles Graner. England was seen in several photographs standing next to hooded, naked prisoners while pointing to their private parts. Graner, on the other hand, was the dope who posed for photographs while standing next to a prisoner with a leash around his neck.

The conduct of both is inexcusable and an embarrassment to the United States. But let's not forget, as Karpinksi told me in an interview, "The pictures that we saw come from Abu Ghraib would pale in comparison to some of the other atrocities either under Saddam or still taking place in Iraq or in other locations now."[1]

Yes, they disgraced their uniforms, and they were both severely punished for what they did. England was found guilty of one count of conspiracy to maltreat prisoners, four counts of maltreatment, and one count of committing an indecent act. She was sentenced to three years in prison. Graner was found guilty of numerous crimes, including assault, and was sentenced to ten years in prison. Having played out thus, the entire Abu Ghraib matter should have been a blip on the radar screen in the context of war and true incidents of barbaric sadism, such as Nick Berg's being decapitated on television.

Nine Army reservists have been convicted of abusing detainees at the Abu Ghraib Prison in Iraq,[2] and Karpinski was served up as scapegoate—demoted and relieved of her command. That should have been the end of the story.

But the media wouldn't let it go. The media still won't let it go. Calls for Donald Rumsfeld's resignation have been everywhere in the mainstream media, and moral outrage has become quite fashionable—with the editorial pages of liberal flagships such as the *New York Times* and *Washington Post* wearing their indignation like the latest from Versace. It is just too easy to rip U.S. efforts to bring democracy to Iraq and to fight the war on terror—to paint an entire nation's efforts with the same brush used for a handul of idiots in a Baghdad prison.

Little did we know at the time, but the coverage of Abu Ghraib was just a preview of coming attractions, a timid introduction for the spin that was to come with regard to our detainment of terror suspects at Guantanamo Bay. There is no better example of what I am talking about than the aforementioned

Time magazine issue of June 12, 2005, which boasted of an "exclusive" with its cover story titled "Detainee 063, Inside the Wire at Gitmo."

As I have previously explained, Detainee 063 is none other than Mohammed al-Kahtani. (*Time* spelled his name Qahtani.) If he'd gotten past a custom's officer named Jose Melendez-Perez when he sought entry to our country in Orlando on August 4, 2001, he would have ended up among the terrorists aboard Flight 93 on 9/11. Thankfully, Melendez-Perez would not let him pass.

Now comes *Time* magazine, anxious to evoke sympathy for a man they call Detainee 063—that same individual who would have been cutting somebody's throat with a box cutter on board Flight 93 had Jose Melendez-Perez not sent him packing for Saudi Arabia. The same man who, after being rejected for admission to the United States one month before 9/11, was captured on a battlefield fighting our soldiers in the battle at Tora Bora in December of 2001. In other words, after failing to become the twentieth hijacker, he went right back to being a soldier in the terrorist war against the United States.

Only in that context can anyone evaluate the treatment he has received while incarcerated. What, exactly, does our treatment or, as some are describing, our "torture" include? How about the atrocity of making him stand. And shaving his beard. Hanging pictures of scantily clad women around his neck. Pinning a photo of a 9/11 victim to his trousers. Interrogating him in a room filled with 9/11 victim photos. Dripping water on his head. And playing Christina Aguilera music.[3]

If anything, when I read the story, I wondered why we had shown him so much benevolence. And I was dying to say so to a national audience. I soon got my chance.

The very week the magazine came out, I had the chance to express my opinion of the manufactured controversy with Chris Matthews on *Hardball*. Joining me in the segment—which I did not know until the camera was turned on— were Gary Schroen who served as the CIA station chief in Pakistan and who was tasked with killing bin Laden after 9/11 (he wrote a good book about his service called *First In*) and William Schulz, the executive director of Amnesty International, who was, of course, highly critical of the treatment of detainees at Guantanamo Bay.

I want to go now to the transcript because I think, in the span of a ten-minute debate on national TV, we got right to the heart of this issue. Here is the way the segment began.

Chris Matthews: So, let's start right now with Michael Smerconish. Should Guantanamo be kept as a detention camp for terrorists?

Smerconish: Absolutely. And, you know, *Time* magazine this week, Chris, finally gives us a name that we can talk about instead of debating this in the abstract. Mohammed al-Qahtani would have cut someone's throat with a box cutter on September 11 and perhaps would have allowed Flight 93 to crash into the Capitol or the White House but for an astute INS agent who kept him out of the country on August 4 of 2001. This is the kind of a guy that we're talking about. And I, for one, am sick and tired of all the kvetching over his rights and his liberties. People have already forgotten what occurred and it has not even been four years.[4]

Damn if it didn't feel great to drop that on national TV! Chris Matthews turned to the fellow from Amnesty International for a response on the question of whether Guantanomo should be closed. It was exactly what you'd expect.

William Schulz: Yes, it should be. It has become the best recruiting tool for al Qaeda that the United States could possibly have provided. It's also become a symbol of U.S. recklessness and hypocrisy in promoting what we claim is a war in defense of the rule of law.

Then Matthews asked him the appropriate follow-up:

Matthews: What do we do with the detainees who are down there now?

Schulz: We bring them—we do one of two things. We either charge them with a crime, bring them to the U.S. mainland and put them on trial, or we have to release them. Now, the *Time* magazine . . .

Matthews: We have to release people, even if they're dangerous?

(CROSSTALK)

Schulz:	No. No. Absolutely not. If we—we then have to charge them with a crime.
Matthews:	Suppose they haven't committed a crime. Suppose they're simply dangerous.
Schultz:	That's a serious problem, then. We can't hold them.
Matthews:	Why not?
Schulz:	What—on what charge? On what charge?
Matthews:	Well, this guy, al-Qahtani, who may have been the twentieth hijacker . . .

(CROSSTALK)

Schulz:	And that's right. And if that's the case, he should be charged, as Moussaoui is being charged as this twentieth hijacker.

(CROSSTALK)

Matthews:	What do we do with people who are members of al Qaeda and openly so?
Schulz:	We charge them with crimes.
Matthews:	And that is a crime—to be a member of al Qaeda?
Schulz:	It may well be a conspiracy, absolutely, if there's evidence to show that they have been involved with violence or potential violence, or planning of violence against the United States or against innocent civilians.
Matthews:	By that argument, the people coming in this country on 9/11, if we had picked them up twenty-four hours before 9/11, we couldn't have kept them, because you say they wouldn't be able to be charged with a crime yet.
Schulz:	I didn't say that. I said they might very well be able to have charged them with a crime.
Matthews:	But if they haven't committed the crime of 9/11 yet, how did we—how could we have kept them?

Schulz: Well, look, this is just like in domestic situations where someone is suspected that they may commit a crime. But we don't then throw them in jail indefinitely. Look, the *Time* magazine article was very interesting. It did three things. It documented a pattern of abuse, so no one can question that any longer. It showed that some of the most effective interrogation of al-Qahtani was nonviolent interrogation. And, finally, it demonstrated that once al-Qahtani had been made a psychological misfit, psychotic, psychological trauma, hearing voices, then his evidence was used to convict or to keep others at Guantanamo in prison. In other words, we were using a psychotic, and evidence from a psychotic, against other people. That's the problem with not bringing people to trial. There may well be dozens more who are not like al-Qahtani and who ought not to be at Gitmo.

Later in the segment, Matthews returned to me:

Matthews: You're shaking your head in disgust, Michael.

Smerconish: I'm shaking my head because I've read the *Time* magazine piece. Where is the abuse? We shaved the guy's beard. We played Christina Aguilera music and we pinned 9/11 victim photos to his lapel. That's abuse? Abuse to me is cutting off Nick Berg's head. Abuse to me is cutting somebody's throat with a box cutter. I mean, what's wrong with sending a message to radical Islam that says "we are going to play hardball with you if you do bad things to the United States"?

Matthews: Well, one—one problem with it, Michael, though I love your spirit, is that you're creating attitude on the other side that—that escalates. They see us making fools of their people. They cut off a few more heads.

Smerconish: You are presupposing that, if you fed them a nice warm piece of quiche and gave them a soft blanket . . .

Matthews: No.

(CROSSTALK)

> Smerconish: . . . then that wouldn't be the case. That's already the
> case, Chris.

There you have it. That *Hardball* is itself a summary of the way in which political correctness threatens our ability to win the war on terror. You have Amnesty International's executive director telling the national cable audience that Guantanamo needs to be closed; we can't hold suspected terrorists even if we believe them to be dangerous; and that *Time* had documented a "pattern of abuse." And there I am reminding people that radical Islam cut the throats of Americans with box cutters and crashed airplanes in order to kill innocent civilians; so we must do whatever it takes to prevent it from happening again.

The *Time* publication was the focus of my radio program in Philadelphia for several straight days. And, in thinking about the attention it was receiving from me and others in the media, I wanted to hear from the one man who could share a unique perspective on Detainee 063, someone *Time* magazine did not seek to interview. I was anxious to go back to Melendez-Perez and ask him for his perspective, which has been missing from the media accounts about alleged abuse at Guantanamo. He told me he had not read the *Time* splash, but was puzzled by the controversy surrounding the interrogation of the man he kept out of our country. While I find that others may have forgotten the horror of what happened on 9/11, even before its four-year anniversary, Melendez-Perez is not one of them.

"This guy was a person coming in to the United States to do some harm, and we need some information to see what was going on—did they have future plans to come back to the United States—I think we can't just treat him with soft gloves," said the man who kept al-Kahtani out of the United States.[5]

"A lot of people are forgetting what happened on 9/11," he continued. "They want to treat these people with so much respect, and that is the way we went previously with Saudi Arabia and other countries and look what happened. We could have treated those people a little different and held them accountable for their actions and maybe we could have precluded 9/11 from happening. And here, we go back and try to say he has rights. In my opinion, I don't think so. I think we should have done something a long time ago to get him to confess. I understand he has provided valuable information, and we have been waiting for that information for three or four years."

With Melendez-Perez's comments fresh in my mind, one week after the *Time* publication, I had the opportunity to chat with Secretary of Defense Donald Rumsfeld about the Guantanamo controversy. Needless to say, he shares the perspective of Melendez-Perez. (And Yours Truly.)

He responded by saying he recently took comfort in reading what David McCullough had pointed out: "If the Revolutionary War had been covered the way this war is being covered, and if people had seen how difficult the conditions are, and how badly things were run, and the difficulty of the task, people would have tossed it in." He continued:[6]

> You're right. The people down there at Guantanomo Bay, under the president's orders, have been treated humanely, and they should be treated humanely. But these are terrorists, trainers, bomb makers, suicide bombers, UBL's, bodyguards, the twentieth hijacker (as you point out), recruiters, and facilitators. These are bad people. These are people who want to go out and kill innocent men, women, and children. We have been letting a number of them go back to their home countries, in the custody of their countries, and already we have found twelve who were let go by mistake, probably because they were using an alias and we weren't able to sort it out, back on the battlefield, trying to kill our people. So this is a tough business. It is a difficult world. The struggle against extremists is not an easy thing. And those who are suggesting that the management, or handling, by our military of what's going on in Guatanamo Bay is not the way it should be are flat wrong.

He got a laugh out of my telling him that, after hearing Amnesty International's complaints, I then read the *Time* magazine piece, thinking I had missed something, and was reminded of the old Peggy Lee song, "Is That All There Is."

"There's no torture going on down there, and there hasn't been," said the secretary of defense.

I told him I had defended the practices at Guatanamo Bay the prior week on *Hardball* and was confronted with the usual rebuttal, that our interrogation techniques don't generate results. He said the interrogation methods are indeed successful.

There is no question but that the United States is learning a great deal.

We've learned the organization structure of al Qaeda and other terrorist groups; we've learned the extent of the terrorist presence in Europe, the U.S., and the Middle East. We have information on al Qaeda's pursuit of weapons of mass destruction, information on recruiting and recruitment centers, on terrorist skill sets, and financing. This information has saved American lives, the information that has been gained down there.

No one wants to hold these people, no one wants to spend time interrogating these people, but we simply have to do it. We are in a long struggle against violent extremists who are anxious, and financed, to kill innocent men women and children in our country and other Western countries across the globe.

Days after this conversation with the secretary of defense, the *New England Journal of Medicine* came out with an article titled "Doctors and Interrogators at Guantanamo Bay."[7] It was probably the height of the asinine sympathy that has been generated on behalf of those who seek to kill us. And the *New York Times*—surprise, surprise—made it a page-one story.[8] The *NE Journal* reported that interrogators at Guantanamo had sought and relied upon the counsel of medical professionals in determining how best to extract information from suspected terrorists.

For example, a psychologist, Major John Leso, a specialist in assessing aviators' fitness to fly, attended the interrogation of Mohammed al-Qahtani. The *New York Times* gave other examples. It reported that, in another case, a detainee's medical files showed he had a severe phobia of the dark and suggested ways in which that could be manipulated to make him cooperate. In another circumstance, the *Times* reported that a doctor read the medical file of yet another detainee and learned he had a particular longing for his mother, and suggested ways that could be exploited to persuade him to cooperate.

Allow me two observations: First, the fact that our detainees have medical records should tell you all you need to know. They are being observed and cared for! It's not as if they were captured at Tora Bora or wherever and presented their Independence Blue Cross cards with x-rays and urine specimens. This means we are monitoring the health of those we think want to cut our throats. And, secondly, I say this is absolutely ingenious. Why not use the information available to us to try to prevent another 9/11?

My friend Joe Scarborough from MSNBC said it best in discussion about torture on my show: "In some circumstances, our interogators should come into the room riding a pig. Whatever it takes."

Surprise, surprise again, that is not the way the *New York Times* spun it, and certainly not the take of the two bleeding hearts who wrote for the *NE Journal*. They saw this as a violation of the confidentiality of medical records: "Wholesale rejection of clinical confidentiality at Guantanamo also runs contrary to settled ethical precepts. At Guantanamo, the fear-and-anxiety approach was often favored. The cruel and degrading measures taken by some, in violation of international human rights law and the laws of war, have become a matter of national shame." Ethical precepts? We're cruel and degrading? National shame?

One word springs to mind: MUZZLED.

Back to my conversation with Secretary Rumsfeld. With all this garbage in mind, I asked him, what does he say to those who would close Guantanamo Bay? The secretary answered with a question of his own:

Then the question is, "What is the alternative?" He who would tear down what is has the responsibility of recommending something better. And I haven't heard anybody who said anything like that who has any idea at all, unless you want to let all these people go and let them kill another 3,000 or 10,000 Americans.

This facility is needed. It is housing people who have done great damage to our country, who are determined to go out and kill additional people if they have the chance: bomb-makers and terrorist financers, and suicide bombers. And they need to be kept off the street. And they are being kept off the street in Guantanamo at a facility being operated by young men and women from our armed services who are doing a fine job. They are treating them in a humane way, but they are keeping them off the street, and they are interrogating them to find out additional information so we can prevent future terrorist acts.

I shared with the secretary my concern that, close in time to the fourth anniversary of 9/11, people have already forgotten as evidenced by this orchestrated debate about prisoner rights. Said the secretary of our war on terror:

No, I'm not worried, and I guess the reason I am not worried is that I have been around a long time. I will be seventy-three next month, and

I have so much confidence in the basic center of gravity of American people. They seem to have a good inner gyroscope that centers them and, while it can be blown off to the side for a while in a rash of bad news, it doesn't take them long to get recentered and understand what is important and what isn't.

I go visit the families of the wounded in Bethesda and Walter Reed and other hospitals, and those families—here their young ones are injured and in some cases with an leg off or arm off or blinded in one eye—and the families are so strong and so supportive, and understand from their sons and daughters who are soldiers, they understand from them, what is actually happening, how well they are doing, and the importance of what they are doing. I am absolutely convinced that, in five or ten years, people will look back and be so proud of what they have done in that conflict. The men and women in uniform, we are so proud to have them.

I pray he is correct. If he is it will only be because our leaders refused to bow to political correctness.

But we need to be on our guard. Think about what happened to Janis Karpinski. "People . . . are no longer interested in the leadership responsibilities [because] they are looking at the political correctness of their decisions," Karpinski told me.[9]

If she's right, in the long run we're dead.

As a closing note about this torture debate: it apparently works!

In December of 2005, ABC News revealed that of eleven top al Qaeda figures who were held in secret Eastern European jails by American forces, all but one were water boarded.[10] Water boarding is a means of interrogation that simulates a feeling of drowning and creates a sense of panic. ABC News reported, "According to sources directly involved in setting up the CIA secret prison system, it began with the capture of Abu Zabayada in Pakistan. After treatment there for gunshot wounds, he was whisked by the CIA to Thailand where he was housed in a small, disused warehouse on an active airbase. There, his cell was kept under 24-hour closed circuit TV surveillance and his life threatening wounds were tended by a CIA doctor specially sent from Langley headquarters to assure Abu Zubaydah was given proper care, sources said. Once healthy, he was slapped, grabbed, made to stand long hours in a cold cell, and finally handcuffed and strapped, feet up, to a water board until after 0.31 seconds he begged for mercy and began to cooperate."[11] ABC went on to report that of the twelve high value targets housed by the CIA, only one did not require water boarding before he talked. Ramzi bin al-Shibh broke down in tears after he was walked past the cell of Khalid Sheif Mohammed, the operational planner for September 11. Visibly shaken, he started to cry and became as cooperative as if he had been tied down to a water board.

Okay, let's think about this for a moment. One dozen dirt bags with information. Eleven get water boarded. Presumably the only reason number twelve doesn't get the treatment is that he spills his guts just by seeing one of his colleagues in the pokey. What does that tell us? It tells me that water boarding works. If the first guy were water boarded without result, and the second guy were water boarded without yielding good intelligence, and the third and the fourth, do you really think they would continue to try the technique with numbers five, six, seven, eight, nine, ten, and eleven? Of course not. Obviously, this is a method that is efficacious.

I had the opportunity to ask U.S. Senator John McCain about this issue. Specifically, I said to him: "On the subject of torture, the question I have as a layperson who lacks your military credentials—Why if it always yields unproductive information is it a recurring subject? Why are there people who apparently have expertise in interrogation who seem to always want to have it at their disposal?"

His reply really didn't address the substance of what I was saying. He told me: "I think because there is a near desperation in the Pentagon to try to get intelligence to try to foil these attacks that are so insidious and so awful and so terrible and tragic that are inflicted upon young Americans. . . . There's this incredible and understandable desire to catch some of these guys and find out where these bombs are being made, where these people are being recruited, where do they come from. We've got to get this intelligence so I understand that, I mean, my God, we're talking about our most precious asset . . . any information that we could find out could never ever make up for the damage that the image of the United States suffers throughout the world by doing it. I can tell you that the image of the United States is not good."[12]

Epilogue:
A Letter to My Son

My aim throughout MUZZLED has been to do more than entertain you with some rants about political correctness. I hope it also motivates you. Together we must end the MUZZLED mind-set. More than taking it in the pants for telling a good joke, these days you can lose your pants thanks to PC skittishness about dealing with terrorism and terror suspects.

My wife and I have four kids: three boys ages five, seven, and nine, and a girl who is seventeen-going-on-thirty. When Wilson, our seven-year-old, was just shy of his second birthday, I got to thinking pessimistically about all the changes around us (keep in mind this was pre-9/11), and I decided to write him a letter dated to coincide with his graduation from college which, fingers crossed, will be in the year 2020. I hope this motivates you the way I hope it will motivate him—because I fear this is our future if we don't break the muzzles:

June 1, 2020

Dear Will,

Your mother and I am so proud of you on this, your graduation date from college.

It's a funny world that you're now entering, and one your dear old dad sometimes has difficulty understanding.

My God, has there been change in this country since you were born on January 8, 1998.

Your mom says I should have stopped being surprised a long time ago.

Heck, I was shocked when you began your education.

I almost passed out that day in 3rd grade when we met your teacher, what was her name, the husky woman with a 5 o'clock shadow?

Who would've believed that she had been a he until just a few weeks before class began!

That reminds me of the time I had to pick you up at the campsite in the middle of the Boy Scout sleepover when you called to say that the scoutmaster had brought his significant other along and they were fighting over the shaving cream.

Now, don't get me wrong, I was as thrilled as anyone when we wiped out the AIDS virus. I just never understood why we stopped spending on research to fight heart disease, cancer, and stroke—which are still the number 1, 2, and 3 killers in this country.

Hey, did I ever tell you that one of the Boy Scouts' core beliefs used to be a faith in God?

Oh, now we're going way back.

I mean, we're talking about the days when Congress still began each day with a prayer, kids in school started each morning with a Pledge of Allegiance, and some of the older court houses, I know you'll never believe this, actually posted the Ten Commandments.

That is, of course, until the ACLU was successful in getting eight of the commandments declared illegal.

Oh well, things change.

But we're excited about your future.

We can't wait for you to settle down.

Maybe meet a woman who might let you work outside the home instead of just relying on her salary.

And I know it's politically incorrect for me to say it, but we look forward to your making us grandparents.

We only hope that, when the time comes, you'll skip all that genetic engineering business.

Did I tell you that a fellow at work just announced the birth of his daughter's first baby? The infant was born just as they had ordered. You know: the blue eyes, the full head of blond hair, and the guaranteed height of 6'2". I know that they were able to ensure the baby will never have the gene for baldness but still, something about it strikes me as unnatural.

Beauty, after all, isn't everything.

I mean, hey, when you were a baby, they had something called the

Miss America Pageant. This was long before what they now have, what's it called—"Which Feminist Is Best Intellectually Suited to Save the World"?

I don't know. I would never have guessed that the day would arrive when the point system used to grade contestants would actually penalize a gal for the way she looks in a bathing suit!

Sometimes I think that all started with the Clinton administration. The Hillary Clinton administration.

What an eight years that was. And then to have Bill come back into office after Hillary was finished.

I would never have believed that America could elect him again. I mean, even after the divorce, Monica was never my idea of a first lady.

But back to Hillary, you know the one thing I can never forget? It's the art she hung in the Oval Office. That picture of Christ on the crucifix with cattle dung all over it. That was too much!

People tell me to just give the lady her due.

After all, she was elected in that memorable campaign when all the candidates admitted to doing Quaaludes and America said, well, that's no big deal.

Ah well, I really just wanted to write and say that I am proud that you performed so well in college.

I know, I know, they don't give grades anymore, so we really can't say how well.

But that was no surprise. I mean, when they finally got rid of the SATs, we all knew that letter grades would soon be a thing of the past.

Some people like the system of deciding who gets into college based on race, gender, and ethnicity alone.

Heck, you were lucky to get admitted to college. If it hadn't been for the implementation of a small quota for white males, I doubt you would have made it.

I can remember when athletes were given scholarships to colleges.

Who would have believed you would turn out to be the athlete you are?

I never knew.

But how could I?

I mean, all those soccer games when you were growing up, they never kept score because they thought it would scar the losers for life. I still don't know if you won or lost most of the games. But hey, at least everyone always got a trophy.

Oh, it's a funny world.

Too bad it's still such a dangerous place; sometimes I just don't get it.

Call your dad a Neanderthal, but I always believed in the death penalty.

I mean, if you told me that in the year 2020 we'd still be arguing about what to do with Mumia Abu-Jamal, I would never have believed it.

Nor would I have believed that the stiffest sentences would be reserved for people who continue to disregard the illegality of smoking cigarettes. Call me a liberal, but the sentencing guideline of one year for every pack that's confiscated—that's just too much.

I know, I know. We had to get rid of the death penalty because the only people to get the sentence had tough childhoods. I just thought we should have given the same attention to the victims of crimes that we gave to the perpetrators.

Ah well, at least our country is safe.

The UN peacekeepers and their outposts in all fifty states must have been a good idea. After all, the Chinese have really only taken control of California and Texas.

I just wish the UN hadn't taken control of local law enforcement too.

You know your dad; I was never comfortable when they passed the mandatory handgun hand-in.

Maybe I should have seen it coming.

I mean, when Congress finally declared the NRA to be a hate group, the handwriting was on the wall.

But they really took the gun outlawing too far. I mean, when the citizen ban was expanded to police, that was just too much for me.

Ah, well, I feel as if I have strayed from just offering my heartfelt congratulations on this rite of passage.

We love you. Good luck, and dare I say, God bless.

Love,
Dad

Acknowledgments

For a talk show host and author, I have a kitchen cabinet that should be the envy of many an elected official. Each of these colleagues is both "book" *and* street smart, they are engaged in the world around them, and I enjoy having each in my circle of influence. It's an eclectic bunch, ranging from an English PhD candidate at an Ivy League institution to ninth grade intern, who, for no more than bragging rights, has each carried the laboring oar for this book. I want to acknowledge their efforts with my heartfelt thanks.

Elliot Avidan is my self-described "bastard intern." That's because he claims he's the only one in the group who's never been invited to my house. (Maybe so, Elliot, but you did get mentioned here first!) Now check out these credentials: This Philadelphia native is a graduate of the U.S. Naval Academy and a former Surface Warfare Officer. Elliot took a Masters in Public Policy from the University of Chicago before graduating from my alma mater, the University of Pennsylvania Law School. He began work as a Presidential Management Fellow with the U.S. Department of State in September of 2005. Elliot worked in support of my radio program throughout his studies at Penn Law. He's an engaging fellow with a great intellect and healthy sense of wonderment. Elliot's role here was primarily in the area of legal analysis of many of the subjects covered.

Josh Belfer was a full member of the team before he got out of the ninth grade. This (now) sixteen-year-old is a student at Akiba Hebrew Academy in Lower Merion, Pennsylvania. He told me he first got into my radio program because of his hour bus ride to school every morning at 6:30 and his father's insistence that he listen. There is nothing I am reluctant to assign to him: radio show research, chapter summarizing, special projects. In eighth grade, Josh and his classmates at Kellman Academy participated in a Mini-Model Congress with other middle schools, held at the New Jersey Statehouse in Trenton, where he was named an Outstanding Debater. He has already been recognized for his leadership, achievement in mathematics and English, and commitment to Jewish education. The most common refrain around my studio: "Are we sure Josh is only sixteen??"

Paul DiMaggio is a newer recruit. (BTW, right now Elliot is reading this and saying, "damn it, it's an alphabetized list and I am still the bastard intern!") Another native of Philadelphia, Paul is a 2003 graduate of St. Joseph's Preparatory School which has been responsible for turning out more than one of my guys. During high school, Paul experienced many academic and athletic successes. He rowed for St. Joseph's on the world famous Schuylkill River throughout his four years in high school. During his junior and senior years, Paul earned a most notable seat on St. Joseph's Varsity 8 boat. Having been nationally recognized for his rowing talents, Paul was recruited to row at Harvard University as an undergraduate. Paul is currently an undergraduate at Harvard University studying government. He intends to attend law school and begin a career in politics. He's proof positive that not all Harvard guys are geeks. He was of great help on the Getting Maid on Campus chapter in particular.

Ben Haney: Ah Ben, the pride and joy of Notre Dame. What can you say about a guy who, while an undergraduate at Notre Dame, was so moved by the passing of Ronald Reagan that he put on a suit and, in the summer heat and humidity, went and stood for hours outside the Capitol Rotunda just to pay his respects to the president (despite having been born after Reagan was first elected president). Ben's another graduate of St. Joseph's, where he was a member of the National Honor Society. Then he joined the Fighting Irish (oops, am I still allowed to call them that?). He's been active in politics on a local level and spent a portion of his sophomore year interning with Senator Richard Lugar (R-IN). After graduating with a BA in political science and a minor in anthropology, he was accepted into St. Joseph's prestigious Alumni Service Program for 2005–2006, and is teaching government to juniors/seniors while assisting the school where needed. Next up, law school, then politics. Someday you will have the chance to vote for him—here's hoping you do. Ben had a variety of hands in this project, while doing the primary legwork for my next book. More to come on that.

Anthony Mazzarelli: Wait until you hear about him. Dr. Mazz was my original intern. In fact, I never even considered having interns until Mazz, a stranger at the time, contacted me out of the blue and raised the possibility. He was then a student at Penn Law and simultaneously a student in medical school. Mazzarelli earned a medical degree from Robert Wood Johnson Medical School, a law degree from Penn, and a master's degree in bioethics from the University of Pennsylvania Center for Bioethics. So, when writing a book, what do you do with a guy who's a lawyer and a doctor? You ask him to look at why law enforcement now sports women who are too short to do the job, and why Miss America is more interested in brains than beauty, of course. He did, and you will enjoy those chapters. Dr. Mazz is currently chief resident in Emergency Medicine at Cooper University Hospital in Camden, New Jersey. He hopes to practice medicine while also having a hand in influencing public policy. He's also got the media bug. I suspect he becomes the most credentialed talk-radio host in America some day soon.

Kurt Schreyer: So far, it sounds like a bunch of rocket scientists working in support of a guy who gets all the glory and only achieved 990 on his SAT. Well, that trend continues with Kurt. Ready for this? This West Virginian graduated from the University of Notre Dame in 1992 where he majored in chemistry and German, and served as the executive officer of the Naval ROTC Battalion during his senior year. Following nuclear power and submarine officer training, he reported to the USS *Albany* (SSN 753) in Norfolk, Virginia. During his forty-two-month tour he held senior positions in both the Engineering and Weapons Departments and was twice awarded the Navy Achievement Medal. Later, as a seminarian at Notre Dame, Kurt rediscovered his love of learning and, after teaching high school, he received his Master's in English while simultaneously serving as the executive producer of Notre Dame's Summer Shakespeare Festival. He is now a PhD candidate and lecturer at the University of Pennsylvania, specializing in Shakespearean drama. I want to acknowledge many people here, but truth be told, I leaned on Kurt the most, and yet I know him the least. Nevertheless, he understands my view of the world (right or wrong though it may be) and is an extraordinary researcher and writer. You'll detect more than a passing hand from Kurt when you get to the chapter on Intelligent Design, among others. I am very grateful to Kurt for his fine work.

TC Scornavacchi: Yes, we have a female in the cabinet. (I did say *kitchen*, cabinet, didn't I!) TC is the producer of my radio program. She's also the Harvard educated, former teacher of our children at the Gladwyne Montessori School. I was lucky to entice her out of teaching and into the media just after she got a taste of the bright lights while doing some on-air work at QVC. No one sells candles better! Effervescent, smart, funny, as pleasant as anyone could be at 4 AM when we put our show together. We keep our guest Rolodex active by giving people the TC treatment after I am all too often abrupt and abrasive. TC procured many of the interviews that I rely on here, transcribed more than a few, and was a constant sanity check for the chapters in early formation. Within nine months of her leaving teaching and producing my radio program, a national show made her an offer to do likewise (the bastards), and she balked. Enough said.

Mary Russel: While I was still in private practice at what is now the Beasley Law Firm in Philadelphia, I had an extraordinary secretary. Mary Russel is old school, which is a good thing. We worked together for several years, and then I reduced my role at the firm to concentrate on talk radio, and she later retired from her position. When this project got rolling, I begged her to let me send a computer to her house so we could work together again. She obliged. Good thing. Her command of the English language is much better than my own. She's been invaluable.

There are others who played more targeted roles but, nevertheless, are important to me in the writing of the book and I wish to thank them, too: **Buz Teacher**, who continues to be my publishing consigliore; **Michael Schefer** is my editor at the *Philadelphia Daily News*, and a darn good one—he keeps me steady, cleans up my work, and makes me look good, and was supportive of many of the columns that I wrote which were expanded into chapters here; **Zack Stalberg** is the former editor of the *Daily News* and is owed the credit (or blame) of bringing me into the newspaper; **Michael S. Katz, Esq.**, is another former colleague from the Beasley Law Firm, a lawyer who used to work in support of my cases. I found myself reaching out for him time and again when I needed to double-check something in the law and wanted to know I could rely on the information; speaking of lawyers, **Steven A. Lerman** and **David S. Keir** provided me with an important sanity check (and it was nice to speak to them about something other than litigation.); **Joey Callahan** (www.joeycallahan.com) is a funny, Philadelphia-based comedian who supplied the comedy you will enjoy in the chapter about the death of the joke; **Carter Cox** is a bright, high-school junior at The Episcopal Academy who, at my request, delved into the world of Intelligent Design; **Michael Maggitti** is an undergraduate at Villanova University who spent some time in the summer with me and did a fine job researching the absence of God in the classroom; **Dave Butts** is a radio listener who made himself known to me, asked to get involved, and provided some helpful analysis; **Mike Dougherty** is yet another St. Joseph's Prep guy, now studying communications at LaSalle University, who supported my interest in the death of the joke, the campaign mounted against a Mexican cartoon character, and several other projects; attorney

Thomas R. Kline, with whom I shared the book concept on the beach at LBI, at a time when I was struggling for a title, and who instantly said, "MUZZLED," and attorney **Paul Lauricella** who similarly came up with the subtitle. (I hope they don't each expect one-third of the revenues.)

I also wish to extend my thanks to those whose efforts are responsible for the success of my radio program. They include: **David Yadgaroff, Mike Baldini,** and **Grace Blazer** in management; **Joan Jones** who ably delivers the news on my program; **Greg Stocker,** a superb technical producer; **Lorraine Ranalli** who does traffic; and there is **Frank Canale, Dave Skalish, Pete Nelson, Sandy Zubyk, Walter Kosc,** and **Bart Feroe** whose joint efforts actually keep me on the air.

I also wish to express my sincere gratitude for my editor, **Joel Miller,** who was very patient, deliberate, and thoroughly engaged in this project.

Finally, there is George. **George Hiltzik:** ah, George, my agent. What can I say about him? Simply the best. Everyone in the business knows him. That is because he and his firm, N.S. Bienstock, represent everyone in the business! George is my uncle. He is my rabbi. He is my personal consigliore. He is my friend. And he is a pain in the ass. This exchange of e-mail between us sums up the special bond we share. You can read it from top to bottom. Enjoy:

—— Original Message ——
From: Michael Smerconish
Sent: Friday, July 15, 2005 4:26 AM
To: George Hiltzik
Subject: Good am

Pls finish the thomas nelson contract.

—— Original Message ——
From: George Hiltzik
Sent: Fri, 15 Jul 2005 10:22:59
To: Michael Smerconish
Subject: RE: Good am

They have our comments. We are following up today. BTW, Peter Kosann from Westwood was with O'Reilly last night and they spoke about you

—— Original Message ——
From: Michael Smerconish
Sent: Friday, July 15, 2005 10:31 AM
To: George Hiltzik
Subject: Re: Good am

Yeah, and what????

—— Original Message ——
From: George Hiltzik
Sent: Fri, 15 Jul 2005 10:31:59
To: Michael Smerconish
Subject: RE: Good am

Ah, for that you will have to return my calls

—— Original Message ——
From: Michael Smerconish
Sent: Friday, July 15, 2005 10:38 AM
To: George Hiltzik
Subject: Re: Good am

J— off

—— Original Message ——
From: George Hiltzik
To: Michael Smerconish
Sent: Friday, July 15, 2005 10:50 AM
Subject: RE: Good am

Some creativity, please, in your insults to me

—— Original Message ——
From: Michael Smerconish
Sent: Friday, July 15, 2005 10:56 AM
To: George Hiltzik

Subject: Re: Good am
Importance: High

You want creativity? Here is what I get if I call you.

MAS: So, ok, I called you back. Now what is it all about?

GH: Kozan spoke to Bill last night and Bill really likes you.

MAS: And what?

GH: And nothing, that's pretty good, eh? It's a good day for the Jews.

MAS: George, Bill liking me doesn't pay the mortgage. Now get me that 3rd hour.

GH: This is all good. Linda likes me. Things are happening. Be patient. You are a putz.

MAS: I got yer putz right here. Just get the show syndicated.

GH: I hear you.

MAS: Have a good weekend.

GH: You too.

—— Original Message ——
From: George Hiltzik
To: Michael Smerconish
Sent: Friday, July 15, 2005 11:05 AM
Subject: RE: Good am

Thanks. Now we don't have to speak

About the Author

MICHAEL SMERCONISH is the Philadelphia radio market's premier talk host who is heard daily on Infinity Radio's 50,000-watt WPHT, found at 1210 AM. The program reaches Pennsylvania, New Jersey, and Delaware. Smerconish is also a frequent guest host for Bill O'Reilly on the nationally syndicated *Radio Factor*. For several years, Smerconish has been a popular columnist for the *Philadelphia Daily News*. In 2003, author Bernard Goldberg republished one of Smerconish's *Daily News* columns in his book *Arrogance*, a follow-up to his bestseller *Bias*. Smerconish is a familiar face on Fox News, MSNBC, and CNN where he provides commentary on current events.

Michael Smerconish graduated Phi Beta Kappa from Lehigh University and then attended the University of Pennsylvania Law School. Thereafter, at the age of twenty-nine, he became the youngest subcabinet level appointee to the administration of George Herbert Walker Bush when he was named Regional Administrator of the Department of Housing and Urban Development. He maintains an of-counsel relationship with the Beasley Law Firm in Philadelphia.

Muzzled is the perfect follow-up to Smerconish's successful first book: *Flying Blind: How Political Correctness Continues to Compromise Airline Safety Post 9/11*. About that book, *Publisher's Weekly* wrote: "Flying with his family, Smerconish, a radio talk-show host and newspaper columnist based in Philadelphia, twice had his eight-year-old son chosen for 'secondary screening'—and was twice able to substitute himself without incident despite his carrying odd-looking electronic broadcast gear. Mulling the ease with which he made it though the process, he then learned of a federal policy to fine airlines 'if they have more than two young Arab males in secondary questioning.' (The actual testimony from an airline industry rep was that the Justice Department said a screening system would be discriminatory if it flagged more than three people of the same ethnic origin.) Contacting the Department of Transportation, Smerconish was told secondary screening is random or behavior-based. Tracking down the decisions that led to these policies in detail—and decrying the policies themselves—Smerconish argues that the U.S. should give some weight to stereotypes. His hero is an immigration inspector in Orlando who, in 2001, stopped a Saudi national (likely the twentieth hijacker) who became visibly upset when asked why he lacked a return ticket. Designed to provoke Congress to address the tension between non-discrimination and airlines' capacity to refuse passengers, this book, with its senatorial foreword, may do just that."

In promotion of *Flying Blind*, Smerconish appeared on Fox News's *The O'Reilly Factor*, CNN's *Paula Zahn*, and MSNBC's *Scarborough Country*. He was also interviewed on countless major market talk-radio programs. C-SPAN's popular *Book TV* program recorded a one-hour presentation made by Smerconish at the Union League of Philadelphia, and rebroadcast the speech several times on national cable television. Smerconish also spoke to the City Club of Cleveland, a presentation then rebroadcast to hundreds of radio stations in the Midwest. *Philadelphia Magazine* positively reviewed *Flying Blind* with a several page pictorial.

Smerconish accepted none of the proceeds from *Flying Blind*, choosing to give his advance and all royalties to The Garden of Reflection, a 9/11 charity in his home community built for the seventeen individuals from Bucks County, Pennsylvania, who perished at Ground Zero.

Notes

INTRODUCTION

1. Todd Murphy, "Rescue Workers Itch to Help Out," *Portland Tribune*, September 16, 2005.

CHAPTER ONE—Photo Finish

1. I confess that I've pulled a Joe Biden with the naming of this chapter. "Photo Finish" is the way the *Financial Times* headlined a February 2, 2005, story on this subject. I tried. I can't do better. It's perfect. But stealing titles is a particularly sensitive subject for me, so I want to confess my misappropriation. My first book, *Flying Blind*, came out on 9/11/04. On 9/15/04, *Investor's Business Daily* titled an editorial on the exact same subject—political correctness in airline security—"Flying Blind," but gave me no credit, even though a staff writer sent me an e-mail and told me that my book was sitting on the desks of the guys who wrote the editorial. Me, I'm stealing with attribution.

2. Banc of America Securities LLC, "Banc of America Securities and Bank of America," www.bofasecurities.com, 2005.

3. http://goldentree.com/index.cfm?sid=850&ctid=15&cid=4579&catID=42.

4. "Bank of America Securities Has No Sense of Humor That We're Aware Of," (financial wire.net via COMTEX) Investors.com, January 18, 2005.

5. Interview with an anonymous source conducted by Michael Smerconish on July 20, 2005.

6. Ibid.

7. Interview with Joel Krasner conducted by Michael Smerconish on August 19, 2005.

8. Interview with an anonymous source conducted by Michael Smerconish on August 19, 2005.

9. Interview with an anonymous source conducted by Michael Smerconish on September 16, 2005.

10. Interview with an anonymous source conducted by Michael Smerconish on August 19, 2005.

11. "Firms Adopting Zero-Tolerance Policies after Scandals," Landon Thomas Jr. of the *New York Times*, as published in the *Seattle Post Intelligencer*, April 4, 2005.

12. "BofA Unit Fired Top-Ranked Analyst," *Charlotte Business Journal*, January 14, 2005.

13. Interview with an anonymous source conducted by Michael Smerconish on July 20, 2005.

14. "Bank of America Securities Has No Sense of Humor That We're Aware Of," (financial wire.net via COMTEX) Investors.com, January 18, 2005.

15. "Senior Staffers Leave Banc of America," *Wall Street Journal*, January 17, 2005.

16. Ibid.

17. Daniel Dunaieff, "Snake Eyes on Wall St. BofA Sacks Analyst over Photo," *New York Daily News*, January 15, 2005.

18. Ibid.

19. Ibid.

20. "Firms Adopting Zero-Tolerance Policies after Scandals," Landon Thomas Jr. of the *New York Times*, as published in the *Seattle Post Intelligencer*, April 4, 2005.

21. Ibid.

22. "Firm Taps Analyst Fired over Picture," *Wall Street Journal*, February 1, 2005.

23. "Observer: Photo Finish," *Financial Times*, February 2, 2005.

24. Clay Harris, "Companies UK: Where His Face Fits," *Financial Times*, February 3, 2005.

25. PRNewswire: "Andrew Susser, Former Head of HighYield Research at Banc of America Securities, Joins GoldenTree Asset Management," www.forrelease.com, February 2, 2005.

26. Interview with James J. Cramer, Esquire, The Michael Smerconish Show, The Big Talker WPHT 1210 AM, Philadelphia, July 23, 2005.

27. "Banc of America Securities Has No Sense of Humor That We're Aware Of," (financial wire.net via COMTEX) Investors.com, January 18, 2005.

CHAPTER TWO—The Payback

1. http://www.whizzinator.com.

2. Mark Craig, "Vikings' Smith May Face Yearlong Suspension," *Minneapolis Star-Tribune*, May 12, 2005.

3. Linda Robertson, "As Smith Found, Whizzinator Not the Best Choice," *Miami Herald*, June 14, 2005.

4. Milo F. Bryant, "Life Still Tough for Gay Male Athletes," *Fresno Bee*, November 1, 2002.

5. Jim Buzinski, "Hearst Apologizes for 'Faggot' Comment," Outsports.com, November 23, 2002.

6. Dave Stinton, "A List of Terrell-able Acts by Owens," The Produce Section, 2004.

7. Kevin Lynch, "49'ers Players Defend Video as Owners Apologize for It, *San Francisco Chronicle*, June 2, 2005.

8. Phillip Matier and Andrew Ross, "York Could Have Avoided Humiliating Team over Video; 49'ers Owner Viewed Tape 5 Months Ago but Didn't Take Action," *San Francisco Chronicle*, June 2, 2005.

9. "The 49'ers' Embarrassing Training Tape View the Team Training Video in Segments," *Chronicle* and SFGate.com Staff Report, June 1, 2005.

10. Ibid.

11. Ibid.

12. Ibid.

13. Ibid.

14. Kevin Lynch, "49'ers Players Defend Video as Owners Apologize For It," *San Francisco Chronicle*, www.sfgate.com, June 2, 2005.

15. "The 49'ers' Embarrassing Training Tape View the Team Training Video in Segments," *Chronicle* and SFGate.com Staff Report, June 1, 2005.

16. Ibid.

17. Ibid.

18. Ibid.

19. Ibid.

21. Ibid.

21. Ibid.

22. "The 49'ers Offense," *Chronicle* Staff Writer, *San Francisco Chronicle*, www.sfgate.com, June 2, 2005.

23. "SF Mayor, 49'ers Owners Offended By 'Training' Video," NBC11.com, http://www.nbc11.com/news/4555452/detail.html?subid=10101681, June 1, 2005.

24. Ibid.

25. Daniel Brown and Sean Webby, "Reaction: Firestorm Rages From Affronted Groups to Mayor's Office," *Mercury News*, June 2, 2005, www.mercurynews.com.

26. "49'ers' Raunchy Video Was 'Terrible Mistake,' MSNBC, Associated Press, http://msnbc.msn.com/id/8059077/, June 2, 2005.

27. "SF Mayor, 49'ers Owners Offended by 'Training' Video," NBC11.com, http://www.nbc11.com/news/4555452/detail.html?subid=10101681, June 1, 2005.

28. Team Statement on Video Controversy, Denise and John York, The San Francisco 49'ers, http://www.ktvu.com/nfl084/4557124/detail.html, June 1, 2005.

29. "Gay Trainer Lindsy McLean Defends San Francisco 49'er Publicist Kirk Reynolds," www.Queerday.com, June 3, 2005.

30. Garance Burke, "49'ers Go to Chinatown to Tackle Hard-Feelings over Training Video," San Francisco Chronicle, www.sfgate.com, June 14, 2005.

31. Ibid.

32. Ilene Lelchuk, "49'ers Can't Say 'Sorry' Enough: Owner is Asked for Jobs, More At Chinatown Forum on Video," San Francisco Chronicle, www.sfgate.com, June 15, 2005.

33. Ibid.

34. Phillip Matier and Andrew Ross, "Training Video Prequel: 49'ers Apologize Anew, Earlier Tape Made by Outgoing PR Director," San Francisco Chronicle, www.sfgate.com, June 8, 2005.

35. Ibid.

36. Kevin Lynch, "49'ers Players Defend Video as Owners Apologize for It," San Francisco Chronicle, http://www.sfgate.com, June 2, 2005.

37. Phillip Matier and Andrew Ross, "49'ers' Personal Foul Team's In-House Training Video Includes Lesbian Porn, Racial Slurs, Barbs at Newsom," San Francisco Chronicle, www.sfgate.com, June 1, 2005.

38. Kevin Lynch, "49'ers Players Defend Video as Owners Apologize for It," San Francisco Chronicle, http://www.sfgate.com, June 2, 2005.

39. "49'ers' Raunchy Video Was 'Terrible Mistake,'" MSNBC, Associated Press, http://msnbc.msn.com/id/8059077/, June 2, 2005.

40. "SF Mayor, 49'ers Owners Offended by 'Training' Video," NBC11.com, http://www.nbc11.com/news/4555452/detail.html?subid=10101681, June 1, 2005.

41. Interview with Kirk Reynolds conducted by Michael Smerconish on August 16, 2005.

42. Interview with Ray Didinger conducted by Michael Smerconish on August 16, 2005.

43. Dr. Z, "While I Was Away," "Inside the NFL," Sports Illustrated.com, June 7, 2005.

44. Jaxon Van Derbeken, Rachel Gordon, and Trapper Byrne, "Video Scandal Rocks S.F. Police," San Francisco Chronicle, December 8, 2005.

45. Ibid.

46. Carolyn Marshall, "San Francisco Police Officers Are Suspended over Skits," New York Times, December 9, 2005.

47. "Police Video a Matter of Respect," editorial, San Francisco Examiner, December 8, 2005.

48. Jaxon Van Derbeken, "New Images Found in Police Scandal," San Francisco Chronicle, December 9, 2005.

49. Justin Jouvenal, "SFPD Videotape Shows Much More," San Francisco Examiner, December 8, 2005.

50. Jaxon Van Derbeken, "New Images Found in Police Scandal," San Francisco Chronicle, December 9, 2005.

51. Ibid.

52. Ibid.

53. Ibid.

54. Justin Jouvenal, "City Suspends Officers for Videotaped Antics," San Francisco Examiner, December 8, 2005.

55. Ilana DeBare, "Workplace Ethics: Videos Violate Most Companies' Harassment Rules, Experts Say," San Francisco Chronicle, December 9, 2005.

56. Jaxon Van Derbeken, "New Images Found in Police Scandal," *San Francisco Chronicle*, December 9, 2005.

57. Ibid.

58. Justin Jouvenal, "City Suspends Officers for Videotaped Antics," *San Francisco Examiner*, December 8, 2005.

59. Jaxon Van Derbeken, "New Images Found in Police Scandal," *San Francisco Chronicle*, December 9, 2005.

60. Ibid.

61. Jaxon Van Derbeken, Rachel Gordon, and Trapper Byrne, "Video Scandal Rocks S.F. Police," *San Francisco Chronicle*, December 8, 2005.

62. Justin Jouvenal, "SFPD Videotape Shows Much More," *San Francisco Examiner*, December 8, 2005.

63. Ibid.

64. Ibid.

65. Justin Jouvenal, "City Suspends Officers for Videotaped Antics," *San Francisco Examiner*, December 8, 2005.

66. Jaxon Van Derbeken, Rachel Gordon, and Trapper Byrne, "Video Scandal Rocks S.F. Police," *San Francisco Chronicle*, December 8, 2005.

67. "Producer Responds to SFPD Video Scandal," CBS5, www.cbs5.com, December 8, 2005.

68. "Police Video a Matter of Respect," editorial, *San Francisco Examiner*, December 8, 2005.

69. David Chanen, "Vikings Cruise Was Allegedly a Sex Party," *StarTribune*, October 12, 2005.

70. Ibid.

71. Greg Bock, "Four Vikings Face Party-Boat Charges," *USA Today*, December 16, 2005.

CHAPTER THREE—Sorry We Got It Correct

1. Remarks of Lawrence H. Summers at the National Bureau of Economic Research Conference on Diversifying the Science and Engineering Workforce, January 14, 2005.

2. Letter to Faculty Regarding NBER Remarks, Lawrence H. Summers, February 17, 2005.

3. Michael Smerconish, "Reparations: Ending the Guilt Trip," *Philadelphia Daily News*, August 22, 2002.

4. Mark Angeles, "Fugitives Among Us, Sometimes Murder Suspects Hide in Plain Sight," *Philadelphia Daily News*, August 22, 2002.

5. Mark Angeles, "Strong Reaction to People Paper Fugitive Cover," *Philadelphia Daily News*, August 23, 2002.

6. Ibid.

7. Ibid.

8. Ellen Foley, "To Our Readers: An Apology," *Philadelphia Daily News*, August 30, 2002.

9. Michael Smerconish, "That Apology—It's Bunk," *Philadelphia Daily News*, September 5, 2002.

10. Joseph P. Tierney, Wendy S. McClanahan, and Bill Hangley Jr., *Murder Is No Mystery: An Analysis of Philadelphia Homicide, 1996-1999*, a publication of Public/Private Ventures, 2001.

11. G. W. Miller III, "Teen Thuggery in Chestnut Hill," *Philadelphia Daily News*, August 11, 2005.

12. Michael J. Mishak, "New Wave of Assaults Hits Hill," *Chestnut Hill Local*, August 11, 2005.

13. Interview with George Miller, *The Michael Smerconish Show*, The Big Talker WPHT 1210 AM, Philadelphia, August 15, 2005.

CHAPTER FOUR—Dressing for Political Correctness

1. Findings of Fact, Opinion of The Commonwealth of Pennsylvania Human Relations Commission, Docket No. E99572D, February 28, 2005.

2. Ibid.

3. Ibid.
4. John T. Molloy, *(New) Dress for Success* (Warner Books), 1998, pp. 234-35.
5. Ibid., at pp. 235-36.
6. Maryclaire Dale, "Radio Salesman Awarded $600,000 in Racial Hostility Complaint," Associated Press, published at TimesLeader.com on April 19, 2005.
7. Interview with John T. Molloy, *The Michael Smerconish Show*, The Big Talker WPHT 1210 AM, Philadelphia, April 27, 2005.

CHAPTER FIVE—Oh, Yes, It's Ladies' Night
1. "Ladies' Night" by Kool and The Gang.
2. Interview with Chris Mourtos, *The Michael Smerconish Show*, The Big Talker WPHT 1210 AM, Philadelphia, June 4, 2004.
3. "Ladies' Night Nixed in NJ," Associated Press, *USA Today*, June 3, 2004.
4. Troy Graham and Jennifer Moroz, "Ladies' Night on Hold at Bar," *Philadelphia Inquirer*, June 3, 2004.
5. Ibid.
6. Interview with Chris Mourtos, *The Michael Smerconish Show*, The Big Talker WPHT 1210 AM, Philadelphia, November 10, 2004.
7. *Ladd v. Iowa West Racing Assn*, 438 N.W.2d 600 (IA 1989), p. 602.
8. *Koire v. Metro Car Wash*, 40 Cal.3d 24 (1985), p. 135.
9. *Pennsylvania Liquor Control Bd. v. Dobrinoff*, 471 A.2d 941 (Pa.Cmwlth., 1984), p. 457.
10. Ibid.
11. *Dock Club, Inc. v. Illinois Liquor Control*, 101 Ill.App.3d 673 (Ill.App., 1981), p. 676.
12. *MacLean v. First Northwest Industries of America, Inc.*, 635 P.2d 683 (WA 1981).
13. "Return of Ladies' Night Advances in Trenton," Associated Press, June 18, 2004.
14. Robert Moran, "'Ladies' Night' Restoration Goes to Full Senate," *Philadelphia Inquirer*, November 9, 2004.

CHAPTER SIX—It's All about Me
1. Kathy Boccella, "District Suited over Bible Ban," *Philadelphia Inquirer*, May 12, 2005.
2. Interview with Donna Busch, *The Michael Smerconish Show*, The Big Talker WPHT 1210 AM, Philadelphia, May 26, 2005.
3. United States Constitution, Amendment I.
4. *Donna Kay Busch v. Marple Newtown School District*, Complaint filed in the Eastern District of Pennsylvania on May 2, 2005.
5. Pattie Price, "MN Says the Bible Is Illegal," *County Press*, Press Newspapers of Delaware County, May 18, 2005; Volume 74, No. 42.
6. Interview of Donna Busch, *The Michael Smerconish Show*, The Big Talker WPHT 1210 AM, Philadelphia, May 26, 2005.
7. Letter of Robert A. Mesaros dated May 15, 2005.
8. Interview of Edward Partridge conducted by Michael Maggitti on May 26, 2005.
9. News of Delaware County, Mid-Delco Edition article, Wednesday, May 18, 2005; Volume 70, No. 24.
10. Interview of Donna Busch, *The Michael Smerconish Show*, The Big Talker WPHT 1210 AM, Philadelphia, May 26, 2005.
11. Ibid.
12. Ibid.
13. Mark A. Sereni, "Doing Right by Students, Law," *Philadelphia Inquirer*, May 31, 2005.
14. Pattie Price, "MN Says the Bible is Illegal," *County Press*, Press Newspapers of Delaware County, May 18, 2005; Volume 74, no. 42.

15. Ibid.

CHAPTER SEVEN—God Bless Patrick Cubbage

1. Memorandum from Joan L. Edwards, Affirmative Action Officer, to Iven C. Dumas, Senior Honor Guard, October 24, 2002; See also, "Honor Guardsman is Fired for Blessing," David O'Reilly, *Philadelphia Inquirer*, January 22, 2003.
2. Military Funeral Honors, "Honoring Those Who Served," the Department of Defense.
3. Ibid.
4. David O'Reilly, "Honor Guard Gets His Job Back, The Northeast Philadelphia Man Had Been Fired for Offering a Blessing at Graveside Services," *Philadelphia Inquirer*, August 8, 2003.
5. Memo from Stephen G. Abel to Iven C. Dumas, October 20, 2003.

CHAPTER EIGHT—Political Correctness in Full Bloom

1. Interview with Collin Kelly, *The Michael Smerconish Show*, The Big Talker WPHT 1210 AM, Philadelphia, May 27, 2005.
2. Rob Haneisen, "Boy, 9, Plants Flowers on Soldier's Graves," *MetroWest Daily News*, http://www.metrowestdailynews.com/localRegional/view.bg?articleid=99256.
3. Interview with Collin Kelly, *The Michael Smerconish Show*, The Big Talker WPHT 1210 AM, Philadelphia, May 27, 2005.
4. Ibid.
5. Matt Viser, "For 9-year-old, Patriotism Flowers," *Boston Globe*, http://www.boston.com/news/local/articles/2005/05/27/for_9_year_old_patriotism_flowers.
6. Rob Haneisen, "Cemetery Thwarts Boy's Effort to Put Flowers on Graves," *MetroWest Daily News*, http://www.metrowestdailynews.com/localRegional/view.bg?articleid= 99456.
7. Rob Haneisen, "Flower Power," *MetroWest Daily News*, http://www.metrowestdailynews.com/localRegional/view.bg?articleid=99716.
8. Rob Haneisen, "Boy, 9, Plants Flowers on Soldier's Graves," *MetroWest Daily News*, http://www.metrowestdailynews.com/localRegional/view.bg?articleid=99256.
9. Ibid.
10. Matt Viser, "For 9-year-old, Patriotism Flowers," *Boston Globe*, http://www.boston.com/news/local/articles/2005/05/27/for_9_year_old_patriotism_flowers.
11. Rob Haneisen, "Cemetery Thwarts Boy's Effort to Put Flowers on Graves," *MetroWest Daily News*, http://www.metrowestdailynews.com/localRegional/view.bg?articleid=99456.
12. Ibid.
13. Ibid.
14. Interview with Collin Kelly, *The Michael Smerconish Show*, The Big Talker WPHT 1210 AM, Philadelphia, May 27, 2005.
15. Rob Haneisen, "Cemetery Thwarts Boy's Effort to Put Flowers on Graves," *MetroWest Daily News*, http://www.metrowestdailynews.com/localRegional/view.bg?articleid=99456.
16. Rob Haneisen, "Flower Power," *MetroWest Daily News*, http://www.metrowestdailynews.com/localRegional/view.bg?articleid=99716.
17. Ibid.
18. "About-Face over Salute to Vets," CBS News, http://www.cbsnews.com/stories/2005/05/26/earlyshow/main697923.shtml.
19. Rob Haneisen, "Flower Kid Honored in Veterans Parade," *MetroWest Daily News*, http://www.metrowestdailynews.com/localRegional/view.bg?articleid=101619&format=text.
20. Interview with Lynn Kelly by Josh Belfer, July 5, 2005.
21. Richard Lodge, "Marine to Aid Boy's Tribute After Cemetery Relents," *Boston Herald*, http://news.bostonherald.com/localRegional/view.bg?articleid=84847.

22. Ibid.
23. Interview with Collin Kelly, *The Michael Smerconish Show*, The Big Talker WPHT 1210 AM, Philadelphia May 27, 2005.
24. Interview with Lynn Kelly by Josh Belfer, July 5, 2005.
25. Ibid.
26. Mary Kate Dubuss, "Vets Group Breaks Cemetery Rules," *MetroWest Daily News*, http://www.metrowestdailynews.com/localRegional/view.bg?articleid=100125.
27. Norman Miller, "Cemetery Plants Will Stay Put," *MetroWest Daily News*, http://www.metrowestdailynews.com/localRegional/view.bg?articleid=100470&format=text.
28. Interview with Lynn Kelly by Josh Belfer, July 5, 2005.
29. Tyler B. Reed, "Boy Marches with Troops," *MetroWest Daily News*, http://www.metrowestdailynews.com/localRegional/view.bg?articleid=100134&format=text.
30. Rob Haneisen, "Flower Kid Honored in Veterans Parade," *MetroWest Daily News*, http://www.metrowestdailynews.com/localRegional/view.bg?articleid=101619&format=text.
31. Interview with Lynn Kelly by Josh Belfer, July 5, 2005.
32. Ibid.
33. Ibid.
34. Ibid.

CHAPTER NINE—Seeing Purple

1. Ben Feller, "Hue Knew? Red Pen Out of Favor with Teachers," *Chicago Sun-Times*, April 4, 2005, http://www.findarticles.com/p/articles/mi_qn4155/is_200504/ai_n13614641.
2. Sarah Rabovsky, "Seeing Red?" *NEA Today*, March 1, 2005, http://www.findarticles.com/p/articles/mi_qa3617/is_200503/ai_n11826925.
3. Ben Feller, "Hue Knew? Red Pen Out of Favor with Teachers," *Chicago Sun-Times*, April 4, 2005, http://www.findarticles.com/p/articles/mi_qn4155/is_200504/ai_n13614641.
4. Sean Kennedy, "Seeing RED," *Tahlequah Daily News*, Tahlequah OK, May 13, 2005, http://www.tahlequahdailypress.com/articles/2005/05/13/news/top_stories/aaaaaink.txt.
5. Christina Hoff Sommers, "Enough Already with Kid Gloves," *USA Today*, May 31, 2005, http://www.usatoday.com/news/opinion/editorials/2005-05-31-kid-gloves-edit_x.htm.
6. Sarah Rabovsky, "Seeing Red?" *NEA Today*, March 1, 2005, http://www.findarticles.com/p/articles/mi_qa3617/is_200503/ai_n11826925.
7. Interview with Leatrice Eiseman, *The Michael Smerconish Show*, The Big Talker WPHT 1210 AM, Philadelphia, November 26, 2004.
8. Ben Feller, "Hue Knew? Red Pen Out of Favor with Teachers," *Chicago Sun-Times*, April 4, 2005, http://www.findarticles.com/p/articles/mi_qn4155/is_200504/ai_n13614641.
9. Ibid.
10. Interview with Leatrice Eiseman, *The Michael Smerconish Show*, The Big Talker WPHT 1210 AM, Philadelphia, November 26, 2004.
11. Karl Zinsmeister, "Political Fashion Can Hurt, Even Kill," *The American Enterprise*, June 2005, http://www.taemag.com/issues/article Ibid.18521/article_detail.asp.
12. Sarah Rabovsky, "Seeing Red?" *NEA Today*, March 1, 2005, http://www.findarticles.com/p/articles/mi_qa3617/is_200503/ai_n11826925.
13. Interview with Leatrice Eiseman, *The Michael Smerconish Show*, The Big Talker WPHT 1210 AM, Philadelphia, November 26, 2004.
14. Ibid.
15. Ibid.
16. Kellie Patrick, "School Retesting Policies Stir Debate," *Philadelphia Inquirer*, February 27, 2005.

17. Ibid.
18. Nirvi Shah, "A-B-C Letter Grades Changing to 1,2,3," *Palm Beach Post*, May 10, 2005.
19. Ibid.
20. Terry Bitman, "No Kidding: No Finals," *Philadelphia Inquirer*, June 15, 2005.
21. "Teaching Group to Consider Banning the Word 'Fail,'" Reuters, July 19, 2005.
22. D. L. Stewart, "Red-Ink Dispute Gets Low Marks," *Dayton Daily News* (Ohio), April 12, 2005.
23. Dale McFeatters, "Red is Apparently a Little Too In-Your-Face for the Younger Generation," *Sun Herald*, Biloxi MS, May 3, 2005, http://www.sunherald.com/mld/the sunherald/news/editorial/11548720.htm.
24. Christina Hoff Sommers, "Enough Already with Kid Gloves," *USA Today*, May 31, 2005, http://www.usatoday.com/news/opinion/editorials/2005-05-31-kid-gloves-edit_x.htm.

CHAPTER TEN—Trophy Mania
1. Nancy Ann Jeffrey, "Trophy Overload," *Wall Street Journal*, March 11, 2005.
2. Interview with Steve Rosenberg, *The Michael Smerconish Show*, The Big Talker WPHT 1210 AM, Philadelphia, March 28, 2005.
3. *Advertising Age Magazine*, American Demographics, April, 2005.
4. Nancy Ann Jeffrey, "Trophy Overload," *Wall Street Journal*, March 11, 2005.
5. Letter to editor of WSJ from the league founders and commissioners of MLGBA.
6. Interview with an anonymous source conducted by Michael Smerconish, March 30, 2005.
7. E-mail from my same friend, who may have to join the Witness Protection program.
8. Rules of the Main Line Girls Basketball League (www.mlgba.com).

CHAPTER ELEVEN—Getting Maid on Campus
1. Pam Belluck, "At Harvard, an Unseemly Display of Wealth or Merely a Clean Room?" *New York Times*, March 22, 2005.
2. Interview with Michael Kopko, *The Michael Smerconish Show*, The Big Talker WPHT 1210 AM, Philadelphia, June 20, 2005.
3. Pam Belluck, "At Harvard, an Unseemly Display of Wealth or Merely a Clean Room?" *New York Times*, March 22, 2005.
4. Interview with Michael Kopko, *The Michael Smerconish Show*, The Big Talker WPHT 1210 AM, Philadelphia, June 20, 2005.
5. Ibid.
6. "Maid for Harvard?" staff editorial, *Crimson*, March 10, 2005.
7. Meredith Trezise, "Capitalism at Harvard: Now with Bleach!" *Vanderbilt Torch*, March 31, 2005.
8. Pam Belluck, "At Harvard, an Unseemly Display of Wealth or Merely a Clean Room?" *New York Times*, March 22, 2005.
9. Ibid.
10. Interview with Michael Kopko, *The Michael Smerconish Show*, The Big Talker WPHT 1210 AM, Philadelphia, March 28, 2005.
11. Ibid.
12. Interview with Michael Kopko, *The Michael Smerconish Show*, The Big Talker WPHT 1210 AM, Philadelphia, June 20, 2005.

CHAPTER TWELVE—Naked Tigers
1. Viola Huang, "Streakers Disbanded Following Complaints," *Daily Princetonian*, May 26, 2005, http://www.dailyprincetonian.com/archives/2005/05/26/news/13001.shtml.
2. Interview with Scott Welfel, *The Michael Smerconish Show*, The Big Talker WPHT 1210 AM, Philadelphia, April 21, 2005.

3. Jennifer Epstein, "Hamilton Streakers Strike Campus," *Daily Princetonian*, April 19, 2005, http://www.dailyprincetonian.com/archives/2005/04/19/news/12657.shtml.

4. Interview with Scott Welfel, *The Michael Smerconish Show*, The Big Talker WPHT 1210 AM, Philadelphia, April 21, 2005.

5. E-mail from Scott Welfel to Michael Smerconish dated Septembver 17, 2005.

6. Cici Zheng, "Taking It All Off: Students Strip Down for Streaking Competition," *Daily Pennsylvanian*, February 23, 2005, http://www.dailypennsylvanian.com/vnews/display.v/ART/421c34d0b9a74?in_archi.

7. Interview with Scott Welfel, *The Michael Smerconish Show*, The Big Talker WPHT 1210 AM, Philadelphia, April 21, 2005.

8. Viola Huaang, "Streakers Disbanded Following Complaints," *Daily Princetonian*, May 26, 2005, http://www.dailyprincetonian.com/archives/2005/05/26/news/13001.shtml.

9. Ibid.

10. Ibid.

CHAPTER THIRTEEN—A Behemoth of an Incident

1. Laura Gitlin, "The 'Water Buffalo' Incident Through the Eyes of Jacobowitz," *Daily Pennsylvanian*, April 15, 2003, http://www.dailypennsylvanian.com/vnews/display.v/ART/3e9bd4af5fdd7?in_archive=1.

2. Ibid.

3. Lisa Levenson, "'Water Buffalo' Case Not Forgotten," *Daily Pennsylvanian*, January 14, 1994, http://www.dailypennsylvanian.com/vnews/display.v/ART/3adb1ee28417f?in_archive=1.

4. Alissa Kaye, "Controversial 'Water Buffalo' Case Continues," *Daily Pennsylvanian*, May 14, 1993, http://www.dailypennsylvanian.com/vnews/display.v/ART/3adb1cd90f271?in_archive=1.

5. Quoted from Peter Berkowitz, "Educating the University," June 1, 2005. This article is a book review of Donald Alexander Downs' *Restoring Free Speech and Liberty on Campus*, http://www.thefire.org/index.php/article/5699.html.

6. Eden Jacobowitz e-mail to Michael Smerconish dated September 12, 2005.

7. Lara Gitlin, "The 'Water Buffalo' Incident Through the Eyes of Jacobowitz," *Daily Pennsylvanian*, April 15, 2003, http://www.dailypennsylvanian.com/vnews/display.v/ART/3e9bd4af5fdd7?in_archive=1.

8. Interview with Eden Jacobowitz conducted by Michael Smerconish, September 6, 2005.

9. Lara Gitlin, "The 'Water Buffalo' Incident Through the Eyes of Jacobowitz," *Daily Pennsylvanian*, April 15, 2003, http://www.dailypennsylvanian.com/vnews/display.v/ART/3e9bd4af5fdd7?in_archive=1.

10. Interview with Eden Jacobowitz conducted by Michael Smerconish, September 6, 2005.

11. Lara Gitlin, "The 'Water Buffalo' Incident Through the Eyes of Jacobowitz," *Daily Pennsylvanian*, April 15, 2003, http://www.dailypennsylvanian.com/vnews/display.v/ART/3e9bd4af5fdd7?in_archive=1.

12. Ibid.

13. Christopher Pryor, "Guest Column: The Other Water Buffalo," *Daily Pennsylvanian*, September 9, 1993.

14. Peter Berkowitz, "Educating the University," June 1, 2005, http://www.thefire.org/index.php/article/5699.html.

15. "Black Co-eds Drop Their Racial Complaint Against White Man at U. of Penn—University of Pennsylvania," *Jet*, June 14, 1993, http://www.findarticles.com/p/articles/mi_m1355/is_n7_v84/ai_13920446.

16. Interview with Eden Jacobowitz by Michael Smerconish, September 6, 2005.

17. Peter Berkowitz, "Educating the University," June 1, 2005, http://www.thefire. org/index.php/article/5699.html.

18. Lara Gitlin, "The 'Water Buffalo' Incident Through the Eyes of Jacobowitz," *Daily Pennsylvanian*, April 15, 2003, http://www.dailypennsylvanian.com/vnews/display.v/ART/3e9bd4af5fdd7?in_archive=1.

19. Peter Berkowitz, "Educating the University," June 1, 2005, http://www.thefire. org/index.php/article/5699.html.

20. Interview with Eden Jacobowitz by Michael Smerconish, September 5, 2005.

21. Lara Gitlin, "The 'Water Buffalo' Incident Through the Eyes of Jacobowitz," *Daily Pennsylvanian*, April 15, 2003, http://www.dailypennsylvanian.com/vnews/display.v/ART/3e9bd4af5fdd7?in_archive=1.

22. Daniel Gingiss, "Nearly 14,000 DP's Stolen From Racks," *Daily Pennsylvanian*, April 16, 2005, http://www.dailypennsylvanian.com/vnews/display.v/ ART/3adb1ce1 49d6e?in_archive=1.

23. Ibid.

24. Gregory Pavlik, "An Unsaintly Camp," *Daily Pennsylvanian*, November 30, 1993, http://www.dailypennsylvanian.com/vnews/display.v/ART/3adb1c59c53e8?in_archive=1.

25. Gregory Pavlik, "Protecting Yourself, Protecting the Country," *Daily Pennsylvanian*, November 2, 1993, http://www.dailypennsylvanian.com/vnews/display.v/ ART/3adb1c 842a19f?in_archive=1.

26. Lisa Leverson, "Just Doing My Job," *Daily Pennsylvanian*, April 1, 1996, http:// www.dailypennsylvanian.com/vnews/display.v/ART/3adb2269ab067?in_archive=1.

27. Interview with Eden Jacobowitz conducted by Michael Smerconish, September 6, 2005.

28. Alissa Kaye, "Controversial 'Water Buffalo' Case Continues," *Daily Pennsylvanian*, May 14, 1993, http://www.dailypennsylvanian.com/vnews/display.v/ART/3adb1cd90f271?in_archive=1.

29. Interview with Eden Jacobowitz conducted by Michael Smerconish, September 6, 2005.

30. Alissa Kaye, "Controversial 'Water Buffalo' Case Continues," *Daily Pennsylvanian*, May 14, 1993, http://www.dailypennsylvanian.com/vnews/display.v/ART/3adb1cd90f271?in_archive=1.

31. Interview with Eden Jacobowitz conducted by Michael Smerconish, September 6, 2005.

32. Alissa Kaye, "Controversial 'Water Buffalo' Case Continues," *Daily Pennsylvanian*, May 14, 1993, http://www.dailypennsylvanian.com/vnews/display.v/ART/3adb1cd90f271?in_archive=1.

33. Laura Gitlin, "Media Buffaloes Penn: A University in the National Spotlight," *Daily Pennsylvanian*, April 15, 2003, http://www.dailypennsylvanian.com/vnews/display.v/ART/3e9be148b9173? in_archive=1.

34. Ibid.

35. Jeremy Kahn, "'Water Buffalo' Sides Discuss Inquiry Board," *Daily Pennsylvanian*, September 15, 1993, http://www.dailypennsylvanian.com/vnews/display.v/ART/3adb1cce97850? in_archive=1.

36. Jeremy Kahn, "Panel to Review Judicial Process," *Daily Pennsylvanian*, September 14, 1993, http://www.dailypennsylvanian.com/vnews/display.v/ART/3adb1ccfbc287?in_archive=1.

37. Lisa Levenson, "'Water buffalo' Case Not Forgotten," *Daily Pennsylvanian*, January 14, 1994, http://www.dailypennsylvanian.com/vnews/display.v/ART/3adb1ee28417f?in_ archive=1.

38. Interview with Eden Jacobowitz conducted by Michael Smerconish, September 6, 2005.

39. Ibid.

40. Jenny Axt, "Student Sues U. For Breach of Contract," *Daily Pennsylvanian*, June 30,

1996, http://www.dailypennsylvanian.com/vnews/display.v/ART/3adb21f8024a0? in_archive=1.

41. Kate Khatib, "Jacobowitz Claims Breach of Contract," *Daily Pennsylvanian*, April 9, 1996, http://www.dailypennsylvanian.com/vnews/display.v/ART/3adb225263a41? in_archive=1.

42. Scott Lanman, "Jacobowitz Settles 'Water Buffalo' Lawsuit," *Daily Pennsylvanian*, September 9, 1997, http://www.dailypennsylvanian.com/vnews/display.v/ART/3adb2453877ce? in_archive=1.

43. Spencer Willig, "Issues of Free Speech Confronted at Colleges," *Daily Pennsylvanian*, April 17, 2003, http://www.dailypennsylvanian.com/vnews/display.v/ART/3e9e836149979? in_archive=1.

44. Ronald Bailey, "The Shadow University: The Betrayal of Liberty on America's Campuses," *The Chief Executive*, November 1999, http://www.findarticles.com/p/articles/mi_m4070/is_1999_Nov/ai_58056112.

45. Alanna Kaufman, "Rights Expert to Represent Photographer," *Daily Pennsylvanian*, December 1, 2005.

46. Jason Schwartz, "Racy Photo Lands Student in Trouble," *Daily Pennsylvanian*, November 30, 2005.

47. Pressed Ham is the appearance of a bare buttock against a clear firm substance such as glass. It's a medical term . . .

48. Picture was printed on the cover of the December 1, 2005, *Philadelphia Daily News.*

49. Jason Schwartz, "Racy Photo Lands Student in Trouble," *Daily Pennsylvanian*, November 30, 2005.

50. Interview with Andrew Geier, *The Michael Smerconish Program*, recorded December 1, 2005, aired December 2, 2005.

51. Ibid.

52. Alanna Kaufman, "Rights Expert to Represent Photographer," *Daily Pennsylvanian*, December 1, 2005.

53. Jason Schwartz, "Racy Photo Lands Student in Trouble," *Daily Pennsylvanian*, November 30, 2005.

54. Alanna Kaufman, "Rights Expert to Represent Photographer," *Daily Pennsylvanian*, December 1, 2005.

55. Interview with Andrew Geier, *The Michael Smerconish Program*, recorded December 1, 2005, aired December 2, 2005.

56. *Philadelphia Daily News*, December 1, 2005.

57. Jason Schwartz, "News Analysis: Media Attention Pressured Officials to Dismiss Charges," *Daily Pennsylvanian*, December 2, 2005.

58. Ibid.

59. Jason Schwartz, "Photographer Escapes Charges," *Daily Pennsylvanian*, December 2, 2005.

60. "Indecent Treatment," editorial, *Daily Pennsylvanian*, December 1, 2005.

CHAPTER FOURTEEN—Cops and Dancers

1. "Atlanta's 26 Hours of Fear," CNN, March 15, 2005, http://www.cnn.com/2005/LAW/03/14/atlanta.summary.

2. "Man Flees after Killing Judge and 2 Others at Atlanta Court," *New York Times*, March 11, 2005, http://www.nytimes.com/2005/03/11/national/11cnd atla.html?pagewanted=1&ei=5070&en=1f9311817bf56b05&hp&ex=1113537600.

3. Ann Coulter, "Freeze! I Just Had My Nails Done," *Pittsburgh Tribune Review*, March 20, 2005.

4. Mean Body Weight, Height, and Body Mass Index (BMI) 1960-2002: United States, prepared by CDC's National Center for Health Statistics.

5. John Lott Jr., "Affirmative Action Has Mixed Results for Cops," FOX News, March 29, 2005, http://www.foxnews.com/story/0,2933,151748,00.html.

6. Ibid.

7. Ibid.

8. Barry Bearak and David Lauter, "Tense Steps to Ending Racial Bias: The Goal of Eliminating Discrimination has Forced Tough Choices. An Important Part of the Story Begins with a Group of Black Janitors at a Steam Plant in North Carolina," *Los Angeles Times*, November 3, 1991, p. A1.

9. Ibid.

10. *Griggs v. Duke Power Company*, 292 F.Supp, 243 (M.D.N.C. 1968).

11. *Griggs v. Duke Power Company*, 401 U.S. 424 (1971), p. 432.

12. "The Supreme Court's 1989 opinion in *Wards Cove Packing Co. v. Atonio* [490 U.S. 642 (1989)] had placed the burden on the plaintiff to show the lack of business necessity. The Civil Rights Act of 1991 returned employment discrimination law to the earlier understanding of the meaning of *Griggs* and overturned that part of *Wards Cove* by defining 'demonstrate' to mean 'meets the burden of production and persuasion.'" Elaine W. Shoeben, "Disparate Impact Theory in Employment Discrimination: What's Griggs Still Good For? What Not?" 42 Brandeis L.J. 597, p. 606.

13. *Guardians Association of the New York City Police Department v. Civil Service Commission of the City of New York*, 431 F. Supp. 526 (S.D.N.Y. 1977), p. 550.

14. Ibid.

15. *Pennsylvania v. Flaherty*, 404 F. Supp. 1022 (W.D. PA 1975), p. 1026.

16. (k) Burden of proof in disparate impact cases.

   (1) (A) An unlawful employment practice based on disparate impact is established under this title only if-

   (i) a complaining party demonstrates that a respondent uses a particular employment practice that causes a disparate impact on the basis of race, color, religion, sex, or national origin and the respondent fails to demonstrate that the challenged practice is job related for the position in question and consistent with business necessity; or

   (ii) the complaining party makes the demonstration described in subparagraph (C) with respect to an alternative employment practice and the respondent refuses to adopt such alternative employment practice.

   (B) (i) With respect to demonstrating that a particular employment practice causes a disparate impact as described in subparagraph (A)(i), the complaining party shall demonstrate that each particular challenged employment practice causes a disparate impact, except that if the complaining party can demonstrate to the court that the elements of a respondent's decision-making process are not capable of separation for analysis, the decision-making process may be analyzed as one employment practice.

   (ii) If the respondent demonstrates that a specific employment practice does not cause the disparate impact, the respondent shall not be required to demonstrate that such practice is required by business necessity.

   (C) The demonstration referred to by subparagraph (A)(ii) shall be in accordance with the law as it existed on June 4, 1989, with respect to the concept of "alternative employment practice."

   (2) A demonstration that an employment practice is required by business necessity may not be used as a defense against a claim of intentional discrimination under this title.

270

(3) Notwithstanding any other provision of this title [42 USCS §§ 2000e et seq.], a rule barring the employment of an individual who currently and knowingly uses or possesses a controlled substance, as defined in schedules I and II of section 102(6) of the Controlled Substances Act (21 U.S.C. 802(6)), other than the use or possession of a drug taken under the supervision of a licensed health care professional, or any other use or possession authorized by the Controlled Substances Act or any other provision of federal law, shall be considered an unlawful employment practice under this title only if such rule is adopted or applied with an intent to discriminate because of race, color, religion, sex, or national origin, 42 U.S.C. §2000e-2(k) (2005), v 29 C.F.R. 1607.4(C) (2005).

17. The data available showed that for one three-year period during this time only 12 percent of women police applicants passed while over 60 percent of male applicants did so. *Lanning v. Southeastern Pennsylvania Transportation Authority,* 181 F.23d 478 (3rd Cir. 1999), p. 482-83.

18. Ibid. p. 489.

19. *Southeastern Pennsylvania Transportation Authority v. Lanning,* 528 U.S. 1131 (2000).

20. 1973 Op.Atty.Gen. No. 57.

21. Press Releases, theborgata.com, May 26, 2005, http://www.theborgata.com/main. cfm?Section=media01&TabType=A&SideNav=pressreleases&Content=media01&CS SID=306.

22. Ibid.

23. Ibid.

24. Suzette Parmley, "Borgata Babes Sell Brand Image," *Sun News,* June 1, 2005, http:// www.myrtlebeachonline.com/mld/myrtlebeachonline/business/11785401.htm.

25. Donald Wittkowski, "Jurisdictional Issues Weigh Down Lawsuit Against Borgata," Press of Atlantic City.com, February 23, 2005, http://www.pressofatlanticcity .com/news/atlantic/022305BORGATABABES_F23.cfm.

26. Ibid.

27. Ibid.

28. Ibid.

29. Ibid.

30. "Cocktail Waitresses Get Fat Fiat," CBS News, February 18, 2005, http://www. cbsnews.com/stories/2005/02/18/national/printable674879.shtml.

31. Ibid.

32. "Weight Watching: Hiring Only Svelte Servers May Shut Out Someone with Superb Skills," *Nations Restaurant News,* March 14, 2005, http://www.findarticles.com/p/articles/ mi_m3190/is_11_39/ai_n13471181.

33. Ibid.

34. Ibid.

35. Suzette Parmley, "Fit the Mold—or Else," *Philadelphia Inquirer,* May 22, 2005.

36. Interview with Professor Motman, *The Michael Smerconish Show,* The Big Talker WPHT 1210 AM, Philadelphia, March 15, 2005.

37. April Washington, "Diversity Worries Set Off Alarms," *Rocky Mountain News,* August 6, 2005, http://www.rockymountainnews.com/drmn/local/article/0,1299,DRMN_15_ 3982015,00.html.

38. Ibid.

39. Profile of General Demographic Characteristics for the Year 2000, Denver County, CO, http://www2.census.gov/census_2000/datasets/demographic_profile/Colorado/ 2kh08.pdf.

40. April Washington, "Diversity Worries Set Off Alarms," *Rocky Mountain News,* August 6,

2005, http://www.rockymountainnews.com/drmn/local/article/0,1299,DRMN_15_3982015,00.html.

41. Ibid.
42. Ibid.
43. Ibid.
44. Ibid.
45. Bob Egelko, "Woman's Suit Against L'Oreal to Go to Trial, Court Rules Alleged Retaliatory Actions a Civil Rights Matter," *San Francisco Chronicle*, August 12, 2005.
46. Ibid.

Chapter Fifteen—There She Isn't

1. Pamela M. McBride, "Here She Comes, Miss America 2003, Erika Harold," http://www.black-collegian.com/issues/2ndsem03/america2003-2nd.shtml.
2. Michael Smerconish, "Want Ratings? Bring Back the Beauty," *Philadelphia Daily News*, September 26, 2002.
3. Anne-Marie Bivans, "The 1920's: The Roaring Twenties and a Promotional Gimmick Birth a Great American Tradition," *The History of Pageants*, 1999, http://www.pageantcenter.com/history.html.
4. "The Changing Ideal," Public Broadcasting Service Online, http://www.pbs.org/wgbh/amex/missamerica/sfeature/sf_decades.html#.
5. "Cartoon Fun and the History of the Miss America Pageant," Brownielocks and the 3 Bears, 2004, http://www.brownielocks.com/americapageant.html.
6. "Cartoon Fun and the History of the Miss America Pageant," Brownielocks and the 3 Bears, 2004, http://www.brownielocks.com/americapageant.html.
7. "The Changing Ideal," Public Broadcasting Service Online, http://www.pbs.org/wgbh/amex/missamerica/sfeature/sf_decades.html#.
8. Ibid.
9. Ibid.
10. Ibid.
11. Ibid.
12. "Encyclopedia: Miss America," NationMaster.com, 2005, http://www.nationmaster.com/encyclopedia/Miss-America.
13. "The Changing Ideal," Public Broadcasting Service Online, http://www.pbs.org/ wgbh/amex/missamerica/sfeature/sf_decades.html#.
14. Kari Huus, "Miss America Seeks Relevance and Ratings," MSNBC, September 17, 2004, http://www.msnbc.msn.com/id/5954542/.
15. "The Changing Ideal," Public Broadcasting Service Online, http://www.pbs.org/wgbh/amex/missamerica/sfeature/sf_decades.html#.
16. Ibid.
17. Ibid. (The swimsuit segment was actually shared with a brief interview portion which were judged together but the interview portion was later done away with.)
18. Olivia Barker, "Here She Is: 'Miss America' on CMT," *USA Today*, June 28, 2005.
19. Ibid.
20. Joe Whiteko, "An Honest Look at Miss America (2005)," Pageant News Bureau, 2005, http://www.pageant.com/missamerica2005/.
21. Olivia Barker, "Here She Is: 'Miss America' on CMT," *USA Today*, June 28, 2005.
22. Ibid.
23. Joe Whiteko, "An Honest Look at Miss America (2005)," Pageant News Bureau, 2005, http://www.pageant.com/missamerica2005/.

24. Interview with Leonard Horn, *The Michael Smerconish Show*, The Big Talker WPHT 1210 AM, Philadelphia, September 17, 2004.
25. Kari Huus, "Miss America Seeks Relevance and Ratings," MSNBC, September 17, 2004, http://www.msnbc.msn.com/id/5954542/.
26. Interview with Leonard Horn, *The Michael Smerconish Show*, The Big Talker WPHT 1210 AM, Philadelphia, September 17, 2004.
27. Miss America Pageant FAQ's, http://www.missamerica.org/competition-info/faq.asp.
28. "1990's Decade in Review," Miss America Organization, http://www.missamerica.org/our-miss-americas/1990/review.asp.
29. Olivia Barker, "Here She Is: 'Miss America' on CMT," *USA Today*, June 28, 2005.
30. Interview with Leonard Horn, *The Michael Smerconish Show*, The Big Talker WPHT 1210 AM, Philadelphia, September 17, 2004.
31. Jacque Steinberg, "Miss America as She Used to Be," *New York Times*, December 22, 2005.

CHAPTER SIXTEEN—Will the Real Rob Morris Please Rise

1. Joseph N. DiStefano, "Wachovia Finds Role in Slavery in its Past," *Philadelphia Inquirer*, June 2, 2005.
2. "Wachovia Summary of the Work of the History Factory," http://www.wachovia.com/misc/0,,877,00.html?DCMP=ILL2433&ATTINFO=7759-personal1.
3. Ibid.
4. Ibid.
5. "Wachovia Corporation and Its Predecessor Institutions," Prepared by the History Factor, p. 1, May 2005.
6. Interview with Blondell Reynolds-Brown, *The Michael Smerconish Show*, The Big Talker, WPHT 1210 AM, Philadelphia, June 8, 2005.
7. Press release titled "Goode to Introduce Financial Reparations Bill," issued June 8, 2005, from the office of Councilman W. Wilson Goode Jr.
8. Interview with Bruce Crawley, *The Michael Smerconish Show*, The Big Talker WPHT 1210 AM, Philadelphia, June 22, 2005.
9. Jeff Jacoby, "The Slavery Shakedown," *Boston Globe*, June 9, 2005.
10. Interview with Rob Morris, *The Michael Smerconish Show*, The Big Talker WPHT 1210 AM, Philadelphia, June 22, 2005.
11. Rob Morris, "Wachovia Supports a Blood Libel Against the United States," unpublished, 2005.
12. E-mail from Rob Morris to Michael Smerconish dated September 9, 2005.

CHAPTER SEVENTEEN—It's All about the Wampum

1. David B. Caruso, "Judge Rules against Tribe in Land Dispute," Associated Press, *Philadelphia Inquirer*, December 3, 2004.
2. Mario F. Cattabiani and Carrie Budoff, "Indians Seek N.E. Pa. Land for Casino," *Philadelphia Inquirer*, May 15, 2003.
3. Michael Smerconish, "Indian Gambling Mess: Blame Congress," *Philadelphia Daily News*, May 22, 2003.
4. *Delaware Nation v. Commonwealth of Pennsylvania*, 2004 WL 2755545 (E.D.Pa. November 30, 2004).
5. Michael Janofsky, "Many Millions in Kickbacks from Tribes," *New York Times*, January 4, 2006.
6. Steve Wieberg, "NCAA Lets FSU Keep 'Seminoles,'" *USA Today*, August 24, 2005.
7. Leilana McKindra, "MOIC Forwards Recommendations from Mascots Review," The NCAA News Online, July 4, 2005.

8. Mrkr Alesia, "Bradley Loses Its Mascot Appeal to NCAA," *Indianapolis Star*, October 21, 2005.

9. Pat Borzi, "A Dispute of Great Spirit Rages On," *New York Times*, November 26, 2005.

10. "NCAA Executive Committee Issues Guidelines for Use of Native American Mascots at Championship Events" by NCAA Executive Committee, The NCAA News Online, August 5, 2005.

11. Ibid.

12. Jim Shore, "Play With Our Name," *New York Times*, August 27, 2005.

13. Robert Andrew Powell, "Florida State Can Keep Its Seminoles," *New York Times*, August 24, 2005.

14. Ibid.

15. Anthony Mague, "Florida State Has Used the Seminole Nickname with the Tribe's Consent Since 1947," DailyOrange.com, October 8, 2004.

16. Bill Vilona, "Seminole Tribe Supports FSU Nickname, Logo," *Pensacola* (FLA.) *News Journal*, June 18, 2005.

17. Ibid.

18. "FSU Appeals NCAA Policy on Use of Native American Names and Symbols," by FSU President T. K. Wetherell, FSU.com, August 12, 2005.

19. Ibid.

20. Ibid.

21. Robert Andrew Powell, "Florida State Can Keep Its Seminoles," *New York Times*, August 24, 2005.

22. Interview with Congressman Tom Feeney by Michael Smerconish for the Bill O'Reilly *Radio Factor*, August 11, 2005.

23. Ibid.

24. Steve Wieberg, "NCAA lets FSU keep 'Seminoles,'" *USA Today*, August 24, 2005.

25. Eddie Pellis, "An Air Force Coach Reprimanded after Comments about Black Athletes," *USA Today*, October 26, 2005.

CHAPTER EIGHTEEN—Intelligently Designing a Curriculum

1. All quotations about the Scopes Trial are from "Scopes Trial" at http://www.pbs.org/wgbh/evolution/library/08/2/l_082_01.html.

2. Jerry Coyne, "The Case Against Intelligent Design: The Faith That Dare Not Speak Its Name," The New Republic Online, post date August 11, 2005, issue date August 22, 2005, http://www.tnr.com.

3. Quoted from: "Harvard Enters Debate on Evolution," Daisuke Wakabayashi, Reuters, August 15, 2005, http://today.reuters.com/news/newsArticle.aspx?type=science News&storyID=2005-08-15T233839Z_01_HO585023_RTRIDST_0_SCIENCE-EVOLUTION-DC.XML.

4. John Agnus Campbell and Stephen C. Meyer, "Evolution: Debate It," *USA Today*, August 15, 2005, http://www.usatoday.com/news/opinion/editorials/2005-08-14-evolution-debate_x.htm.

5. Ibid.

6. Michael Powell, "Evolution Shares a Desk with 'Intelligent Design,'" *Washington Post*, December 26, 2004, http://www.washingtonpost.com/wp-dyn/articles/A25961-2004 Dec25.html.

7. Geoff Brumfiel, "Intelligent Design: Who Has Designs on Your Students' Minds?" Nature.com, April 28, 2005, http://www.nature.com/nature/journal/v434/n7037/full/4341062a.html#a1.

8. Interview with Michael Behe, *The Michael Smerconish Show*, the Big Talker WPHT 1210 AM, Philadelphia, January 6, 2005.

9. "School Board OKs Challenges to Evolution," AP press writer Martha Raffaele on msnbc.com, November 12, 2004, http://msnbc.msn.com/id/6470259/.

10. Jerry Coyne, "The Case against Intelligent Design: The Faith That Dare Not Speak Its Name," The New Republic Online, post date August 11, 2005, issue date August 22, 2005. http://www.tnr.com.

11. Ibid.

12. Ibid.

13. Interview with Jeff and Carol Brown, *The Michael Smerconish Show*, The Big Talker WPHT 1210 AM, Philadelphia, November 22, 2004.

14. "School Board OKs Challenges to Evolution," AP press writer Martha Raffaele on msnbc.com, November 12, 2004. http://msnbc.msn.com/id/6470259/.

15. Interview with Jeff and Carol Brown, *The Michael Smerconish Show*, The Big Talker WPHT 1210 AM, Philadelphia, November 22, 2004.

16. Anna Badkhen, "Anti-evolution Teachings Gain Foothold in U.S. Schools, Evangelicals See Flaws in Darwinism," *San Francisco Chronicle*, November 30, 2004, http://sfgate.com/cgi-bin/article.cgi?file=/c/a/2004/11/30/MNGVNA3PE11.DTL.

17. Ibid.

18. Interview with Michael Behe, *The Michael Smerconish Show*, The Big Talker WPHT 1210 AM, Philadelphia, January 6, 2005.

19. "Pennsylvania Parents File First-Ever Challenge to 'Intelligent Design' Instruction in Public Schools," ACLU.org, December 14, 2004, http://www.aclu.org/ReligiousLiberty/ReligiousLiberty.cfm?ID=17207&c=139.

20. Ibid.

21. Interview with Jeff and Carol Brown, *The Michael Smerconish Show*, The Big Talker WPHT 1210 AM, Philadelphia, November 22, 2004.

22. Michael Powell, "Evolution Shares a Desk with 'Intelligent Design,'" *Washington Post*, December 26, 2004, http://www.washingtonpost.com/wp-dyn/articles/A25961-2004Dec25.html.

23. John Agnus Campbell and Stephen C. Meyer, "Evolution: Debate It," *USA Today*, August 15, 2005, http://www.usatoday.com/news/opinion/editorials/2005-08-14-evolution-debate_x.htm.

24. Jerry Coyne, "The Case Against Intelligent Design: The Faith That Dare Not Speak Its Name," The New Republic Online, post date August 11, 2005, issue date August 22, 2005. http://www.tnr.com.

25. Stephen Jay Gould, "Darwinian Fundamentalism," *New York Review of Books*, Vol. 44, No. 10, June, 1997, http://www.nybooks.com/artlcles/1151.

26. "Convergent Evolution," http://www.pbs.org/wgbh/evolution/library/01/4/1014 01.html. On "cladists" or "cladistics"; also see http://en.wikipedia.org/wiki/Cladist.

27. John Agnus Campbell and Stephen C. Meyer, "Evolution: Debate It," *USA Today*, August 15, 2005, http://www.usatoday.com/news/opinion/editorials/2005-08-14-evolution-debate_x.htm.

28. Ibid.

29. Laurie Goodstein, "Judge Rejects Teaching Intelligent Design," *New York Times*, December 21, 2005.

30. Opinion of Judge John E. Jones III, *Tammy Kitzmiller et al. vs. Dover Areas School District et al.*, United States District Court for the Middle District of Pennsylvania, December 20, 2005.

31. Ibid.

CHAPTER NINETEEN—I Wish I Were Joking

1. http://www.menofmysteryoc.com.
2. http://www.randomhouse.com/bantamdell/koontz/meet_dk.html.
3. Steven Barrie-Anthony, "Koontz Talk Brings Claims of Racism," *Los Angeles Times*, November 10, 2005.
4. Interview with Charles Fleming, *The Michael Smerconish Show*, The Big Talker WPHT 1210 AM, Philadelphia, November 16, 2005.
5. Interview with Dean Koontz, *The Michael Smerconish Show*, The Big Talker WPHT 1210 AM, Philadelphia, December 2, 2005.
6. Steven Barrie-Anthony, "Koontz Talk Brings Claims of Racism," *Los Angeles Times*, November 10, 2005.
7. Ibid.
8. Ibid.
9. Interview with Dean Koontz, *The Michael Smerconish Show*, December 2, 2005.
10. Steven Barrie-Anthony, "Koontz Talk Brings Claims of Racism," *Los Angeles Times*, November 10, 2005.
11. Ibid.
12. Interview with Charles Fleming, *The Michael Smerconish Show*, November 16, 2005.
13. Ibid.
14. Ibid.
15. Ibid.
16. Ibid.
17. Warren St. John, "Seriously, The Joke Is Dead," *New York Times*, May 22, 2005.
18. Tom Shales, "Rock, Well . . . Didn't," *Washington Post*, February 28, 2005.
19. "Robin Reveals Banned Oscars Song," published September 3, 2005, on contactmusic.com. Also posted at Hollywood.com, http://www.hollywood.com/news/detail/ article/ 2436196&f%3D4.
20. Mark Armstrong, "'South Park' Guys: Bleep the Oscars!" published March 3, 2000 on EOnline.com http://www.eonline.com/News/Items/0,1,6110,00.html.
21. John Lahr, "The Goat Boy Rises," *The New Yorker*, Issue of 1993-11-01, posted online 2004-08-02.
22. Ibid.
23. Gail Shister, "War at Home Producers Cut 'Fag' Reference from Pilot," *Philadelphia Inquirer*, August 1, 2005.
24. Christopher Noxon, "Television without Pity," *New York Times*, October 17, 2004.
25. Ibid.
26. Interview with Jackie Mason, *The Michael Smerconish Show*, The Big Talker WPHT 1210 AM, Philadelphia, July 29, 2005.
27. Ibid.
28. Robert Strauss, "So Jersey, He Deserves His Own Rest Area," *New York Times*, August 7, 2005.
29. Interview with Joe Piscopo, *The Michael Smerconish Show*, The Big Talker WPHT 1210 AM, Philadelphia, August 12, 2005.

CHAPTER TWENTY—Stamps of Disapproval

1. "Group Decries Urban Outfitters T-Shirt Making Fun of Mexico," AP News story posted 7/22/05 at http://www.9news.com/acm_news.aspx?OSGNAME=KUSA&IKOBJECTID =4005ecfa-0abe-421a-00e5-ec7865b5f242&TEMPLATEID=0c76dce6-ac1f-02 d8-0047-c589c01ca7bf.
2. Ibid.

3. Interview with José Quiñonez, *The Michael Smerconish Show*, The Big Talker WPHT 1210 AM, Philadelphia, August 1, 2005.

4. Ibid.

5. "Mexico Backs Stamps Amid Race Row" at BBC News, http://news.bbc.co.uk/2/hi/americas/4637943.stm.

6. James C. McKinley Jr., "New Racial Gaffe in Mexico; This Time It's a Tasteless Stamp Set," *New York Times*, June 30, 2005.

7. Mark Stevenson of Associated Press, "Stamps Renew Racial Tensions with Mexico," *Bakersfield Californian*, June 30, 2005.

8. Ibid.

9. Ibid.

10. NLPC Press Release: Jesse Jackson Complaints About Racist Mexican Stamps Ring Hollow, published June 30, 2005, on NLPC.org.

11. "Mexico Backs Stamps Amid Race Row," BBC News, http://news.bbc.co.uk/2/hi/americas/4637943.stm.

12. Mark Stevenson of Associated Press, "Mexico Defends Stamp of Black Character," published on-line, Yahoo News, June 30, 2005.

13. Wikipedia.org, http://en.wikipedia.org/wiki/Mem%C3%ADn_Pingu%C3%ADn.

14. Laurence Iliff, "Caricature Called Racist by Some, Beloved by Others," *Charlotte Observer*, July 24, 2005, http://www.charlotte.com/mld/charlotte/news/world/ 12212459.htm.

15. Mary Lou Pickel, "For Blacks, Stamps Jab at Old Wounds," *Atlanta Journal Constitution*, July 27, 2005, http://www.ajc.com/news/content/news/stories/0705/27 caricatures.html.

16. Gregory Kane, "Mexican Stamp Is Bad, but U.S. Rappers Have It Licked," *Baltimore Sun*, July 6, 2005.

17. Quoted from "Memín Pinguin and Mexico's National Myth," Cristobal Cavazos, *People's Weekly World*, July 23, 2005, http://www.pww.org/article/articleview/7437/1/279.

18. Hector Ayala, "Sorry, Jesse, But Comic Book Hero Deserves a Stamp," *Tucson Citizen*, July 22, 2005, http://www.tucsoncitizen.com/index.php?page=opinion&story_id= 072205b5_ayala&page_number=0.

CHAPTER TWENTY-ONE—Can't We All Just Get Along?

1. Quote from Rodney King; from the cover of *Time*, May 11, 1992.

2. Rick Santorum, *It Takes a Family*, ISI Books, 2005, p. 23.

3. Stephen D. Levitt and Steven J. Dubner, *Freakonomics*, William Morrow (2005)

4. Ibid. 138.

5. Jane Gross , "U.S Fund for Tower Victims Will Aid Some Gay Partners," *New York Times*, May 30, 2002.

6. Ibid.

7. Ibid.

8. "WEDDINGS/CELEBRATIONS; Gregory Krzyminski, Raymond Konz," *New York Times*, Section 9; Column 2; Society Desk; Pg. 10, July 6, 2003.

9. Michael Smerconish, "Summer & Smoke: My Gay Epiphany," *Philadelphia Daily News*, August 28, 2003.

10. Chebium, Raju, "High Court Allows Boy Scouts to Exclude Gays," June 28, 2000, http://archives.cnn.com/2000/LAW/06/28/scotus.gay.boyscouts.01/.

11. Ibid.

12. Linda K. Harris, "Boy Scout Council 'Devastated' by United Way Cuts," *Philadelphia Inquirer*, August 2, 2003.

13. Ibid.

14. Ibid.

15. Ibid.
16. Michael Smerconish, "00076: Save the Scouts from the United Way," *Philadelphia Daily News*, November 20, 2003.
17. Ibid.
18. Ibid.
19. Linda K. Harris, "Boy Scout Council 'Devastated' by United Way Cuts," *Philadelphia Inquirer*, August 2, 2003.

CHAPTER TWENTY-TWO—Up in Smoke
1. National Cancer Institute, "Cancer Facts," http://cis.nci.nih.gov/fact/10_14.htm#3, accessed on August 13, 2005.
2. "Major Cause of Heart Attacks in Younger Patients? Smoking," http://heartdisease.about.com/od/smokingandheartdisease/a/smokeyoungMI.htm, accessed on August 13, 2005.
3. R. J. Ignelzi, "What to Do to Shoo Away Flu, Sans Shot," *San Diego Union Tribune*, October 19, 2004, p. E1.
4. "Enrollment Completed in Study of Vaccine to Prevent and Treat Nicotine Addiction," *Drug Week*, August 19, 2005, p. 710.
5. "Exposing the Myth of Medical Marijuana," http://www.usdoj.gov/dea/ongoing/marijuanap.html, accessed on August 13, 2005.
6. *U.S. v. Randall*, 104 Daily Washington Law Reporter 2254 (D.C. Sup. 1976) *cited in* Andrew J. LeVay, "Urgent Compassion: Medical Marijuana, Prosecutorial Discretion, and the Medical Necessity Defense," 41 B.C. L. Rev. 699 (2000), p. 715.
7. 21 C.F.R. §312.34(b)(i)-(ii) (2005). The explicit restrictive language was added in 1987. There are additional restrictions: "(iii) The drug is under investigation in a controlled clinical trial under an IND in effect for the trial, or all clinical trials have been completed; and (iv) The sponsor of the controlled clinical trial is actively pursuing marketing approval of the investigational drug with due diligence."
8. "Irvin Rosenfeld and the Compassionate IND—Medical Marijuana Proof and Government Lies," http://blogs.salon.com/0002762/stories/2005/02/18/irvRosenberg AndTheCompassi.html, accessed on 15 August, 2005.
9. "Marijuana as Medicine: A Plea for Reconsideration," *JAMA*, June 21, 1995, pp. 1875-76.
10. Ibid.
11. Job 1:21, *New King James Bible*.
12. Christopher Krohn, "Why I'm Fighting Federal Drug Laws from City Hall," *New York Times*, September 21, 2002, §A1, p. 15.
13. John Ritter, "Pot Raids Anger State, Patients," *USA Today*, September 17, 2002, p. 3A. Interestingly, the raid played so poorly, with the image of armed DEA agents confronting patients in wheelchairs stuck in everyone's mind, that Santa Cruz County won a temporary injunction halting future raids. Steve Wishnia, "The Cannabis War," *In These Times*, Institute for Public Affairs, July 11, 2005, p. 8.
14. Evelyn Nieves, "I Really Consider Cannabis My Miracle; Patients Fight to Keep Drug of Last Resort," *Washington Post*, January 1, 2005, p. A3.
15. "Supreme Court to Rule on Federal Regulation of Medicinal Drug Use," *Daily Bruin Online*, November 17, 2004.
16. Evelyn Nieves, "I Really Consider Cannabis My Miracle; Patients Fight to Keep Drug of Last Resort," *Washington Post*, January 1, 2005, p. A3.
17. Ibid.
18. *Gonzales v. Raich*, 125 S. Ct. 2195 (2005) at 2201.
19. According to the National Organization for the Reform of Marijuana Laws (NORML), with whose general stance I disagree, those states are Alaska, Arizona, California, Colorado,

Hawaii, Maine, Maryland, Montana, Nevada, Oregon, Vermont, and Washington; http://www.norml.org/index.cfm?Group_ID=3391, accessed on August 15, 2005.

20. Ken Kobayashi, "Medical Cannabis Outlook Clarified," *Honolulu Advertiser*, June 11, 2005, p. 1A.

21. If you guessed that Column "A" referred to tobacco and Column "B" to marijuana, congratulations. Of course, many of the side effects of marijuana that the federal government cites result from smoking the plants' leaves. There are numerous efforts to develop alternate means of administering the drug, but they are obviously hampered by the fact that the act of procuring the marijuana is criminal.

22. Hendrik Hertzberg, "Watched Pot," *New Yorker*, June 27, 2005.

23. From *Caddyshack* (1980). Source: http://www.imdb.com/title/tt0080487/quotes.

24. Geoffrey Cowley and Claudia Kalb, "The Deadliest Cancer," *Newsweek*, August 22, 2005, p. 42.

25. Garrett Condon, "Lung Cancer, Oft-ignored, Still Deadliest," *Hartford Courant*, August 16, 2005, p. D3.

26. Geoffrey Cowley and Claudia Kalb, "The Deadliest Cancer," *Newsweek*, August 22, 2005, p. 42.

27. Ibid.

28. George Hesselberg, "Critics of Smoking Ban Air Ad Radio Spots, Telephone Calls Spread Job Loss Crisis Message," *Wisconsin State Journal*, September 2, 2005, p. C1.

29. Jacqueline Shoyeb, "Some Look to Tighten Proposed Smoking Ban in State," *Times Leader*, September 6, 2005, p. C7.

30. Ibid.

31. Stuart Eskanazi, "There's Danger in the Air," *Seattle Times*, September 7, 2005, p. F1.

32. Elvia Diaz, "Ballot Initiative Filed to Ban Public Smoking Statewide," *Arizona Republic*, September 1, 2005, p. A1.

33. Wendy Koch, "39% Live in Areas Limiting Smoking; Six More States Pass Restrictions in 2005," *USA Today*, December 29, 2005.

34. As part of an effort called "Lights for the Cure" the city of Philadelphia turns pink for one month every year as more than thirty-seven buildings and landmarks are "bathed in pink light, including City Hall, Battleship New Jersey, National Constitution Center, Ben Franklin Bridge, Love Park Fountain, as well as office towers like Bell Atlantic Tower, One Commerce Square, One and Two Liberty Place, and Mellon Bank Center, among others." "Pink Skyline Planned for Breast Cancer Awareness," *Philadelphia Business Journal*, September 29, 2003.

35. Interview with John McKeon, *The Michael Smerconish Show*, The Big Talker 1210 WPHT, Philadelphia, July 21, 2005.

CHAPTER TWENTY-THREE—Mumidiots

1. Sworn testimony of Reginald Thompson, Police Dispatcher, *Cmwlth. PA v. Mumia Abu-Jamal*, (N.T. 6/19/82, 3.106).

2. Sworn testimony of Michael Scanlan, Witness, *Cmwlth. Pa. v. Mumia Abu-Jamal*, (N.T. 6/25/82, p. 18).

3. Ibid. p. 6.

4. Mumia Abu-Jamal: "I for one feel like putting down my pen. Let's write epitaphs for Pigs!" *The Black Panther*, 4/18/70, p. 12.

5. Sworn testimony of Joseph Kohn, *Cmwlth. Pa. v. Mumia Abu-Jamal*, (N.T.6/21/82, pp. 32-37).

6. Sworn testimony of Michael Scanlan, Witness, *Cmwlth. Pa. v. Mumia Abu-Jamal*, (N.T.6/25/82, pp. 6-7).

7. Sworn testimony of Cynthia White, Witness, *Cmwlth. Pa. v. Mumia Abu-Jamal*.

8. Sworn testimony of Anthony Paul, Supervisor, Firearms Identification Unit, Philadelphia Police Department, *Cmwlth. Pa. v. Mumia Abu-Jamal,* (N.T. 6/23/82, pp. 102-107).

9. Sworn testimony of Michael Scanlan, Witness, *Cmwlth. Pa. v. Mumia Abu-Jamal,* (N.T. 6/25/82, p. 8).

10. Sworn testimony of Anthony Paul, Supervisor, Firearms Identification Unit, Philadelphia Police Department, *Cmwlth. Pa. v. Mumia Abu-Jamal,* (N.T. 6/23/82, 6.110, 6.168).

11. Sworn testimony of Charles Tumosa, criminalist for the City of Philadelphia, *Cmwlth. Pa. v. Mumia Abu-Jama,* (N.T. 6/26/82, pp. 16-17).

12. Sworn testimony of Priscilla Durham, security officer, Thomas Jefferson University Hospital, *Cmwlth. Pa. v. Mumia Abu-Jamal,* (N.T. 6/24/82, p.28).

13. Transcript from *20/20,* December 9, 1998, ABC Transcript # 1879.

14. Ibid.

15. Elizabeth Kolbert, "Public Radio Won't Use Commentary by Inmate," *New York Times,* May 17, 1994.

16. "Public Radio Hires Officer's Killer as a Death Row Commentator," *New York Times,* May 15, 1994.

17. Interview of Maureen Faulkner by Michael Smerconish, January 17, 2005.

18. Ibid.

19. Dan Ashley, KGO-TV San Francisco Investigative Report, May 7 and 8, 1998.

20. ABC News: *20/20 Wednesday,* "Hollywood's Unlikely Hero," Producer Harry Phillips with Correspondent Sam Donaldson, December 9, 1998, ABC Transcript # 1879.

21. Ibid.

22. Dan Ashley, KGO-TV San Francisco Investigative Report, May 7 and 8, 1998.

23. ABC NEWS: *20/20 Wednesday,* "Hollywood's Unlikely Hero," Producer Harry Phillips with Correspondent Sam Donaldson, December 9, 1998, ABC Transcript # 1879.

24. Sworn testimony of Dr. Paul Hoyer, *Cmwlth. Pa. v. Mumia Abu-Jamal,* (N.T. 8/9/95, p. 186).

25. Ibid. pp. 191-92.

26. Sworn testimony of Anthony Paul, Supervisor, Firearms Identification Unit, Philadelphia Police Department, *Cmwlth. Pa. v. Mumia Abu-Jamal,* (N.T. 6/23/82, 6.110).

27. Ibid. 6.168.

28. Sworn testimony of George Fassnacht, *Cmwlth. Pa. v. Mumia Abu-Jamal, PCRA Hearing,* (N.T. 8/2/95, p. 158).

29. Buzz Bissinger, "The Famous and the Dead," *Vanity Fair,* August 1999.

30. Statement of Decision: Request for Clemency by Stanley Williams, December 12, 2005. http://ww.governor.ca.gov/govsite/pdf/press_release_2005/Williams_Clemency_Statement.pdf

31. Ibid.

32. Interview of Maureen Faulkner by Michael Smerconish, January 17, 2005.

CHAPTER TWENTY-FOUR—The Parade at PC and Main Streets

1. Editorial note: Kurt Schreyer, a Naval Academy graduate and current PhD English candidate at Penn, refused a sobriety test after preparing that warning.

2. Interview with David Kozinski conducted by Josh Belfer, August 4, 2005.

3. Interview with Penny Kozinski, *The Michael Smerconish Show,* The Big Talker WPHT 1210 AM, Philadelphia, August 2, 2005.

4. Ibid.

5. Ibid.

6. Interview with David Kozinski, by Josh Belfer, August 4, 2005.

7. Ibid.

8. Ibid.

9. Diane K. Spivak, "'Osama' Parade Float Draws Negative Image in Chesterton," July 7, 2005, *Post Tribune*, http://www.post-trib.com/cgi-bin/pto-story/news/z1/07-07-05_z1_news_05.html.

10. David Rutter, "Osama-on-a-rope A Poor Example of Patriotism," *Post Tribune*, July 10, 2005, http://www.post-trib.com/cgi-bin/pto-story/columns/rutter/z1/07-10-05_z1_rutt_1.html.

11. "Bin Laden Float Sparks Debate," AP Story at IndyStar.com, July 7, 2005, http://www.indystar.com/apps/pbcs.dll/article?AID=/20050707/NEWS01/50707014/1006.

12. "Parade Float Depicting Bin Laden Sparks Debate," TheIndyChannel.com, July 7, 2005, http://www.theindychannel.com/print/4695918/detail.html.

13. Ibid.

14. Ibid.

15. Interview with Penny Kozinski, conducted by Josh Belfer, August 2, 2005.

16. Ibid.

17. Ibid.

18. Ibid.

19. Interview with David Kozinski, conducted by Josh Belfer, August 4, 2005.

CHAPTER TWENTY-FIVE—*24* and There's So Much More

1. Interview with Shohreh Aghdashloo, *The Michael Smerconish Show*, The Big Talker WPHT 1210 AM, Philadelphia, January 25, 2005.

2. Interview with Roger Cross, *The Michael Smerconish Show*, The Big Talker WPHT 1210 AM, Philadelphia, January 14, 2005.

3. "Fox's '24' airs Muslim disclaimer: CAIR consulted on text read by Kiefer Sutherland," WorldNetDaily.com, February 9, 2005.

4. Ibid.

5. Michael Smerconish, "Fox Undercuts '24' on Radical Islam," *Philadelphia Daily News*, January 20, 2005.

6. Debbie Schlussel, "Jihad on Fox's '24,'" DebbieSchlussel.com, February 10, 2005.

7. Robert Spencer, "CAIR Intimidates Fox TV," www.aim.org, Guest Column, January 27, 2005.

8. The words of Geoff Brock, Lehigh University Class of 2005, September 1, 2005.

CHAPTER TWENTY-SIX—The T-Word, Shhhh!

1. *The American Heritage Dictionary of the English Language*, Fourth Edition, Copyright @2000 by Houton Mifflin Company.

2. "Police: Did 4 London Bombers Die?" CNN, July 12, 2005, http://www.cnn.com/2005/WORLD/europe/07/12/london.attacks/index.html.

3. "G8 Leaders Condemn 'Barbaric' Attacks," CNN, July 7, 2005, http://www.cnn.com/2005/WORLD/europe/07/07/blair.statement/index.html.

4. Tom Gross, "The BBC Discovers 'Terrorism,' Briefly," *Jerusalem Post* Online, July 11, 2005, http://www.jpost.com/servlet/Satellite?pagename=JPost/JPArticle/ShowFull&cid=1121048976775&p=1006953079865.

5. Chris Muir, "The T-word," *Day By Day*, July 8, 2005, http://www.yourish.com/archives/2005/july3-9_2005.html.

6. Interview with Tom Gross, *The Michael Smerconish Show*, The Big Talker WPHT 1210 AM, Philadelphia, July 13, 2005.

7. Tom Gross, "The BBC Discovers 'Terrorism,' Briefly," *Jerusalem Post* Online, July 11, 2005, http://www.jpost.com/servlet/Satellite?pagename=JPost/JPArticle/ShowFull&cid=1121048976775&p=1006953079865.

NOTES

8. Interview with Tom Gross, *The Michael Smerconish Show*, The Big Talker WPHT 1210 AM, Philadelphia, July 13, 2005.

9. Ibid.

10. Ibid.

11. Interview with James O'Brien, *The Michael Smerconish Show*, The Big Talker WPHT 1210 AM, Philadelphia, July 22, 2005.

12. Chris Muir, "The T-word," *Day By Day*, July 8, 2005, http://www.yourish.com/archives/2005/july3-9_2005.html.

13. Tom Gross, "The BBC Discovers 'Terrorism,' Briefly," *Jerusalem Post* Online, July 11, 2005, http://www.jpost.com/servlet/Satellite?pagename=JPost/JPArticle/ShowFull&cid=1121048976775&p=1006953079865.

14. Tom Leonard, "BBC Edits Out the Word 'Terrorist,'" *Telegraph*, http://news.telegraph.co.uk/news/main.jhtml?xml=/news/2005/07/12/nbbc12.xml.

15. Tom Gross, "The BBC Discovers 'Terrorism,' Briefly," *Jerusalem Post* Online, July 11, 2005, http://www.jpost.com/servlet/Satellite?pagename=JPost/JPArticle/ShowFull&cid=1121048976775&p=1006953079865.

16. Tom Leonard, "BBC Edits Out the Word 'Terrorist,'" *Telegraph*, http://news.telegraph.co.uk/news/main.jhtml?xml=/news/2005/07/12/nbbc12.xml.

17. Tom Gross, "The BBC Discovers 'Terrorism,' Briefly," *Jerusalem Post* Online, July 11, 2005, http://www.jpost.com/servlet/Satellite?pagename=JPost/JPArticle/ShowFull&cid=1121048976775&p=1006953079865.

18. Feedback [NewsWatch], MAS Listener, e-mail to NewsOnline Complaints.

19. RE: Feedback [NewsWatch], NewsOnline, e-mail to MAS Listener, July 13, 2005.

20. "Blair Calls BBC Coverage 'Full of Hate of America,'" Murdoch, Yahoo News, September 17, 2005.

21. Definition and Use of the Word "Terrorist" from *The Inquirer*'s Stylebook, July 18, 2005, *Philadelphia Inquirer* Online, http://www.philly.com/mld/inquirer/news/editorial/12162820.htm.

22. Ibid.

23. Tim Johnson and Matthew Schofield, "As Bomb Toll Reaches 50, Stoic Londoners Carry On," *Philadelphia Inquirer* Online, July 9, 2005, http://www.philly.com/mld/inquirer/2005/07/09/news/nation/12089856.htm.

24. Ken Dilanian and Matthew Schofield, "London Awash in Worry for Missing," *Philadelphia Inquirer* Online, July 18, 2005, http://www.philly.com/mld/inquirer/2005/07/10/news/front/12095287.htm.

25. Matthew Schofield, "Four Tied to London Bombings," *Philadelphia Inquirer* Online, July 13, 2005, http://www.philly.com/mld/inquirer/news/front/12117931.htm.

26. General Information, *Telegraph* Online, http://www.telegraph.co.uk/portal/main.jhtml?menuId=652&menuItemId=-1&view=HELP&grid=P9&targetRule=.

27. "Al Qa'eda Brings Terror to the Heart of London," *Telegraph* Online, July 8, 2005, http://www.telegraph.co.uk/news/main.jhtml?xml=/news/2005/07/08/nbomb08.xml.

28. Philip Johnston, "They Will Not Change Our Way of Life, Says the Queen," *Telegraph* Online, July 9, 2005, http://www.telegraph.co.uk/news/main.jhtml?xml=/news/2005/07/09/nbomb09.xml.

29. Hugh Muir and Rosie Cowen, "Four Bombs in 50 minutes—Britain Suffers Its Worst-ever Terror Attack," *Guardian* Unlimited, July 8, 2005, http://www.guardian.co.uk/uk_news/story/0,,1523819,00.html.

30. Interview with Tom Gross, *The Michael Smerconish Show*, The Big Talker WPHT 1210 AM, Philadelphia, July 13, 2005.

31. "Piggy Banks Banned on Muslim Fear," Free Republic, quoting the *Daily Express*, October 24, 2005.

32. Kate O'Hara, "St. George's Cross Charity Tie-Pins Racists—Prison Chief," *Yorkshire Post Today*, October 4, 2005.

33. Russell Jenkins, "Hit-and-Run Victim Ends Up in PC Trap for Calling Driver Fat," *London Times* online, October 14, 2005.

34. "Camilla's Protector Paid Out," Herald Sun (Australia), January 8, 2006.

35. Anthony Browne, *The Retreat of Reason* (Civitas: Institute for the Study of Civil Society, 2006).

36. Adam Sherwin, "Outlook Is Suddenly Brighter," *London Times*, October 5, 2005; Suzanne Finney, "Always Look on the Bright Side of Life," *Daily Mail*, October 5, 2005.

37. Text: Tony Blair's Statement, CBS News, July 7, 2005, http://www.cbsnews.com/stories/2005/07/07/world/main707101.shtml.

38. "G8 Leaders Condemn 'Barbaric Attacks,'" CNN.com, July 7, 2005, http://www.cnn.com/2005/WORLD/europe/07/07/blair.statement.

39. Transcript of Statement Made by PM Tony Blair, Incidents in London, July 21, Directgov, http://www.number10.gov.uk/output/Page7858.asp.

40. Statement to Parliament on the London Bombings, Directgov, http://www.number10.gov.uk/output/Page7903.asp.

CHAPTER TWENTY-SEVEN—Still Flying Blind

1. Running Press: Philadelphia, 2004.

2. "Bin Laden Determined to Strike in US," President's Daily Briefing, August 6, 2001.

3. Questioning of Dr. Condoleezza Rice by The Honorable John F. Lehman, Ninth Public Hearing of the National Commission on Terrorist Attacks Upon the United States, April 8, 2004.

4. Interview with The Honorable John F. Lehman, *The Michael Smerconish Show*, The Big Talker WPHT 1210 AM, Philadelphia, April 10, 2004.

5. Statement by the Department of Transportation Office of Public Affairs Rep. Brian Turmail to the *Philadelphia Daily News*, e-mail from Brian Turmail to Michael Smerconish dated April 23, 2004.

6. 49 USCS 44902, Refusal to Transport Passengers and Property.

7. Statement of José Melendez Perez to the Seventh Public Hearing of the National Commission on Terrorist Attacks upon the United States, January 26, 2004.

8. Interview with José Melendez-Perez, *The Michael Smerconish Show*, The Big Talker WPHT 1210 AM, Philadelphia, September 20, 2004.

9. Statement of Richard Ben-Veniste at the Seventh Public Hearing of the National Commission on Terrorist Attacks Upon the United States, January 26, 2004.

10. "Exclusive: Detainee 063 Inside the Wire at Gitmo," *Time*, June 20, 2005.

11. Interview with José Melendez-Perez, *The Michael Smerconish Show*, The Big Talker WPHT 1210 AM, Philadelphia, September 20, 2004.

12. Interview with Michael Tuohey, *The Michael Smerconish Show*, The Big Talker WPHT 1210 AM, February 21, 2005.

13. Ibid.

14. Jules Crittenden, "Radio Man Flies High to Launch Racial Profiling," *Boston Herald*, September 5, 2004.

15. Testimony of Edmond Soliday, United Airlines, the National Commission on Terrorist Attacks Upon the United States, January 27, 2004.

16. Paul Sperry, *Infiltration* (Nashville: Nelson Current, 2005), p. 240.

17. Ibid., 240-41.

18. Ibid., 241.
19. Ibid., 245.
20. Interview with Sgt. Peter DeDominica, *The Michael Smerconish Show*, The Big Talker WPHT 1210 AM, Philadelphia, October 5, 2004.
21. Ibid.
22. Robert Anglen, "Agent Says Terrorists Will Hit Again," *Arizona Republic*, November 21, 2004.
23. Jeffrey Leib, "Airports Aim to Cut Hated Pat-Downs," *Denver Post*, March 29, 2005.
24. Annie Jacobsen, "Terror in the Skies—Again?" WomensWallStreet.com, July 16, 2004.
25. Audrey Hudson, "Passengers Describe Flight as a Terrorist Dry Run," *Washington Times*, April 27, 2005.
26. "U.S. Blocks Dutch Flight Over Passengers," Associated Press, posted at MSNBC.com, April 10, 2005.
27. Mark Hosenball and Michael Hirsh, "Terrorism: Mystery Flight," *Newsweek*, April 25, 2005.
28. Leslie Miller, "U.S. Weighs Boosting Aviation Security," Associated Press, posted at MSNBC.com, April 21, 2005.
29. Interview with Roger Depue, *The Michael Smerconish Show*, The Big Talker WPHT 1210 AM, Philadelphia, March 17, 2005.

CHAPTER TWENTY-EIGHT—Is That All There Is?

1. Interview with Janis Karpinski, *The Michael Smerconish Show*, The Big Talker WPHT 1210 AM, Philadelphia, December 15, 2005.
2. "Soldiers Convicted in the Abu Gharaib Case," Associated Press, *New York Times*, September 27, 2005.
3. Adam Zagorin and Michael Duffy, "Inside the Interrogation of Detainee of 063," *Time*, June 12, 2005.
4. *Hardball* with Chris Matthews, MSNBC, June 15, 2005.
5. Interview with José Melendez-Perez, *The Michael Smerconish Show*, The Big Talker WPHT 1210 AM, Philadelphia, June 14, 2005.
6. Interview with Donald Rumsfeld, *The Michael Smerconish Show*, The Big Talker WPHT 1210 AM, Philadelphia, June 21, 2005.
7. M. Gregg Bloche, M.D., J.D. and Jonathan H. Marks, M.A., B.C.L., "Doctors and Interrogators at Guantanamo Bay," *New England Journal of Medicine*, July 7, 2005.
8. Neil A. Lewis, "Interrogators Cite Doctors' Aid at Guantanamo," *New York Times*, June 24, 2005.
9. Interview with Janis Karpinski, The *Michael Smerconish Show*, The Big Talker WPHT 1210 AM, Philadelphia, December 15, 2005.
10. Brian Ross and Richard Esposito, "Exclusive: Sources Tell ABC News Top Al Qaeda Figures Held in Secret CIA Prisons," December 5, 2005.
11. Ibid.
12. Interview with John McCain on Friday, December 2, 2005.

Index

24, 200–2, 204–5

50 Cent, 150

9/11, vii, x, 1, 49–50, 166–67, 194–95, 199, 201, 205, 217–22, 224–27, 229–30, 234, 236, 238, 240, 242–43, 246

9/11 Commission, 217–18, 221–22, 225

ABC, 36, 108, 187–88, 207, 244–45

Abramoff, Jack, 127–28

Abu Ghraib (Prison), x, 173, 194, 234–35

Abu-Jamal, Mumia, 183–93, 249

Academy Awards, 149

Adams, Belinda, 58

Adams, Dave, 229

Addison Wesley Publishers, 183–84

Africa, Ramona, 192

Africa, John, 192

Aghdashloo, Shohreh, 200–1

Ahmed, Rabiah, 201

Alger, Horatio, 73

Allengheny Airlines, 223

Al-Kahtani, Mohammed, 221–22, 236–40, 242

Al-Mujahid, Dhoruba, 192

Al Omari, Abdul Aziz, 223

al Qa'eda/al Qaeda, 217, 222, 227, 237–38, 242, 244

al Shehri, Wail, 224

al Shehri, Waleed, 244

al Suqami, Satam, 224

America West Airlines, 231

American Academy of Family Physicians, 177

American Academy of HIV Medicine, 177

American Airlines, 218–20, 222, 224

American Arbitration Association, 100

American Association for Nude Recreation, 79

American Civil Liberties Union (ACLU), 46, 89, 137, 140–41, 226, 247

American Demographics, 68

American Nurses Association, 177

American Public Health Association, 177

American Revolution, 56, 119

Americans for Nonsmokers' Rights, 179

Americans United for Separation of Church and State, 140–41

American West Airlines, 231

American with Disabilities Act, 100

Amnesty International, 234, 236–37, 240–44

Anderson, Elijah, 88

Angelou, Maya, 183

Anti-Defamation League, 157

Arizona Republic, 227

Articles of Confederation, 120

Asner, Ed, 183, 187, 191

Associated Press (AP), 18, 197–98, 207

Atlantic City Airport, 217

Atta, Mohammed, 103, 221, 223–24, 229

Ayala, Hector, 161

Aykroyd, Dan, 155

Aziz, Abdul, 223

Badge of Slavery/Thirteenth Amendment, 117

Baghdad, 235, 239

Baker, Nicole Johnson, 108

Baldwin, Alec, 183

Banc of America Securities, LLC, 3–6, 8–9, 172

Bank of Charleston, 114

Bank of North America, 114, 119–22

Bantam Dell, 147

Barkocy, Frank, 6

Barnes, Judge Rowland, 93–94

Bashur Airfield, 54

Bauer, George, 105

Bauer, Jack, 200, 202–3

Beastie Boys, 183–84

Bechtold, Victoria, 108

Behe, Michael, 138, 141

Belushi, John, 155

Ben-Amos, Dan, 88

Ben-Veniste, Commissioner Richard, 222

Berg, Nick, 235

Between Good and Evil, 232

Bible, ix, 45–48, 54, 99, 137–38, 143–45, 150

Bic, 60

Bill of Rights, 178

Bingham, Mark, 222

bin al-Shibh, Ramzi, 245

Bin Laden, Osama (UBL), 194–99, 208, 218, 236, 241–42

Bissinger, Buzz, 191

Black Guerilla Family, 193

Blair, British Prime Minister Tony, 206, 210, 215

"Blame Canada", 149

Bland, Larry, 9

Bloomberg News, 3, 6

Blue Latinos, 158

Bluffs' Run Racetrack, 42

Bonnicklewis, Colleen, 84

Borgata Hotel and Casino, 99–101

Boston Globe, 119

Boston Herald, 225

Bowser, Charles, 36

Boy Scouts of America (BSA), 167, 169–70, 247

Brady, Bob, 222
Brandau, Julie, 94
Brigadier General William C. Doyle Veterans Memorial
   Cemetery, 50
British Broadcasting Company (BBC), 207–10,
   212–13
Britt, Bill, 30
Brock, Geoff, 204
Brome, Danny, 78
Brooks, Shawn, 35–40
Brown, Carol and Jeff, 140–41
Brown, J. Edward, Esq., 116, 118
Brown, Mayor Willie, 183
Browne, Anthony, 214
Bruce, Captain Rick, 25
Bryan, William Jennings, 137
Burger, Chief Justice Warren, 96
Burlingame, Debra, 222
Burlingame, Chic, 222
Busch, Donna Kay, 45–48, 53
Busch, Wesley, 45–48, 53
Bush administration, 163, 229, 230
Bush, Governor Jeb, 134
Bush, President George W., 13, 137, 144, 160, 210
Business Ethics, 7
Byrne, David, 183

Cagney, James, 127
California Medical Association, 177
California Supreme Court, 43, 103–04
Camp of the Saints, The, 86
Campbell, Naomi, 183
Capitol (U.S.), 222, 237
Cappaert, Barbara, 4
Carlson, Sharon, 60
Carter, Judge Robert, 96–97
Carter Ledyard & Milburn, 7
Castro, Fidel, 163
CBS, 150–52
Central Intelligence Agency (CIA), 236, 244, 245
Chambers, Ken, 132
Chan, Doug, 18
Chappelle, Dave, 14
Charlie's Angels, 25
Chartered Financial Analyst (CFA), 4
Chestnut Hill Local, 32–33
Cheney, Dick, 204
Chinese American Citizens Alliance Hall, 17
Chinese American Voter Education Committee, 18
Chomsky, Noam, 183
Chriskey, Tim, 7
Chung, George, 13–14, 21
Churchill, Winston, 159, 213
Civil Rights Act of 1964, 95–96
Civil Service Commission, 102
Civil War, 57, 115, 119, 126
Clinton, President Bill, 1, 46, 210, 248
Clinton Global Initiative, 210
CNN, 88, 207, 223
Coastline Restaurant, 41–42, 100

Code of Federal Regulations, 97
Cohen, Officer Andrew, 25–26
Cohen, Secretary of Defense William, 231
Cohen, Ben, 183
Colin, Lieutenant Colonel Cynthia, 53
Commission on the Status of Women, 26
Commonwealth Court (of New Jersey), 43
Communist Party, 184
Computer Assisted Passenger Pre-screening System
   (CAPPS), 232
Congressional Black Caucus, 36
Connecticut, 60
Constitution (U.S.), 47, 120, 136, 145
Constitutional Convention, 121
Continental Airlines, 224
Continental Congress, 120
Cook, Thomas, 45, 47
Cook, Wesley, 182–84
Cook, William, 182
Cordova, Salvador, 138
Corral, Mike, 175
Corral, Valerie, 175
Council for American-Islamic Relations (CAIR)
   201–02, 204
Counter Terrorist Unit (CTU), 200
Coviello, Patrick, 169
Coyne, Dr. Jerry, 139
Cozen, Steve, 126–27
Cradle of Liberty Council, 169–70
Cramer, Jim, ix, 8
Crawley, Bruce, 118
Crimson, 74–76
Croce, Pat, 29
Cross, Roger, 200–1
Crow, Jim, 117
Crown Point, 198
Cuba, 163
Cubbage, Captain Adam, 49, 54
Cubbage, Patrick, 49–55, 172
Culpepper, Daunte, 27
Curtain, Jane, 155
Customs Declaration Form, 221
Cutler, Eddy, 59

Daily Pennsylvanian (*DP*), 85–87, 90–92
Daily Worker, 184
Dangerfield, Rodney, 180
Darrow, Clarence, 137
Darwin's theory of evolution, 137–39, 142–43
Davidson, Lisa, 179
Davis, Angela, 192
Davis, Dr. Paul, 97
D.C. Superior Court, 173–74
D-Day, 55
DeBerry, Coach Fisher, 135
Declaration of Independence, 120
DeDominica, Sergeant Peter, 226–27
Delagnes, Gary, 26
Delta Airlines, 224
Delta Sigma Theta, 81, 84

Denver Fire Department, 101, 103
Department of Defense (DOD), 51–52, 54
Department of Transportation (DOT), 218–20, 224–25, 229
Depue, Roger, 232
Deutsche Bank, 4
Devlin, Kevin, 57
Didinger, Ray, 22–23
Dinkins, David, 183
Discovery Institute, 142
Dock Club, 43
Doctorow, E. L., 183
Donahue, Terry, 12–13, 21
Donaldson, Sam, 187–88
Douglas, Hugh, 12
Douglas, Michael, 13
Dover County School Board, District, 140–141, 144
Dowling, Judge John, 43
Drug Enforcement Administration (DEA), 174–76
Dubner, Stephen, 164
Dumas, Iven, 51, 54

Ebert, Roger, 183
Ed Sullivan Theatre, 150
Edgel Grove Cemetery, 56–57
Edwards, Joan L., 51–52
Eiseman, Leatrice, 61–63
Eldredge, Niles, 143
Elliot, Dr. John P., 231
Emergency Committee (of England), 215
Emergency Operations Center (Fort Dix), 49
Engelstad, Ralph, 130
England, Private First Class Lynndie, 235
English, Diane, 152
Encyclopedia Britannica, 38
Equal Employment Opportunity Commission (EEOC), 97, 101
Equal Rights Advocates, 25
Erickson, Dennis, 12
ESPN, 11, 27
Establishment Clause (First Amendment), 46

Farrakhan, Louis, 122–24, 160
Farrell, Mike, 183, 191
Farrell, Noreen, 25
Fassnacht, George, 190
Faulkner, Maureen, 183–86, 191, 193
Faulkner, Officer Daniel (Danny), 182–92
Favre, Brett, 12
Federal Air Marshal Service, 229
Federal Bureau of Investigation (FBI), 227, 232
Federal Emergency Management Agency (FEMA), x
Feeney, Representative Tom, 134
Feinberg, Kenneth R., 166
Ferdinand, Archduke Francis, 211
Fighting Irish, 134
Finn, Michael, 61
"Financial Reparations Bill," 115
Fiore, Dave, 19
Fireman, Cassie, 100

First Amendment, 46, 136, 139
First In, 236
Fleming, Charles, 147–48
Flintlock Inn, 43
Florida State University (FSU), 128–29, 132–35
Flying Blind: How Political Correctness Continues to Compromise Airline Safety Post 9/11, 217, 220–21, 223–25, 230, 232–33
Foley, Ellen, 30
Fong, Chief Heather, 24, 26
Food and Drug Administration (FDA), 174
Ford, Barbara, 57
Foriska, Joseph, 61–62
Forten, James, 121
Fox (network), 200–2, 207
Fox News, 78, 92, 210
Fox, President Vicente, 160
Foundation for Individual Rights in Education (FIRE), 89
Founding Fathers, 122, 197
Fourth of July, 195, 197
Franklin, Bernard, 130, 134
Framingham Memorial, 59
Freakonomics, 164
Fredricksburg, 115
Fresno Bee, 11

G8 (summit), 209, 215
Garcia, Jeff, 11
Geier, Andrew, 90–91
Genesis, 138, 144
Georgia Railroad and Banking Company, 114
Gettysburg, 115
Gillespie, David R., 41–42, 44, 100
Ginsburg, Ruth Bader, 177
Glassman, Stephen A., 38
Gleneagles, Scotland, 215
Glover, Danny, 183
Goode Jr., Councilman W. Wilson, 115, 122
Goldberg, Lee, 147
Goldberg, Whoopi, 183
GoldenTree Asset Management, LP, 7–8
Goldman, David, 4–5
Gonzales, Alberto, 171
Goodman, Mayor Oscar, 110
Gordon, ADA Arnold H., 191
Gordon, Judge Eugene A., 95–96
Gould, Stephen Jay, 143
Graner, Specialist Charles, 235
Grigg, Corporal John, 58
Griggs v. Duke Power Company, 95, 97
Griggs, Willie, 95
Gross, Tom, 207–9, 213
Guantanamo Bay (Gitmo), x, 194, 197, 222, 234–37, 239–43
Guardian, 206, 212–13
Guardians Association of the New York City Police Department, 97
Guither, Peter, 174
Gulf War, 234

Hackney, Sheldon, 87
Halifax bank, 214
Hall, Deputy Cynthia Ann, 93–96, 98
Halliburton, 202
Halvorssen, Thor, 89
Hamas, 211
Hanjour, Hani, 229
Hansen, Joan, 147
Hardball, 236, 240–41
Harmony Grove Community Church, 145
Harold, Erika, 105–6
Harrelson, Woody, 172
Harvard, 9, 28, 73–76, 80–81, 89, 194
Harvard Law Review, 8
Hawkins, Carolyn, 79
Hawthorne, Nathaniel, 86
HBO, 14
Hearst, Garrison, 11
Herbold, Hilary, 80
Hershberger, Jeff, 6
Hicks, Bill, 150–51
Hightower, Jim, 183
Hilell Society, 87–88
History Factory, 114
HIV/AIDS, 109, 112, 168, 174–75, 214, 247
Hoglan, Alice, 222
Holland & Co., 7
Holland, Michael, 7
Hollywood Reporter, 150
Homeland Security Department, 229
Hopkins, Anthony, 232
Horn, Leonard, 108–10
Horowitz, Daniel, 25
Hotel Employees and Restaurant Employees Union, 100
Houldin, Linda, 48
Hoyer, Dr. Paul, 188–90
Hudson, Audrey, 229
Hudson, Yvonne, 155–56
Hughes, Howard, 148
Human Relations Act, 43
Human Rights Commission, 26
Huntington, Pennsylvania, 185
Hurricane Katrina, x, 210
Hussein, Saddam, 199, 234
Hwang, Eileen, 79

Illinois Appeals Court, 44
Infiltration, 225
Infinity Broadcasting, 35, 153
Initiative 901, 179
Inquirer, 29, 210, 212
Institute of Medicine, 174
Intelligent Design (ID), 137–45
Institutional Investor, 8
Intensity, 146
Investigational New Drug program (IND), 174
Iowa Civil Rights Commission, 97
Iowa Supreme Court, 43
Iraq, viii, 54–55, 58, 194, 196, 234, 235

Islam, 132, 206, 215–16, 230, 234, 239–40
It Takes a Family, 164
It Takes a Village, 164
Ivins, Molly, 183
Ivy League, ix, 37, 77–78, 81, 85

Jackson, George, 192–193
Jackson, Janet, 149
Jackson, Jesse, 6, 123, 159
Jackson, Michael, 1
Jackson, Victoria, 156
Jacobowitz, Eden, 81, 83–92
Jacobsen, Annie, 228–29
Jacoby, Jeff, 119
Jaffe, Janine, 79
Jefferson, Thomas, 138
Jenkins, Suzanne, 84
Jerusalem Post, 207
Jezebel's, 43
Jillette, Penn, 149
John Bates Clark Medal, 164
Jones, Joan, 153
Jones III, Judge John E., 144–45
Judicial Inquiry Office (JIO), 83–84, 85–86, 87
Justice Department, 177, 225

Kahrahrah, Bernard, 126
Kane, Gregory, 160
Karpinski, Brigadier-General Janis, 234–35, 244
Kasem, Casey, 183
Katz, Joe, 67
Kazmark, Justin, 62
Kelleher, Herb, 219
Kelly, Collin, 56–59
Kelly, Lynn, 57–59
Kelly, Marjorie, 7
Kennedy, Wally, 36
KGO-TV, 187
Kidd, Judith H., 74–75
King, Rodney, 163
Kinsey, Alfred, 166
Kissimmee, Florida, 79
Kitzmiller et al. v. Dover Area School District et al., 137
KLM Flight 875, 229
Knight-Ridder Inc., 29
Koire, Dennis, 43
Konrath, J. A., 147
Konz, Raymond, 167
Koontz, Dean, 146–48
Kopko, Michael, 73–76
Koran, 46, 194
Korean War, 57
Kors, Alan, 85, 87–90
Kozinski, David, 195
Kozinski, Penny, 195
KPIX-TV, 15
Krasner, Joel, 2, 4–6, 8–9
Kriefman, Mitchell, 155
Krohn, Christopher, 174
Krzyminski, Gregory, 167

Kubo, Ed, 177

Ladies' Day, 42–43
"Ladies Night", viii, 9, 41, 43–44, 100
Lambert, Lester, 29
Lambro, Judge Thomas, 97
Landis, John, 183
Langley, 244
Lansky, Meyer, 127
Late Show, 150
Lattera, Gregory, 169
Law Enforcement Assistance Administration, 97
Lawrence, Andrew, 20
"Learning for Life" program, 169–70
Lee, Spike, 183
Lehman, Secretary John, 218–19, 225
Leno, Jay, 149
Leo, John, 84
Leso, Major John, 242
Letterman, David, 150–51
Letter of Marque, 121
Levitt, Steven, 164–65
Lieberman, Senator Joseph, 231
Life in Prison, 192
Limbaugh, Rush, 84
Lincoln, Abraham, 138
Lind, John Walker, 227
Lin, Tsai-Shai, 192
Lin, Yee-Chen, 192
Lipson Jr., David H., 169–70
Little League, 67–68, 227
Liverpool Privy Council, 121
Logan International Airport, 226–27
Loman, Willy, 38
London, 184, 197, 206–10, 212–13, 215–16
L'Oreal, 104
Los Angeles Times, 91, 147
Lotterstein, Rob, 151–52
Lower Merion, 67–69
Lower Merion Little League, 67, 70
Ludwig, Christian, 29
Lyle, Amaani, 152
Lymphoma Foundation of America, 177
Lynn, Reverend Barry W., 140–41

Mackler, Jeff, 187
Mad Money, 8
Mailer, Norman, 183
Main Line Girls Basketball Association (MLGBA), 70–71
Maine, 223
Malaysia, 85
Malcolm X, 192
Malden, Karl, 13
Mandela, Nelson, 192
Mansmann, Judge Carol, 98
Marines, 53, 58
Mariucci, Steve, 19
Marple Newtown School District, 46
Mason, Jackie, ix, 14, 153–56

Mason, Nick, 213
Matthews, Chris, 236–239
Matzke, Nicholas, 139
McCain, Senator John, 218, 245
McCullough, David, 241
McFerrin, Bobby, 183
McGreevey, Governor Jim, 42
McKeon, Jack, 180
McKinnie, Bryant, 27
McLean, Lindsy, 17
McManimon, Lieutenant Dennis, 79
McNabb, Donovan, 11
McNally, James, 100
Medical Society of the State of New York, 177
Meehan, Billy, 30
Melendez-Perez, Jose, 221–225, 236, 240–241
Men of Mystery, 146–147
Mercer, Wesley, 167
Merrill Lynch, 2
Mesaros, Robert A., 46–48
Metro West Daily News, 56–57
Middle District of Pennsylvania, 144
Miller III, George W., 32, 34
Mineta, Norman, 229–30
Minnesota Vikings, 10, 26
Miss America pageant, ix, x, 105–12, 194, 248
Mohammed, Khalid Sheif, 245
Molloy, John T., 35, 37–39
Monday Night Football, 11
Mondesire, Whyatt, 36
Monson, Diane, 176–77
Montana, Joe, 13
Morgan Stanley, 167
Morris, Robert, 114, 118–22, 126
Morrison, Barry, 157
Morton, Robert, 151
Motman, Maryellen, 100–1
Mourtos, Christos, 41–42
Munich Olympics, 211
Murder Is No Mystery, 32
Murdoch, Rupert, 210
Murphy Brown, 152
Murphy, Eddie, 156
Murray, Jim, 222
Myerson, Bess, 107

National Association for the Advancement of Colored People (NAACP), 36, 129, 159–60
National Cancer Institute, 178
National Center for Science Education, 139
National Congress of American Indians (NCAI), 129
National Enquirer, 58
National Institute on Drug Abuse (NIDA), 174
National Legal and Policy Center (NLPC), 160
National Organization for Women (NOW), 107, 129
National Public Radio (NPR), 183–85, 191
National Rifle Association (NRA), 249
Native Americans, 125–131, 133–34
Nat West bank, 214
Navy, 218

NBA, 11, 28, 135
NBC, 152, 207
NCAA, 128–134
NEA Today, 60, 62
Nelson, Willie, 172
Nepal, 85
(New) Dress for Success, viii, 9, 35, 37–38
New Jersey, 9, 29, 41–42, 44, 49–51, 56, 64, 77–78, 100, 180, 184, 186
New Jersey Council on Indian Affairs, 125
New Jersey Department of Military and Veterans Affairs, 51, 53
Newberry, Jeremy, 18, 23
New England Journal of Medicine, 242–43
Newman, Jonathan, 144
Newman, Paul, 183
Newsom, Mayor Gavin, 12–13, 16, 24
Newsweek, 178
New York Daily News, 3, 7
New York State Association of County Health Officials, 177
New York Times, 24, 78, 110, 146, 167–68, 175, 184, 206, 235, 242–43
NFL, viii, 10, 12–13, 15, 22–23
Niedt, Lieutenant Colonel Roberta, 53
Nichols, Brian, 93–94, 98
Ninth Circuit Court of Appeals, 104, 176
No Child Left Behind, 64
Non-Importation Agreement, 120
Northwest Detectives, 33
Northwest Flight 327, 228
Novella, Don, 156

O'Brien, Dennis, 222
O'Brien, James, 208
Of Pandas and People, 138–39, 141–42, 145
Olson, Chris, 102
Olympia, Washington, 184
One Nation Under Therapy: How the Helping Culture Is Eroding Self-Reliance, 66
O'Reilly Factor, The, 92
Origin of Species, The, 142, 144
Orlando International Airport, x, 221
Osceola, Chief, 128, 132–34
Osceola Jr., Max B., 132
Oval Office, 248
Owens, Albert, 191–92
Owens, Terrell (TO), 11, 15–16, 103

Pacifica Radio, 183, 185
Padilla, Jose, 227
Pageant News Bureau, 108
Palestinian Peace Institute, 77
Pantone Color Institute, 61
Paper Mate, 60–61
Parker, Tom, 6
Parker, Trey, 149–50
Parliament, 215
Parrish, Tony, 14, 20
Partridge, Edward, 47

Paul, Anthony, 189
Pavlik, Gregory, 86–87
Peltier, Leonard, 192
Penalosa, Sergio, 159
Penn, Thomas, 125–26
Penn, William, 125
Pennsylvania Human Relations Commission (PHRC), 36, 38–39
Pennsylvania Liquor Control Board, 43
Pennsylvania Railroad System, 68
Pentagon, 222, 245
Pepper Hamilton LLP, 141
Peters, Charles, 79
Peterson, Heather, 35
Peterson, Julian, 14, 18, 22
"Phoenix Memo", 227
Phoenix Sky Harbor International Airport, 231
Phi Beta Kappa, 105
Philadelphia African American Chamber of Commerce, 118
Philadelphia Eagles, 11, 35–36, 222
Philadelphia Bulletin, 23
Philadelphia Daily News, 1, 23, 28–33, 57, 91, 194, 202, 219
Philadelphia Democratic Party, 222
Philadelphia Inquirer, 3, 29, 53, 169, 210–12
Philadelphia School District, 169
Philips, Brian, 110
Pilot Pen, 60–61
Piscopo, Joe, 155–56
Playboy, 11
Pledge of Allegiance, 247
Podberesky, Sam, 225
Pope John Paul II, 209
Portland Airport, 224
Post-Conviction Relief Act (PCRA), 188–89
Post Tribune, 197
Pratt, Geronimo Ji Jaga, 192
President's Daily Briefing (PDB), 218
Princeton, 73–74, 76, 79–81, 194
Princeton University Varsity Streaking Team, 77–79
Professional Association of Teachers, 65
Proposition 215, 176
Pryor, Christopher, 82–85
Public Health Laboratory Service, 214
Pujol, Claude, 187
The Purpose Driven Life: What on Earth Am I Here For?, 94

Queen Elizabeth, 213
Queer Eye for the Straight Guy, 167
Quiñonez, José, 158

Rabinowitz, Dorothy, 88
Radner, Gilda, 155
Ragone, Peter, 16–17
Rage Against the Machine, 183–84, 186
Raich, Angel, 176–77
Randall, Robert, 173–74
Randolph, William, 167

Raspail, Jean, 86
RBC Capital Markets, 8
Read, Robin, 87
Reagan, Ronald Wilson, 129, 218
Real Money, 8
Real World, 111
Reconstruction, 117
Red Hot Chili Peppers, 77
Rehm, Bryan, 141
Rehnquist, William, 177
Reid, Andy, 12
Reid, Richard, 227
Rendell, Ed, 122, 126, 191
Research Triangle Institute, 174
Reuben, Jason, 76
Rickles, Don, 148–49
Ridge, Tom, 144
Rubenstone, Edward, 89
Revolutionary War, 57, 119–21, 241
Reynolds, Kirk, 10–23, 26–27, 172
Reynolds-Brown, Blondell, 113, 115–16
Rice, Dr. Condoleezza, 218–19, 225
Rita Cosby Live & Direct, 92
Rizzo, Frank L., 164, 222
Rock, Chris, 14, 153
Roe v. Wade, 165
Rolling Stone, 88
Roosevelt, President Theodore, 138
Robbins, Tim, 183
Rocket, Charles, 156
Rosato, Tony, 155
Rosenberg, Steve, 67–71
ROTC, 49, 54
Rumph, Mike, 18
Rumsfeld, Donald, ix, 135, 241, 243
Running Press, 220
Rushdie, Salman, 183
Rutherford Institute, 46–47, 53–54
Rutter, Dave, 197

Salon.com, 174
Sands Atlantic City Hotel and Casino, 156
San Francisco Chronicle, 12, 16
San Francisco Examiner, 24
San Francisco 49ers, 10–11, 16–17, 194
San Francisco Police Department (SFPD), 24, 26
San Quentin Prison, 193
Santorum, Senator Rick, 164, 167
Saracini, Ellen, 222
Saracini, Victor, 222
Sarandon, Susan, 183
Saturday Night Live, 155–56
Scales, Alton, 103
Scarborough Country, 92
Scarborough, Joe, 242
Schefer, Michael, 29, 31
Schifter, Catherine, 86
Schirripa, Steven R., 148
Schroen, Gary, 236
Schulz, William, 236–239

Schulze, Mal, 57
Schwarzenegger, Arnold, 191–193
Scopes, John, 137, 144
Scotland Yard, 214
Second Amendment, 195
Seminoles, 128, 132–34
Seminole Nation General Council, 133
Seminole Nation of Oklahoma, 133
Seminole Tribe of Florida, 134
Sereni, Mark A., 48
The Shadow University: The Betrayal of Liberty on American Campuses, 89
Shahbandar, Tarek, 198
Shaiman, Marc, 149–50
Shakur, Assata, 192
Sharpie, 11, 60
Shearman & Sterling, 3
"Sheldon Award", 87
Sheridan, Nicollette, 11
Shindle, Kate, 110, 112
Silberman, Robert, 61
Silence of the Lambs, 232
Silvergate, Harvey, 90
Simon, Randall, 7
Sitting Bull, 130
Sky Soldiers, 54
Smith, Ashley, 104
Smith, Doug, 125
Smith, Onterrio, 10
Smoot, Fred, 27
Soliday, Edmond, 225–26
Sommers, Christina Hoff, 66
Sopranos, 125, 148
Sorkin, Ira Lee, 7
Sottosanti, Joseph, 64
Southeastern Pennsylvania Transit Authority (SEPTA), 97–98
South Park: Bigger, Longer, and Uncut, 149
Southwest Airlines, 219
Spanish-American War, 57
Specter, Arlen, 225
Spencer, Robert, 202
Sperry, Paul, 225
Spitz, Dr. Margaret, 178
Sports Illustrated, 20, 23
Standing Rock Sioux tribe, 130
State Department, 227
Stocker, Greg, 153
Steinem, Gloria, 183
Stepford Wives, The, 110
Stevens, John Paul, 177
Stone, Oliver, 183
Street, John, 30, 113
Street, Sharif, 30
Strojny, Greg, 59
Sullivan, Joseph, 33
Summers, Larry, 28
Sunoco, 54
Sunshine State Standards, 64
Supporters of the Military (SOM), 195–98

INDEX

Supreme Court (of U.S.), 48, 96–98, 104, 167, 169, 175, 177
Susser, Andrew, 2–9, 172
Sutherland, Kiefer, 200, 202

Tannanbaum, Steven A., 7
Taylor, Ayanna, 84
Taylor, Nikki, 84
Teasley, Hoyt, 94
Telegraph, 212
Tetamy, Chief Tundy, 125
Thomas, Clarence, 177
Thomas, Denita, 84
Thompson, Bill, 64
Thompson, Kennedy, 113, 119, 122
Time magazine, 222, 226, 236–37, 239–41
Timoney, John, 32
Tobacco Free Dan County Coalition, 179
Today show, 58
Tonight Show, The, 149
Toyota, 160
Transportation Safety Administration (TSA), 10, 227–28, 232
Trudeau, Gary, 84
Trujillo, Larry, 101–3
Tualo, Esera, 11
Tuohey, Michael, 223–25

Ulbrich, Jeff, 15
United Airlines, 219, 224–26
United Nations (UN), 249
United States Commission on Civil Rights (USCCR), 129
United Way, 169–70
University of North Dakota (UND), 130, 134–35
University of Pennsylvania (UPENN), 2, 76, 81–82, 85, 90, 128
UN Summit, 210,
Urban Outfitters, 157–58
US Airways, 223–24
U.S. District Court, 95, 144
U.S. Supreme Court, 47, 169

Vail Resorts, 3
Vargas, Manelick De La Parra, 159
Vassar Spectator, 2
Vespa-Papleo, J. Frank, 41–42
Veterans of Foreign Wars Parade, 59
Viacom, 35
Vietnam, 55–57, 85
Village Voice, 6
Villanova, Pennsylvania, 68

Wachovia Corporation, 113–16, 118–20, 122, 126
Wagner, Leon, 7
Walczak, Witold, 140
Walker, Alice, 183
Wall Street, viii, 2, 4, 6–9
Wall Street Journal, 7, 67, 69–70, 85, 88
Walters, Barbara, 153–54

War at Home, 151
War on Drugs, 172, 177
Warner Brothers, 152
Washington, President George, 138
Washington Post, 88, 91, 150, 176, 239
Washington Times, 229
Weathers, Patrick, 156
Weinglass, Leonard, 187–90
Welfel, Scott, 78
West, Paul, 142
Western District of Pennsylvania, 97
Wetherell, T. K., 132
White House, 218, 221–22, 237
White, John, 160
Whitehead, John, 46–48, 53
Wilhelm, David, 94
Will, George, 84
William Penn Foundation, 32
Williams, Ken, 227
Williams, Moe, 27
Williams, Robin, 149
Williams, Stanley "Tookie", 191
Williams, Vanessa, 107
Willing & Morris, 114
Willing, Thomas, 114, 121–22
Wilson, James, 121
Wiswall, Jack, 104
Wittman, Scott, 149
Wo/Men's Alliance for Medical Marijuana, 175
WomensWallStreet.com, 228
Wong, Reverend Norman, 18
Woodrow Wilson School of Public and International Affairs, 77, 79
Woods, James, 229
Woodward, Joanne, 183
World Health Organization (WHO), 171, 181
World War I, 57, 126, 196
World War II, 55, 57, 59, 126, 146, 196

XXL magazine, 160

Yale Law Journal, 183–85
Yang, Yen-I, 192
Yanowitz, Elysa, 104
Yarrow, Peter, 183
Yayo, Tony, 160
Yocum, Frank, 231–32
York, John, 12–13, 17–18

Zinsmeister, Karl, 62
Zubaydah, Abu, 244
Zurzolo, Joe, 35–36, 38, 40